SECURING ETERNITY

SECURING ETERNITY

Ancient Egyptian Tomb Protection from Prehistory to the Pyramids

Reg Clark

The American University in Cairo Press
Cairo New York

First published in 2019 by
The American University in Cairo Press
113 Sharia Kasr el Aini, Cairo, Egypt
200 Park Ave., Suite 1700, New York, NY 10166
www.aucpress.com

Dar el Kutub No. 13060/18
ISBN 978 977 416 902 1

Dar el Kutub Cataloging-in-Publication Data

Clark, Reg
Securing Eternity: Ancient Egyptian Tomb Protection from Prehistory to the Pyramids / Reg Clark.— Cairo: The American University in Cairo Press, 2019.
p. cm.
ISBN 978 977 416 902 1
1. Egypt—Antiquities
I. Title
932

1 2 3 4 5 23 22 21 20 19

Designed by Adam el-Sehemy
Printed in the United States of America

But with regard to any man who shall do anything evil to my tomb,
or who shall enter it with the intention of stealing,
I shall seize his neck like a bird's, and I shall be judged with him in
the court of the Great God . . . .[1]

Inscription from the private tomb of Herymeru at Saqqara[2]

Contents

List of Illustrations ix
Preface xix
Introduction 1
Abbreviations and Glossary 3
Maps 7

1 The Purpose and Context of the Egyptian Tomb and the Need for It to Be Secure 9
2 Securing the Early Tomb: Prehistory to the End of the Predynastic Period 13
3 Defending the Pit Tomb: From Egypt's Unification to the Mid-First Dynasty 35
4 Portals, Passages, and Portcullises: The Second Half of the First Dynasty 69
5 Subterranean Sepulchers: New Security Developments in the Second Dynasty 129
6 A Parting of the Ways: Step Pyramids and Mastabas in the Third Dynasty 169
7 Pyramids and Plug-Stones: Security Innovations in the Early Fourth Dynasty 223
8 Conclusion 269

Chronology 277
Notes 281
Bibliography 325
Index 353

List of Illustrations

Maps

1. Map of Egypt, drawn by the author after Bard (2007, map 5.4). 7
2. Map of Lower Nubia, drawn by the author after Bard (2007, map 5.2). 8

Figures

1. Stone slabs over the graves at Site 117 at Jebel Sahaba, drawn by the author after Wendorf (1968, fig. 4). 14
2. A shallow pit burial at Merimde (Junker 1929, plate IIa), courtesy of the Österreichische Akademie der Wissenschaften. 15
3. Assorted Badarian graves (Brunton and Caton-Thompson 1928, plate 9). 16
4. Burial at al-Omari Cemetery F (Debono and Mortensen 1990, plate 42.1, fig. 5), courtesy of the German Archaeological Institute (DAI) Cairo. 18
5. Burial with grave goods at Maadi (Rizkana and Seeher 1990, plate 3), courtesy of the DAI Cairo. 19
6. Rectangular-shaped graves from Naqada (Petrie and Quibell 1896, plate 83). 20
7. Typical section through a late Naqada II grave, drawn by the author. 22
8. Plan of tomb 23 at Cemetery HK6 at Hierakonpolis (Friedman 2005, 4), courtesy of the Hierakonpolis Expedition. 23
9. Tomb 26 at Cemetery HK6 at Hierakonpolis (Friedman 2008b, fig. 11), courtesy of the Hierakonpolis Expedition. 24
10. Tomb U-j at Umm al-Qa‘b (Dreyer 1998, plate 3b), courtesy of the DAI Cairo. 26
11. Grave 85 at al-Kab, adapted by the author from Hendrickx and van Rossum (1994, plates 63 and 64). 27

12. Tomb 6 in Cemetery 137 at Seyala (Firth 1927, 211). 28
13. Tomb L23 at Qustul (Williams 1986, fig. 159), courtesy of the Oriental Institute of the University of Chicago. 29
14. Burial 8 at Kom al-Ahmar (de Morgan 1909, fig. 130). 30
15. Photograph of tomb 2 at Locality HK6 at Hierakonpolis (Adams 2000, plate 6a), courtesy of British Archaeological Reports. 31
16. Grave 1845 at Tarkhan (Petrie 1914, plate 12). 32
17. Tomb B0/1/2, the tomb of King Iry-Hor (Kaiser and Dreyer 1982, fig. 12 and plate 55A), courtesy of the DAI Cairo. 36
18. Tomb B7/9, the tomb of King Ka (Kaiser and Dreyer 1982, fig. 12 and plate 56B), courtesy of the DAI Cairo. 37
19. Tomb B17/18, the tomb of King Narmer (Kaiser and Dreyer 1982, fig. 12 and plate 56C), courtesy of the DAI Cairo. 38
20. Tomb B10/15/19, the tomb of King Hor-Aha (Kaiser and Dreyer 1982, fig. 12 and plate 56C), courtesy of the DAI Cairo. 40
21. The tomb of King Djer at Umm al-Qa'b (Kaiser and Dreyer 1982, fig. 12), courtesy of the DAI Cairo. Photograph by the author. 42
22. The tomb of King Djet at Umm al-Qa'b (Kaiser and Dreyer 1982, fig. 12; Dreyer 1991, fig. 7), courtesy of the DAI Cairo. 43
23. The tomb of Queen Merneith at Umm al-Qa'b and a general view of Umm al-Qa'b looking southwest toward the wadi (Kaiser and Dreyer 1982, fig. 12), courtesy of the DAI Cairo. Photograph by the author. 44
24. Grave 63 at Tell al-Farkha (Dębowska-Ludwin 2011b, fig. 3). 47
25. Tomb 1 at Tell Ibrahim 'Awad (Haarlem 1996, fig. 1). 49
26. Mastaba V at Nazlet Batran (Daressy 1905, fig. 1; Petrie 1907, fig. 6). 51
27. Mastaba XVII at Abu Ghurab (Radwan 2000, fig. 2). 52
28. Tomb S 3357 (Hor-Aha) at Saqqara (Emery 1939, plate 1). 53
29. Tomb S 3471 at Saqqara (Emery 1949, plate 2). 54
30. Tomb S 2185 at Saqqara (Quibell 1923, plates 5 and 6.2). 55
31. Tomb S 3504 at Saqqara (Emery 1954, plates 1 and 3), courtesy of the Egypt Exploration Society. 56
32. Tomb S 3503 at Saqqara (Emery 1954, plate 38), courtesy of the Egypt Exploration Society. 58
33. Tomb 68.H.4 at Helwan, drawn by the author after Saad (1951, plan 5). 59
34. Mastaba 1060 at Tarkhan (Petrie et al. 1913, plates 16.1 and 18). 61
35. Tomb II at Awlad al-Sheikh (Ranke 1926, figs. 3–4), courtesy of Walter de Gruyter. 62

36. Tombs N 1506 and N 1532 at Naga al-Deir (Reisner 1908, fig. 53 and plate 77, plan 2). 63
37. Tomb IV at Abydos (Hussein 2011, fig. 9). 64
38. The Naqada 'Royal Tomb' after Borchardt (1898, plate 14). 66
39. Tombs 1207 and 1208 at Armant (Mond and Myers 1937, plate 5), courtesy of the Egypt Exploration Society. 67
40. The tomb of King Den at Umm al-Qa'b (Dreyer et al. 1998, plate 9a; Dreyer 2003b, 69), courtesy of the DAI Cairo. 70
41. The tomb of King Adjib (Petrie 1900, plate 15; Kaiser and Dreyer 1982, fig. 12), courtesy of the DAI Cairo. 73
42. The tomb of King Semerkhet (Dreyer 2005, fig. 19; Dreyer et al. 2006, fig. 7), courtesy of the DAI Cairo. 74
43. The tomb of King Qa'a (Kaiser and Dreyer 1982, fig. 12; Dreyer et al. 1996, plate 10a), courtesy of the DAI Cairo. 77
44. Tomb 2897 at Minshat Abu Omar (Kroeper 1992, fig. 12). 80
45. Graves 50 and 55 at Tell al-Farkha (Dębowska-Ludwin 2009, plate 3; 2012, fig. 17). 81
46. Tomb MO25 at Cemetery M in Abu Rawash (Klasens 1961, fig. 2), courtesy of the Rijksmuseum van Oudheden. 82
47. Tombs MO1 and MO2 in Cemetery M at Abu Rawash, drawn by the author after Montet (1938, plate 2). 83
48. Tomb MO10 in Cemetery M and 'locking mechanisms,' drawn by the author after Montet (1938, 51–52 and plate 6). 85
49. Tomb 1056 at Tura al-Asmant, drawn by the author after Yacoub (1981, plate 17). 87
50. Tomb 130 at Tura al-Asmant, drawn by the author after Yacoub (1981, plate 18). 88
51. Tomb 249 at Tura al-Asmant, drawn by the author after El-Khouli (1968, plate 5). 89
52. Tomb S 3507 at Saqqara and its hidden 'mound' (Emery 1958, plates 85 and 86), courtesy of the Egypt Exploration Society. 90
53. Tomb S 3506 at Saqqara and axionometric view (Emery 1958, plates 40 and 43), courtesy of the Egypt Exploration Society. 91
54. Tomb S 3035 (Hemaka) at Saqqara (Emery 1938, plates 1 and 2). 93
55. Tomb S 3036 (Ankha) at Saqqara (Emery 1949, plates 14 and 15). 95
56. Tomb X at Saqqara (Emery 1949, plate 43). 97
57. Tomb S 3338 at Saqqara (Emery 1949, plate 55). 98
58. Tomb S 3500 at Saqqara (Emery 1958, plate 114), courtesy of the Egypt Exploration Society. 99

59. The twin portcullises of tomb S 3500 at Saqqara (Emery 1958, plate 119b), courtesy of the Egypt Exploration Society. 100
60. Tomb S 3505 (Merka) at Saqqara (Emery 1958, plates 2–4), courtesy of the Egypt Exploration Society. 101
61. Tomb S 2105 at Saqqara and a view of its portcullis (Quibell 1923, plate 16.2; Reisner 1936, fig. 52). 103
62. Tomb S 3121 at Saqqara (Emery 1949, plate 48). 105
63. Tomb S 3120 at Saqqara (Emery 1949, plate 53). 106
64. Tomb 423.H.9 at Helwan (Saad 1969, plate 13). © 1969 University of Oklahoma Press. Reproduced with permission. All rights reserved. 108
65. Interior of tomb 1390.H.2 at Helwan (Saad 1969, plate 16). © 1969 University of Oklahoma Press. Reproduced with permission. All rights reserved. 109
66. Tomb 1.H.4 at Helwan, drawn by the author after Saad (1951, plan 3). 110
67. Tomb 150.H.5 at Helwan, drawn by the author after Saad (1951, plan 15). 110
68. Tomb 407.H.4 at Helwan, drawn by the author after Saad (1951, plan 9). 111
69. Tomb 785.H.5 at Helwan, drawn by the author after Saad (1969, plan 9). 111
70. Tomb 355.H.4 at Helwan, drawn by the author after Saad (1951, plan 7). 112
71. Tombs 1371.H.2 and 1502.H.2 at Helwan, drawn by the author after Saad (1947, plates 38 and 40). 112
72. Tomb 553.H.2 at Helwan, drawn by the author after Saad (1947, plate 36). 113
73. Interior of tomb 385.H.4 at Helwan (Saad 1969, plate 17). © 1969 University of Oklahoma Press. Reproduced with permission. All rights reserved. 114
74. Tomb 40.H.3 (Op. 2/1) at Helwan, drawn by the author after Köhler (2005, plate 13). 115
75. Tomb 1.H.3 at Helwan, drawn by the author after Saad (1947, plate 61). 116
76. Tombs 2038 and 2050 at Tarkhan (Petrie 1914, plate 18). 118
77. Tomb III at Awlad al-Sheikh (Ranke 1926, figs. 5–6), courtesy of Walter de Gruyter. 119
78. Tomb N 1581 at Cemetery 1500 at Naga al-Deir (Reisner 1908, figs. 65–66). 120

79. Tomb M1 at Mahasna (Reisner 1936, fig. 49). 121
80. Tomb 1 at Abydos (Hussein 2011, fig. 4). 122
81. Tomb b 91 at al-Amra (Randall-MacIver and Mace 1902, plate 4, fig. 8). 123
82. Plan of the tomb of King Hotepsekhemwy/Raneb at Saqqara (Lacher 2008, fig. 2), courtesy of the DAI Cairo. 130
83. The entrance stairway to the subterranean tomb of King Hotepsekhemwy/Raneb at Saqqara (Dreyer 2003b, 74), courtesy of the DAI Cairo. 132
84. Plan of the tomb of King Ninetjer at Saqqara (Lacher 2011, fig. 2), courtesy of the DAI Cairo. 133
85. The tomb of King Peribsen at Umm al-Qa'b (Dreyer et al. 2006, fig. 13 and plate 22b), courtesy of the DAI Cairo. 136
86. The tomb of King Khasekhemwy at Umm al-Qa'b after Dreyer (et al. 2003, fig. 16 and plate 23a) and Dreyer (2003a, 77), courtesy of the DAI Cairo. 137
87. Tombs 10B–4 and 12B–6 at Abusir (Bonnet 1928, plate 2). 141
88. Tomb S 3024 at Saqqara (Emery 1949, fig. 9). 142
89. An unidentified 'house-type' subterranean stairway tomb at Saqqara (Emery 1961, fig. 96), from *Archaic Egypt* by W.B. Emery (Penguin Books, 1961, 2nd ed. 1991). Reproduced by permission of Penguin Books. © Estate of Walter B. Emery, 1961, 1991. 143
90. Assorted subterranean substructures at Saqqara (Quibell 1923, plate 30). 144
91. Tomb S 2302 at Saqqara, adapted by the author from Quibell (1923, plate 30) and Reisner (1936, fig. 60). 145
92. The 'end-on' flagstones used to block the passage of tomb S 2171 at Saqqara (Quibell 1923, plate 15.1) 146
93. Tomb S 3477 at Saqqara (Emery 1962, plate 4), courtesy of the Nederlands Instituut voor het Nabije Oosten. 147
94. Tomb 25.H.5 at Helwan, drawn by the author after Saad (1951, plan 13). 149
95. Tomb 505.H.4 at Helwan, drawn by the author after Saad (1951, plan 11). 150
96. Tomb Op. 4/94, drawn by the author after Köhler (2007, fig. 2). 151
97. Tomb Op. 4/4 plan and portcullis sketch, drawn by the author after Köhler (2000, 40; 2003, fig. 2). 152
98. Tomb Op. 4/123 at Helwan, drawn by the author after Köhler (2008b, fig. 17). 153

99. The 'deep staircase' tomb Op. 4/148 at Helwan, drawn by the author after Köhler (2009, fig. 4). 154
100. Tomb 256.H.8 at Helwan, drawn by the author after Saad (1957, plan G). 155
101. Grave 240 at Tarkhan/Kafr Amar (Petrie and Mackay 1915, plate 12.5). 156
102. Graves 771 and 821 at the Bashkatib Cemetery, Lahun (Petrie et al. 1923, plate 42, figs. Q and S). 157
103. Tomb 560 at Sedment (Petrie and Brunton 1924, plate 81). 159
104. Tombs 562, 429, and 507 at Qau (Brunton 1927, plate 12.1, 4, and 5). 160
105. Tomb 3112 at Spur 5 in Cemetery 3100 at Badari (Brunton 1927, plate 24). 161
106. Tomb N 1586 from Cemetery 1500 at Naga al-Deir (Reisner 1908, figs. 71 and 73). 162
107. Tomb 205 at Armant (Myers and Fairman 1931, plate 41), courtesy of the Egypt Exploration Society. 163
108. Grave 64 in Cemetery 24 at al-Kab (Hendrickx and van Rossum 1994, plate 54). 164
109. The stone-lined tomb 2 at al-Qara (de Morgan 1908, fig. 40). 165
110. Section facing west of the Step Pyramid at Saqqara after Lauer (1936, plate 19). © IFAO. 170
111. Plan of the substructure of the Step Pyramid after Lauer (1936, plate 15). © IFAO. 171
112. Axonometric view of Step Pyramid stages and the granite vault (Lauer 1936, plate 18.2; 1962, fig. 20). © IFAO. 172
113. Enlarged sections of the Step Pyramid shaft and descent after Lauer (1936, plate 17). © IFAO. 175
114. Plan and cross-section of the Step Pyramid South Tomb after Lauer (1936, plate 31). © IFAO. 177
115. Plan and cross-section of the pyramid of Sekhemkhet, drawn by the author after Goneim (1957, plate 4) and Lauer (1979, fig. 7). 180
116. Exposed corner of the unfinished pyramid of Sekhemkhet and the unopened alabaster sarcophagus (Goneim 1957, plates 16 and 51). 182
117. Plan and section of the Layer Pyramid at Zawiyat al-Aryan (Dodson 2003, 46). 185
118. The remains of the Brick Pyramid at Abu Rawash and section drawing (Lepsius 1897, fig. 12; Dodson 2003, 48). 187
119. Covington's Tomb, also known as tomb no. 1 or Mastaba T, at Giza (Reisner 1936, fig. 73). 192

120. Tomb S 2405 (Hesyra) at Saqqara (Quibell 1913, plate 2). 194
121. Tomb S 3050 at Saqqara, adapted by the author from Martin (1974, figs. 7 and 8a), courtesy of the Egypt Exploration Society. 196
122. Tomb S 3070 at Saqqara (Emery 1968, plate 2), courtesy of the Egypt Exploration Society. 197
123. Tomb S 3518 (Imhotep?) at Saqqara (Emery 1970, plates 19 and 20), courtesy of the Egypt Exploration Society. 199
124. Plan and section of tomb 287.H.6 at Helwan, drawn by the author after Saad (1951, plan 2) with view of stone-lined shaft (Saad 1951, plate 2a). 201
125. Shaft tombs 735 and 769 at the Bashkatib cemetery in Lahun (Petrie et al. 1923, plate 43, figs. AA–BA). 202
126. Stairway tombs 3227 and 3228 at Badari (Brunton 1927, figs. 12.1 and 12.6). 203
127. Tombs N 574, N 599, and N 573 + 587 in Cemetery 500-900 at Naga al-Deir (Reisner 1932, figs. 137a–137b and 157; 1936, fig. 86). 205
128. Tomb N 593 in Cemetery 500-900 at Naga al-Deir (Reisner 1932, fig. 149). 206
129. Tombs R1 and R40 at Reqaqnah (Garstang 1904, plates 4a and 4b). 208
130. Plan and section of tomb K1 at Beit Khallaf (Garstang 1903, plate 7), courtesy of Bernard Quaritch. 210
131. Plan and section of tomb K2 at Beit Khallaf (Garstang 1903, plate 18), courtesy of Bernard Quaritch. 212
132. Sketch drawings of the descent to and entrance of an unidentified stairway tomb at al-Kab (Quibell 1898, plate 12). 213
133. Plan of the superstructure of tomb 274 at the rock necropolis al-Kab and internal view of the stair-shaft during the substructure's excavation (Limme 2008, fig. 31). © L. Moelants, F. Roloux & MRAH, Brussels. Photograph © Royal Museums of Art and History, Brussels. 215
134. Section of the pyramid of Meidum looking west, drawn by the author after Maragioglio and Rinaldi (1964b, plate 2, fig. 2). 224
135. The pyramid of Meidum in recent times, photographed by the author, and close-up section of its substructure looking west, drawn by the author after Maragioglio and Rinaldi (1964b, plate 4, fig. 1). 225
136. The Bent Pyramid at Dahshur, photographed by the author. 227
137. The two substructure systems in the Bent Pyramid, drawn by the author after Maragioglio and Rinaldi (1964b, plate 9, figs. 1–2, and plate 11, figs. 3–4). 228

138. Close-up plan and section of the portcullis arrangements in the Bent Pyramid, drawn by the author after Maragioglio and Rinaldi (1964b, plate 13, fig. 2). 230
139. Section view of the Bent Pyramid's satellite pyramid, drawn by the author after Maragioglio and Rinaldi (1964b, plate 15, figs. 1–2). 232
140. Section through the Red Pyramid at Dahshur, drawn by the author after Maragioglio and Rinaldi (1964b, plate 18, fig. 3). 233
141. The Red Pyramid, photograph by the author, and section view drawn by the author after Maragioglio and Rinaldi (1964b, plate 18, figs. 4–5). 234
142. Plan and section of tomb AS 33 at Abusir, adapted by the author from Bárta, Coppens, and Vymazalová (2010, figs. 3.1, 3.18, and 3.21). 237
143. Plan and section of the tomb of Hetepi (AS 20) at Abusir (Bárta, Coppens, and Vymazalová 2010, figs. 2.1 and 2.2). 238
144. Plan and section of the 'Lake of Abusir' tomb 1 (Bárta 2000, fig. 2). 240
145. The substructure of tomb no. 1 at Dahshur (de Morgan 1895, figs. 3–5). 241
146. Plan and section of tomb DAS 9 (Ipy) at Dahshur, adapted by the author from Alexanian and Seidlmayer (2002, figs. 1 and 4), courtesy of the DAI Cairo. 242
147. Section through the substructure of DAS 32-4 (Iinefer) at Dahshur (Barsanti 1902b, figs. 5–6). 243
148. Plan and section of DAS II/1 (Netjer-Aperef) at Dahshur (Alexanian 1999, figs. 4–5), courtesy of the DAI Cairo. 244
149. Interior view of the burial chamber of DAS II/1 (Netjer-Aperef) at Dahshur (Stadelmann et al. 1993, plate 57c), courtesy of the DAI Cairo. 246
150. Plan and sections of the tomb of Rahotep and Nefert at Meidum, drawn by the author after Harpur (2001, fig. 61), sections after (Petrie 1892, plate 7) and Reisner (1936, fig. 110), respectively. 247
151. Substructure sections of the tomb of Ranefer at Meidum (Petrie 1892, plate 7; Reisner 1936, fig. 111). 250
152. Section through tomb 51 from the Far Western Cemetery at Meidum (Petrie et al. 1910, plate 17). 252
153. Plan and section of tomb A in the Great Western Cemetery at Meidum (Petrie et al. 1910, plate 15). 253
154. Mastaba 17 exterior today and tomb section (Petrie et al. 1910, plate 12). Photograph by Dyan Hilton. 255

155. Mastaba 17 interior layout and plug-stones (Reisner 1936, fig. 105; Jánosi 2006, fig. 32a). 256
156. Plan and sections of burial chambers in Nefermaat and Atet's tomb at Meidum. Plan by the author after Harpur (2001, fig. 38; Jánosi 2006, fig. 33) and sections after Petrie et al. (1910, plate 4; 1912, plate 15). 258
157. Tombs N 546 + 604 and N 739 at Cemetery 500-900 at Naga al-Deir (Reisner 1932, figs. 161 and 200–201, respectively). 262
158. The superstructure and tomb plans of Kamena at al-Kab (Quibell 1898, plates 1.4 and 23). 264

Preface

I had just given a talk on tomb security at the International Congress of Egyptologists in Florence in 2016 when Nigel Fletcher-Jones of AUC Press approached me and suggested that I might write a book on Egyptian tomb security aimed at the Egyptophile, student, and general reader, which AUC Press would publish. I was delighted at his offer. My doctoral thesis on this topic was already in print, but it is an expensive book for an individual, and, as one of my friends who purchased it commented, "fairly hard going for a layperson." This was therefore a golden opportunity for me to share my research with a broader audience, who I was sure would be as fascinated to read about the methods the ancient Egyptians used to defend their tombs as I was when I started my research ten years ago, especially as there is so little written about it that is properly researched and accurate.

My interest in tomb security began after my first visit to Egypt at the beginning of the 1990s. I visited all the usual sites, but by taxi, which permitted me more time than with a tour group. Moreover, the first Gulf War was in full swing and most of the sites deserted, so I explored at leisure, aided by a copy of William Murnane's marvelous *The Penguin Guide to Ancient Egypt* (1983). Of all the sites I visited, the two that inspired me the most were Saqqara and Meidum, the latter made memorable by an exciting descent, via a robbers' tunnel, deep underground into the plundered, stone-lined burial chamber of the enormous Mastaba 17. Upon my return to the UK, I determined to find out more about the wonderful things I had seen and began attending evening classes in Egyptology—the rest being history.

During my studies over the years, I was especially interested in tomb security and architecture. The trouble was, with the exception of A.J. Spencer's excellent chapter "Security of the Tomb" in his *Death in Ancient Egypt*,[1] and Dieter Arnold's section on "Securing Tombs" in his *Building in Egypt*,[2] there was hardly anything published on the subject. Most authors devoted no more than a paragraph or two to the topic—some as much as a page! Therefore, when I finally got around to considering a topic for my Egyptology PhD, tomb security immediately sprang to mind. Here was something that had been largely ignored by most Egyptologists, for whatever reasons, which I could now explore in depth. Some six years later it was complete, and many of the results of the research are presented in this book.

Over the years, many people have helped me in the course of my research, and I would like to acknowledge them here. First and foremost, my PhD supervisors, Professor Martina Minas-Nerpel and Dr. Troy Sagrillo, for their expert guidance, comments, and advice. Also, Professor Alan Lloyd and Associate Professor Kasia Szpakowska, who taught me during my first degree course in Egyptology at Swansea University.

I should also like to thank the following scholars for taking the time and trouble to answer the many questions that arose during my research: Dr. Joanna Dębowska-Ludwin, Professor Günter Dreyer, Dr. Eva-Maria Engel, Dr. Bernd Fitzner, Dr. Renée Friedman, Professor Stan Hendrickx, the late Dr. Dirk Huyge, Professor Christiana Köhler, Dr. Claudia Lacher-Raschdorff, Dr. Luc Limme, Colin Reader, Dr. Ilona Regulski, Dr. Jane Smythe, the late Dr. Nabil Swelim, and Dr. Katharina Zinn. Additionally, I'm also grateful to Dr. Carl Graves of the Egypt Exploration Society (EES), London, and Dr. Daniela Rosenow of the German Archaeological Institute (DAI), Cairo, for their help in granting permission for some of the images in this book.

Last, but not least, my warmest thanks go to my good friend Professor Aidan Dodson, who taught me at Bristol University in the late 1990s, when I first began my Egyptological studies, and has been a steadfast mentor ever since.

Finally, in the descriptions of the tombs in this book, where possible and space permits, I have tried to include details of any robberies that may have taken place. I feel this helps with our appreciation of what the tomb builders were up against and why they needed to invest in security measures. As the reader will see, these paint a rather unflattering picture of the darker side of human nature that has plagued the funerary culture of ancient Egypt from its very beginning, and indeed sadly, when times are troubled, occasionally continues to this day. . . .

Introduction

Ancient Egyptians went to great lengths to protect their dead from the ever-present threat of tomb robbery by incorporating special architectural features in their tombs. However, tomb security has rarely been considered a topic in its own right and is usually treated as a secondary subject in Egyptological works, which tend to regard its role as incidental to the design of the tomb, rather than perhaps being the driving force behind it.

The issue was raised in the early twentieth century by the great Egyptologist George Reisner,[1] who suggested that the rapid evolution of the Egyptian tomb substructure was a result of the desire for tomb security and more ostentatious tombs, rather than a development spurred by religious or funerary practices.

This book takes Reisner's proposition much further and presents a chronological survey of Egyptian tomb development from a security point of view from the Predynastic Period (about 5000–4000 BC) to the early Fourth Dynasty (about 2500 BC). By first describing and then thematically analyzing these features, it demonstrates that many aspects of the architecture of Egyptian tombs over this period, both royal and private, were indeed—subject to changing tastes, needs, and ideologies—a result of the need to protect the tomb or improve its security.

As mentioned above, this book covers the period from the Predynastic up until the early Fourth Dynasty. This is because the fundamental elements of tomb architecture chiefly develop during this roughly twenty-five-hundred-year time span, so that by the end of the reign of King Sneferu, the Egyptian grave had progressed from a simple backfilled pit, with perhaps a mound, to a massive limestone pyramid with a complex substructure. The majority of Egyptian tomb development from then on, up until the Ptolemaic Period, consisted of variations on a theme based on already established architectural and security principles.

The book is divided into eight chapters. Chapter 1 looks at the purpose and context of the Egyptian tomb in order to 'set the scene' for the remainder of the book. After a general overview of the Predynastic Period in Chapter 2, the book then progresses through the dynasties. A chapter is devoted to each, with the exception of the First Dynasty, which merits two chapters due to the complex developments that take place in that period. In the dynastic chapters, royal tombs are described first, and then a selection of private tombs by necropolis location, north to south—including many from the less well-known cemeteries, as these are usually ignored in the mainstream literature. At the end of each section, the main developments are thematically summarized so as to highlight the key architectural and security innovations of the period. And at the end of the book, the whole is drawn together in a conclusion that covers the entire two-and-a-half millennia of Egyptian tomb development discussed in the text.

Throughout the work, in order to make it accessible to as wide an audience as possible, I have opted to describe the various tomb 'types,' rather than allocate a 'type number,' which is common in Egyptological circles. Thus, a subterranean tomb with stairway access is described as exactly that, rather than as a 'Reisner Type IVa' and so on, which can confuse the non-specialist.[2] Wherever possible, I have also incorporated appropriate tomb plans or images, but as the reader will appreciate, in a book of this size it is not possible to include everything; where there is no illustration, a quick glance at the footnotes will usually point to another suitable source.

Finally, spread among the chapters there are three short sections dealing with the main methods used to secure the passageways in Egyptian tombs, namely backfills, blockings, portcullises, and plug-stones. These are included as they are rarely discussed in standard Egyptological publications. They also provide important background material that is relevant to Chapters 4 to 7 but applies across the dynasties, and so would be difficult to fit in the chronological sequence.

Abbreviations and Glossary

Archéo-Nil	Archéo-Nil: Bulletin de la société pour l'étude des cultures prépharaoniques de la vallée du Nil
AJSL	American Journal of Semitic Languages and Literatures
ASAE	Annales du Service des antiquités de l'Egypte
BACE	Bulletin of the Australian Centre for Egyptology
BIFAO	Bulletin de l'Institut français d'archéologie orientale
BMFA	Bulletin of the Museum of Fine Arts (Boston, MA)
BMSAES	British Museum Studies in Ancient Egypt and Sudan
BSFE	Bulletin de la Société française d'Égyptologie
CDE	Chronique d'Égypte; bulletin périodique de la Fondation égyptologique reine Élisabeth
CCE	Cahier de la céramique Égyptienne
CRAIBL	Comptes-rendus des séances de l'Académie des inscriptions et belles-lettres
DAI	German Archaeological Institute, Cairo
DE	Discussions in Egyptology
DÖAW	Denkschrift der Österreichischen Akademie der Wissenschaften in Wien
EA	Egyptian Archaeology: Bulletin of the Egypt Exploration Society
ENiM	Égypte nilotique et méditerranéenne
GM	Göttinger Miszellen
JEA	Journal of Egyptian Archaeology

JARCE	Journal of the American Research Center in Egypt
JEOL	Jaarbericht van het Vooraziatisch-egyptisch Genootschap Ex Oriente Lux
JNES	Journal of Near Eastern Studies
Kêmi	Kêmi: revue de philologie et d'archéologie égyptiennes et coptes
KMT	KMT: A Modern Journal of Ancient Egypt
MDAIK	Mitteilungen des Deutschen Archäologischen Instituts Abteilung Kairo
MOSAIK	MOSAIK Journal
MIFAO	Mémoires publiés par les membres de l'Institut français d'archéologie orientale du Caire
MIO	Mitteilungen des Instituts für Orientforschung
OMRO	Oudheidkundige Mededelingen uit het Rijksmuseum van Oudheden
RdE	Revue d'Égyptologie
Rec. de Trav	Recueil de traveaux relatifs à la philologie et à l'archéologie égyptiennes et assyriennes
SAAC	Studies in Ancient Art and Civilization
SAK	Studien zur Altägyptischen Kultur
Sokar	Sokar Magazine
ZÄS	Zeitschrift für ägyptische Sprache und Altertumskunde

Glossary

'Backfill'	The loose material used to fill a grave pit or access route to both physically close it and make it secure against robbery.
'Cover'	The thickness of geological material above the substructure of a subterranean tomb, between it and the surface.
'Emplacement'	The grooved housing in which a portcullis can both slide and be secured once it is in place.
'Footprint'	The area defined by the perimeter of a structure, in this book usually a superstructure.

'Footprint overhang'	The shortest distance from the perimeter of a superstructure (usually the longest edge) to the edge of the void of its underlying pit or substructure.
'Plug-stone'	The cuboid stone block inserted into descending corridors in pyramids and some private tombs.
'Secondary blocking'	Usually, a mud-brick or stone blocking behind a 'primary blocking' such as a portcullis.
'*Tafl*'	A soft sedimentary rock consisting of mud or clay and calcium carbonate, often found in limestone beds. It can range in composition from a calcerous shale to a muddy or salty limestone.
'Tongue wall'	A projecting mud-brick wall within the burial chamber of a substructure that usually abutted a wooden shrine.
'Tonne'	The metric tonne of one thousand kilograms, as opposed to the 'imperial ton' of the British and American *avoirdupois* system, which is one thousand and sixteen kilograms.
'Twin mastaba'	A single superstructure with twin offering niches serving two separate substructure systems and burials, usually of the tomb owner and spouse.

Maps

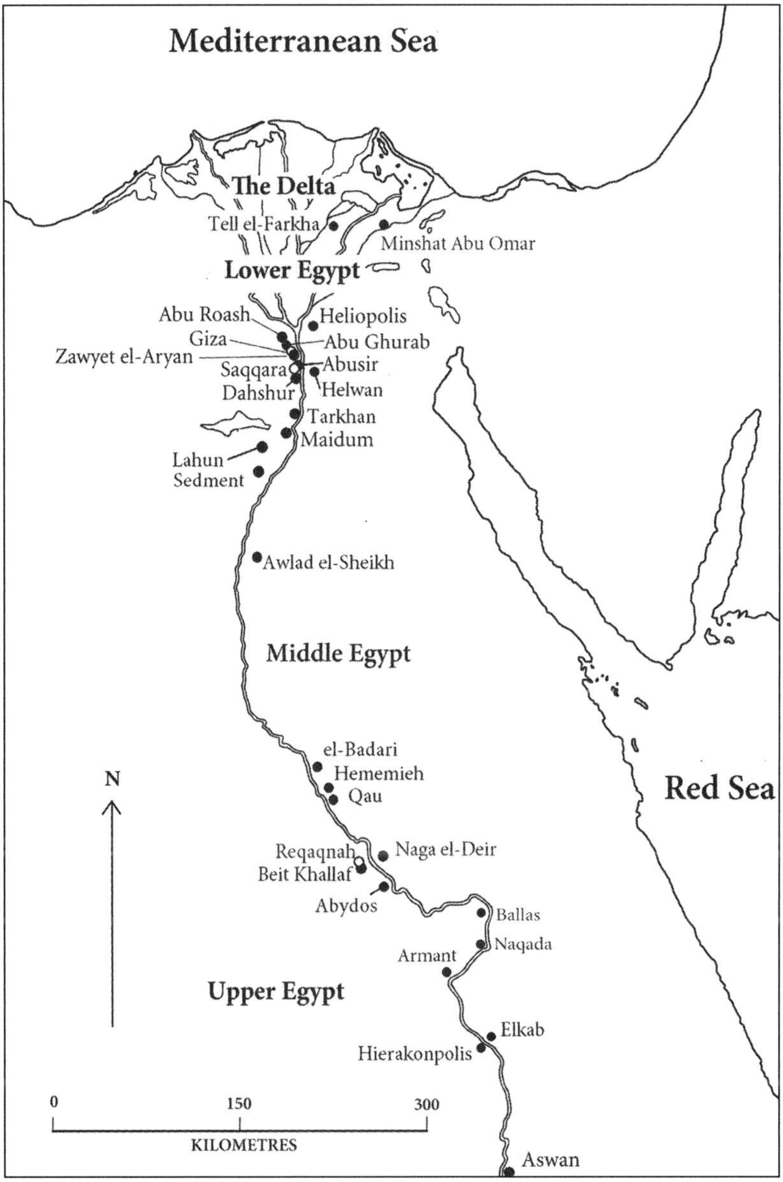

Map 1. Map of Egypt, with the key sites in the book from Minshat Abu Omar in the Delta to Aswan before the first cataract.

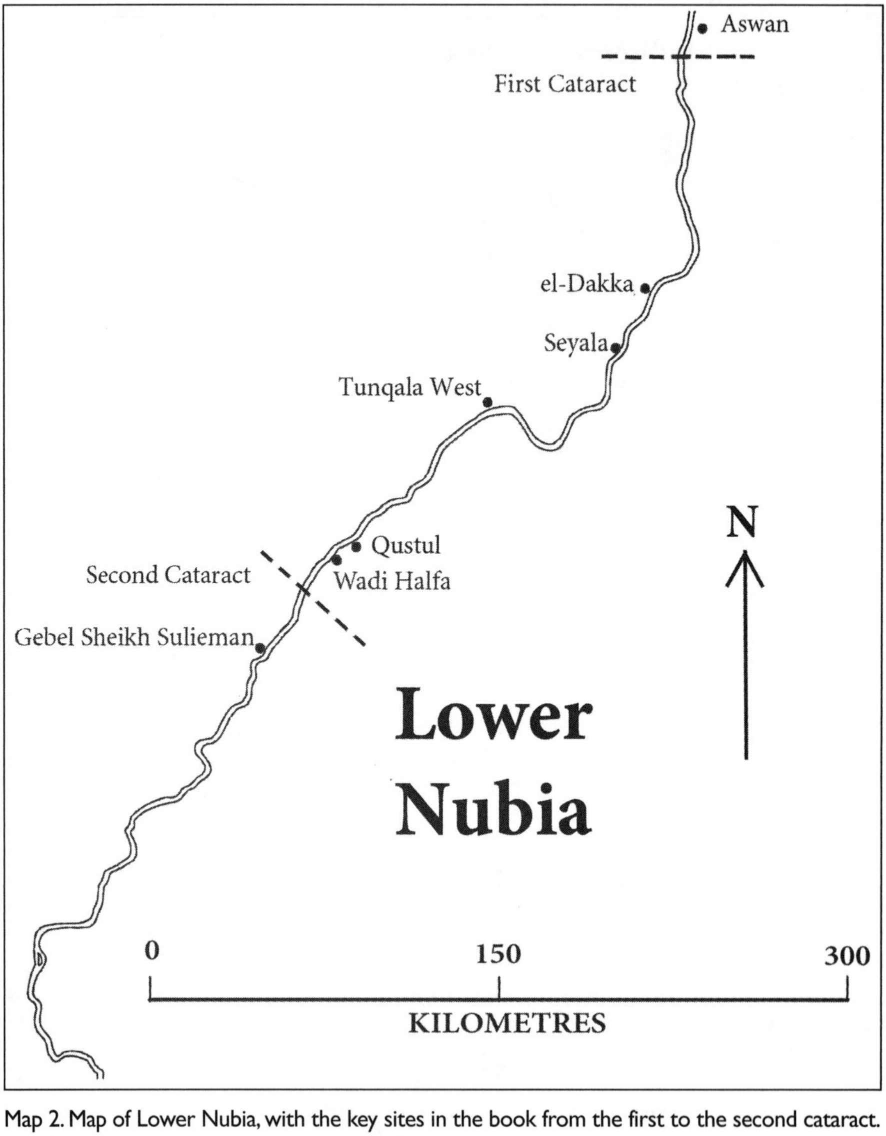

Map 2. Map of Lower Nubia, with the key sites in the book from the first to the second cataract.

1

The Purpose and Context of the Egyptian Tomb and the Need for It to Be Secure

The overwhelming evidence of the investment made by the ancient Egyptians in the construction, decoration, and protection of their tombs suggests that for them, the tomb was far more than just a practical method of hygienically disposing of their dead. It is evident from the care taken by the Egyptians to respectfully inter their corpses and equip their tombs with grave goods, from the Badarian culture (about 5000–4000 BC) onward, that during the Predynastic Period they were developing a funerary culture with particular beliefs, but precisely what these were remains open to debate.[1] Moreover, and importantly from the tomb security point of view, we also know from excavations that these Predynastic graves were being systematically robbed of their valuables, almost as soon as they were completed.[2]

We can surmise that by the end of the Predynastic Period (about 3150 BC), with the emergence of bipartite (two-part) tombs comprising a substructure for the burial and an aboveground offering place, usually allied with some form of protective superstructure,[3] the Egyptians believed in a form of afterlife[4] in which the tomb played an essential part. It did this by both protecting the body and enabling the deceased to be provided with food and drink offerings by the living, which benefited the tomb owner by providing 'magical' sustenance in the hereafter.[5] Following on, the Early Dynastic Period saw a rapid upsurge in the number of these types of tombs, which were now built in a wide variety of styles and differing locations, many of which retained the bipartite form of a concealed substructure to contain the body and a visible protective superstructure above with a defined offering place. Additionally, in a few elite necropoleis, some large tombs now also incorporated storehouses for vast numbers of grave goods, which were concealed in magazines both above- and belowground.[6] However, in parallel with these developments, it is also apparent from the increasing number of security features that were being incorporated in the tombs to protect them, such as reinforced substructures, access route blockings, and protective superstructures, that wholesale tomb robbery was rampant and a serious ongoing problem.

This substantial investment in tomb security raises two important questions. First, what was it in the tomb that needed protecting? Second, why did the tomb continue to be used in its bipartite form and remain partly visible on the surface rather than being totally concealed and hidden from view, which would have been a far more effective form of defense? These questions are best answered by looking at the mortuary beliefs and customs of the ancient Egyptians that may have influenced the tomb's design.[7]

Although there is little written evidence from the Early Dynastic Period or the Third and Fourth Dynasties concerning mortuary beliefs, later Old Kingdom inscriptions, such as the Pyramid Texts,[8] reveal that the corpse of the deceased was associated with two spiritual elements, the *ba* and the *ka*. These were an integral part of a human being in life but separated from it at death.[9] Moreover, we know that the ancient Egyptians believed that once a corpse was interred within its tomb, the structure formed not only a secure repository for the body but also a dwelling for the *ka* and the *ba*.[10] The *ka* remained in the tomb with the body; the *ba* could leave during the day to join the world of the living but had to return at night.[11] However, both had to be able to reunite with the body in the tomb every day in order for the deceased to attain the highest desirable form in the afterlife, which was an *akh*, or 'effective' spiritual being, able to enjoy an eternal existence both on earth and among the gods in the cosmos.[12] In this context, perhaps the tomb was therefore the place where, in a daily reenactment of this process, the Egyptologist Harold Hays had suggested "the hidden deceased becomes effective after rebirth."[13] Consequently, in order that this crucial cycle could take place, it would have been essential for the body, or at least its substitute in the form of a statue or relief depicting the deceased,[14] to remain in situ and undamaged in its final resting place, which undoubtedly was one of the key reasons that the tomb needed to be made secure.

In addition, from early on, personal property in the form of valuables and prized domestic objects was often included with the burial as, from the Egyptian viewpoint, the deceased was still regarded as an entity in his or her own right and would use those items in the afterlife.[15] The nature of the grave goods varied over time. In the Predynastic Period, dependent on their owner's status, graves might contain variously: stone bead necklaces; mudstone palettes for grinding cosmetics; copper fish hooks; needles; axe heads; ivory bracelets, pins, and spoons; ornamental flint tools; stone unguent and cosmetic jars; and sundry items decorated with gold foil.[16] By the Early Dynastic Period, the inventory of items deposited in high-status graves had increased considerably and included: jewelry of gold and semi-precious stones; cosmetic and toilet articles of ivory, bone, and stone; ornamental hard stone jars and vases; copper tools and vessels; furniture, games, boxes, and weapons in ivory and wood; and woven goods such as linen, clothing, and basketwork.[17]

These valuable accoutrements attracted grave robbers,[18] who sought items of portable wealth that could be easily recycled, such as jewelry, amulets, copper, silver, and gold—although ivory, textiles, and furniture, together with fresh oils and unguents, were also desirable.[19] Therefore, depending on the location of these commodities within the tomb, it also became necessary for appropriate security measures to be put in place to protect them.

Finally, both the *ba* and the *ka* could partake of sustenance by absorbing the 'essence' of food offerings provided for them in actual or symbolic form,[20] accessed through a portal that was typically marked by a stela, offering niche, or false door. Usually set into a superstructure, the portal formed a liminal zone that connected this world with the world of the dead and provided a focus where the cult of the deceased could be celebrated, offerings left, and the living could interact with the dead.[21] The visible aboveground elements therefore formed an important focal point and memorial, where the dead, although secure deep within their substructures, were still approachable and able to be communicated with,[22] cared for, and remembered as an integral part of the living community.[23]

From the tomb security point of view, the presence of such a conspicuous structure was arguably counterproductive, as it would have drawn unwelcome attention to the tomb. But, undoubtedly aware of this shortcoming, rather than discard the aboveground element altogether, the ancient Egyptians sought to make the best of both worlds by exploiting the protective potential of the superstructure and using its architecture to increase the tomb's security levels instead.

Conclusion

It would seem, therefore, that the choices made by the Egyptians in relation to their tombs' architecture, location, and contents were governed by the pursuit of their beliefs regarding the afterlife, which paradoxically rendered many of these elements vulnerable to the depredations of tomb robbers, vandals,[24] and, in times of war or civil disorder, perhaps even bands of looters.[25] To prevent this happening, and to compensate for their inherent vulnerabilities, these structures therefore needed to be made more secure, which was achieved by modifying their architecture in ways that up until the early Fourth Dynasty significantly affected the design and development of the Egyptian tomb in general, which is the topic explored in the rest of this book.

2

Securing the Early Tomb: Prehistory to the End of the Predynastic Period

This chapter traces the early development of tomb security in ancient Egypt from the Late Paleolithic Period (about 21,000–12,000 BC) up until the end of the Naqada IIIA Period (about 3300–3150 BC) to see what effect, if any, these security precautions had on the architecture of the Egyptian tomb. To put these developments into broader perspective, it concomitantly traces the development of grave architecture as a whole within the context of the various cultures concerned to 'set the scene' for the analysis and discussion in the chapters that follow.

The Late Paleolithic: An Early Beginning

The earliest intentional burial discovered in the Nile Valley appears to be that of a child, found at Taramsa Hill near Qena, which dates to the mid-Middle Paleolithic Period (about 55,000 BC). It consisted of little more than a scrape in the ground hastily filled with gravel.[1] Later graves from the Upper Paleolithic Period have also been excavated at the sites of Nazlet Khater 4 (about 31,000 BC) in Upper Egypt and Wadi Kubbaniya (about 19,000 BC) near Aswan.[2]

It is not until the Late Paleolithic Period (about 21,000–12,000 BC) that we have perhaps the first evidence of humans in the Nile Valley taking any further steps to protect their dead, over and above the provision of the usual backfilled pit by way of burial. It occurs in some graves found in a cemetery in Lower Nubia. The area, known as Site 117, is situated three kilometers north of Wadi Halfa on the east bank of the Nile, and is just south of Jebel Sahaba.[3] Here, some twelve to fourteen thousand years ago, fifty-eight bodies were interred in shallow oval pits. In addition to their soil backfill, in the majority of the burials thin undressed flat sandstone slabs (Fig. 1), varying from 0.25 to

Figure 1. Sketch section of the typical arrangement of stone slabs over the graves at Site 117 at Jebel Sahaba.

0.5 m in width, had been used to cover the graves.[4] These preparations indicate a desire to protect the interment beyond the level one might ordinarily expect at this early date. Indeed they are the first instance of a culture doing so in the area of the Upper Nile,[5] as most early graves usually consisted of no more than a shallow pit scooped out of the desert that was backfilled with spoil from the excavation, then perhaps covered with a mound of the excess soil or gravel.[6] As for the purpose of the slabs, one possibility is that they were placed there to protect the burials from the depredation of wild animals, hunting dogs, or possibly wind erosion, as due to their shallow nature the graves would have been inherently vulnerable to disturbance. Alternatively, the slabs may have been placed simply to form a memorial. But if their purpose was only that, then there would be no need to cover the entire grave; a simple grave marker would have sufficed.

The Neolithic and Predynastic Periods

The Fayum Neolithic Culture

The appearance of this culture occurred in the north of Egypt shortly before 5000 BC, suggesting a complete change in the nature of habitation in the Nile Valley, from what was fundamentally an Epipaleolithic hunter-gatherer society to an economy based mainly on the production or obtaining of food.[7] However, this society seems not to have established any permanent settlements, but rather to have relied on transient cereal cropping and fishing. As a result, no evidence has been found of any cemeteries or burials from excavations of the lakeside settlements.[8]

Merimde Beni Salama

Evidence of the very first burials associated with settlements (about 5000 BC) was found at one of the earliest established communities in Egypt, situated some sixty kilometers to the northwest of Cairo at Merimde Beni Salama in Lower Egypt.[9] For about one thousand years the inhabitants interred their dead in graves, most probably within the abandoned remains of their settlements. When excavated, the graves were found to consist of shallow oval pits (Fig. 2) in which bodies, wrapped in either skins or mats, were placed in a contracted position and sometimes covered with the vestiges of plant remains before the pits were backfilled.[10] It appears that no attempts were made to protect or secure these burials in any other way.

The Badarian Culture

In Upper and Middle Egypt the earliest phase of the Predynastic era is the Badarian, about 5000–4000 BC, named after the Middle Egyptian site at al-Badari. The main sites were Deir Tasa, Hemamieh, Matmar, and Mostagedda, which were most likely settled by about 4000 BC.[11] During the Badarian Period, the typical burial was made in an oval or circular pit, with the contracted body swathed in a mat or goatskin

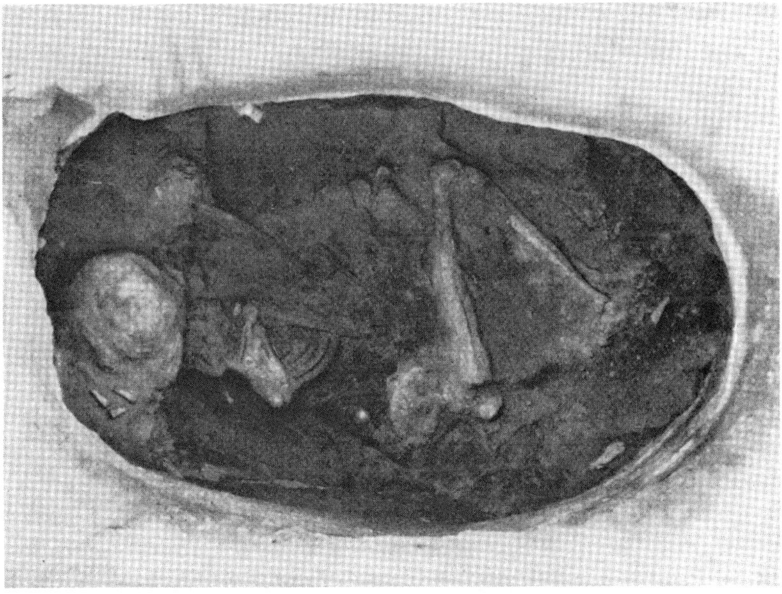

Figure 2. A shallow pit burial at Merimde with the body in a contracted position.

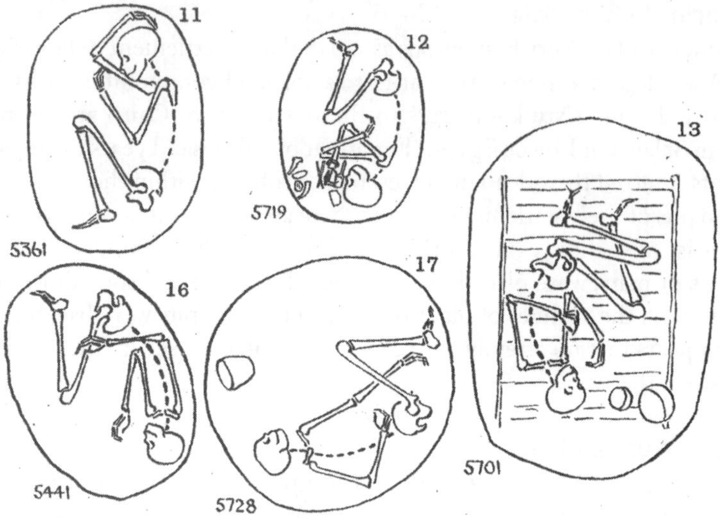

Figure 3. Assorted Badarian graves.

(Fig. 3) and accompanied by an assortment of grave goods. After interment had taken place, the grave would be backfilled and, it is generally thought, covered with a mound of gravel or sand.[12]

From the viewpoint of tomb security, the great Egyptologist George Reisner suggested that the function of a grave mound during the Predynastic Period was twofold, in that it provided further protection for the burial itself and acted as a focus for the provision of cult offerings for its occupant. Moreover, he proposed that this mound may have provided the prototype on which the majority of later Egyptian grave superstructures were based.[13] But while a mound of gravel would hinder a grave robber or foraging animal to an extent, the underlying reasons for this practice may initially have been utilitarian. First, there would have been a greater volume of excess soil from the pit than was necessary to backfill it, due to the addition of the body and grave goods. This excess may simply have been piled on top. Second, the mound may have been left there so that the extra soil would eventually compensate for the otherwise inevitable depression that would have been caused by the settling of the backfill over the grave's surface. Such depressions in graves are well known and caused by two factors: 'primary depressions' are caused by settling of the backfill in the pit, and 'secondary depressions' are caused by the decomposition and collapse of the abdominal cavity and the concomitant release of gases.[14] This 'mounding' can be seen in modern graves, which, once dug and subsequently closed, have the excess fill piled up over the burial to allow for settlement.[15] In addition, the mound also minimizes the problem of cracking along the edge of the pit where the looser new fill breaks away from the compacted surround.[16]

Concerning Predynastic burials, the presence of such a mound is still a matter of debate.[17] Whether this architectural feature was retained or leveled out is unknown, and it is not easy to ascertain today whether it existed at all.[18] In either case, there is ample archaeological evidence from the period that contemporary grave robbery was taking place and was developing into one of the most enduring and unfortunate aspects of ancient Egyptian culture.[19] At al-Badari, for example, Guy Brunton reported that a grave at Cemetery 5100 "contained a plundered female body, showing that the robbing of these graves began soon after the actual interments."[20] Indeed, more recently, Wendy Anderson, in her quantitative analysis of the Badarian burials excavated by Brunton, demonstrated that grave robbers were regularly robbing the "highly visible tombs" of high-status individuals during this period. Her statistics show that larger graves possessing in excess of three grave goods were more frequently either robbed or "disturbed" than those containing less, and that the looting was actually occurring during the Badarian Period itself.[21] As a result, it is tempting to wonder whether, from the point of view of the security of the Predynastic grave, such a 'telltale' mound was all that desirable in the long term, and to speculate that perhaps the grave was simply left to settle out level, as in the cemeteries of today.

Some of the burials excavated by Brunton at al-Badari were found to contain sticks and matting at the sides of the graves, which he concluded might have been the remains of some sort of collapsed "roofing," intended to prevent sand and gravel from falling on the body. These, Brunton suggests, may have been made into a type of rigid "tent" to keep the body free of sand, which would explain the apparent lack of any other roofing arrangements in the graves.[22] Another possibility is that this sort of 'tent' structure may have also been introduced to preempt other post-internment problems likely to arise with a burial. First, it may have been intended to prevent disruption by animals, which is a common cause of disturbance in burials, as scavenging carnivores, omnivores, and rodents are all known to consume corpses.[23] Second, perhaps it formed a secondary physical barrier in addition to the backfill to deter the intrusions of grave robbers. Last, it could also have

Figure 4. Burials at al-Omari Cemetery F, showing heaps of stones covering the graves.

circumvented the need for a 'giveaway' mound over the pit by obviating the inevitable 'depression' over the grave by preventing the fill from settling and compacting. This would have offered additional security from the risk of being located by tomb robbers. Alternatively, if the mound *was* indeed considered to be a desirable feature of the grave, and concealment was not an issue, the 'tent' may have been installed as a support to prevent the mound's collapse from the aforementioned effects of primary depression.

Al-Omari

In Lower Egypt, just northeast of Saqqara and located at the base of Jebel Tura near Helwan, three settlement sites and two cemeteries dating to around 4000 BC mark the remains of the al-Omari culture. Contemporary with the late phase of Merimde Beni Salama, at al-Omari the dead were buried in shallow graves or in the remains of old storage pits adjacent to the settlement or the individual habitation.[24] In the graves, some of the bodies were found covered in reed mats and occasionally accompanied by a pot, or a sporadic flint. The interments themselves were backfilled with sand or domestic debris. It is noteworthy that a number of the graves were covered by mounds of stones (Fig. 4). The limestone blocks used in their construction were randomly placed

Figure 5. Burial with grave goods at Maadi, grave MA45.

and varied in size and number, with some being quite large, such as in graves F1–11.[25] It may be that these stones were intended to protect the grave from disturbance by erosion, animals, or robbers. Their like is not seen again until the Early Dynastic Period, where they are found protecting graves at Abu Rawash.[26]

The Buto Maadi Culture

Also in Lower Egypt, at the start of the fourth millennium BC, evidence of another distinct but slightly later culture appears with the Buto Maadi culture, the sites of which are located to the east of the Nile, south of Cairo. The major evidence comes from the three main cemeteries at Maadi, Heliopolis, and Wadi Digla, where, unlike at Merimde Beni Salama, cemeteries were distinctly separated from the settlement. The six hundred burials recorded so far have shown no evidence of any sophisticated grave architecture (Fig. 5), as the majority of the interments were solitary burials in simple oval pits. It appears from vestiges of wood found in some of the graves that a few of the bodies discovered may have been wrapped in mats and possibly covered in branches.[27] However, unlike their contemporaries in Upper Egypt and Nubia, whose burials were now becoming progressively more elaborate, these graves are notable for the comparative paucity

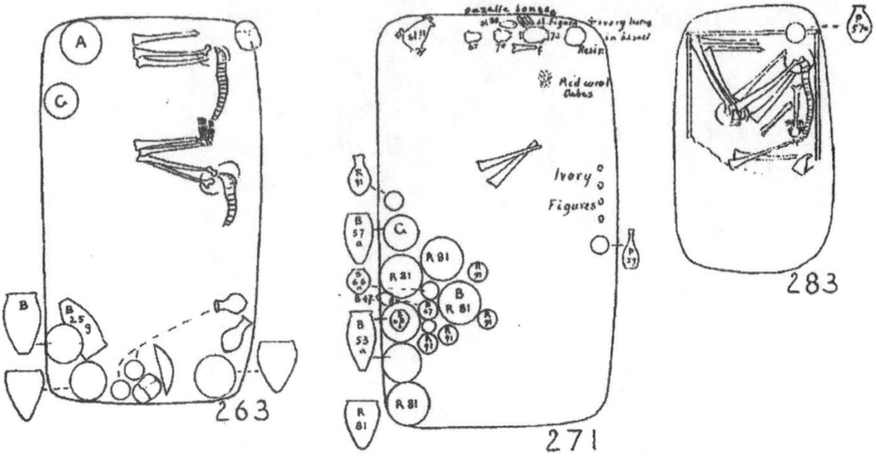

Figure 6. Rectangular-shaped graves from Naqada.

of grave goods or personal adornments.[28] In this case no attempt seems to have been made to improve the security of the grave other than the aforementioned branches, which may have been placed there to thwart scavenging animals or the casual grave robber.

Naqada I

The next phase of the Predynastic era in Upper Egypt is the Naqada I Period, which dates to about 3900–3650 BC. The period was named after the largest of the Predynastic burial sites in Upper Egypt, which was Naqada, and the majority of related sites can be found along the Nile from Hierakonpolis in the south to Abydos in the north. Although there are other sites at al-Badari and the Fayum, the three key centers are located at Abydos, Hierakonpolis, and Naqada.[29]

The majority of burials were simple oval or rectangular graves, covered by rudimentary roofs of wood branches and twigs (Fig. 6) supporting a covering of soil.[30] Flinders Petrie and James Quibell described the typical tombs as "vertical pits, with the body laid on the floor; and the pit in all wealthy tombs was roofed over with beams and brushwood."[31] The inclusion of these roofs in the grave suggests that the previous discussion regarding the security aspects of the Badarian period applies here too: it may be that the roof was designed to thwart tomb robbers and scavenging animals, as well as to prevent primary and secondary depressions. Therefore, it could be regarded as another form of defensive measure to protect the tomb itself. In addition, the need to support a grave mound, if it existed, should not be excluded from the realm of possibility.

Naqada II

In the Naqada II Period (about 3650–3300 BC), the majority of burials take the form of the now ubiquitous grave pit, each containing a single body in a crouched position.[32] That a number of ordinary, non-elite graves were also being systematically targeted by robbers during this period is particularly evident from an excavation at Cemetery HK43 at Hierakonpolis, which is dated to Naqada IIA–IIC. Here, the pattern of soil disturbance indicates that the robbers knew exactly where individuals were buried, and that what they were searching for (possibly a copper necklace) was situated around the deceased's neck. In some cases, a cut in the fabric and matting surrounding the neck is the only indication that tomb robbers had been there at all, such was the accuracy of their digging.[33] Moreover, it is likely that the graves at HK43 were marked with a mound of sand or stones, though no trace remains today.[34] As suggested earlier, this may have assisted the robbers in locating their booty.

It is during Naqada II that improvements in construction methods in tombs of the elite become increasingly discernible. For example, grave walls in some of the more sophisticated tombs were now reinforced with liners. These, when present, were made either of a wattle of sticks and wicker or of wooden boards that kept the surrounding soil or sand away from the body. In both cases the tomb would have been roofed over with mats or sticks and possibly plastered with mud.[35] While linen shrouds or mats were generally preferred to animal skins for wrapping the body during this period, the appearance of 'wealthier' burials also signals the first emergence of coffins. Initially these were made of basketwork, later also clay, and eventually wood. Additionally, for perhaps the select few, the use of brick lining in graves was now increasingly frequent.[36] Its function was to consolidate the sides of the grave, prevent the collapse of the surrounding soil or gravel, and possibly support a roof (Fig. 7).[37] Depending on a mud-brick liner's thickness, it may also have provided a degree of protection against lateral tunneling by robbers.[38]

One of the purposes behind many of these innovations, which permitted a larger grave to be constructed, may have been the further segregation of the body from contact with the surrounding ground and the provision of additional storage space for grave goods, which were

Figure 7. A typical section through a late Naqada II grave lined with mud-brick. It is shown here with a wood and brick roof, covered by a mound.

now more often placed farther from the body.[39] However, much as these innovations may have seemed desirable at the time, one unintended and unfortunate consequence of this enlarged capacity for grave goods may of course have been that of attracting more tomb robbers!

These developments and their increased levels of sophistication can be seen, for instance, at Naqada with the appearance of a segregated elite burial ground known as Cemetery T. The burials located there were generally larger than those of the adjacent non-elite cemeteries and accompanied by numerous grave goods.[40] Most notable are tombs T10, T15, T20, and T23, in which brick linings were employed that no doubt supported beams bearing wooden roofs.[41] In other high-status cemeteries, roofs were also used to close a few graves without the benefit of a supporting brick liner, as for example in tomb B101 in Cemetery B at 'Abadiya and tombs U-133 and U-149 in Cemetery U at Umm al-Qa'b.[42]

Although the incorporation of a roof in a tomb's design was undoubtedly successful in concealing and protecting the body and its grave goods, in the long term it actually proved counterproductive. This was probably because a roof, however strong, made it easier to rob the contents: it was now simply a case of tunneling sideways into the void

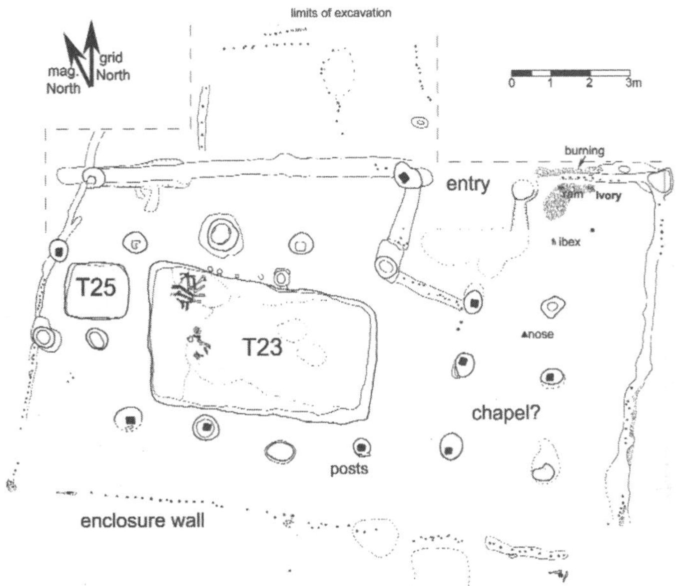

Figure 8. Plan of tomb 23 at Cemetery HK6 at Hierakonpolis. The postholes for the superstructure and enclosure can be clearly seen.

of the grave cyst, avoiding the roof itself, and then looting it in comfort, rather than having to excavate the whole burial pit of its backfill.[43]

While there is no evidence of a roof per se over its burial pit, perhaps the earliest example of an elite or royal grave, and certainly the largest, is tomb 23, found in the elite cemetery HK6 at Hierakonpolis, which dates to Naqada IIA–B. It possesses one of the first examples of a superstructure and funerary enclosure (in wood and wicker) found to date (Fig. 8). Although this superstructure is not definitely identified as a 'temple' for its associated tomb, evidence from its surroundings demonstrates that the tomb belongs to a long-established 'ritual precinct.'[44] While these types of decorated lightweight superstructures may not have offered much physical protection to the burial itself, one might suggest that from the point of view of security, the location of the tomb within a sacred space such as the cemetery would have offered a degree of protection from disturbance and robbery, at least in times of political stability, when presumably the cemetery would have been policed in some way.[45]

A further example of this type of tomb complex, perhaps dating to Naqada IIB, can be seen from the excavation of tomb 26, also at

Figure 9. Tomb 26 at Cemetery HK6 at Hierakonpolis, showing the ledge for supporting the roofing beams, along with the surrounding postholes.

cemetery HK6. This has revealed remains of wooden boards preserved on a ledge running around the perimeter of the tomb (Fig. 9), suggesting that, like the tombs at Naqada Cemetery T, the burial chamber had a roof.[46] It is not known whether these roofs were topped with a mound, perhaps retained with a wooden or wicker wall as Reisner speculated,[47] or surmounted with a lightweight superstructure, as may have existed over the earlier tomb 23 at Hierakonpolis.[48]

Slightly later in date, and contemporary with the other elite tombs from Cemetery T at Naqada, is the famous decorated tomb 100 at Hierakonpolis, located in the 'Painted Tomb Cemetery' some two kilometers from the elite Cemetery HK6.[49] This grave was cut into the hard desert sand and lined with mud-brick, and it almost certainly had a wooden roof—as did many of its neighbors, such as tomb 500, which, when excavated, still had the remains of wooden beams and posts to support roof planking.[50] More important for this discussion is that the geographical location, decoration, and architecture of tomb 100 may demonstrate a security response to an external threat. Evidence of burning from recent excavations of the complexes of tombs 23 and D9 in Cemetery HK6 has led Renée Friedman to suggest that the relocation of elite or royal burials from their traditional location at HK6 to the cemetery of the Painted Tomb, and the concurrent moving of the previously painted superstructure, decoration, and 'chapel' underground, may have been a response to the deliberate burning and destruction of the lightweight superstructures and funerary artefacts at HK6.[51] This damage was possibly caused by the destructive results of an unknown political upheaval or some other catastrophic event.[52] Indeed, that instability and disorder existed during this period is evident from the investment in fortifications for 'royal' cities, such as Hierakonpolis, Naqada, and Abydos, which seems to demonstrate the response of these communities to frequent threats.[53]

This change in the level of investment from the aboveground to the subterranean complex could be regarded as one of the earliest tangible responses to a threat to the security of the elite or 'royal' tomb. Consequently, it may signal a marked change in approach toward high-status and elite tomb architecture, as it would appear that from this period onward security considerations necessarily became an important factor in tomb design.

Naqada IIIA to the start of Naqada IIIB

During this period, which begins around 3300 BC,[54] while for the vast majority of the non-elite the simple pit burial undoubtedly remained the norm,[55] we have evidence of further developments in higher-status interments, two examples of which are found at Cemetery HK6 in Hierakonpolis. The first is the mud-brick-lined and wooden-roofed tomb 11, which dates to Naqada IIIA1–2. Interestingly from the tomb security perspective, excavations revealed that the tomb was robbed via trenches cut into both the northeast and southwest edges of its pit, which had been deliberately dug to avoid its protective roof.[56] The second, tomb 16, whose restored structure dates to Naqada IIIA2,[57] was discovered fully lined with "Flemish bonded" bricks. Remains suggest that its roof was supported by a large central wooden beam of cedar that ran the length of its burial chamber.[58] Aboveground, the tomb was surrounded by fence posts of unknown date, like much of the rest of HK6.[59]

Corresponding to, and indeed contemporary with, tombs 11 and 16 is the famous tomb U-j in Cemetery U at Umm al-Qa'b, Abydos, which has been dated to Naqada IIIA2. According to U-j's excavators, the layout of this rectangular, brick-lined, and multi-chambered tomb may have been modeled on a small palace of the period (Fig. 10). It still possesses the vestiges of its roof, made of layers of mat and plastered mud-bricks supported by acacia-log beams between 0.15 and 0.2 m in diameter, which overhung the grave pit by between 0.2 and 0.35 m. The

Figure 10. Tomb U-j at Umm al-Qa'b, showing its thick mud-brick liners and their position below the ancient desert levels.

existence of these layers of roofing material and the location of the top of the tomb's 0.45 m thick mud-brick liner at 0.6 m below the original desert surface suggest a roof and accompanying backfill of substantial dimensions. These, together with the grave's liner, were intended to offer a considerable degree of security for the tomb's occupant, who was interred in a wooden shrine in the largest of the chambers and accompanied by numerous grave goods.[60] It is therefore possible that, as in the case of tomb 100 at Hierakonpolis, we may be seeing a further development for security reasons of the move underground of the earlier complex superstructure arrangements seen in the high-status tombs at HK6. The return of such superstructures as a 'model palace' aboveground probably does not occur again until the reign of King Hor-Aha and his successors at Umm al-Qa'b, in the form of their associated funerary enclosures at nearby Abydos North.

While these developments signal the appearance of larger and more complex elite or high-status graves during this period, also of specific interest for this discussion are the contemporary graves just to the north of Hierakonpolis, across the Nile on the east bank at al-Kab. Here the remains of a Naqada IIIA cemetery, containing nearly fifty tombs, have been discovered, together with a smaller number of Naqada IIIB–D graves,[61] many of which have security-related features. Some of the most important graves—gauged by tomb size and the value of the funerary goods—are pit burials that incorporate undressed sandstone slabs. Rectangular in form, these tombs vary in their use of the stone. The slabs were used either to partially line the smaller graves or as coverings for the graves themselves, where the excavators note that their placement preponderated over the funerary goods.[62]

Of particular interest at this site are two large graves dating to Naqada IIIA2. No. 69, although disturbed, was found partially covered with two stone slabs, the largest of which was 1.4 m long, 0.3 m wide, and 0.14 m thick. In much better condition and undisturbed by tomb robbers, no. 85, the larger of the graves, was roofed over entirely with four large sandstone slabs after being backfilled (Fig. 11).[63] Although the use of stone like this is not generally characteristic for tombs of this period,[64] it provides an interesting addition to the emerging battery of defensive

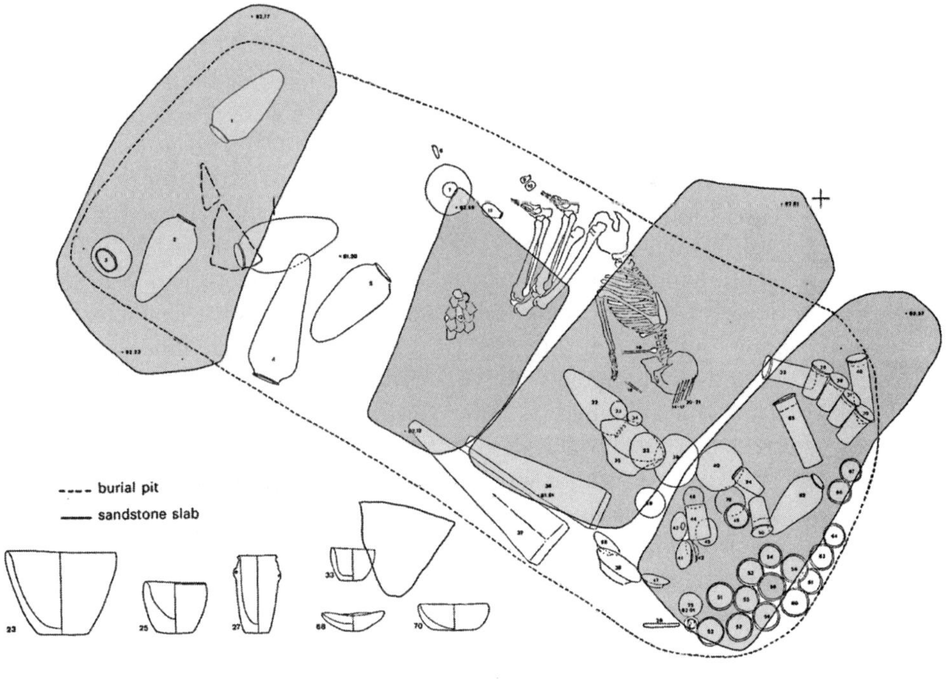

Figure 11. Grave 85 at al-Kab, showing the large sandstone slabs laid over the grave. The pottery dates the burial to Naqada IIIA2.

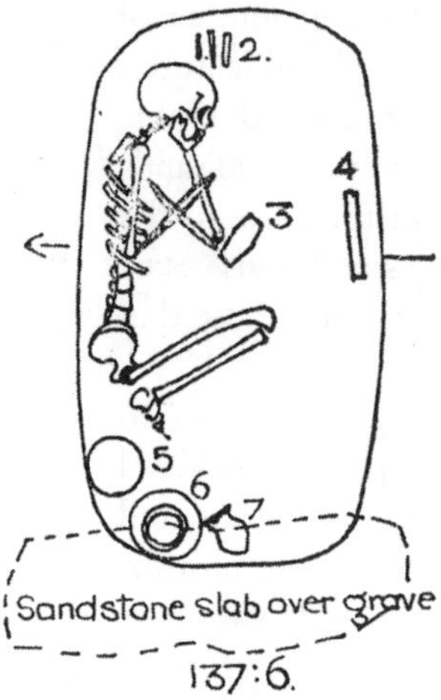

Figure 12. Tomb 6 in Cemetery 137 at Seyala, showing a sandstone slab in position over the grave.

measures in Egyptian tombs. The added benefits of using stone in this fashion to provide security are obvious, and while it has been acknowledged that the function of the stones at this site may also have been as grave markers, the sheer weight and solidity of the slabs would have provided a physical barrier to the depredations of tomb robbers. Indeed, the effectiveness of the stones in grave no. 85 is attested by the undisturbed state of its contents, which were found intact.[65]

Contemporaneously, in Lower Nubia security arrangements similar to those at al-Kab were used for the burials of the so-called 'princes' of Seyala, at Cemetery 137, half a kilometer from Seyala at Nag' Umm Agag. Here three generations of nobles and their retainers belonging to the Late A-Group culture, which dates from Naqada IIIA1 to Naqada IIIA2, had their tombs dug into the local clay and alluvium on the east bank of the Nile.[66] Like some of the tombs at al-Kab, these pit graves were also roofed with "sandstone slabs of considerable size and length."[67] The largest, tomb no. 1, was originally roofed over with sandstone slabs, one of which collapsed into the grave. When the slab was finally removed during the excavation, many artefacts in Egyptian style were revealed, including gold-handled maces, copper items, stone vessels, and Naqadan pottery.[68] A smaller tomb nearby, no. 6,[69] illustrates the characteristic roofing arrangement (Fig. 12). Farther south, there are nine similarly dated graves protected with stone slabs in Cemetery 268 at Tunqala West. A typical example is grave 3, whose pit was protected by sandstone slabs, one of which was 2 m long and 0.88 m wide. Like many of the graves at this site, it was once protected by a superstructure consisting of a low perimeter wall of fieldstones filled with a sand core.[70]

Meanwhile, farther south, contemporary with the tombs at Seyala and Tunqala West, several large high-status tombs, some of which have been dated to Naqada IIIA–B, were being prepared at Cemetery L at Qustul, also in Lower Nubia.[71] The graves took the form of large rectangular pits excavated into the alluvium, into the sides of which were dug burial chambers or loculi, whose entrances were blocked with layers of enormous stones.[72] Out of the twenty-five tombs found

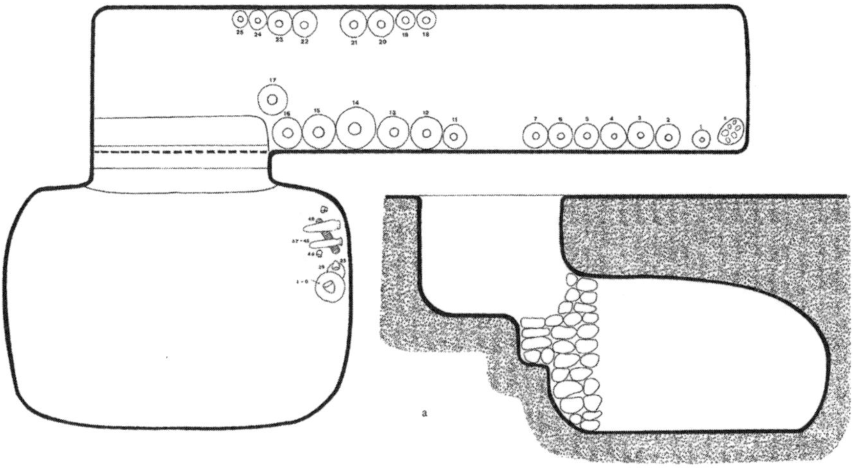

Figure 13. Plan and section of tomb L23 at Qustul, showing the stone blocking to the burial chamber.

dating to this period, the most notable examples are L2, L5, L9, L11, L19, L22, L23, and L24. These are believed to be contemporary with the royal or elite tombs of Locality HK6 at Hierakonpolis, and Bruce Williams has suggested that the largest examples, such as L23, are the direct forerunners of the HK6 tombs.[73] The biggest of all, tomb L24, is regarded as broadly contemporaneous with tomb U-j at Umm al-Qa'b and dates to Naqada IIIA2.[74] Tomb L23 consists of a pit with a stepped-down side chamber, or loculus, cut in one end (Fig. 13). Apart from the usual soil fill, it is not clear if any special arrangements were made to close off access to the pit itself, but the side chamber, which contained the burial and other items, had been deliberately sealed off with stone blocks, while the remainder of the tomb was used for the storage of large quantities of grave goods.[75] This separation may have been intended to isolate the body from the grave goods, but from the tomb security point of view the real benefit of the side chamber type of construction is that it took advantage of the surrounding geology to form a strong natural roof over the burial itself, and thus offered more protection to the body than a simpler pit grave. Additionally, in order to rob the tomb, the pit would first have to be cleared of its backfill and grave goods and any intervening blocking would have to be removed before access could be made to the burial itself.

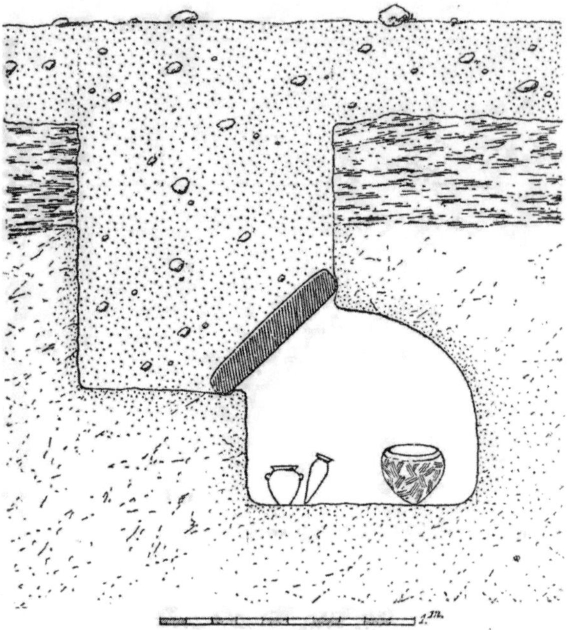

Figure 14. Cross section of burial 8 at Kom al-Ahmar (Naqada III), showing large stone slabs blocking access to the burial loculus.

A comparable and contemporary grave may signal that the sealed side burial chamber was also adopted as a means of security further north, in Upper Egypt. Known as burial 8, the grave was found intact by Henri de Morgan at Kom al-Ahmar opposite al-Kab (Fig. 14). It can be dated to Naqada IIIA from its finds.[76] Once the burial had been made and the grave goods installed, the loculus was closed with stone slabs laid to form an angle and sealed with Nile mud. The whole was then concealed by filling the pit with backfill to the surface.[77] Therefore, at both Kom al-Ahmar and Qustul it appears that we have some of the earliest examples of a specific architectural attempt not only to enhance the security of the body but concomitantly to part the corpse from its accompanying funerary provisions by using a separate chamber with a blocking. Notably, both contained a mixture of Naqada III and A-Group pottery,[78] which may indicate a high degree of interaction between the two cultures.[79]

Nearby, an example of what may be the earliest use of a stone portcullis occurs in a higher-status (in terms of size and location) tomb of similar design situated at Locality HK6 at Hierakonpolis.[80] Tomb 2 possibly dates to Naqada IIIA–B,[81] and was entirely excavated into the surrounding sandstone and shale strata (Fig. 15). The tomb's pit

Figure 15. Tomb 2 at Locality HK6 at Hierakonpolis, showing the niche in the base and side and one of its associated 'portcullis' stones propped up at one end.

descended through a 0.65 m top layer of gravel and silt, into the rock, to reach a total overall depth of 3.5 m. Around its upper edge, a 0.2 m deep step was cut to accommodate roofing beams. A hole cut into the base of this pit, at the southeastern end, had a small 1.7 m high side chamber excavated on its eastern face whose ceiling tapered internally down to a height of 0.5 m. Inside the pit, two portcullises of cherty limestone were found propped up, which the excavators assumed were intended to close off the side chamber, in a manner comparable to the stone walling of tomb L23 at Qustul. Presumably the side chamber would have then contained the deceased. One of the portcullises was 1.4 m long, 0.9 m wide, and 0.2 m thick and would have weighed approximately 0.8 metric tonnes.[82] It is also possible, given that remains of mud plaster were found on the walls, that the portcullises were concealed by plastering, which could have increased the security of the burial chamber by hiding it from the view of potential plunderers. Therefore, not only did this tomb benefit from the additional security provided by the natural stone roof created by its niche, but its use of shaped embryonic 'portcullis' slabs to prevent access to the burial also demonstrates a marked evolutionary progression from the earlier use of dry stone as at Qustul and the 'lean-to' use of stone slabs at Kom al-Ahmar. This was a technological advance that would only

Figure 16. The excavated grave 1845 at Tarkhan, with the mud-brick superstructure wall now missing its gravel fill.

be realized to its full potential many years later with the development of the sliding portcullis in the Early Dynastic Period.

Apart from these exceptional developments, we have already seen that the majority of contemporary elite pit tombs elsewhere in Egypt were protected from above by little more than a wooden roof, backfill, and possibly a mound. However, although details are scarce, there is evidence that the first mud-brick superstructures were beginning to make an appearance during this period. The pit tomb 563.H.11 at Helwan, which dates to Naqada IIIA2 by its contents, was recorded by Zaaki Saad in his unpublished field diaries as possessing a mud-brick superstructure of some kind.[83] In addition, small mud-brick-walled superstructures were noted by Petrie at Tarkhan, overlying pit tombs 852 and 1845, which also date to this period (Fig. 16). These structures were filled with sand and gravel,[84] and would have provided a certain degree of additional protection to the underlying grave, as well as providing a focus for food offerings.[85] Therefore, these developments signal the emergence of another defensive measure for the protection of the tomb, namely the mud-brick mastaba, which, unlike a tumulus (the overlying mound formed from the excavation spoil), was designed to be permanent and was soon to become an essential part of a tomb's frontline defenses.

Conclusion

The need for better security arrangements had been accelerated by the emergence of an elite class in a socially differentiated Egypt from the Naqada I Period onward. In the larger tombs of the elite, greater quantities of valuable commodities were being included in the burial, leading to the concomitant problem of increased levels of tomb robbery.[86] As Egyptian society evolved, with ever-increasing amounts of grave goods being deposited in tombs, providing yet more opportunities for the unscrupulous, it is reasonable to link the development of these early security measures with an urgent need to ward off the predations of grave robbers. This rapid development of architectural solutions to address the problem of tomb security would continue in the Early Dynastic period and Old Kingdom, with ever more complex and innovative measures being introduced in royal and private tombs, the evolution of which is described in the following chapters.

3

Defending the Pit Tomb: From Egypt's Unification to the Mid-First Dynasty

The last chapter looked at the development of the Egyptian tomb and its security measures in the most formative epochs in Egyptian history, the Neolithic and Predynastic Periods, during which Egypt progressed from a land inhabited by wandering hunter-gatherers to a fully stratified society based in settlements. In the discussion it became apparent that from the Naqada II Period onward many architectural features in tombs evolved as a direct response to escalating levels of robbery, which resulted from the increased material wealth deposited in the burials of the emerging elite.

At the end of the Predynastic, the next phase is the Early Dynastic Period, which is marked by the emergence of the first kings of Egypt in Dynasty '0' (about 3150 BC). They are followed by King Narmer, who both unified Upper and Lower Egypt into a single state and founded the First Dynasty (about 2190 BC). These political developments brought for the privileged few a greater material prosperity that was reflected in their wealthier burials and increasingly lavish tombs, which now required even greater protection from robbery.

This chapter looks at the measures used to defend royal and private tombs in the first half of the Early Dynastic Period,[1] from Dynasty '0' to the mid-First Dynasty (Naqada IIIB–IIIC2),[2] to see what architectural features were introduced to protect them against robbery and how these influenced the development of the ancient Egyptian tomb. The first part deals with tombs of the kings and queens of the period in the royal cemetery at Abydos. The second part discusses selected examples from the far greater number of private tombs found throughout the whole of Egypt.

Royal Tombs

Abydos, Umm al-Qa'b

The first royal tombs of the Early Dynastic Period are situated at Umm al-Qa'b in Abydos, just south of their Predynastic forebears in Cemetery U. Along the path of the great wadi to its west, the royal necropolis had developed progressively southward from Naqada I onward, beginning with Cemetery U in the north and ending with the graves of the last six kings and one queen of the First Dynasty and the final two kings of the Second. Between them in Cemetery B are the tombs of Dynasty '0' and the earliest kings of the First Dynasty.[3] The earliest tombs in Cemetery B are those of the Dynasty '0' kings Iry-Hor and Ka, followed by that of Narmer of the First Dynasty.

Iry-Hor

Designated as tomb B0/1/2 and dated to Dynasty '0,' the pit tomb of King Iry-Hor comprises three mud-brick-lined pits, of which B2 is the burial chamber,[4] with B0 and B1 acting as magazines (Fig. 17).[5] The top of the mud-brick lining of B2, which is only one-and-a-half bricks thick, originally sat 0.8 m under the ancient desert level and supported a wood and mud-brick roof. This was probably composed of closely spaced crossbars covered with at least two layers

Figure 17. Tomb B0/1/2, the tomb of King Iry-Hor.

of brick that overlapped the pit by 1.25 to 1.45 m. This in turn was covered with a layer of mud that ran into the desert floor and was most likely concealed from view by the spoil from the pit, so nothing remained visible.[6]

Ka

Little remains of the tomb of King Ka, numbered B7/9 (Fig. 18). Of its two pits, B7 is considered to be the burial chamber due to its superior construction, while B9 was intended for storage. Internally, both pits were lined with sloping mud-brick walls of one brick's thickness. It is suggested that the roof, like that of Iry-Hor's tomb, comprised a framework of beams overlaid with one or two layers of brick,[7] set at 0.5 m below the level of the desert, where it overlapped the brick lining by 0.5 m all round. Once the burial had taken place, the remainder would have been filled up to the desert level with backfill from the excavation, as with all of the tombs at Umm al-Qa'b.[8]

Narmer

Tomb B17/18 is ascribed to King Narmer,[9] the founder of the First Dynasty. It initially consisted of two separate chambers, but the

Figure 18. Tomb B7/9, the tomb of King Ka.

Figure 19. Tomb B17/18, the tomb of King Narmer.

original mud-brick liners were only a single brick's length in thickness, and—due to ancient repairs to the original collapsed wall between the two—now form a single chamber separated by a dividing wall. In burial chamber B18, remains indicate that the roof was set 0.3 m below the original desert level and was similar to those of Iry-Hor's and Ka's tombs (Fig. 19). Two postholes in the floor of B17, the adjacent subsidiary chamber, suggest some sort of tent-like structure may have been erected within it, but it is unlikely that these posts were intended to support a roof.[10]

The thin brick linings and the compacted sand surrounding these tombs would not have offered much more protection than those of their Predynastic predecessors in Cemetery U, although it is reported that the desert sand surrounding Narmer's tomb is the consistency of soft sandstone,[11] which suggests that tunneling through it would require a certain degree of effort. Indeed, the main problem with these mud-brick liners seems to have been their tendency to collapse under lateral pressure from the surrounding sand,[12] which would presumably have affected their roofs as well, thus creating a giveaway depression and possibly inviting the attention of grave robbers. Nonetheless, with their roofs set well down and their pits backfilled and brought level with the desert, the substructures of these early royal tombs would have been well concealed and probably difficult to enter.

Aboveground, there is little tangible evidence of the existence of defensive superstructures over the tombs of the early kings at Abydos;[13]

therefore, the discussion of this topic will rely on recent scholarship on the royal cemetary at Umm al-Qa'b regarding the possible forms of any such structures. To date, no superstructures have been proposed for the tombs of Iry-Hor, Ka, or Narmer, but it is reasonable to suppose that their graves would have been covered with some sort of low mound,[14] even if it were just the excess backfill from their grave pits. However, with the tombs of the next three monarchs at Umm al-Qa'b—Hor-Aha, Djer, and Djet—major changes and improvements to the defensive architecture of the royal tomb are introduced, most notably the introduction of the protective tumulus, and possibly the first royal superstructures.[15]

Hor-Aha

Although essentially still a pit grave, it is with the tomb of Hor-Aha that we see a noticeable increase in the overall size, strength, and solidity of the royal sepulcher's construction in comparison to its immediate predecessors (Fig. 20). Located in Cemetery B, chambers B10/15/19 are attributed to the king, of which the midmost B15 is considered to be the burial chamber,[16] with B10 and B19 functioning as magazines. Additionally, for the first time, two other chambers and thirty-five subsidiary tombs containing members of the royal household accompany the complex to its east.[17] In a significant strengthening of the structure in comparison to its earlier neighbors, chambers B10/15/19 were lined with thick, sloping mud-brick walls approximately 1.5 to 2.1 m thick, set 0.6 to 0.8 m below the ancient desert surface. Internally, the three chambers contained wooden structures or 'shrines,' which were supported by columns within the pits along their longer sides.[18]

In burial chamber B15, the roof was built of stout wooden crossbars supporting a mat overlay over which further layers of mud-brick were built up to form a slightly curved cover perhaps 0.3 to 0.4 m thick. The whole was then mud-plastered down to the desert edge. The other chambers, B17 and B19, were similarly covered, albeit with flatter roofs of lighter construction. Due to the lack of erosion of the mud plaster on these roofs, Werner Kaiser and Günter Dreyer, the tomb's excavators, have suggested they were probably protected with a large sand tumulus formed from the excavation spoil,[19] thus creating what may have been the earliest protective superstructure over a royal tomb.

The enormous increase in the thickness of Hor-Aha's mud-brick tomb liners provided several benefits. First, they shored up the surrounding desert matrix and prevented the collapse of the tomb's internal

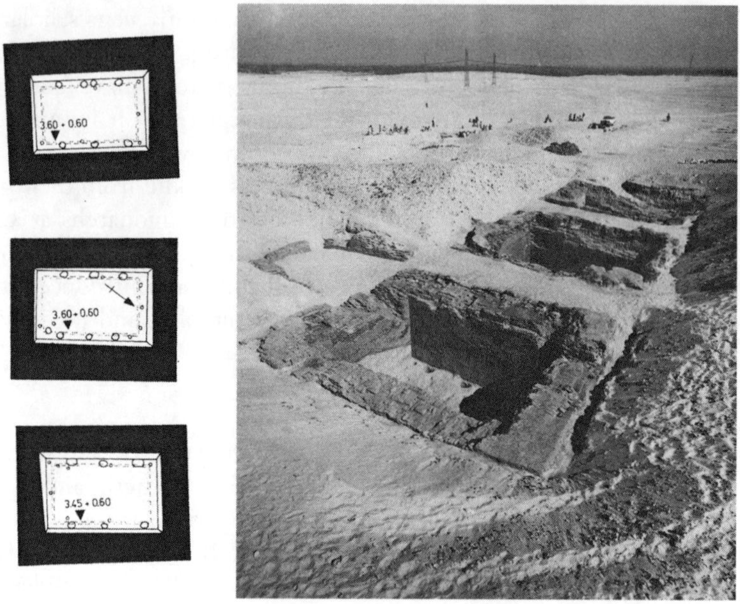

Figure 20. Tomb B10/15/19, the tomb of King Hor-Aha, with its massive mud-brick liners.

walls. Second, they provided support for the stronger roof, which would have been more resistant to penetration from above and capable of bearing the enormous weight of the tumulus.[20] Finally, they provided important lateral protection by hindering any tunneling through the side of the tomb.[21] However, ancient robbers' tunnels in the sides of chambers B15 and B19[22] suggest that even walls of this thickness were not entirely effective.

The entrances of the abovementioned robbers' tunnels start at some distance from the edge of the burial chambers' mud-brick liners, which suggests that the tomb's protective sand tumulus was roughly forty meters long, sixteen meters wide, and approximately two meters high. Its volume would have been around thirteen hundred cubic meters, which, assuming it consisted of desert sand, would have weighed about two thousand and eighty tonnes. Albeit simple in concept and execution, this mound would have provided an extremely effective obstacle to potential plunderers, as any disturbance would have started dangerous avalanches of loose sand flowing toward the perpetrator. Moreover, its protective 'footprint' would have overlapped the chambers' outermost edges by around two meters. Allowing for the mud-brick liners, this would have created a 'footprint overhang'[23] 3.5 to 4.1 m wide, which, as we have already noted, seems to have forced the robbers that tunneled into Hor-Aha's tomb to start digging from well beyond its perimeter.

Djer

Tomb O, the nearby grave of Aha's successor King Djer, represents a radical change in design compared to its predecessors in Cemetery B. It is also accompanied by over two hundred subsidiary burials, making it the largest complex at Umm al-Qa'b.[24] Rather than two or three separate chambers as before, Djer's tomb's substructure consisted of a single large pit lined with substantial 2.6 m thick mud-brick liners, against which mud-brick tongue walls were built on three sides to abut a central wooden shrine. These formed buttress-like dividers that functioned as storage magazines for grave goods,[25] provided a support for the roof and an internal sand tumulus, and probably gave additional reinforcement for the inward thrust of the walls (Fig. 21). The roof, which sat about one meter below the ancient desert level, was formed of roof beams twelve to twenty-four centimeters in diameter covered in mats and two layers of mud-brick. Recent excavations have demonstrated that it is possible a hidden sand tumulus up to 0.5 m thick may have been built over the underlying shrine, similar to that found in the later tomb of Djet.[26] This would have provided an additional layer of defense and is more fully discussed below.

Additionally, it is possible that Djer's tomb, and indeed all subsequent royal tombs at Umm al-Qa'b, were protected by a structure similar to the one that Dreyer has suggested once covered the tomb of Djet (see below).[27]

Therefore, Djer's tomb relied for its security on the strength of its thick mud-brick liners and a substantial roof that was perhaps covered by an internal sand mound. While aboveground, it may have been protected from overhead and lateral attack by an overlying tumulus or superstructure. Of course the tomb was robbed at some point, and the culprits must have been disturbed: Petrie discovered a mummified arm, which may have belonged to the king himself, still wearing four gold bracelets with lapis, amethyst, turquoise, and ivory details,[28] hidden in a hole in the brick liner to the rear of the chamber.[29]

Djet

More is known about the architecture of the tomb of Djer's successor Djet, which is very similar in design. Tomb Z is surrounded by

Djer

Figure 21. The tomb of King Djer at Umm al-Qa'b. The 'tongue' walls surrounding the shrine can be clearly seen.

a hundred and seventy-four subsidiary graves and consists of a large pit lined with a stoutly built mud-brick wall 2.5 to 2.75 m thick. Projecting internal mud-brick tongue walls created buttress-like storage magazines for grave goods, enclosed a wooden shrine chamber, and supported both the roof and an internal tumulus (Fig. 22).[30] Over the pit, remains indicate that a wooden roof closed the tomb and that after it had been sealed an encircling sloping mud-brick retaining wall was built over the top, the upper edge of which sat 0.7 m below the ancient desert surface.[31] It is assumed the cavity created by this

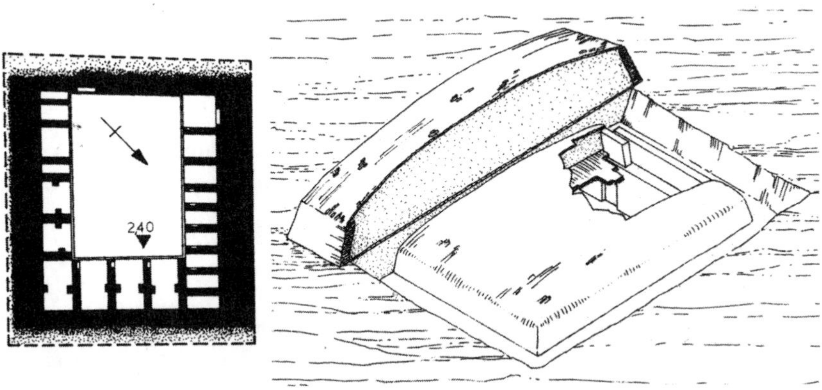

Figure 22. The tomb of King Djet at Umm al-Qa'b, with a sketch of the 'hidden' tumulus and superstructure.

wall was filled with sand, creating a form of mound, which, although possibly there for religious reasons,[32] would have contributed to the security of the tomb both during construction and after it was completed.[33] This may have been covered with a single brick layer on its surface, but whether it was flat or curved is unknown. The remaining void left in the pit above the mound was then probably filled with gravel or sand and brought level with the desert surface with another brick and mat roof, possibly supported by timber, leaving nothing visible of the substructure.[34]

There are no traces of any superstructure above the tomb of Djet, but Dreyer has suggested—based on parallels at other First Dynasty cemeteries, the enormous quantities of of excess sand that surround the royal tombs at the desert level, and the previously mentioned positions of tomb robbers' tunnels—that the whole substructure, including the tomb's concealed mound, may have been covered with a sand tumulus up to 2.5 m high, possibly sheathed in a slightly curved mud-brick casing, as shown in his reconstruction drawing (Fig. 22).[35] Such a casing would have provided not only extra protection but also a degree of permanence by consolidating the sand and preventing aeolian drift.

The substructure of Djet's tomb (and likewise possibly Djer's tomb before it) was therefore protected from lateral attack by its thick mud-brick liners and from above by a strong roof supporting the internal sand mound, which was in turn covered with its own wood and mud-brick roof. The sand in this mound, while not forming a resistant barrier in itself, would still have been troublesome for tomb robbers to deal with, as digging through over a hundred cubic meters of loose sand would have been extremely hazardous. Moreover, the possible presence of an overlying mud-brick-clad superstructure would have provided additional protection to the whole from above, and its footprint overhang would have deterred lateral tunnelers.

Figure 23. The tomb of Queen Merneith at Umm al-Qa'b and a general view of Umm al-Qa'b looking southwest toward the wadi.

Merneith

The tomb of Queen Merneith, the putative successor to Djet, was accompanied by forty-one subsidiary burials. Differing in design from its predecessors, tomb Y comprised a single burial chamber enclosed by mud-brick walls 1.22 to 1.32 m thick (Fig. 23). These were encircled by eight rectangular storage magazines, whose mud-brick walls varied from 1.2 to 1.3 m thick. Like its predecessors, the inner burial chamber contained shallow brick tongue walls, wooden posts, and the remains of a wooden floor. Faint traces of matting suggest it also had a roof.[36] In all probability the tomb contained a wooden shrine, as had its immediate predecessors. Therefore, it would have been protected laterally by its stout mud-brick walls and magazine chambers and from above by a concealed roof, perhaps backed up with a hidden sand tumulus. Aboveground, like the other First Dynasty royal tombs at Umm al-Qa'b, Merneith's tomb could possibly have been protected by a sand tumulus or superstructure of some sort, although there are no remains to confirm this.[37]

Thematic Analysis: The Architecture and Security of Royal Tombs to the Mid-First Dynasty

It appears that the tombs of Kings Iry-Hor, Ka, and Narmer hardly differ from their Predynastic forebears and were no more solidly built than those of their predecessors in Cemetery U.[38] They too relied on the surrounding sand and thin brick liners for lateral defense and a wood and mud-brick roof to provide protection from above, together with a certain degree of concealment.

With the tombs of Hor-Aha and his successors Djer, Djet, and Merneith, there is a discernible change in the strength of the construction. Now their substructures were built with more substantial mud-brick liners and magazines designed both to protect them from lateral tunneling or collapse and to support the increased load of a more substantial roof and protective internal sand tumulus. They were possibly further protected with an overlying mound or superstructure.

Whether these putative royal superstructures, if they existed, comprised poured sand or a mud-brick-clad tumulus is uncertain, but if the latter did exist it would certainly have offered a degree of permanence and monumentality. Whatever their form, if we accept that these tumuli or superstructures existed, they would have protected their substructures from overhead attack, and their large footprint overhangs would have made lateral tunneling by robbers more difficult by forcing the start point outward for their excavations.

Private Tombs

The usual method of building an elite private tomb during this period—in contrast to the simple unlined and backfilled pit grave that was the dominant tomb type in dynastic Egypt for the non-elite[39]—was to cut a rectangular pit and line it with a half or single thickness of mud-brick to consolidate its sides.[40] This formed a retaining wall within the substructure that prevented the collapse of the surrounding matrix and provided a degree of security against lateral tunneling.[41] After the burial was installed, the grave mouth was usually covered with branches or wooden beams and perhaps a layer of mud-brick or mud, before the remaining backfill was heaped over the whole or covered with a superstructure. However, the builders of some higher-status tombs went much further in the provision of security measures and incorporated specific architectural features designed to protect the tomb, and it is these that are discussed here.

Unlike royal tombs, which were largely restricted to Abydos during this period, the geographical distribution of private tombs is far wider and the methods used to protect them greater in variety. Therefore we will now look at tombs in the whole of Egypt, from north to south, where it soon becomes clear that differences in local customs, necropolis geology, and the availability of building materials resulted in a variety of architectural security measures in response to the threat of tomb robbery.

Tomb Security in the Delta

Some of the earliest and most northerly pit tombs with improved security measures are to be found in the Delta, where a distinctive style of tomb architecture develops, slightly different from that in the rest of Egypt.

Tell al-Farkha

The cemetery with the most numerous examples is the Eastern Kom cemetery at Tell al-Farkha, which dates to Naqada IIIB-C1[42] and where the tombs are cut into what the excavators describe as 'compact ground.'

Among these there are two distinct categories. The first type had substructures that were poorly defended laterally with just a single mud-brick liner, but were protected by a larger superstructure, such as grave 9, whose 1.07 m high mastaba overlapped its pit by approximately 0.75 m.[43] The superstructures of the second type of tomb did not overlap, but matched the dimensions of their substructure's more substantial mud-brick liners exactly, such as the intact grave 6,

Figure 24. Grave 63 at Tell al-Farkha with its 0.75 to 1 m thick walls, which were the same thickness in both the substructure and the superstructure.

which was protected by mud-brick liners 0.5 m thick and closed with a 0.5 m high mud-brick superstructure of the same dimensions.[44] Even stronger were the liners of contemporary graves 63 and 100, which varied between 0.75 and 1 m and from 1 to 2 m thick, respectively, and mirrored the perimeters of their overlying superstructures precisely. Those in grave 100 also incorporated woven mats between its courses for reinforcement.

The unusual design of this second type of tomb incorporated an internal 'shaft' that led straight down into the grave pit (Fig. 24),[45] which suggests the core may have been backfilled after the burial had been lowered through. This differs from most mastaba tombs of this period, where the whole superstructure was usually built over an already closed grave.

Here too, in a defensive measure peculiar at this time to the tombs of the Eastern Delta (but adopted elsewhere in later dynasties), liquid mud was used in a number of graves to improve their security, such as in grave 99 at Tell al-Farkha.[46] Excavations have shown that once the body and grave goods were interred in the tomb, they were coated in a thick layer of greasy mud, reported as "a very compact cover that made any robbery hardly effective," thus protecting the burial and perhaps, it has been suggested, also acting as a magical security measure.[47] The efficacy of this type of defense is confirmed in the aforementioned grave 100, which was protected by a layer of Nile mud. It appears that in ancient times robbers attempted to cut into this mud after digging through the tomb's superstructure, but their progress was halted by its density—as indeed was the case during the tomb's more recent excavation in the twenty-first century, which proved a lengthy and difficult process.[48]

Tell Ibrahim 'Awad

Also in the Eastern Delta, at site B at Tell Ibrahim 'Awad, a slightly younger tomb dating to Naqada IIIC2 not only incorporated stout walls but also used mud for protection, as at Tell al-Farkha (Fig. 25). Tomb 1 was dug in the sand and lined with mud-brick walls between 0.9 and 1.95 m thick that also incorporated internal magazines. Although disturbed, the grave was found to be largely intact, as it was filled with "tightly packed" clay and roofed with layers of reed mats supported by beams. In addition, aboveground, like graves 63 and 100 at Tell al-Farkha, the tomb's mud-brick liners were mirrored by the walls of its overlying superstructure, which shared the same outer perimeter, thus offering its burial a considerable degree of protection.[49]

Kafr Hassan Dawud

Southeast of Tell Ibrahim 'Awad at Kafr Hassan Dawud, the burials in two large earlier graves dated to the reign of Narmer were also secured with Nile mud. Graves 913 and 970 were dug into the alluvial sand of the Nile terrace, but were entirely unlined. However, once the burials were installed they were backfilled with mud, which set rock-hard and protected their contents. Presumably at this site, this measure alone was considered a sufficient defense, as aboveground these graves were merely covered by a simple mound consisting of sand, gravel, and silt.[50]

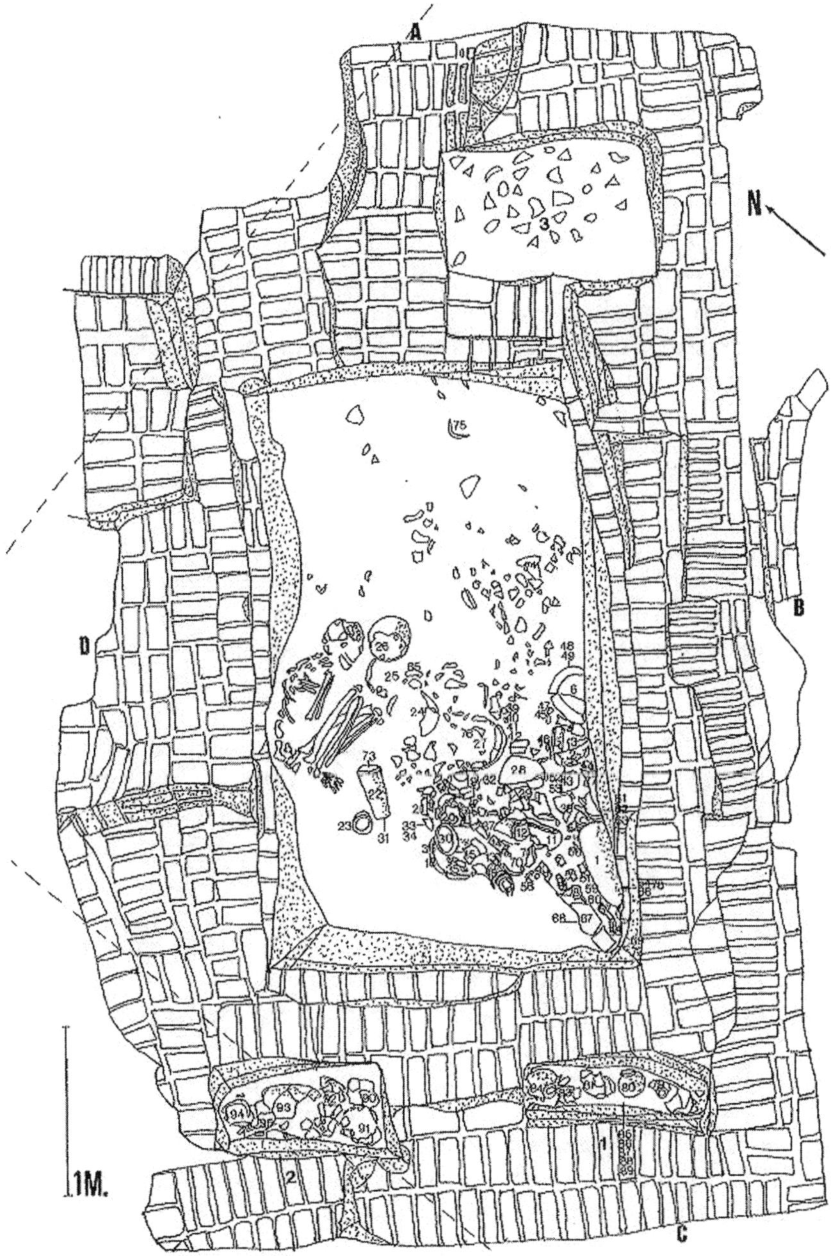

Figure 25. The massive mud-brick walls of tomb 1 at Tell Ibrahim Awad, with internal magazines built within them.

Tomb Security in Lower Egypt

Further south in Lower Egypt, slightly different methods from those in the Delta were developed to protect tombs against robbery. Although they use broadly similar technologies, their designs vary widely, presumably depending on the status and wealth of the owner, the availability of materials, and the strength of the surrounding geology.

Abu Rawash

One simple way to defend a pit tomb from robbery during this period was to reinforce its closure. At some sites this could take the form of a double roof, the most northerly example of which is in the large tomb 389 in Cemetery 300 at Abu Rawash, which dates to Naqada IIIB–C1. Its 1.8 m deep gravel-cut pit was lined with 0.5 m mud-brick walls for lateral protection and subdivided internally with two magazines at either end. It was closed from above with twin wooden roofs that were placed at heights of 1.1 to 1.3 m and 1.6 m from its base,[51] which would theoretically have offered its burial twice the protection from overhead attack. In this case, there is no record of any superstructure, but presumably one would have protected the substructure, as in the double-roofed tombs from Saqqara and Naga al-Deir, discussed below.

Nazlet Batran

On a much larger scale, at Nazlet Batran near Giza, which is approximately 1.2 kilometers south of the pyramid of Khufu, is a large tomb known as Mastaba V, which dates to the reign of Djet (Fig. 26). Within a rectangular pit excavated in the desert gravel, a further pit was dug to create a three-meter-deep burial chamber, leaving a raised platform at either end for magazines. The whole pit was lined with mud-brick walls approximately one meter thick, which consolidated the gravel and provided lateral protection. Inside the burial chamber, projecting mud-brick walls were built to support a large wooden shrine, similar to those in the tomb of King Djet at Abydos. About 2.4 m up from the base of the chamber the whole structure was closed with a roof of wooden beams, mats, and soil, which would have provided a 0.6 m layer of protection and supported the superstructure.

The superstructure consisted of a monumental mud-brick mastaba with a palace façade exterior,[52] whose walls were up to 1.2 m thick and probably enclosed a core of rubble or sand, which sheltered the substructure's wooden roof.[53] Its height is unknown, but its protective footprint overhang can be estimated at approximately 7.75 m on the

Figure 26. The First Dynasty Mastaba V at Nazlet Batran, with a view of the ruined palace façade mud-brick superstructure.

longer sides, thus forming a significant deterrent to lateral tunneling by tomb robbers. This would have offered the tomb's owner, within the limits of the building technology of the time, both a handsome memorial and a high level of protection from robbery.

Abu Ghurab

A more basic style of substructure was used just north of Saqqara in Mastaba XVII at Abu Ghurab (Fig. 27), which dates to the mid-First

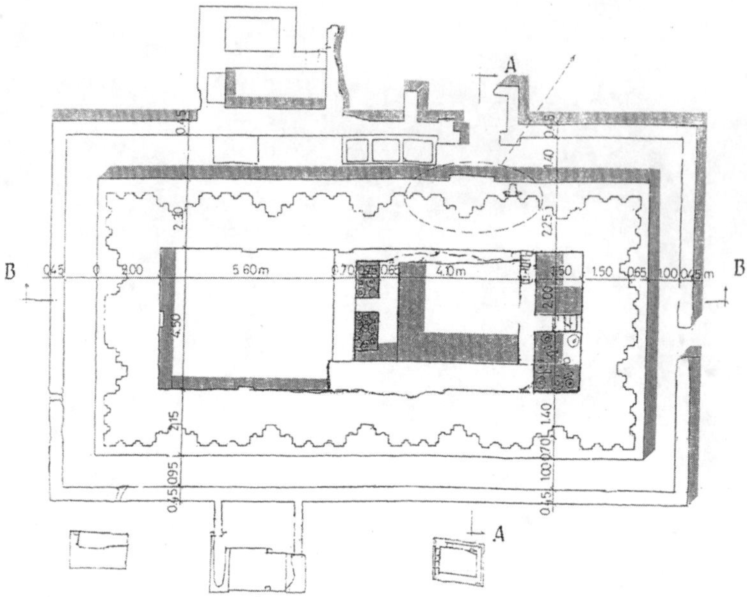

Figure 27. Mastaba XVII at Abu Ghurab, showing the offset substructure.

Dynasty. It comprised a pit in the sandy soil that was lined with 0.7 m thick mud-brick walls to consolidate its sides and provide lateral protection, and subdivided internally to provide four magazines. This pit was then closed with stout wooden beams and a roof and brought level with a substantial layer of *tafl* before being covered by a superstructure. The latter was offset in relation to its substructure (possibly to mislead tomb robbers?) and consisted of 1.8 m thick palace façade mud-brick walls surrounding an internal core of coarse sand. The whole structure was encompassed by a low-level plinth—decorated with a single bull's head, or bucranium—that created a minimum footprint overhang of approximately 1.8 m to defend the substructure against lateral tunneling. Despite these measures, the burial chamber was robbed at some point in antiquity, but unusually the partly mud-filled adjoining magazines and their grave goods remained intact.[54]

Moving southward, we now look at the major cemeteries of Saqqara and Helwan, which are the two most important necropoleis among the several that serviced the ancient city of Memphis and are situated on opposing banks of the Nile.[55]

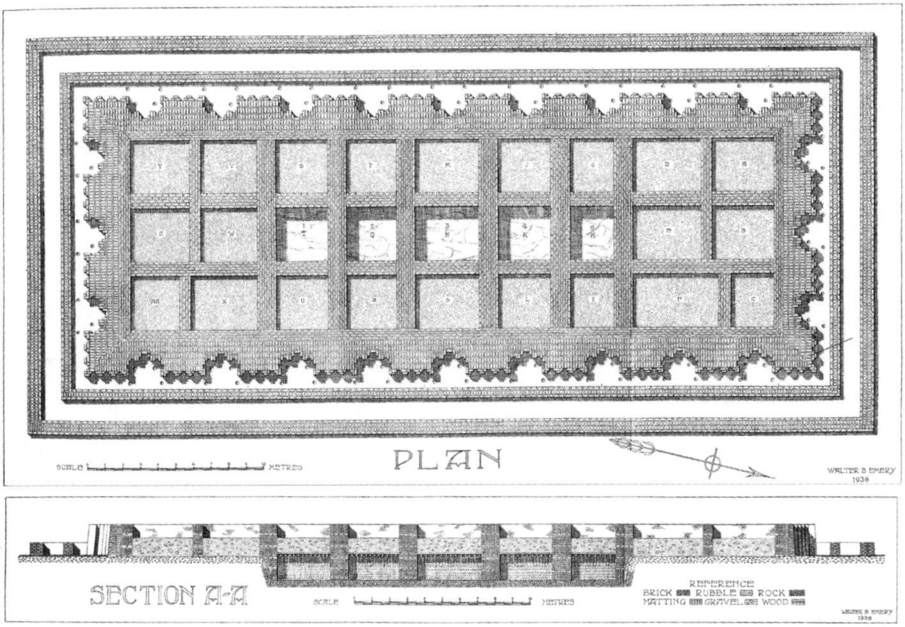

Figure 28. Tomb S 3357 (Hor-Aha) at Saqqara.

Saqqara

On the west bank at Saqqara, the better known of the two sites, the large mastaba tombs of senior officials or members of the royal family occupy the eastern edge of the desert plateau, where they are built in a layer of calcareous limestone topped with gravel. Their large superstructures were between three and five meters in height, so that their fortified walls would have dominated the escarpment and been easily seen from the cultivation.[56]

Their close proximity to each other permits us to trace their architectural development. The earliest of them is tomb S 3357, which dates to the reign of Hor-Aha.[57] The substructure comprised a pit 1.35 m deep excavated through a 0.8 m layer of gravel into the rock beneath (Fig. 28). This was lined with 1 m thick mud-brick walls, which both consolidated the gravel stratum and provided lateral protection against tunneling, although a robbers' tunnel in the burial chamber wall demonstrates that this was sadly unsuccessful. Internally, the pit was subdivided by mud-brick walls into compartments that mirrored those in the superstructure above, the central one of which is assumed to be the burial chamber. Once the burial was installed, it was closed by a

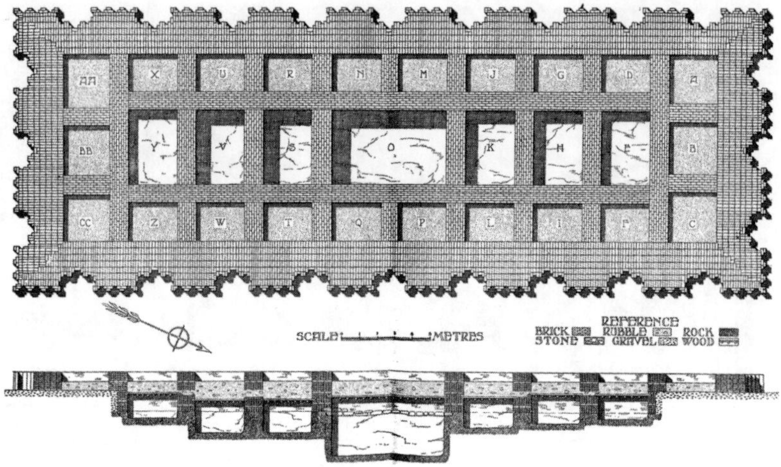

Figure 29. Plan and section of tomb S 3471 at Saqqara.

twelve-centimeter-thick wooden roof supported by beams, which was covered with reed mats and plastered with mud, both defending the chambers below and supporting the superstructure.

Aboveground, the superstructure consisted of 1.75 m high mud-brick palace façade walls 2.4 to 2.65 m thick, backed by an additional internal 0.4 to 0.65 m 'skin' wall, which provided a minimum footprint overhang over the substructure of approximately 6.3 m on the longest side. Internally, mud-brick cross walls formed twenty-seven magazines that provided storage for grave goods and supported a roof. Once filled with food and funerary artefacts, these were filled with one meter of rubble and sand and covered by the wooden roof. Finally, two enclosure walls, estimated at 1.5 m high, surrounded the whole structure and completed the tomb's external defenses.[58]

The slightly later tomb S 3471, which dates to the reign of Djer,[59] has a similar layout. However, in this instance a 1.2 m deep pit was first dug in the gravel down to the underlying rock, into which seven separate chambers were then excavated, with the burial chamber in the center (Fig. 29). The pit was lined with a mud-brick wall approximately one meter thick, which consolidated the gravel and protected against lateral tunneling. In addition, the rock dividers between the chambers were extended in mud-brick to both secure those divisions (albeit unsuccessfully, as robbers tunneled through them!) and support the wooden beams and planks that closed the pit and bore the superstructure.

Figure 30. Tomb S 2185 at Saqqara, with a view of its stone-lined and roofed substructure.

Aboveground, the superstructure's 2 to 2.75 m thick walls were slightly thinner than those of S 3357, as they lacked the internal skin wall. The inner core was subdivided by internal cross-walls that created twenty-nine magazines, which were filled with 0.5 m of rubble and probably also roofed in wood.[60] Although its height is unknown, its protective footprint overhang was approximately 5.5 m along its longest sides.

In response to the obvious vulnerability of the mud-brick linings in these tombs, the burial chamber and magazines of tomb S 2185 (Fig. 30), which dates to the reign of Djer, were reinforced for extra protection. They were still cut into the gravel and bedrock, but instead of being lined with mud-brick, they were lined and subdivided with coursed masonry to improve their lateral defenses in what is undoubtedly one of the earliest architectural uses of stone in Egypt. In addition, instead of a wooden roof, stone slabs 0.2 to 0.32 m thick were used to defend the pit from overhead attack and support the overlying superstructure.

Although stone-lined and roofed, the substructure was still protected by a conventional mud-brick superstructure with palace façade walls approximately 2.4 m thick, which may have stood up to 6 m high. Probably roofed in wood, internally it contained gravel-filled side chambers and a central core of storage magazines that aligned directly with those of the substructure beneath. Its huge area provided a minimum footprint overhang of approximately seven meters, and externally it was surrounded by an enclosure wall not more than a meter high. Despite these mighty defenses, the tomb was still plundered by robbers, who forced their way from chamber to chamber and set fire to the interior, presumably to cover their tracks.[61]

Although the use of stone was one means of bolstering the defenses of a burial chamber, other solutions were also developed at Saqqara to address the problem. The nearby tomb S 3504 dates to the reign of Djet and initially resembled S 3471 in its layout. Following

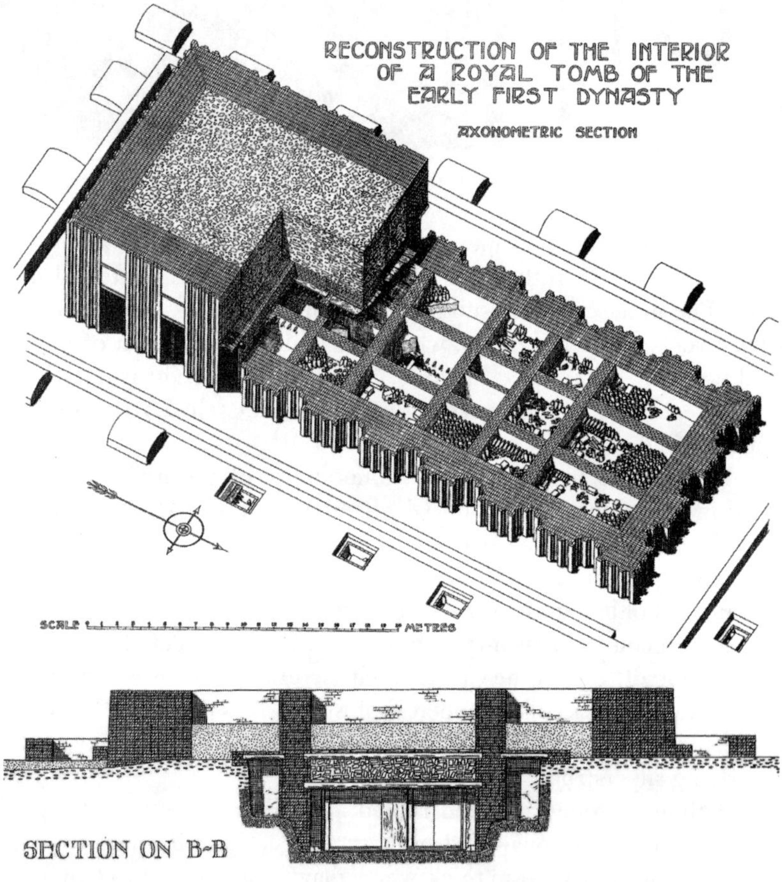

Figure 31. Above: Axonometric view of tomb S 3504 at Saqqara, showing its complex substructure and the magazines for grave goods in its superstructure. Below: Cross-section of the substructure, showing its rubble-filled double roof.

an earlier robbery and the destruction by fire of its single wooden roof, the substructure was reconstructed as a single deep chamber set in the existing gravel and rock-cut pit. This was reinforced with mud-brick walls 1.2 m thick, laid against the original fire-damaged 1 to 1.3 m thick liners, creating a large burial chamber with two magazines at one end (Fig. 31). For extra protection against tunneling, the remaining magazines were then filled up with rubble and sand. Then a new wooden double roof that 'sandwiched' approximately one meter of bricks and rubble was built over the burial chamber for additional security, which suggests that this area was considered to be a particularly vulnerable point, despite the overlying protection of its large superstructure.[62]

The superstructure was built with 2.9 m thick palace façade mud-brick walls, which enclosed and protected forty-five internal magazines separated by cross-walls and holding enormous quantities of grave goods and victuals for the owner's use in the afterlife.[63] Externally, it was surrounded by a raised curb covered with horned bulls' heads (bucrania),[64] which together with the main walls provided a footprint overhang approximately 4.9 m wide. This protection notwithstanding, it is evident from the previously mentioned robbery that the raiders simply tunneled under the superstructure and set fire to the tomb, causing the collapse of the substructure's single wooden roof and the mastaba's inner core. When the restoration took place, the substructure was reroofed and the collapsed cross-walls of the magazines above the burial chamber simply left to act as buttresses.[65]

Lastly, tomb S 3503 is attributed to the reign of Merneith and followed the same lines as S 3357 and S 3471, but with fewer compartments (Fig. 32). It was built within a gravel and rock-cut pit and lined with mud-brick walls 0.65 to 0.8 m thick, then subdivided by cross-walls to form a burial chamber and four magazines. These were covered by a single wooden roof, which both supported and in turn was protected by the superstructure. This contained twenty-one magazines formed by cross-walls, each filled with approximately 0.75 m of rubble.[66] Surrounded by 2.75 m thick palace façade mud-brick walls and an enclosure wall, the minimum footprint overhang of the superstructure was approximately 5.75 m. However, remains of a robbers' tunnel in the southwest corner of subterranean magazine J demonstrates that despite the superstructure's deep footprint overhang, the tomb's plunderers still tunneled beneath it straight into the heart of the complex.[67]

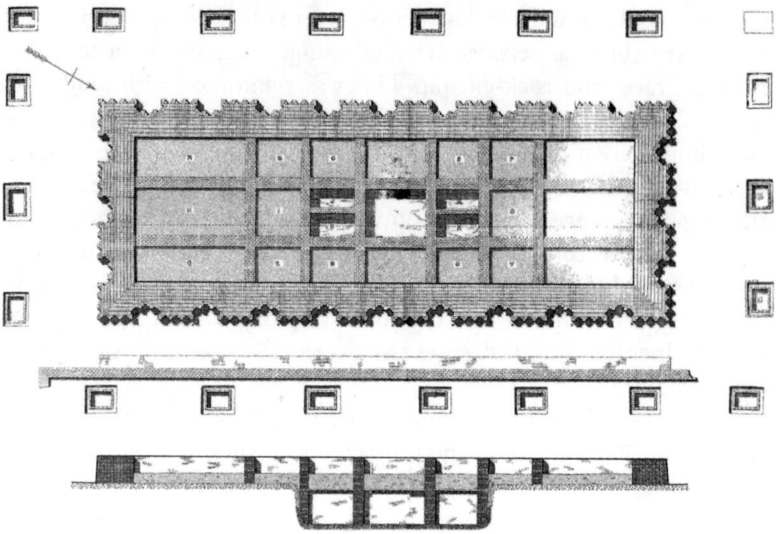

Figure 32. Plan and section of tomb S 3503 at Saqqara.

The large plans and cross sections of the burial chambers in these tombs at Saqqara would have made them vulnerable to lateral tunneling and attack from above, and the limestone into which they were cut would have provided a good degree of defense against the former. However, it is evident from the nature of their architecture that the most vulnerable areas were their wooden roofs and the gravel layer over the limestone stratum. Aboveground, the protective function of their massive overlying superstructures was twofold: besides performing their usual role of protecting the substructures beneath them with their generous footprints, they now also acted as fortified storehouses for the enormous quantities of grave goods and victuals that were amassed for the benefit of their owners in the afterlife.[68]

While the North Saqqara plateau seems to have catered for the higher-status members of Memphite society, on the opposite, eastern bank of the Nile, a far greater number of its citizens seem to have been buried in the gravel paleofan (waterborne conglomerate deposits) of Wadi Hof, which formed the Helwan necropolis.[69]

Helwan

Unlike at Saqqara, where the limestone geology provided a high level of protection to the pit tombs cut into it, the weaker gravel matrix at this site meant that architectural solutions were needed to increase a tomb's security.[70] At Helwan, in addition to the roof, this usually but not always entailed some sort of internal mud-brick liner being used for lateral protection, as can be seen in the numerous pit tombs shown on the site plans drawn by Zaki Saad in the mid-twentieth century, very few of which have been properly published.[71]

However, another method of defending burial chambers in pit tombs at this site was to protect them with a deep backfill as well, as in two mid-First Dynasty examples found by Saad. Tomb 68.H.4 was lined in the usual way with 0.3 to 0.35 m thick mud-brick liners, which would have consolidated the surrounding gravel and provided lateral protection (Fig. 33). On this occasion, within the pit, secondary internal ledges formed by a further 0.4 m thick layer of mud-brick supported the roof and permitted it to be protected by two meters of gravel backfill.[72] Nearby, the larger tomb 185.H.4, although of simpler construction, lacked the lateral protection of a mud-brick liner and instead relied on simple gravel-cut ledges that supported its roof

Figure 33. The gravel-cut and mud-brick-lined tomb 68.H.4 at Helwan. The holes for the deep-set roofing beams are clearly visible in the pit.

and 1.9 m of backfill.[73] There is no record of any superstructures over these particular tombs, but it is likely that their substructures would have been defended from above by a mud-brick mastaba, like most of the tombs at Helwan. Denudation and the *sebbakhin* (local farmers who have broken up the nutrient-rich mud-brick for fertilizer) have taken their toll on most of these mastabas, and there are few traces of them left today.[74]

Therefore, we can see that instead of just being covered by a wooden roof and shallow backfill, like many of the earlier Predynastic tombs that could easily be tunneled under or broken into, these tombs at Helwan were made more secure simply by increasing the depths of their roofs and backfills. This is because any attempt to rob them would involve laboriously digging into the grave pit and then through a couple of meters of loose gravel backfill as well as the supporting roof, or the even more laborious option of tunneling down from outside the pit and then digging sideways through the gravel to enter the void of the chamber laterally. If a superstructure was present, its bulk and footprint would have added to the amount of digging involved in either direction.

Tarkhan

Farther south, the remains of four large mastaba tombs are to be found in the gravel and marly limestone of the 'Hill Cemetery' at Tarkhan. Among these is Mastaba 1060, which dates to the reign of Djet and, like the earlier Saqqara S 2185, is notable for the use of stone to strengthen its security. Its substructure consisted of a rectangular pit and four magazines excavated into the limestone, all of which were plastered (Fig. 34). A ledge at the top of the burial chamber may have supported a 7.5 cm thick wooden roof and 0.3 m thick protective limestone slabs, the broken remains of which were found in the chamber.

Aboveground, it was defended by a palace façade superstructure with 3.4 m thick mud-brick walls, which provided a footprint overhang approximately six meters wide on its longest sides. Cross-walls divided its interior into compartments that were filled with sand, and externally it was surrounded by an enclosure wall. Despite these measures, robbers managed to gain access to the burial chamber by digging down through the mud-brick at point 'A' marked on the plan, but the starting point of the attack is unknown, and whether it came through or under the superstructure is unclear.[75]

Figure 34. Mastaba 1060 at Tarkhan. The robbers entered the substructure via the mud-brick at point 'A' to avoid the stone roof, the remains of which are visible in the photograph of the burial chamber.

Tomb Security in Middle Egypt

Awlad al-Sheikh

As mentioned above, doubling a tomb's defenses would, in theory, offer its burial chamber twice the protection from attack, and tomb II at Awlad al-Sheikh, which dates to the mid-First Dynasty, had both a double roof and a double liner (Fig. 35). Within a pit approximately 2.8 m deep,

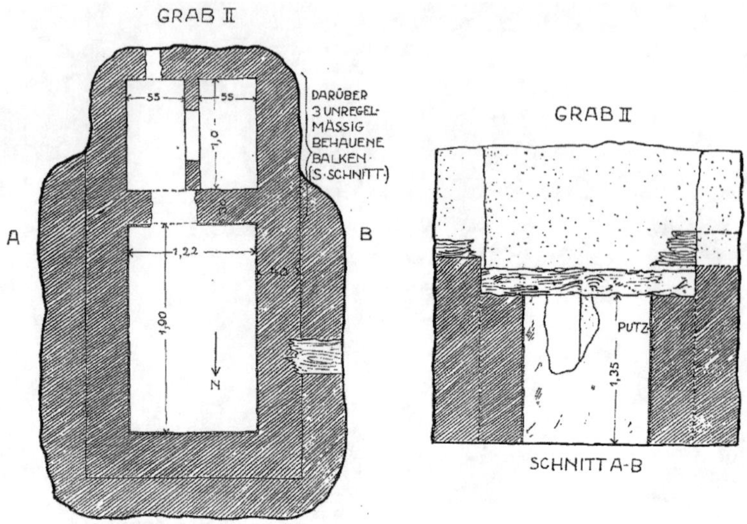

Figure 35. The double-roofed tomb II at Awlad al-Sheikh, with its two layers of mud-brick liners and two sets of wooden roof beams.

two layers of mud-brick walls with a combined thickness of about 0.7 m formed the burial chamber and two magazines. A ledge formed by the 1.35 m high inner wall supported the wooden beams of the first roof. Beams were then inserted 0.25 m higher in the outer wall to support the second roof and the pit brought level with the surface with around a meter of gravel. Although there was no trace of any aboveground monument, presumably a superstructure would have defended the whole. Despite its substructure's twofold layer of protection from above and the sides, the tomb was still robbed in antiquity.[76]

Tomb Security in Upper Egypt

Naga al-Deir

Just north of Abydos, in Cemetery 1500 at Naga al-Deir, there are two pit tombs that date to the reigns of Djer and Djet, respectively, whose roofs were also reinforced for better security (Fig. 36). The first is tomb N 1532, whose 2.7 m deep pit was cut in the sand and gravel and lined with mud-brick walls 0.3 to 0.4 m thick. From remains found in situ, George Andrew Reisner, the tomb's excavator, suggested that the roof of this tomb and its neighbors may have consisted of as many as ten to fourteen brick courses. Indeed, Reisner's drawing tentatively shows the mud-brick roof at around a meter thick, which would have left room for a 0.5 m gravel backfill.[77] The second grave is the nearby tomb N 1506, which was protected by a double roof. A 2.3 m deep pit with slightly sloping sides was excavated in the gravel, within which was built a 1.27 m high mud-brick burial chamber and magazines that were covered by a layer of tree branches. These supported a brick roof that may have been up to seven courses thick (about 0.5 m), then another layer of branches, and yet more mud-brick to provide an extra layer of protection and support the tomb's superstructure.[78]

Aboveground, due to denudation and the *sebbakhin*, the remains of only a few superstructures were found during Reisner's excavations of these tombs, though he suggested that doubtless many more had once existed. No extant remains were found over the first of these (N 1532), but a mud-brick mastaba was built over N 1506 that was set off-center and orientated at a slightly different angle from its burial chamber. Information is scarce, but Reisner described its external walls as "thick" and decorated with "offering niches" and its core as "gravel or rubbish." Its substructure was well protected by a footprint overhang

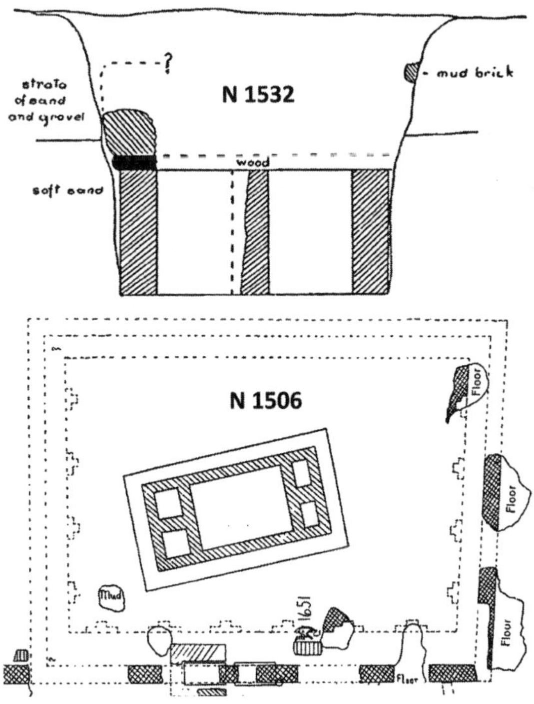

Figure 36. Above: Section through the brick-lined pit tomb N 1532 from Cemetery 1500 at Naga al-Deir, with its thick mud-brick roof. Below: The outline of the palace façade superstructure of the nearby tomb N 1506 in relation to its mud-brick-lined substructure.

of approximately two meters, and the whole was surrounded by an enclosure wall.[79]

Without these strong roofs, these high-status graves would have been quite vulnerable to an overhead attack through their backfill or a lateral approach through the gravel strata. The reason such effort was put into making them secure becomes clear from the contents of N 1532: when it was excavated, considerable amounts of gold jewelry were discovered under its collapsed roof, which had either caved in from decay or been smashed by robbers. On the other hand, N 1506 seems to have survived intact until the twentieth century. Reisner noted during its excavation that it appeared to have suffered from recent plundering.[80]

Abydos

South of Naga al-Deir at Abydos lies an Early Dynastic cemetery approximately 1.5 kilometers southeast of Umm al-Qa'b and 0.5 kilometers south of the temple of Sety I.[81] Within it a large pit grave has been revealed, which demonstrates that this type of private tomb was being constructed at Abydos at the same time as the royal cemetery was being used at Umm al-Qa'b (Fig. 37). Tomb IV consists of a pit in which mud-brick walls approximately 0.5 m thick line both ends of

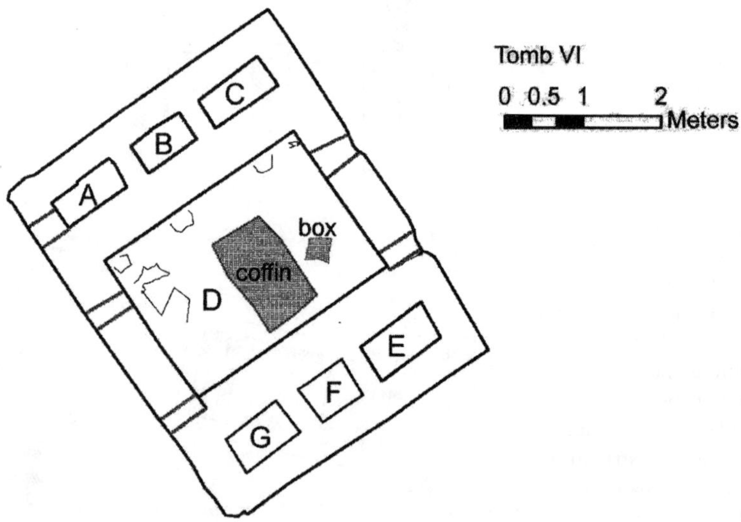

Figure 37. The mud-brick-lined tomb IV at Abydos, showing its six magazines.

the main chamber, which is flanked on its two longest sides by walls 0.5 to 0.6 m thick and three mud-brick magazines that increase the lateral protection to around 1.3 m in total on the northwest flank and 1.5 m on the southeast. The main pit was roofed with beams and wooden planks, but the magazines were less well protected by reeds and mud.[82] Aboveground excavations have shown evidence of a protective superstructure, while other excavations have revealed that the burial chamber was robbed by means of a tunnel cut through from magazine 'G,' which suggests that perhaps daunted by the wooden roof of the main chamber, the robbers may have opted for the more vulnerable reed roof of the magazine as the easiest route into the tomb.

Naqada

One of the earliest monumental tombs in Egypt was located south of Abydos at Naqada. Known as the Naqada 'Royal Tomb,' it is notable for being virtually without a substructure, relying entirely on its aboveground architecture to house and protect its burial and grave goods. Attributed to Queen Neith-hotep 'A,'[83] the putative mother of Hor-Aha and possible wife of Narmer, the tomb is one of two large monuments at the site,[84] which are contemporary with the founding of Memphis and the elite necropolis at Saqqara (Fig. 38).[85] Constructed directly on the gravel of the knoll on which it stood, the tomb was built in two stages without an excavated pit to house its burial compartments, which were instead created aboveground. Mud-brick walls 2.3 to 3.32 m thick were divided internally into five compartments by mud-brick walls accessed by doorways, the middle one being the burial chamber. Once the burial and grave goods were installed, the doorways were sealed and the final phase of the structure completed. This consisted of a large palace façade mastaba with mud-brick walls 3.8 to 4 m thick, which were linked by cross-walls to the core structure to form sixteen separate compartments, probably filled with gravel or sand.[86] The remains of burnt beams, found by Ludwig Borchardt, suggest that a wooden roof was built over the whole tomb; this, in combination with the massive mud-brick walls and their filling of gravel or sand, protected the tomb and created the aboveground equivalent of a six-meter footprint overhang. Possibly because of concerns about the vulnerability of its ground-level magazines, this tomb design seems to have been rapidly superseded by the more conventional pit and superstructure combination, whose construction on two levels also provided more secure storage capacity.[87]

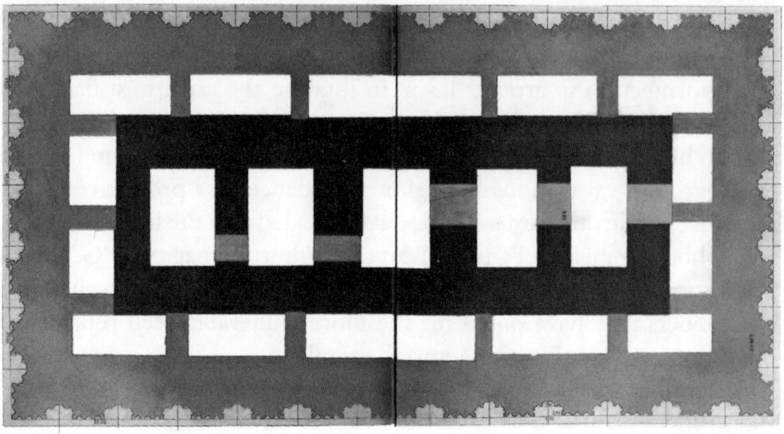

Figure 38. The Naqada 'Royal Tomb,' with its palace façade walls enclosing the inner core (in black). The mud-brick door blockings are shown in lighter tones.

Armant

Lastly, in the southernmost necropolis described in this chapter, are two of the earliest elite graves from Cemetery 1200 at Armant, which date to Naqada IIIB–C1. Tomb 1207 consisted of a large pit cut in the desert that was lined with mud-brick walls 0.2 to 0.25 m thick and set 0.45 m beneath the surface, which may have supported beams for a roof (Fig. 39). On three sides were projecting tongue walls, which may have abutted a wooden shrine similar to those in the contemporary tombs of Kings Djer and Djet at Abydos. Nearby tomb 1208 was slightly larger and lined with mud-brick walls 0.1 to 0.3 m thick. Ledges up to 0.8 m below the surface presumably supported a wooden roof. Unlike 1207, it was subdivided by 0.4 m thick mud-brick walls that created a separate burial chamber and surrounding magazine storage within the pit.[88] Although there is no sign of any superstructures, both tombs would have been protected to some extent by substantial wooden roofs and backfill. This proved not to be enough to save them. Both tombs had been systematically and repeatedly robbed, and we know the robbers gained entry through a tunnel burrowed into the western corner of tomb 1208, obviously dug to bypass the roof.[89]

Thematic Analysis: The Architecture and Security Features of Early First Dynasty Private Tombs

Although in the first half of the dynasty the defenses of some private pit tomb substructures remained virtually unchanged from those of their

Predynastic predecessors, in many cases greater efforts were made to protect tombs, and these varied widely depending on circumstances. In necropoleis with generally weak geology or strata, attempts were made to defend pits against lateral tunneling by reinforcing their liners with materials that were locally to hand. This usually took the form of thick mud-brick liners and, in a very few cases, quarried stone, such as in tomb S 2185 at Saqqara. Exceptionally, in the Delta, the use of liquid mud to form an unyielding and pervasive concretion seems to have been a localized specialty. To defend the burial chamber from above, increased backfill depths were tried, with thicker roofs or sometimes even two roofs for twice the protection. These measures brought another benefit insofar as the deeper a roof was set, the farther down a lateral attack would have to go. Moreover, for additional defense at Saqqara and Tarkhan, some tomb roofs were reinforced with or made entirely of stone.

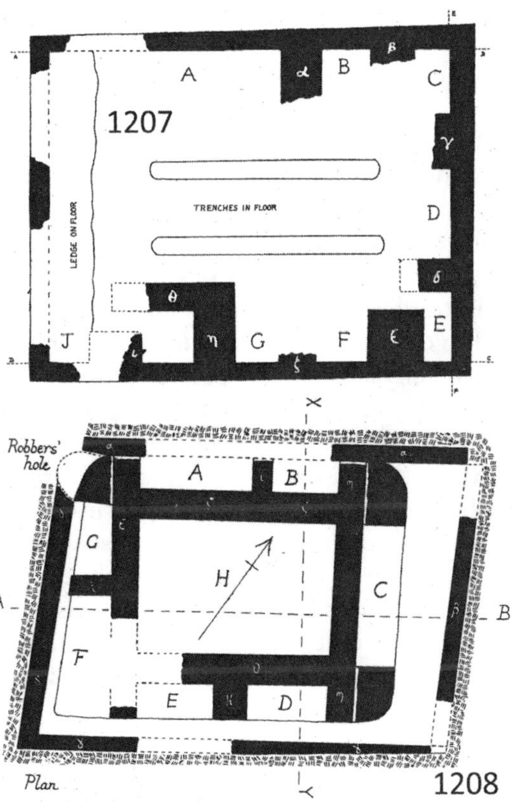

Figure 39. The substructures of tombs 1207 and 1208 at Armant. The projecting 'tongue' walls of 1207 can be clearly seen in the upper drawing.

Aboveground, substructures were now often protected from overhead attack by a filled superstructure built of mud-brick, with the exception of the Naqada 'Royal Tomb,' which lacked a substructure altogether. Moreover, by building the superstructure larger than its substructure, it could also provide a footprint overhang to defend against lateral tunneling. However, this was not always the case in the Delta, where in the early First Dynasty the stoutly built substructures of some graves at Tell al-Farkha and Tell Ibrahim 'Awad were protected with large superstructures that mirrored their plan and dispensed with a footprint overhang altogether. That notwithstanding, the majority of elite pit tombs relied on their superstructure's generous footprint overhangs to protect their substructures. These were provided by mastabas with fortress-like mud-brick retaining walls, which both contained the back pressure of their core fill and protected it from compromise by external incursions. Moreover, the massive superstructures of the high officials at Saqqara additionally secured within their stout walls compartmented interiors that functioned both as storehouses for valuable funerary artefacts and as pantries for the important provision of victuals for the afterlife.

Conclusion

It is evident that during this period, the focus of improvements in the design and security of royal and private tombs was the reinforcement of the grave pit's liner, where the surrounding geology required it, and the strengthening of its roof or closure, which were its most vulnerable points. In all cases, the introduction of a protective superstructure provided an omnidirectional extra layer to a tomb's defensive architecture, and its bulk and footprint protected the substructure from overhead and lateral attack. However, the nature of these defenses meant that the tomb could only be finished after the owner's death. As a result, the disposition of the substructure and its contents was necessarily left exposed to public view until the burial had been installed, thus compromising its security. This particular problem was solved in the second half of the First Dynasty with the introduction of the external entrance, which permitted the tomb to be completed during its owner's lifetime. But as we shall see in the next chapter, these new features created new problems, which inspired further ingenious responses from the tomb makers.

4

Portals, Passages, and Portcullises: The Second Half of the First Dynasty

In the previous chapter we saw how pit tombs during the early part of the First Dynasty evolved from their distinctly Predynastic origins into far more sophisticated structures as a direct response to the persistent threat of tomb robbery. It became evident that high-status and royal tombs were now incorporating specific defensive architectural features such as resistant liners, roofs, and superstructures to compensate for inadequacies in the strength of the surrounding geology, frequently using materials such as wood, mud-brick, and, more rarely, stone. However, one major weakness was that the pit tomb's design meant it could only be fully completed *after* its burial was installed, thus leaving its contents and disposition visible to prying eyes and undoubtedly compromising its security. A solution to this problem was devised by creating an external access route into the substructure, which allowed the whole tomb to be fully completed before its owner's demise. All that needed to be done when the time came, after the grave goods had been deposited and the funeral had taken place, was to secure the tomb's entrance.[1] The first examples of this type of entrance to pit tombs, usually in the form of a stairway or slope, begin to appear in the mid-First Dynasty, in what we shall now refer to as a stairway pit tomb. While this innovation was arguably beneficial from the security point of view, the introduction of external access brought with it attendant problems, which are discussed below.

This chapter looks at the changes to the security and architecture of the tomb in the latter half of the First Dynasty and, as in the previous chapter, begins by discussing royal tombs.

Royal Tombs

Den

The first royal sepulcher to incorporate an external access route is the stairway pit tomb of King Den at Umm al-Qa'b, Abydos. Designated as tomb T, the complex of Den covers a surface area of two hundred square meters,[2] and is partly encircled by a hundred and forty-four subsidiary burials and three storage pits.[3] Its innovative entranceway consisted of a 23.77 m long staircase that descended west directly to the tomb's burial chamber by way of a single landing and passage (Fig.

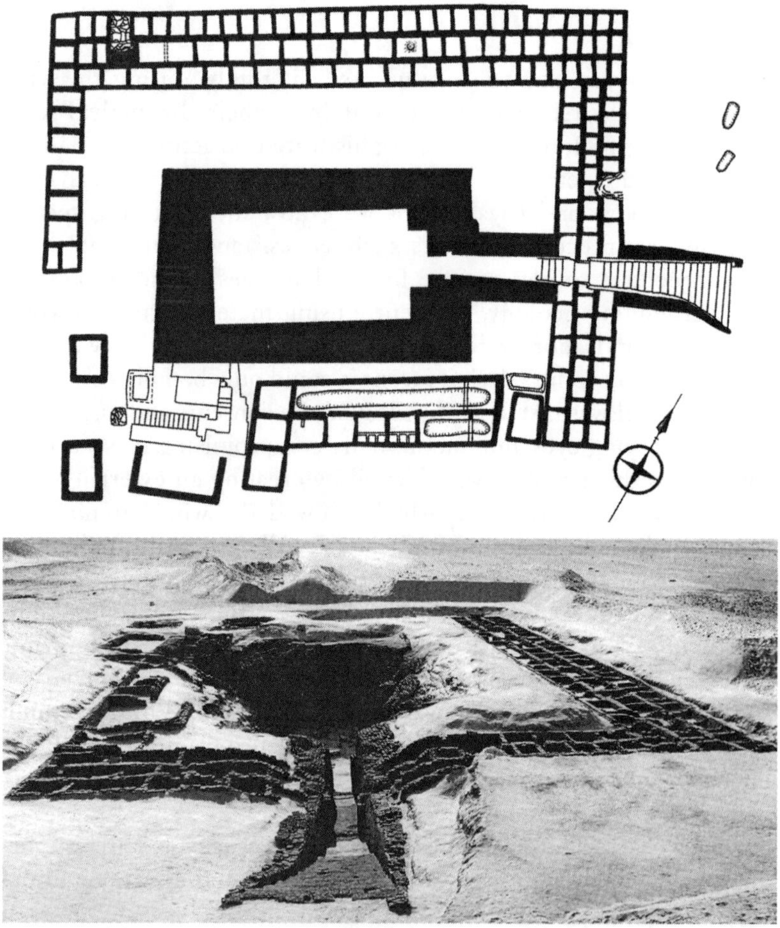

Figure 40. The tomb of King Den at Umm al-Qa'b. The subsidiary graves originally partly concealed the staircase.

40).[4] Because the surrounding ground was compacted sand,[5] the steps and enclosing stairwell were built of mud-brick, which consolidated the surrounding desert matrix,[6] and housed the internal closures that secured the route. The walls of the stairwell also supported a wood and mud-brick roof that protected the descent from above and formed a foundation for the subsidiary graves that partially concealed it. Importantly, as the side walls descended beyond these graves toward the burial chamber they broadened to 1.8 m thick,[7] providing additional protection against lateral tunneling.

Externally, the stairway's entrance would have been just below the ancient desert level and was probably hidden by sand.[8] Internally, after the burial was installed, the descent was blocked in several different ways to secure the stairway. Midway down on the first landing, remains of a wooden hinge pivot plate indicate that a wooden door was used to close the opening. Just before it, residual layers of mud-brick suggest that a blocking wall was built after the door was closed to seal the opening permanently.[9] Further down at the base of the stairway, before the burial chamber entrance, there are vertical grooves forming a portcullis emplacement. Although no trace has been found of the portcullis itself, it is often assumed by scholars that it was made of stone.[10] However, modern excavations have shown that these grooves were reduced in width from their original size, and it has been suggested that a smaller *Holzfalltür* or wooden beam blocking may have been used instead,[11] perhaps similar to that found in the tomb of Adjib, discussed below.[12] Lastly, immediately after the 'portcullis,' a short passage leads to a doorway at the entrance to the burial chamber, where remains of a wooden hinge bracket and striking plate for a bolt suggest that another lockable wooden door was positioned at the threshold.

The burial chamber itself is cut into the compacted sand and lined with massive four-meter-thick mud-brick walls, the tops of which sit approximately one meter below the ancient desert level.[13] They flank the remains of a floor of dressed granite slabs that once covered the entire burial chamber,[14] but it is unlikely that these were provided for security reasons: it would have been easier to enter the tomb through the side walls than to undermine the floor. On the sides of the chamber it appears that mats were hung from timber framing fixed to the mud-brick liners.[15] Attached to this framing and set in by approximately 0.75 m were stout wooden uprights that supported a large wooden shrine. Excavations have shown that on top of the shrine a hidden sand tumulus (perhaps brick-covered) was built, like those in the tombs of Djer and Djet.[16] This was at least 0.85 m thick and, supported by beams, its top would have sat just below the ancient desert level.[17] At the southwest corner of the tomb, a shorter staircase leads to an annex built outside the main burial chamber lining. This annex probably functioned as a 'serdab,' designed to permit the king's spirit to access the wadi. Possessing its own security measures in the form of a mud-brick blocking and wooden portcullis like the main tomb, the annex did not permit access to the burial chamber itself.[18]

Little is known about the tomb's superstructure, apart from the reconstruction of the supporting roof and hidden tumulus discussed earlier. Dreyer estimates, however, that if all the spoil from the grave pit's excavation had been used, the superstructure would have overlapped the outer edge of the pit's brick liner by around one meter and may have been up to four meters high,[19] thus protecting the substructure both from overhead attack and lateral tunneling with its five-meter footprint overhang.

The defenses of this tomb below ground level, although similar in nature to those of the tombs of Djer and Djet, were far stronger. The extra-thick mud-brick walls of the burial chamber deterred lateral penetration, and its strong roof with internal sand mound provided protection from above. Moreover, these features may have been backed up internally by a substantial wooden shrine. However, from a security perspective the introduction of a stairway in the tomb now created a new vulnerability: once discovered by tomb robbers, this route could lead them straight to the burial chamber.

Adjib

The small and simple stairway pit tomb of Den's successor, King Adjib, is known as tomb X. Surrounded by sixty-four subsidiary graves,[20] it was entered by a less complex descent than that of its predecessor. The mud-brick entrance stairway was positioned at the southeastern corner of the tomb and descended west to a depth of 2.46 m (Fig. 41). Although there is no evidence of a roof over its short stairwell, its entrance was probably, like Den's, concealed by sand. Where the base of the stairway met the substructure, the opening to the burial chamber was found blocked by a wooden barrier set within vertical grooves. This comprised five-centimeter-thick wooden boards laid horizontally and held in place by vertical planks in the slots, wedged tight into position using mud-bricks. Against these boards, layers of bricks were then loosely piled on the stair side to complete the closure, after

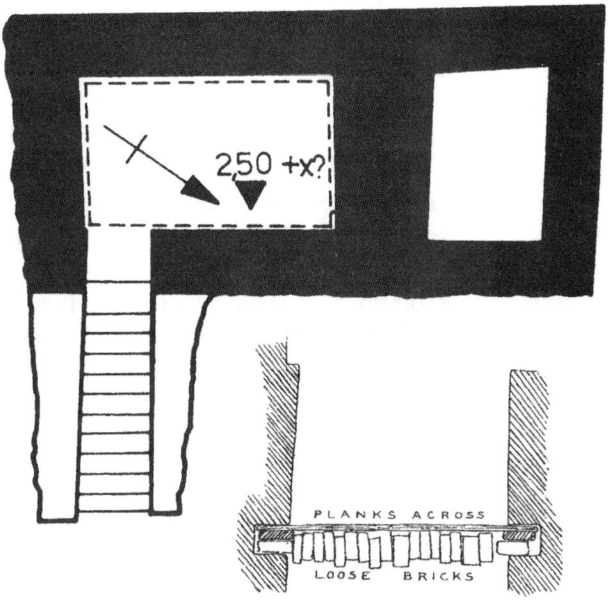

Figure 41. The tomb of King Adjib at Umm al-Qa‘b, with Petrie's sketch of the wood and mud-brick door blocking.

which the remaining length of the stairwell was probably backfilled with sand. Within the grave pit, the 2.46 m deep burial chamber was lined with 1.5 m thick mud-brick walls and floored in wood, a thick mud-brick dividing wall separating it from a smaller adjacent storage magazine. Remains of plastering 1.82 m high suggest that the whole substructure was covered by a roof 0.44 m thick (which could have supported a hidden tumulus), with perhaps another 0.2 m to reach the desert level. No evidence of any internal shrine has been discovered, although Petrie described finding a wooden support post for a roof, which could have been part of such a structure.[21] Aboveground, the tomb was possibly also protected by a tumulus or superstructure like those advocated for its predecessors.[22]

With its unremarkable blockings in the stairway and thin—compared to its forerunners—mud-brick burial chamber walls, this royal tomb is clearly unexceptional in its security measures, even set against some private tombs of the period. Admittedly, its roof and internal mound would have provided a certain level of defense, but at half the thickness of those same structures in Den's tomb, they would not have done a great deal. One can only speculate that perhaps a substantial superstructure provided more solid protection from above.

Semerkhet

Designated as tomb U,[23] the stairway tomb of the next monarch, King Semerkhet, was flanked by sixty-seven subsidiary burials and two magazines,[24] all of which, for the first time, abutted and encircled the burial chamber walls directly and thus formed part of the substructure (Fig. 42).[25] The walls varied in depth from 0.8 to 1.2 m and seem to have been roofed with reeds.[26] Lacking a built stairway, the substructure was entered on its northeast by an irregular desert-cut ramp that descended four meters to the floor of the burial chamber.[27] Although the descent shows no traces of consolidation with mud-brick,[28] its final section was flanked by the mud-brick walls of the tomb's subsidiary burials and the opening to the burial chamber itself. Presumably, once the tomb was sealed, the location of the descent was then concealed by sand in a similar fashion to its predecessors.

Figure 42. The tomb of King Semerkhet at Umm al-Qa'b, with a view of its recently excavated substructure.

As in the tomb of Adjib, the burial chamber entrance was also found stopped up with loose bricks, but this time without the benefit of any wooden backing. However, during the recent re-excavation of the tomb, part of a tree trunk was found embedded in the remains of this blocking and may have formed part of the missing reinforcement.[29]

Regarding these blockings in the tombs of Adjib and Semerkhet, one wonders whether or not they are the originals. Just loosely piling bricks across a doorway seems a rather lax security measure when such time and trouble had been taken to build the rest of the tomb. One plausible explanation might be that they are the remnants of later blockings made during the Middle or New Kingdoms, when the tombs were opened again following revived interest in the necropolis,[30] and that the original blockings were made of stone, like that found in the tomb of the last king of the dynasty, discussed below.

Although the burial chamber of Semerkhet is internally of a similar size to that of Den, its mud-brick walls were only around 1.5 m thick on average.[31] Within them, as in Den's tomb, partial remains indicate that a wooden shrine was erected and bounded by 0.1 m diameter posts.[32] Recent excavations have demonstrated that the tomb's roof was also supported by wooden beams, which were set approximately 0.5 m below the upper edge of the chamber lining.[33] This would have permitted the inclusion of a hidden tumulus, akin to the others mooted at Umm al-Qa'b.

Evidently built in a hurry,[34] Semerkhet's tomb, like Adjib's, was unexceptional in terms of its security features. The blockings to the burial chamber entrance, if they are the original ones, would not have offered much defense. The wooden roof and possible internal sand mound would have had defensive capabilities similar to those in earlier tombs, although they were obviously not as stoutly built as those of Den. The tomb may have benefited from the protection of its encircling subsidiary burials, as the tomb of Merneith was protected by its surrounding magazines. But these graves were only 1.2 m deep and could presumably have been tunneled under quite easily. On the surface, it is suggested that a superstructure of some form provided protection, which some scholars note would also have covered the surrounding subsidiary burials due to their proximity,[35] but it seems unlikely, as these graves were found to be roofed with reeds,[36] which would not have supported a heavy superstructure. It may be that instead these graves were individually capped, as is proposed for the tomb of Qa'a.

Qa'a

The sepulcher of the last king of the dynasty, King Qa'a, is known as tomb Q.[37] It was entered by a mud-brick staircase at its narrow northern end (Fig. 43). Much altered during construction,[38] in its final form, plastered mud-brick stringers defined the beginning of the tomb's descending stairwell. The steps were bounded by the end walls of two external flanking magazines, and in the roofed passage between these the walls and entrances of four internal magazines enclosed the steps that led to the burial chamber.[39] These magazines were in turn enclosed on the west by a row of subsidiary burials and on the east by a single magazine and more burials,[40] so that the staircase was protected laterally by these structures and from above by a wood and mud-brick roof.[41] Although the upper steps and stringers of the outer stairway were unroofed, a lack of weathering on their surrounding plasterwork may indicate that they were filled with sand,[42] and so probably concealed from view. Internally, there was originally a mud-brick blocking at the head of the stairs of the tomb,[43] now missing. Eleven steps down and still visible are the remains of the earliest stone portcullis found in situ at Umm al-Qa'b. This broken limestone slab is 0.98 m high[44] and preserved within mud-brick retaining grooves set in the walls of the stairway. If we assume that the original height of the portcullis was at least two meters and that it weighed around 1.6 tonnes,[45] it would have been a very effective blocking. Finally, further down the descent and past the portcullis, the entrance to the burial chamber was blocked with mud-brick.[46]

The burial chamber, which is approximately three meters deep, is surrounded on three sides by shallower storage magazines. Its mud-brick walls are approximately two meters thick on all but the northern face, which is formed by the 1.2 m thick end walls of the magazines that flank the tomb's staircase.[47] Internally, the chamber was lined with a stout wooden framework upon which mats or leather panels were probably hung, and within this a wooden shrine was erected, supported by posts up to 0.2 m thick.[48] Impressions of beams in the burial chamber walls demonstrate it was roofed with timbers of up to a 0.3 m diameter that spanned the full width of the chamber, smaller sections being used elsewhere over the magazines and subsidiary graves.[49] Over this a hidden sand tumulus was probably constructed, similar to that in the tomb of Djer, with its upper edge set about 0.2 m under the ancient desert surface. Finally, the whole pit may have been leveled off with the excess sand from the original excavation and finished with a layer of Nile mud.[50]

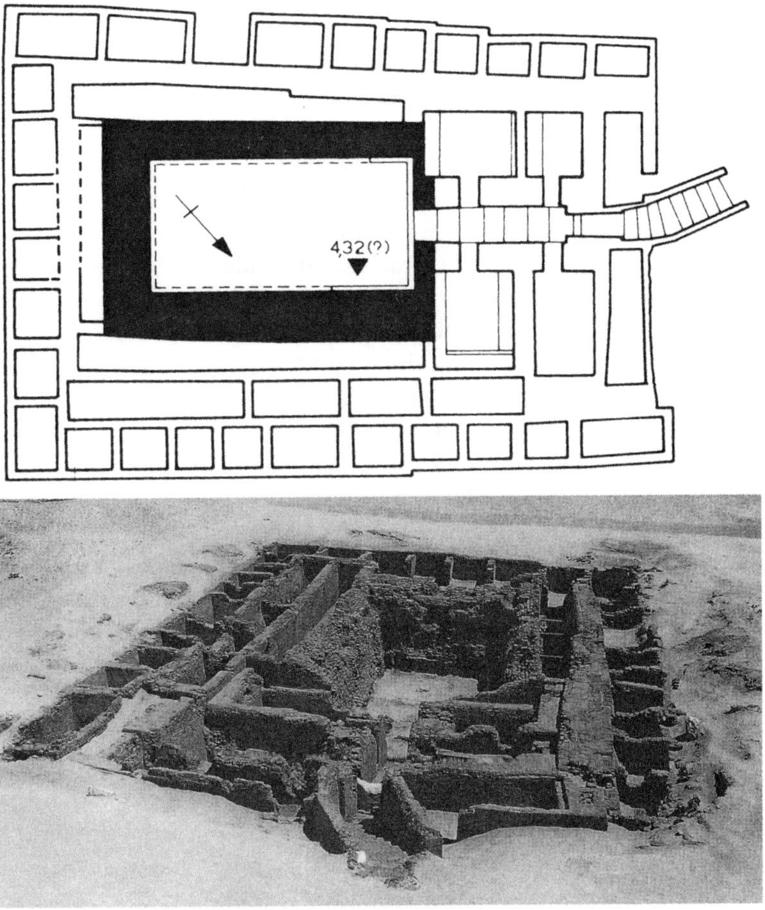

Figure 43. The tomb of King Qa'a at Umm al-Qa'b. The remains of the broken portcullis are visible in the photograph at the base of the stairway.

The burial chamber wall is edged on three sides by long magazines that add another two to three meters to its width, except on the eastern side where a further row increases it to about four meters. The northern entrance wall, meanwhile, is protected by six large magazines that flank the staircase. The whole was then surrounded by a continuous string of twenty-six mud-brick chambers (apart from a gap in the southwest to permit the exit of the king's spirit[51]), which were either subsidiary burials or magazines.[52] Although these were not of the same depth as the burial chamber, they would have provided a degree of extra protection against lateral tunneling like their counterparts did for the tombs of Merneith and Semerkhet.

For protection at the surface, Eva-Maria Engel suggests, based on the entrance holes made by tomb robbers into the surrounding magazines, that the tomb was protected by a single superstructure over the burial chamber and that its encircling subsidiary burials had their own separate covers. Moreover, based on her calculations of the load-bearing capacity of the tomb's roof, Engel estimates that this structure could have been approximately 13 m long, 9 m wide, and 2.5 m high and may have contained about 293 cubic meters of sand and stones,[53] which remarkably would have weighed approximately 470 metric tonnes.[54]

In this last royal tomb of the First Dynasty we see a combination of architectural elements used in earlier tombs of the cemetery brought together into one design: first, a concealed stairway entrance, protected with mud-brick blockings and a stone portcullis; second, an inner burial chamber with thick mud-brick walls, within which was a stoutly built wooden shrine; third, like the tombs of Djer, Djet, and Den, a substantial roof with hidden tumulus; fourth, like the tombs of Merneith and Semerkhet, a ring of magazines and subsidiary tombs that made it more difficult to penetrate laterally into the main tomb; and finally, an enormous superstructure over the whole to protect from overhead and lateral attack. Even with all these defensive elements in place, at some point in antiquity the tomb was plundered by robbers. The evidence suggests that they initially entered by the stairway but, finding their way obstructed by the portcullis, decided to bypass it entirely rather than attempt to move or breach it, choosing instead to tunnel through the surrounding mud-brick into the flanking magazines and work their way around from chamber to chamber.[55]

Thematic Analysis: Architecture and Security Features of Royal Tombs in the Second Half of the First Dynasty

In the latter half of the dynasty, the descents of royal stairway pit tombs such as those of Den, Adjib, and Qa'a relied on the surrounding desert geology and a combination of mud-brick, wood, and sand to defend their access routes from external attack. Internally, to close these passageways after the burial was installed, poured sand was used as a backfill, together with various combinations of mud-brick blockings, wooden doors, and portcullises of wood or limestone. The addition of external access routes permitted royal tombs to be completed before their owners' death and thus theoretically offered greater secrecy about the nature and disposition of their contents. But these new access routes also introduced a potential security flaw, as, once located, they would lead directly to the substructure's core.

While the substructure retained the same defensive elements as its forerunners from the first half of the dynasty, in the tomb of Den we see a significant increase in both the size of the burial chamber and its structural components. These improvements were not implemented in the sepulchers of Adjib and Semerkhet. Although the same defensive elements were present, they were comparatively small, despite the lateral defenses of Semerkhet's tomb being augmented by its encircling retainer burials. The protection offered by placing subsidiary burials next to the burial chamber was retained in the tomb of Qa'a, the most complex royal stairway tomb of the dynasty, where all the defensive elements were combined, albeit on a smaller scale than in the tombs of Den and Semerkhet.

Finally, like their earlier neighbors at Umm al-Qa'b, it's possible that at ground level the substructures of these royal stairway tombs were shielded from overhead and lateral attack by the mass and footprint overhangs of their overlying superstructures, whether in the form of simple sand tumuli or perhaps more monumental mud-brick clad mounds.

Private Tombs

Presumably following royal precedent, the latter half of the First Dynasty saw the widespread adoption of the external entrance and access route among the private tombs of the elite. However, although the simple pit tomb was no longer the most favored design, it had yet to be entirely superseded by the stairway tomb, and, as we shall see, tomb builders in the various necropoleis were experimenting with other security features and architectural innovations, including the first entirely subterranean substructures. As in the previous chapter, the various sites under consideration are discussed in geographical order, from north to south.

Tomb Security in the Delta

When discussing tomb security, it is always tempting to look at the best protected graves, as they permit us to marvel at the ingenuity of the tomb builders and the strategies they employed to defend the tomb. However, the levels of protection did vary, and among the Early Dynastic elite graves at Minshat Abu Omar in the Eastern Delta, there are some rare examples that clearly demonstrate the consequences of building tombs with inadequate defenses.

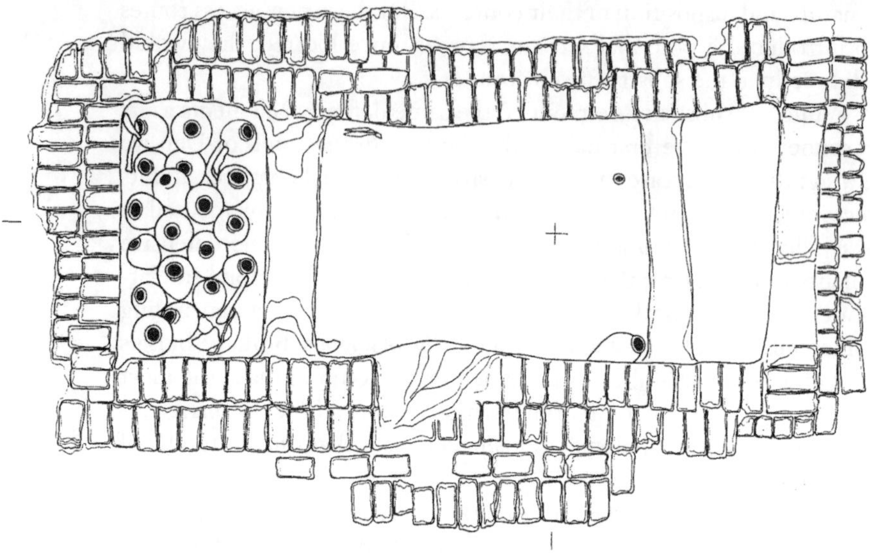

Figure 44. The mud-brick-lined tomb 2897 at Minshat Abu Omar.

Minshat Abu Omar

Dating from the mid- to latter half of the First Dynasty,[56] eight tombs have been found cut into the sand of the Minshat Abu Omar necropolis that were lined with either mud or mud-brick and usually subdivided into two or three chambers, the largest of which was used for the burial. The biggest of these is grave 2897, which was lined with walls two bricks thick (Fig. 44). These supported a wood-framed roof covered with mats, mud-bricks, and mud, which partially collapsed when the tomb was robbed. No remains of any protective superstructures have been discovered at the site. There is debate as to whether they existed, and it could be that the roofs of most of these tombs were like nearby grave 1590, which was set only ten centimeters below the original surface.

It appears that most of these tombs were robbed through their roofs. This may have been because the thefts were carried out soon after the bodies were buried, when the thieves still remembered the locations of the tombs. Or it may be that the shallow roofs eventually collapsed and the resulting depressions gave away the tombs' locations.[57] Either scenario graphically demonstrates the vulnerability of pit tombs when inadequately concealed by far too shallow a roof and backfill and lacking any protective superstructure.[58]

Tell al-Farkha

Farther west at Tell al-Farkha, burial chambers continued to be lined with mud-brick as they had been in the first half of the dynasty, as in graves 50 and 55, which both date to the latter half of the First Dynasty, or perhaps into the Second (Fig. 45).[59] Perhaps to strengthen their lateral protection, the mud-brick liners of both tombs were increased to a thickness of one and a half bricks. Aboveground, grave 50 was reasonably defended by a large mud-brick mastaba 0.9 m high, which overhung its substructure by approximately 0.65 m.[60] However, the superstructure of grave 55 offered its substructure far more protection.[61] Its remains were 1.5 m high and consisted of a loose mud-brick core held together with soil packing and reinforced with mat-work. This was surrounded by an 'adjusting wall' that increased its footprint overhang to an impressive 1.9 to 2 m.[62] Evidence of its effectiveness is demonstrated by an unfinished vertical robber tunnel found in the center of the mastaba over the burial chamber,[63] which suggests that, deterred by the mastaba's footprint overhang, the thief may have decided it was easier to dig through the superstructure rather than to try and undermine it.

Tomb Security in Lower Egypt

Abu Rawash

In Lower Egypt, the most northerly elite necropolis is Cemetery M at Abu Rawash,[64] where the surrounding calcareous rock[65] provided a robust defense against lateral tunneling. This resulted in differing approaches to

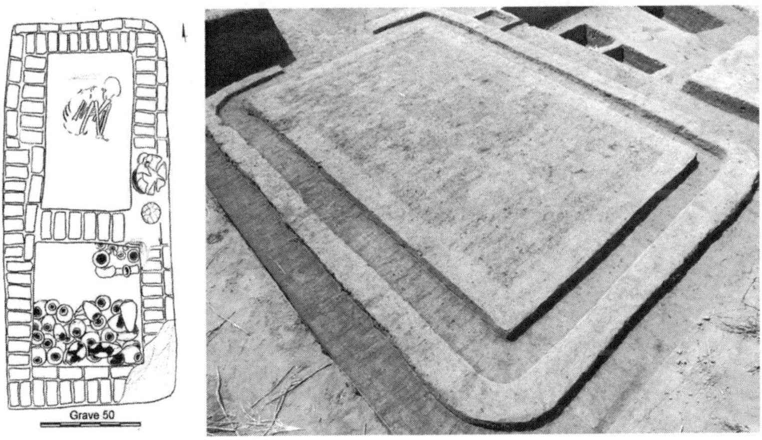

Figure 45. Left: The mud-brick-lined substructure of grave 50 at Tell al-Farkha. Right: The massive mud-brick superstructure and enclosure wall of nearby grave 55.

the security of the substructure. In the case of pit tomb MO25,[66] which dates to Naqada IIIC2,[67] the burial was protected by a double roof, in a similar manner to tomb 389 from the earlier part of the dynasty (see Chapter 3). Here, the usual pit was excavated three meters down into the rock and lined with clay bricks (Fig. 46). Its lower section was then subdivided to provide a burial chamber with four magazines and closed with a planked wooden roof. Above this, sitting 0.3 m below ground level, ledges were built to support large wooden beams and a second roof, which also supported the tomb's superstructure, built from the local clay.[68] Surprisingly, the footprint overhang would have been just over 0.75 m at its narrowest point. However, as the substructure was already well protected by its double roof and the surrounding rock, it is possible that the tomb's builders considered anything larger to be superfluous.

Close by, some of the first elite tombs in the Early Dynastic Period to adopt a subterranean burial chamber (like the Predynastic examples

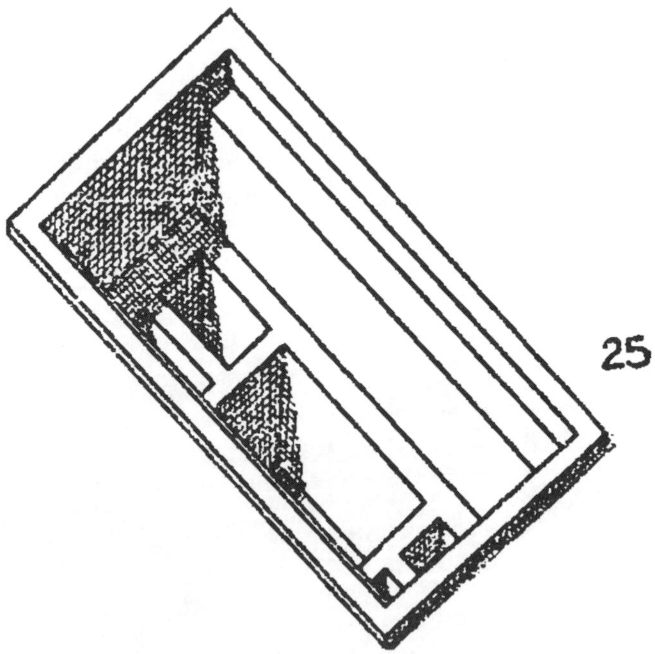

Figure 46. Axonometric drawing of the double mud-brick liners in the double-roofed tomb MO25 at Cemetery M in Abu Rawash.

at Qustul and Kom al-Ahmar discussed in Chapter 1) are also found at Cemetery M. Dating to the reign of Den,[69] they all take a similar form insofar as their substructures comprise a closed main pit from which an internal shaft, usually blocked by a portcullis, leads to a subterranean burial chamber and sometimes adjacent magazines.

The first example is tomb MO1.[70] The upper part of its substructure consisted of a large rock-cut pit that also formed its principal storage magazine, which was lined with mud and wooden boards and surrounded by a brick wall (Fig. 47). Within the pit at its northern end a

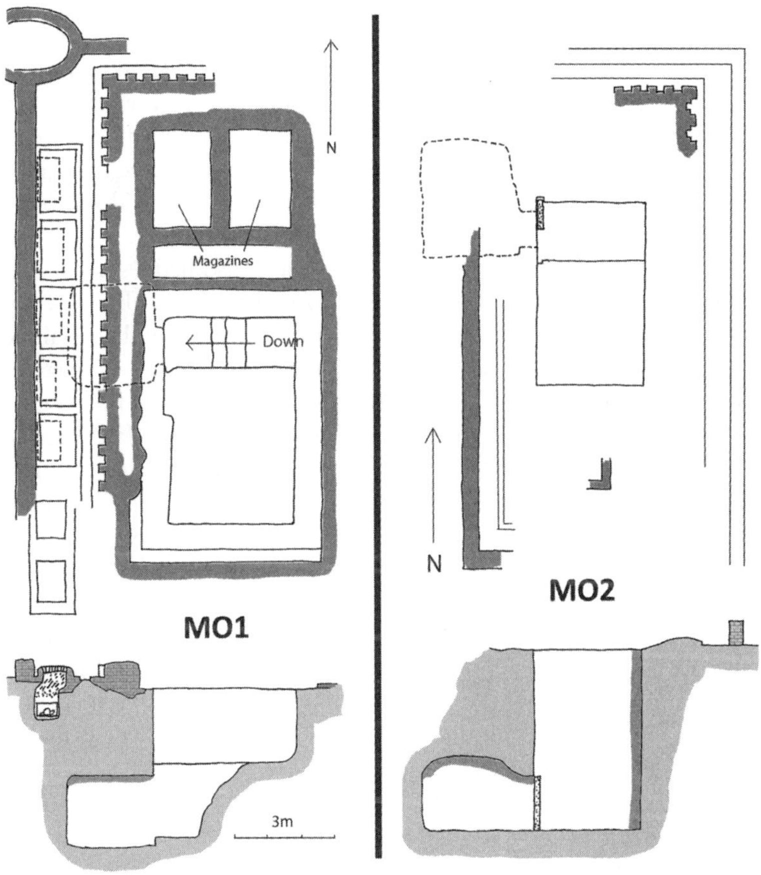

Figure 47. Tombs MO1 and MO2 in Cemetery M at Abu Rawash. In both cases, the rock-cut and roofed magazine pit contained a shaft leading to the subterranean burial chamber.

rudimentary staircase descended west in a shaft, where further progress was blocked by a single stone portcullis set in a grooved emplacement. Beyond this lay a 2.1 m high crudely cut subterranean burial chamber, whose floor was set 4.7 m below ground level. Although the chamber projected beyond the protective footprint of its superstructure, it was protected from above by the cover of the natural rock, which was approximately 2.5 m thick.[71] The whole of the exposed rock-cut pit substructure that led to the burial chamber was then closed by a composite roof of mud, reeds, sand, and mud-brick, supported by beams and sheltered by a protective superstructure. This consisted of a large mud-brick palace façade mastaba that contained three internal storage magazines at its northern end. Its walls were 1.32 m thick, but as with most of the superstructures at Cemetery M, details of its core are unknown. Its footprint overhang was approximately two meters to the edge of the rock-cut pit and magazine. As previously mentioned, this did not totally cover the underlying burial chamber, but that was protected from above by a row of seven subsidiary graves bounded by a 0.6 m wide enclosure wall, which encircled the main body of the superstructure.[72]

Tomb MO2 is adjacent to tomb MO1 and also had a sunken magazine that was probably roofed. Access to its burial chamber was off a deep shaft situated at one end of its magazine, rather than by a staircase (Fig. 47). At the base of the shaft, the entrance to the burial chamber was blocked in an unusual arrangement found only at Abu Rawash: two portcullises set side by side in grooves, of which only the left remained in situ. Made of limestone,[73] it was 0.2 m thick and would have weighed around 0.55 tonnes, making the weight of the pair just over a metric tonne. It was pierced at its bottom right corner with a ten-centimeter-diameter hole, which Pierre Montet, the tomb's excavator, suggested would have been mirrored on the missing slab, enabling the two to be bound together.[74] Beyond this lay a 2.4 m high subterranean burial chamber protected by approximately 3 meters of rock cover. Like tomb MO1, the main body of the substructure was defended by a mud-brick mastaba[75] whose footprint overhang was 1 to 1.4 m, and which also did not cover its burial chamber.

This type of layout is repeated with variations in nearby tombs MO3, MO4, MO6, MO7, MO10, MO11, MO12,[76] and MO19.[77] The portcullises of tombs MO3, MO4, and MO7, like MO1, were furnished with just a single stone fitted into a grooved emplacement,[78] whereas tombs MO6, MO10, MO11, and MO12 possessed twin stones placed side by side,[79] all of which, except MO6,[80] were supported by grooved emplacements. Unusually, in tomb MO19 the pit and shaft leading to the subterranean burial chamber were found entirely blocked with undisturbed stones and rubble instead (discussed below).[81]

Tomb MO10 is important because of its remarkable method of concealing and securing its portcullises (Fig. 48). In the shaft before the burial chamber were two vertical grooves that Montet suggested would have held twin portcullis stones. Above the entrance to the burial chamber and just below the floor edge of the magazine was a horizontal groove 'a' that was matched on the opposite wall of the shaft by a ledge 'c.' One end of a wood or stone floor would have been inserted into groove 'a' with the other end resting on ledge 'c,' thus concealing and securing the two portcullis stones beneath. The purpose of cavity 'b,' which sat over the left-hand vertical groove and ran into the magazine floor, was probably to house some sort of wooden packing to 'lock' the floor into place.[82]

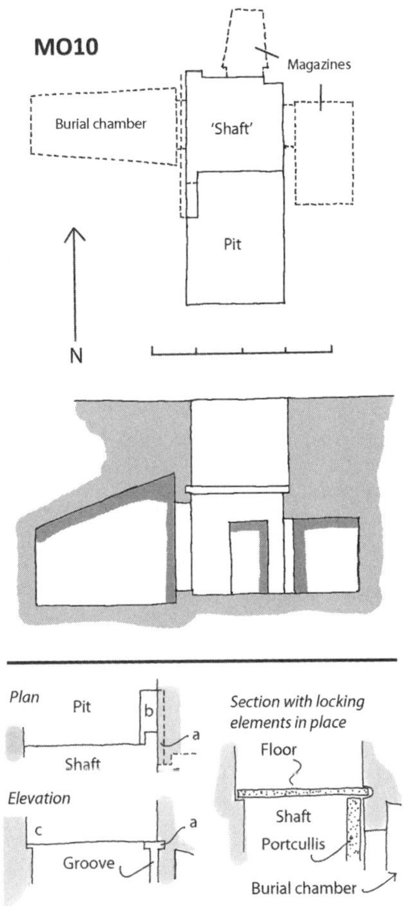

Figure 48. Plan and section of tomb MO10 in Cemetery M at Abu Rawash and its 'locking mechanisms.'

The rock cover over the burial chamber roofs of these tombs varied from 1.3 to 3.2 m thick, and some had subterranean satellite magazines running from their central shafts. In addition, the varying placement of the burial chambers of tombs MO1, MO2, MO4, MO6, and MO7 in relation to their superstructures demonstrates that both their locations and orientation were deliberately diversified, presumably to conceal their whereabouts and misdirect potential tomb robbers. As some of the first tombs in the Early Dynastic Period to adopt the entirely excavated burial chamber, the burial chambers of the Cemetery M group were well defended both by their clever placement and by the cover of their surrounding geology. The overall success of these as security is illustrated by the fact that most of these tombs were robbed through their mud-brick mastabas, underlying magazines, and shafts. However, there is a singular example where the rock cover over the burial chamber was found to have been breached.

The pit substructure of tomb MO19 was sheltered by an overlying superstructure with walls 1 to 1.5 m thick, but the subterranean burial chamber that ran from its shaft extended eastward beyond the mastaba's northeastern edge. The burial chamber had been entered, but unusually not through its superstructure and connecting shaft. Instead, the thieves—who must have been aware of its exact location—avoided the superstructure and tunneled directly through the rock above the burial chamber's northwest corner to plunder it.[83] This leads one to the conclusion that at Cemetery M, the relationship of the superstructure to the burial chamber was like that in many later subterranean tombs insofar as its role was less to protect the burial chamber directly, as was essential with pit graves, and more to conceal the tomb's more vulnerable access route and magazines.

Tura al-Asmant

Some thirty-three kilometers southeast of Abu Rawash at Tura al-Asmant, slightly west of the main site of Tura, a number of stairway pit tombs are excavated in the gravel.[84] There are five published, all of which have gravel-cut mud-brick-lined stairways and burial chambers that would have protected them against lateral tunneling. Perhaps to prevent discovery, their stairways were oriented in differing directions. In tombs 130, 1035, and 1056, they took offset approaches to their burial chambers,[85] whereas those in tombs 986[86] and 249[87] were axially placed. However, all the tombs, with one exception, lack any remains of superstructures, so it cannot be established whether they existed or, if they did, whether their stairwells projected beyond. Some of these tombs had their descents blocked by portcullises. The best protected was 1056, whose mud-brick-lined staircase was blocked at its end by a 0.18 m thick, 1.1-tonne limestone portcullis in a grooved emplacement, and whose burial chamber was sealed by a second portcullis of similar size farther on, at the end of a short passage (Fig. 49).[88]

Many of the burial chambers in these graves were protected by strong mud-brick liners, such as those in tomb 1056, whose 0.8 m thick walls were set 0.8 m down from the desert level, where they supported a wooden roof[89] and presumably a deep gravel backfill. Nearby, although the dimensions are unavailable, tomb 1035 had two thick layers of mud-brick liners in its burial chamber, the innermost of which probably also

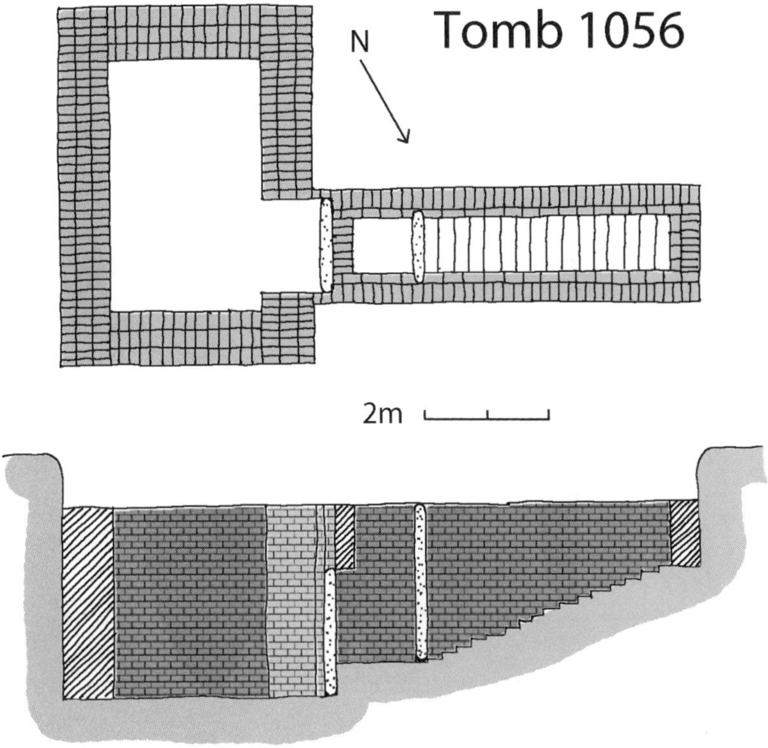

Figure 49. The mud-brick-lined tomb 1056 at Tura al-Asmant, showing the two portcullises in the stairway.

supported a recessed roof and gravel fill,[90] as was the case in the slightly later tomb 986,[91] whose inner mud-brick liner was set down at a lower level within the gravel-cut pit to form the burial chamber.[92]

Two tombs at this necropolis, like those found farther south at Helwan (see below), are notable for their stone linings and worth examining in detail. The first is tomb 130, whose mud-brick-lined stairway was unusually roofed by protective stone slabs, one being approximately 1.3 m long, 0.7 m wide, and 0.15 m thick (Fig. 50). At the foot of the descent, the 2.5 m deep burial chamber was lined with mud-brick walls 0.6 to 1 m thick, within which large limestone slabs roughly 1.1 m high by 0.1 to 0.15 m thick lined the floor and walls. To close the pit from above, it was probably roofed with wood and backfilled to the surface.[93] Larger and more heavily defended is the nearby tomb 249.

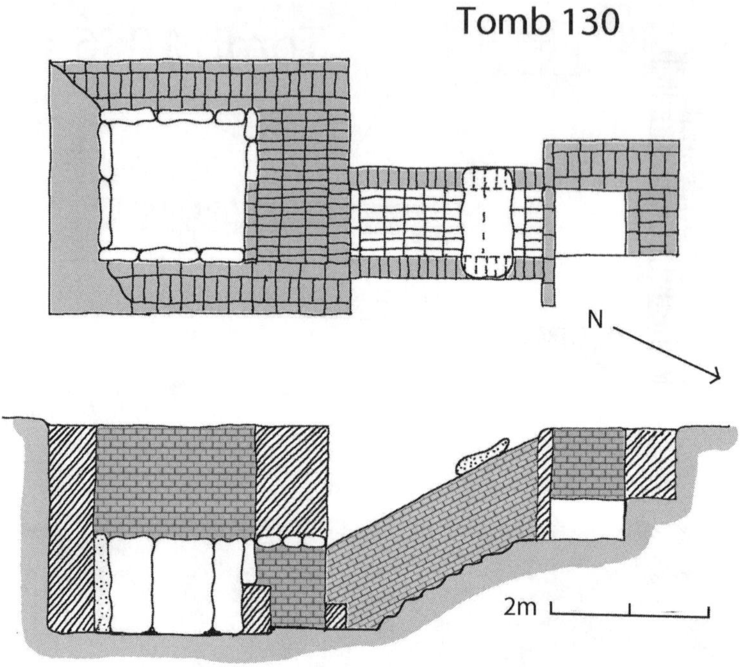

Figure 50. The stone-lined mud-brick tomb 130 at Tura al-Asmant. A stone slab is visible over the mud-brick stairway.

Its mud-brick-lined stairway and passage were blocked by two portcullises (of unknown dimensions) set in grooved emplacements. The first prevented access to the flanking magazines; the second barred access to the burial chamber. Although the drawings of the latter are not entirely clear (Fig. 51), it appears that a 3.4 m deep pit was cut in the gravel and lined with stone slabs approximately two meters high by 0.1 m thick. Above the slabs a ledge was cut in the gravel, presumably to support beams for a wooden roof, and unusually this too was stone clad, presumably to deter vertical tunneling. From it a mud-brick wall of the same thickness rose approximately 0.9 m, which probably formed the foundations of the superstructure and enclosed a gravel backfill.[94]

The unusually thick mud-brick walls and stone liners in these burial chambers at Tura al-Asmant indicate the tomb builders' acute awareness of the vulnerability of the surrounding gravel matrix to *sondages* by tomb robbers. As we shall see below, they were not alone: the necropolis of Helwan suffered from a similar problem.

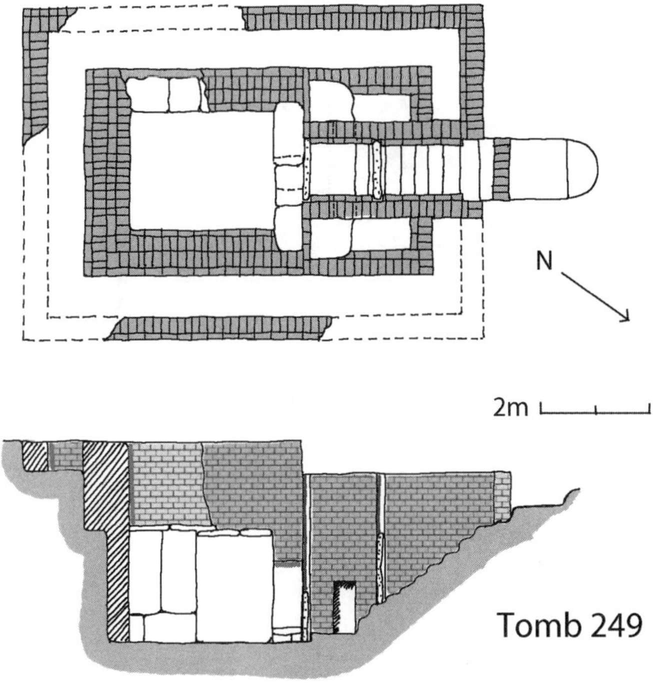

Figure 51. The stone-lined mud-brick tomb 249 at Tura al-Asmant. It may have had two portcullises in its stairway.

Saqqara

Farther south, at the elite cemetery of North Saqqara, new forms of tomb design were also being introduced that differed markedly from their predecessors in the first half of the dynasty and incorporated innovative security measures. Due to the high status of their owners, they are the largest and most complex private tombs of the period, defended by a wealth of defensive features whose development is easily traced thanks to the detailed excavations of Walter B. Emery.

The first four of these tombs date to the reign of Den and vary widely in their layouts. The earliest is S 3507,[95] which was essentially still a pit tomb. However, its burial chamber, rather than taking the form of a long and shallow subdivided trench like the previous tombs at this necropolis, was a rock-cut pit roughly a third the length of its predecessors, but deeper,[96] thus reducing the size of its plan and cross section. The pit was lined with mud-brick at the top to stabilize the surrounding gravel strata (Fig. 52), and within it an internal stairway led to

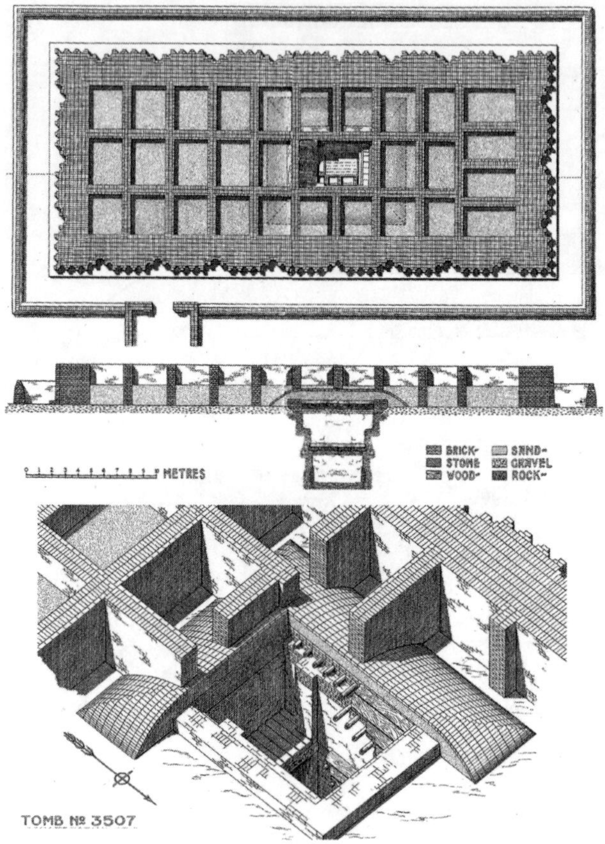

Figure 52. Tomb S 3507 at Saqqara, and a cut-away axonometric view showing its hidden 'mound.'

a wooden floor supported by a rock-cut ledge that formed the roof of the burial chamber and concomitantly created an upper storage magazine. The entire pit was then closed from above by a strong wooden roof supported on beams embedded in the gravel. Remarkably, this bore a rectangular mound of rubble and sand clad in a layer of brick (Fig. 52). Kaiser proposed that its purpose may have been to seal the tomb and make it secure before its superstructure was completed,[97] although others have suggested that it may have been the equivalent of the concealed tumulus in the royal tombs at Abydos or represented a primeval mound of creation.[98]

The tomb's overlying superstructure was similar in size and design to its predecessors, despite the much smaller plan of its innovative substructure, and surrounded by an enclosure wall. Internal cross-walls

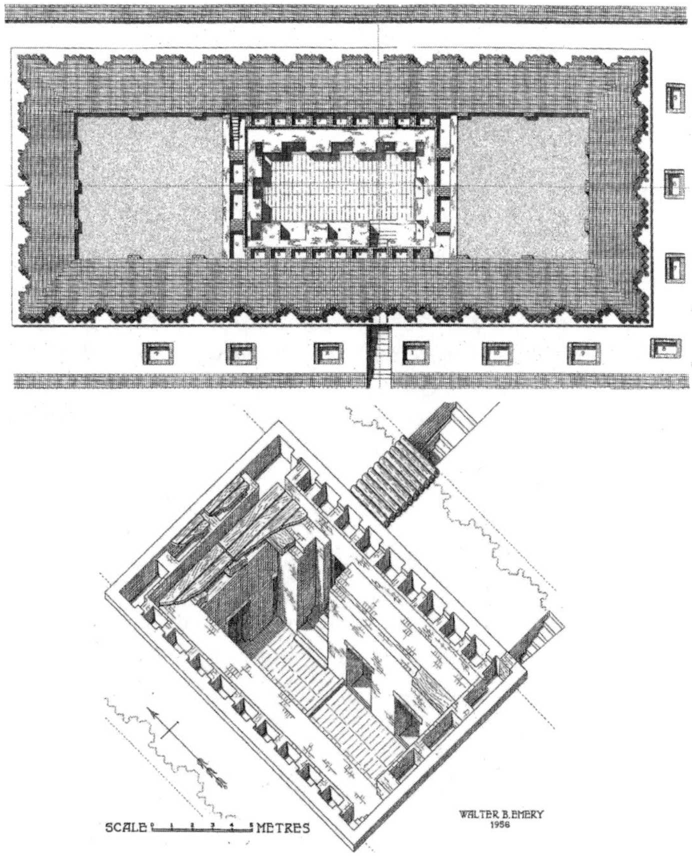

Figure 53. Plan of tomb S 3506 at Saqqara, and an axonometric view of its complex substructure.

divided it into magazines. These were part filled with sand and enclosed by unusually thick 4.5 to 4.7 m wide outer mud-brick walls that were decorated with modeled bucrania, thus creating a 6 m wide footprint overhang that would have deterred a lateral assault on the substructure. Its apparent success in this respect is demonstrated by the route taken by the tomb robbers, who probably entered the pit via the roof of the superstructure and the underlying protective mound that lay below it.[99]

Although apparently unremarkable at first glance, S 3507 is important as it is one of the first tombs to markedly reduce the cross section and plan of its grave pit. This brought security advantages by making the substructure more difficult for robbers to locate by *sondage* from above or from the side, as a greater proportion of its superstructure was able to conceal it.

However, pit tombs at Saqqara such as S 3507 were the exception in this period and were soon superseded and outnumbered by those with external access, with most of the examples published by Emery being of extraordinary size and complexity. We will discuss eight examples whose descents and substructures differ in design, location, and orientation, although it should be noted that their overlying superstructures, though individually different, are invariably orientated north–south.

One of the earliest was tomb S 3506 (Fig. 53).[100] On its east side, slightly north of center, a brick-lined stairway began 10.2 m out from the substructure and descended west through the rock to the pit. Its entrance was concealed under the paving within the enclosure walls, and its stairwell was roofed with wooden logs to bear the weight of the overlying superstructure. Internally, at the base of the stairs, a limestone gateway into the substructure was blocked after the burial from the stair end with a mud-brick wall set behind a wooden door. The stairway was then filled with sand, whose pristine condition upon excavation demonstrated that it had been totally undisturbed.[101] Beyond the stairs, the substructure comprised a large pit excavated 5.15 m into the rock and gravel. At its upper rim, a wide ledge was cut in the surface gravel, which was consolidated and made secure from tunneling by a buttressed mud-brick wall. Within the pit, a massive brick inner structure 1.35 to 1.62 m thick lined the walls up to the level of the gravel ledge and supported wooden beams and a substantial planked roof, which both defended the chamber and formed a foundation for the superstructure.[102]

The mastaba itself was composed of 4.2 to 4.45 m thick mud-brick palace façade walls that, rather than enclosing storage magazines, surrounded a core entirely filled with rubble, thus protecting the substructure from overhead attack. Further encircled by a ledge with applied modeled bucrania, these walls created a 5.5 m footprint overhang to deter lateral tunneling. Despite these mighty defenses, excavations revealed that the tomb, like S 3507, had been robbed by way of the superstructure and the wooden roof of the pit.[103]

A different approach was adopted in the enormous tomb of Hemaka, S 3035.[104] Its offset entrance started nine meters from the superstructure's southern end and descended west for four meters through gravel, which was consolidated by the stairway's mud-brick liners (Fig. 54). The stairwell carried on through the rock that began three meters below the surface and continued to the southern corner

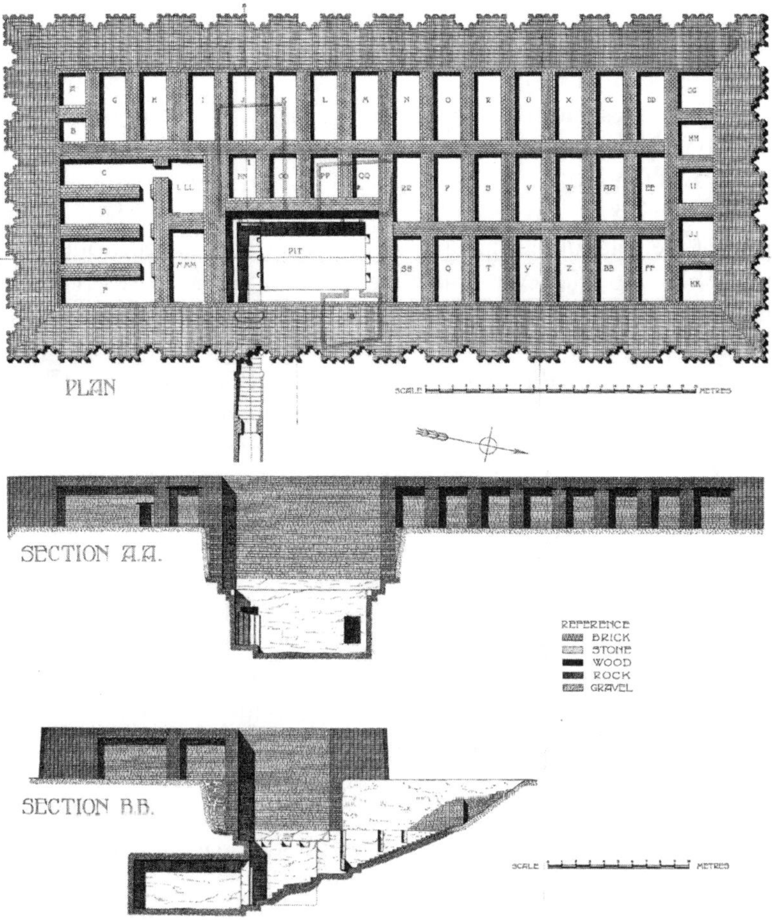

Figure 54. Tomb S 3035 (Hemaka) at Saqqara, showing the offset substructure and the deep internal 'shaft' within the superstructure, which may have been filled with gravel for increased security.

of the main pit. Internally, this descent boasted the largest number of portcullises in the necropolis. About a third of the way down, beyond a brick gateway, three portcullises were set at intervals in grooves in the rock to block the lower part of the stairway. The two upper stones were missing, but the broken section of the lowest was still in situ and measured 2.21 m wide by 0.35 m thick. Although damaged when tomb robbers bored through it, enough remained to show that it had been grooved on both sides to accommodate lowering ropes.[105] The staircase continued down into the main pit and ended in a doorway leading to a rock-cut chamber, which was blocked by yet another large, freestanding portcullis.[106] The stone had holes and grooves for lowering ropes and was 0.25 m thick. Thieves had damaged its base and top,[107] but even in this condition it is estimated to have weighed about two tonnes.[108]

Following the precedent set by the aforementioned S 3507, the plan of the main burial chamber was compact, and in fact smaller than that of S 3506. However, unlike its centrally placed predecessors and in what seems to be an attempt to misdirect tomb robbers, the pit was positioned off-center beneath the southeast section of the superstructure and excavated through a 3.5 m thick layer of loose gravel,[109] 5 m down into solid rock.[110] In the upper edge of the rock layer, a ledge was cut and notched for large beams that supported a substantial wooden roof. Around this rim, a 1 to 1.7 m thick brick wall was built that both consolidated the loose gravel and provided lateral protection. This rose beyond the surface to form part of a seven-meter-high shaft within the superstructure, which was probably backfilled with rubble.[111] Within the pit, three entrances led to separate subterranean 'satellite' chambers excavated in the rock, protected from above by approximately five meters of rock and gravel strata, one of which Emery, the tomb's excavator, hypothesized to be the burial chamber, although it seems equally probable to the writer that the large pit performed this function, like all the other stairway pit tombs nearby, and that these rock-cut chambers were simply magazines.[112]

Overhead lay the largest superstructure at Saqqara from this period, whose perimeter formed by 3.75 to 4.2 m thick mud-brick palace façade walls created a footprint overhang approximately five meters wide from the edge of the offset burial pit.[113] Internally, it was divided by cross-walls into magazines that were filled with rubble, sand, and grave goods. These surrounded the internal shaft over the main burial chamber and also supported the beams, planks, and bricks that formed the roof.[114] As mentioned earlier, as an additional security feature, the internal brick shaft was probably filled with gravel, creating an impenetrable and intimidating 544 cubic meters of combined pit backfill and superstructure core, which would have weighed around 870 tonnes. The success of this innovation is demonstrated by the route selected by the tomb robbers, who, instead of taking the usual overhead or lateral approach, chose to attack the substructure through its heavily defended staircase and three portcullises instead.[115]

Another stairway tomb that incorporated an off-center burial pit, perhaps for security reasons, is S 3036 (Fig. 55).[116] To misdirect thieves its offset entrance staircase was toward the northern end of its mastaba and descended west. Initially lined with mud-brick to a depth of 3.5 m to consolidate the surrounding gravel, the remainder of the stairway was cut in the rock. It was roofed in either stone or wood, and its entrance was hidden under the brick paving of the enclosure ambulatory. Internally, the descent was blocked by a single portcullis (now missing) at the base of

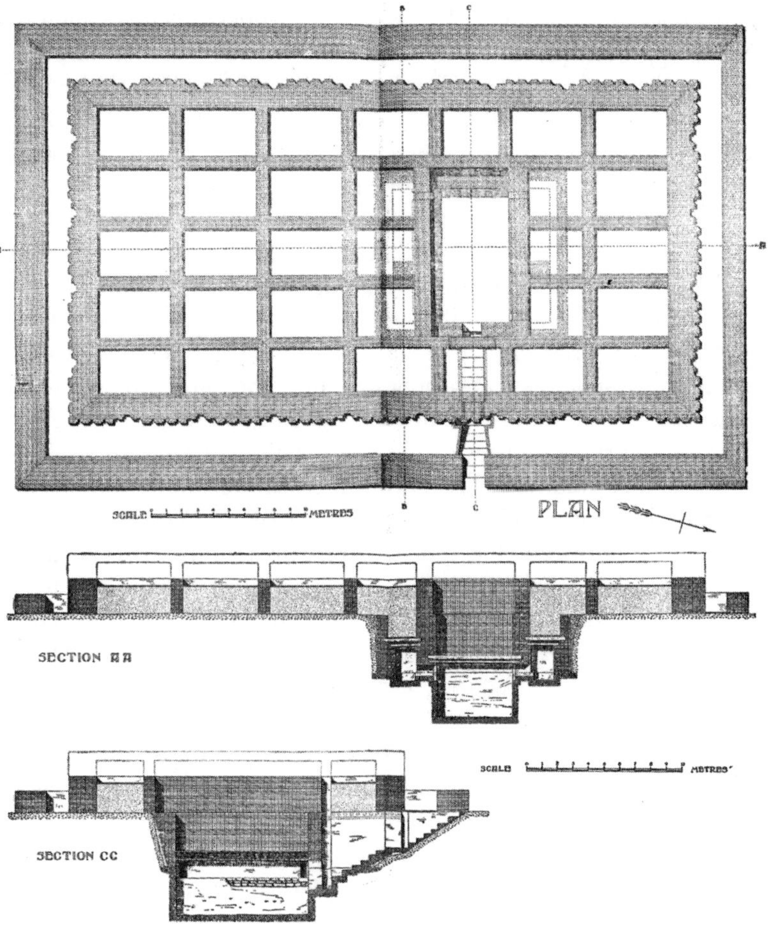

Figure 55. Tomb S 3036 (Ankha) at Saqqara, showing the offset and smaller substructure. The tomb, like S 3035, may have had an internal backfilled 'shaft' in its superstructure.

the stairs, whose enormous size can be envisaged from the large grooves built to accommodate it, which were 0.63 m wide and 2.7 m apart.[117] Based on the average portcullis height of just over 2.5 m at this necropolis, this monolith may have weighed in excess of 8 tonnes![118] At the end of the stairway, a large stepped pit was excavated through the 3.5 m deep gravel layer, then a rectangular burial chamber was dug through its base, at ninety degrees to the long axis of the mastaba, three meters into the bedrock beneath. Within the gravel-cut pit, 0.7 m thick brick liners consolidated the sides and offered lateral protection, but around the rim of the inner burial chamber, 1.2 m thick mud-brick walls were built that rose up into the superstructure, like those in the tomb of Hemaka, which formed a kind of shaft. The chamber was then closed by a 0.14 m thick wooden roof that supported large beams set close together to permit mud-bricks to be laid over them, which then may also have supported a deep gravel fill in the abovementioned shaft.[119]

The deep gravel layer surrounding this tomb would have been vulnerable to lateral tunneling, which may be why the burial chamber was placed well down within the rock strata. If we assume that the brick shaft over the burial was indeed filled with gravel, these combined defenses would have theoretically provided a strong barrier to attack from all directions. Despite these measures, of course, the tomb had been totally plundered, like most of the tombs at Saqqara, and even set on fire.[120]

The next three stairway tombs are tentatively dated to the reign of Adjib[121] and are radically different in their architecture. Taking a completely different approach from that of its neighbors, tomb X was entered from the northern end of its superstructure by steps that descended west and then south through a rock-cut ramp flanked by two high-level magazines to the burial chamber (Fig. 56). The entrance was probably hidden under the pavement and the remainder of the passage roof covered by the solid mud-brick superstructure. Access to the burial chamber was blocked by a 0.3 m thick, 2 tonne limestone portcullis that had two holes drilled in its base for lowering ropes. Beyond, the simple burial chamber was cut through the gravel and rock to a depth of 4.9 m and aligned along the axis of the superstructure. A surrounding ledge on three sides, set 3.35 m above the burial chamber floor, probably supported a wooden roof, but unusually for a tomb at this site, there seem to have been no separate mud-brick liners to consolidate the upper gravel layer to give lateral protection. Although it would appear from Emery's drawing that the brickwork of the overlying superstructure may have been built down into the recess and performed that function instead.

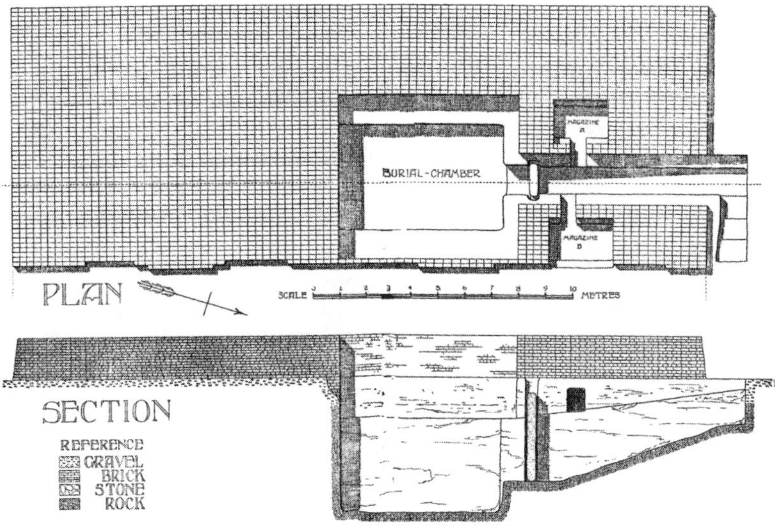

Figure 56. Plan and section of tomb X at Saqqara, showing the unusual solid mud-brick superstructure.

The superstructure of tomb X was also very different from others we have seen at Saqqara. It was constructed of solid mud-brick and entirely lacked internal storage (Fig. 57). The brickwork protected the greater part of the underlying access route and its flanking magazines and, as mentioned above, may also have partially filled the grave pit and acted as a kind of backfill. Although, when excavated, the majority of the mastaba's eastern face was largely missing, if we assume for the sake of this discussion that it was axially placed over its substructure, its protective footprint overhang is likely to have been approximately 4.5 m wide.[122] Predictably, the tomb had been ransacked at some point by robbers, but Emery's excavations revealed no evidence of their point of entry.

Although the substructure of our next tomb, S 3338 was of a similar design to that of tomb X, significantly, its entire L-shaped sloping descent was, for the first time, concealed beneath the core of its superstructure (Fig. 57). First descending west in the gravel layer, it then turned and went south into the rock, in line with the axis of the burial chamber. The whole passage roof was probably protected from overhead attack by stone blocks resting on ledges, and internally vertical grooves were cut to hold two portcullises, one before the flanking magazines and another found in situ at the entrance to the burial chamber, which was 0.25 m thick[123] and would have weighed approximately 1.4 tonnes.[124] Beyond

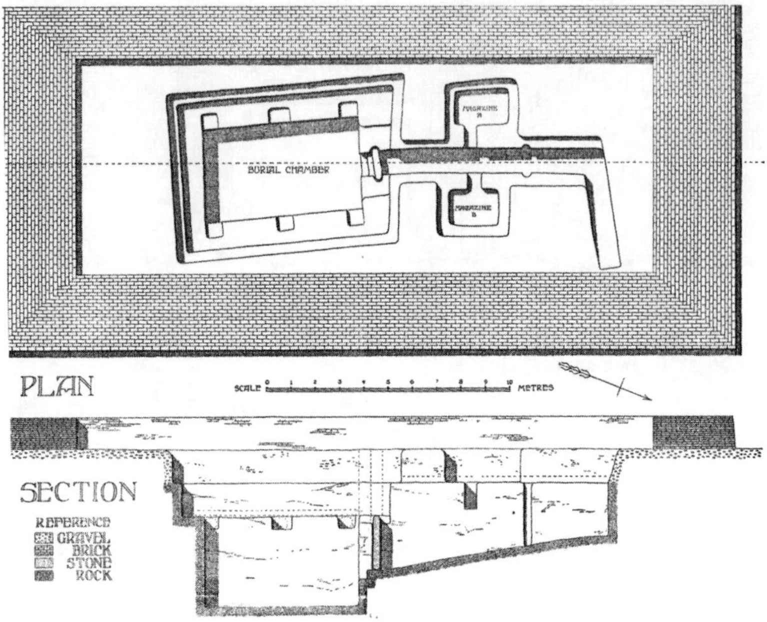

Figure 57. Tomb S 3338 at Saqqara. The stairway is now completely concealed within the superstructure for security reasons.

these, the burial chamber was broadly like that of tomb X and aligned in the same direction. Around the top of its unlined pit, which was sunk through the gravel and rock to a depth of 6.25 m, a ledge intended to support a wooden roof had been cut at 3.55 m from the floor, just below the level of the gravel. Notches carved in this ledge probably supported huge wooden beams that bore both the roof of the chamber and the core fill of the superstructure.

Unusually, the tomb's overlying protective mastaba consisted of 2.3 to 3.4 m thick mud-brick retaining walls, which were devoid of external decoration and whose inner core was filled entirely with rubble. Although this offered the tomb's burial chamber only a relatively small 2.4 m footprint overhang by way of protection from lateral attack, it may be that the massive weight and volume of the rubble covering it, together with the entirely concealed access route, were considered more than adequate compensation. Smashed stone vases found in the burial chamber suggest that the tomb had been robbed,[125] presumably through its roof, as the undisturbed portcullis in the descent precludes this as the route of entry.

The last three tombs in this necropolis all date to the reign of Qa'a[126] and revert to entrances on their eastern sides. Although their burial chambers are similar to those in S 3338 and tomb X, unlike them they are all orientated at ninety degrees to their superstructures, thereby shrinking their pits' cross section and exposure to lateral tunneling on what would usually be the most vulnerable edge under an axially orientated superstructure.[127]

Tomb S 3500[128] was entered from beyond its enclosure wall by means of a staircase 9.3 m long, slightly south of center (Fig. 58). Cut in the

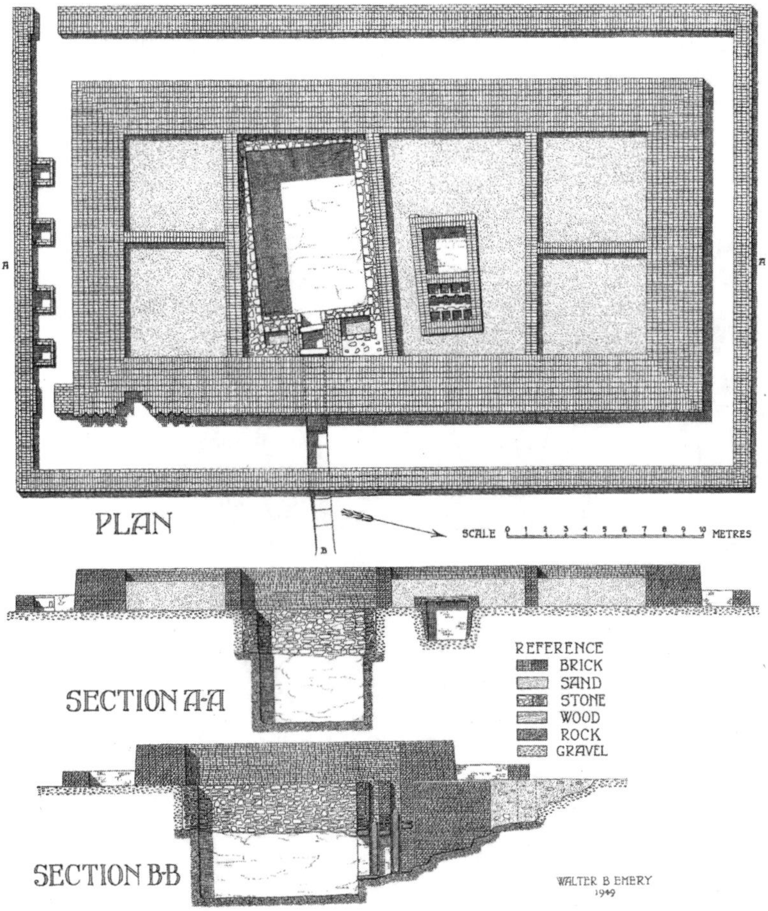

Figure 58. Tomb S 3500 at Saqqara, with its offset burial chamber and internal magazines.

deep gravel, it descended under the wall, down into the rock to the burial chamber. Possibly roofed with wood, rather than being mud-brick-lined, it appears the whole stairwell was filled with solid mud-brick, which both blocked it and consolidated the surrounding gravel. Additionally, just before the entrance to the burial chamber two hefty portcullises sealed the descent, the first and larger of the two was 3.1 m high, 1.35 m wide and 0.3 m thick and would have weighed around 2.7 tonnes (Fig. 59). The smaller second stone, unlike the first, had been drilled with holes to accept lowering ropes and would have weighed approximately 1.68 tonnes.[129] High up, two small magazines flanked the portcullis emplacement, and further north an entirely separate mud-brick-lined pit was roofed with wood for the same purpose. The burial chamber was sunk through the two-meter layer of gravel and a further 3.2 m into the rock.[130] At the top a ledge was cut in the rock that supported a masonry wall, which was intended to consolidate and reinforce the gravel against lateral attack and probably support a wooden roof.

Figure 59. The enormous twin portcullises of tomb S 3500. The holes for lowering ropes are clearly visible.

The overlying superstructure consisted of a plain single-niched mastaba,[131] whose external mud-brick walls were 2.6 to 2.8 m thick and surrounded a core subdivided by cross-walls and filled with sand. This provided the substructure with a protective footprint overhang of approximately three meters, but even so it proved inadequate. Undeterred, thieves had burrowed under the superstructure from the eastern corridor, through the weaker gravel strata, and into the western wall of the burial pit.[132]

Access to the substructure of S 3505,[133] the largest tomb complex in the necropolis, was by way of the eastern corridor that ran between its superstructure and the surrounding inner enclosure wall (Fig. 60). Here, a ramp ran north–south for 7.65 m before, halfway down the mastaba's length, turning ninety degrees and descending west 9.65 m to the burial chamber. The whole of it was roofed in wood and, after the burial, its entrance ramp was backfilled and partly concealed by a bench that supported bucrania. Internally and quite high up, the descent was flanked

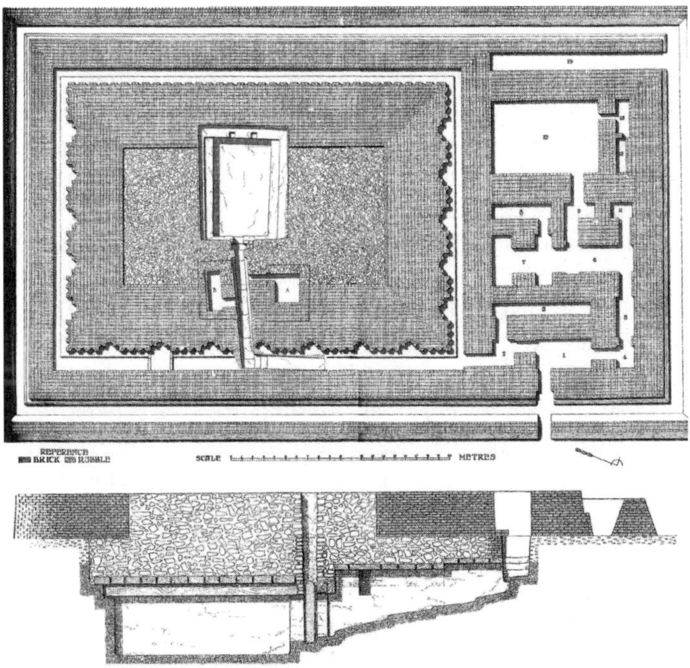

Figure 60. The massive tomb S 3505 (Merka) at Saqqara. The huge wooden thirty-centimeter-thick 'planks' that roofed the substructure are visible in the section drawing.

by two mud-brick-lined rock-cut magazines, which were themselves protected with wooden roofs. At the end of the ramp, a single three-meter-high, 2.25 tonne portcullis was set in an emplacement, blocking the entrance to the rectangular burial chamber, which was sunk 5.75 m down through the gravel and bedrock.[134] Just below the gravel strata, notches and a recess were cut in the rock walls of the chamber to accommodate enormous 0.6 m square wooden beams and a wooden roof.[135] The enormous timber 'planks' that formed this roof were a remarkable 0.3 m thick and 0.9 m wide in section, thus providing the burial chamber with both a significant degree of protection from attack from above and support for the considerable bulk of its overlying mastaba.

Aboveground, the superstructure was located within two sets of enclosure walls that also surrounded an adjacent funerary temple. It consisted of a palace façade mastaba, whose immense mud-brick walls were between 5.15 and 6 m thick (the strongest at Saqqara), and which surrounded an inner core of packed rubble that protected the tomb's substructure and the majority of its access route with a footprint overhang of approximately 4.5 m. But, as was often the case at Saqqara, these mighty defenses were to no avail: the tomb had been completely robbed and ravaged by fire in antiquity.[136]

Finally, the less well-documented tomb S 2105, excavated by Quibell, was entered from the east by a centrally placed stairway, whose entrance was concealed underneath the thick wall of its mastaba (Fig. 61), its roof probably protected by wood and the whole covered by the mastaba's gravel fill. The descent was blocked by a portcullis. Although little detail is available, a photograph of the stone in situ shows that the top corner had been broken at some point (Fig. 61). Beyond it, the burial chamber took the form of a square pit, once roofed by "timber baulks" that covered the chamber and supported the superstructure.[137] The latter had 2.8 to 3.5 m thick mud-brick walls that provided a 2.8 m footprint overhang,[138] covered the entrance, and enclosed a gravel core, which in turn protected the burial pit and a magazine. While there is no concrete evidence of the tomb having been plundered, the tell-tale broken portcullis does suggest that robbers may have gained access by this route.

The access routes to these stairway tombs at Saqqara would have been well protected laterally by their rock surroundings, but it appears from the mud-brick linings used to reinforce the descents that the overlying gravel strata was considered vulnerable to lateral

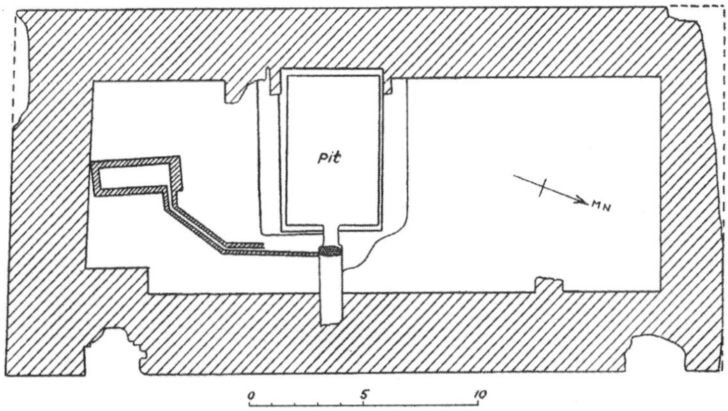

Figure 61. Tomb S 2105 at Saqqara, and a view of its broken portcullis in position at the entrance to the burial chamber.

attack. To foil potential attacks from above, the tomb builders relied on wood or stone roofing and the protective footprint of the superstructure, and it is evident both from the concealed entrances and the diverse locations and orientations of their associated descents that these were deliberately positioned with the intention of frustrating tomb robbers.[139]

As for the security of the burial chambers, the fact that, like the stairways, the overlying gravel stratum into which these pits were cut was reinforced with mud-brick or stone liners points to their innate susceptibility to lateral tunneling. So, in the majority of cases, it seems that the tomb builders relied on the underlying strata of limestone rock to provide lateral security, and accordingly the wooden roofs that closed these chambers were located either below or level with the rock. It also appears that by varying both the location and orientation of burial chambers and progressively reducing their plans and cross sections, they too were being made more difficult to locate. Although they remained vulnerable to attack from above, despite their protective superstructures, as demonstrated by the size and strength of the wooden roofs that were built to close and defend them.

Aboveground, perhaps for security reasons, as the dynasty progresses we see a slight change to the role of the monumental superstructure at Saqqara, from fortified storehouse and protector of the substructure to a more defensive function with fewer grave goods, whose primary function was now to protect the underlying burial chamber, its access route, and flanking magazines.

A further refinement of the stairway tomb, and one that foreshadows future developments, is made at the end of the dynasty with the introduction of the entirely subterranean burial chamber in two tombs that date to the reign of Qa'a.[140] Unlike the slightly earlier tombs in Cemetery M at Abu Rawash, they were connected to stairways with external access.

The earliest of these is S 3121 (Fig. 62).[141] Access was through a concealed entrance that began in the north corridor of its superstructure and led to a 7.6 m long sloping passage that descended toward the face of a rock escarpment, into which was cut the burial chamber. The lower half of the passage was partially dug in the rock, its upper half built of masonry to consolidate the upper strata of the gravel in which it was cut. The whole was roofed and protected by seven large blocks of limestone, each approximately two meters long, one meter wide, and 0.6 m thick, which in turn were protected by the rubble fill of the superstructure. A portcullis at the end of the passage originally blocked the entrance of the burial chamber. The slab had been smashed to pieces, but from the fragmentary remains Emery was able to ascertain that it had been drilled to accept lowering ropes and had been cut with copper chisels. Beyond it, and taking advantage of the natural topography, the trapezoid burial chamber was cut into the

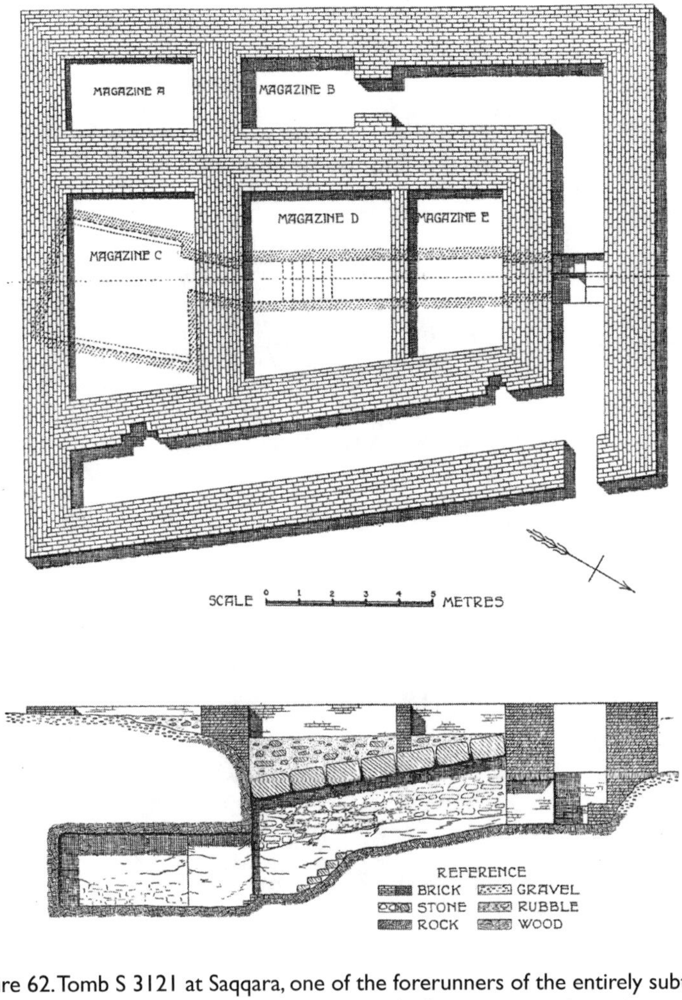

Figure 62. Tomb S 3121 at Saqqara, one of the forerunners of the entirely subterranean tomb. The enormous sixty-centimeter-thick stones over the stairway can be seen in the section drawing.

vertical face of the escarpment and reinforced with masonry on two sides. This left a natural rock cover 3.7 m thick, which was further protected by the tomb's overlying superstructure.[142]

The stairway of adjacent tomb S 3120 followed much the same plan as its immediate neighbor (Fig. 63),[143] but from its concealed entrance took a longer stepped descent southwest from the superstructure's internal passage and then turned southeast under the superstructure

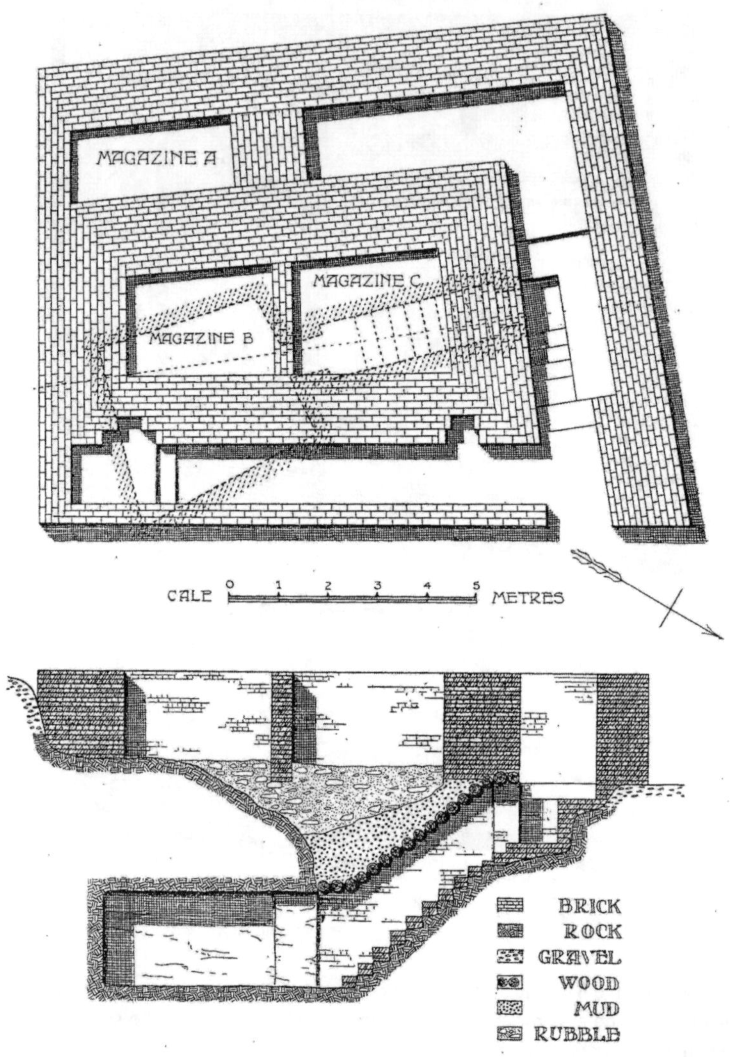

Figure 63. Tomb S 3120 at Saqqara. Its stairway was only roofed with wooden beams.

wall. Its 3.5 m long rock-cut stairwell seems to have been entirely lined with mud-brick and supported a wooden roof that bore a mud and rubble backfill between it and its superstructure. The burial chamber was also similar to that of S 3121, but it was unlined and less well protected by a sloping rock roof and compensatory layer of rubble, approximately 2.6 m thick at its deepest point.[144]

Aboveground, the unusual substructures of both tombs were reflected in the construction of their distinct trapezoid superstructures. Although when viewed externally the upper half of these structures would have seemed level to the viewer, in fact their foundations followed the contours of the escarpment over which they were built. Internally they both contained an L-shaped open corridor that led to a single magazine, creating a kind of inner protective mastaba. Probably roofed in wood, these inner structures contained magazines that were filled with sand and rubble, which both protected the roofs of their underlying trench-cut stairwells and concealed the undulating geology that lay over their subterranean burial chambers.[145]

With their burial chambers well protected by the surrounding rock geology, these unusual tombs mark a transitional phase at Saqqara from the older stairway pit tombs to the entirely underground substructures of the subterranean stairway tomb, a design that was to become commonplace in the tombs in this necropolis and elsewhere during the Second Dynasty.[146]

Helwan

Meanwhile, on the opposite bank of the Nile from Saqqara at the Helwan necropolis, the transition from pit tomb to stairway pit tomb was also not immediate. There are a few examples of traditional pit tombs without external access that incorporate special security measures to compensate for the weaker geology of the cemetery, one of the most notable of which is the use of stone to reinforce the vulnerable walls of the burial chamber.[147] We shall examine two examples here.

The first is 423.H.9, which is dated to the reign of Den. Saad described the tomb's mud-brick-lined burial chamber and four magazines, as "being roofed with limestone" and therefore "intended to protect the tomb from robbery." Aboveground, the substructure was protected by a large mud-brick mastaba with 2.5 m thick palace façade walls, which was presumably filled with gravel, sand, or rubble (Fig. 64). Saad's published dimensions suggest the tomb had an exceptional 11.5 m footprint overhang, which would have provided a major deterrent to lateral attack. But despite this, and perhaps because they were aware of the substructure's stone roof, robbers had still dug three separate tunnels into the burial chamber from "outside the wall" and plundered it.[148]

To prevent this sort of lateral tunneling, stone was also used to protect the burial chamber of tomb 1390.H.2, which dates to the middle

Figure 64. Interior of the superstructure of tomb 423.H.9 at Helwan, which would have been filled with sand, gravel, or rubble. The recess for the burial chamber's roof can clearly be seen and would have been covered by stone slabs.

of the dynasty. It appears from Saad's necropolis plan and photographs to comprise a rectangular mud-brick-lined pit tomb with magazines at either end.[149] The central burial chamber was lined with two courses of large limestone orthostats 2.5 m long, 0.8 m high, and 0.2 m thick, weighing about a tonne each and laid horizontally edge to edge (Fig. 65).[150] Details of the substructure's closure are unavailable, but it may have been done in the usual Helwan manner with a wooden roof brought level with rubble to the surface.[151] Presumably, like most of the tombs at Helwan, it would also have been protected by a superstructure, but no details are available.

Apart from these two tombs, there are far greater numbers of stairway pit tombs at the site, and they vary widely in their architecture and size. Although it can be difficult to date many of them accurately,[152] the majority can be broadly dated to Naqada IIIC–D.[153] Some of their substructures are just gravel-cut, some are mud-brick-lined, and some, more famously, are lined or roofed with stone. In most of these tombs, the longitudinal axis of the burial chamber is roughly north–south, but as at Saqqara, their stairways approach in various orientations and

Figure 65. Interior of the gravel-cut tomb 1390.H.2 at Helwan, lined with twenty-centimeter-thick stone slabs for protection.

positions. It seems that generally the stairway either enters the burial chamber at its narrowest end, in line with the burial chamber's longitudinal axis, or is set at ninety degrees to the axis and joins the burial chamber somewhere along the longest edge of the substructure. However, aboveground, the denudation of the majority of superstructures at Helwan because of erosion, reuse of materials, and the actions of the *sebbakhin* makes it hard to establish the exact relationship of the tomb's superstructures to their burial chambers and stairways.[154]

An early stairway pit tomb with apparently the barest protection was 1.H.4, whose simple gravel-cut stairway descended eastward and was probably blocked with backfill (Fig. 66). At its base, an unlined pit formed the burial chamber, which was provided with internal ledges to accommodate wooden beams that supported a shallow roof and the tomb's superstructure. At first glance, the thin mud-brick walls of the superstructure, only 0.75 m thick, also suggest little investment in the tomb's defenses, yet its 2.4 m footprint overhang and gravel core would actually have provided decent lateral protection for both the pit and its stairway.[155]

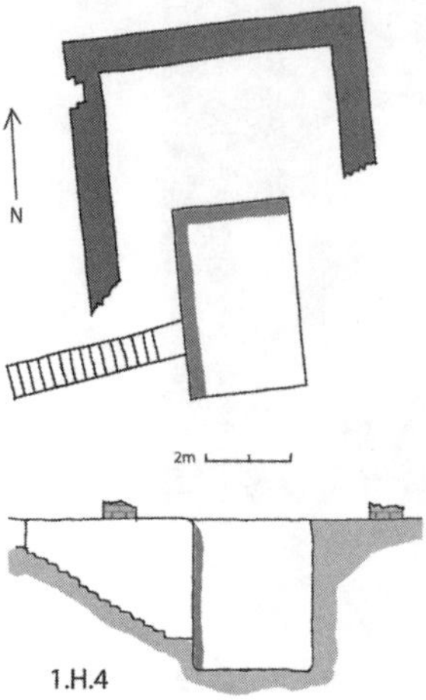

Figure 66. The unlined gravel-cut tomb 1.H.4 at Helwan.

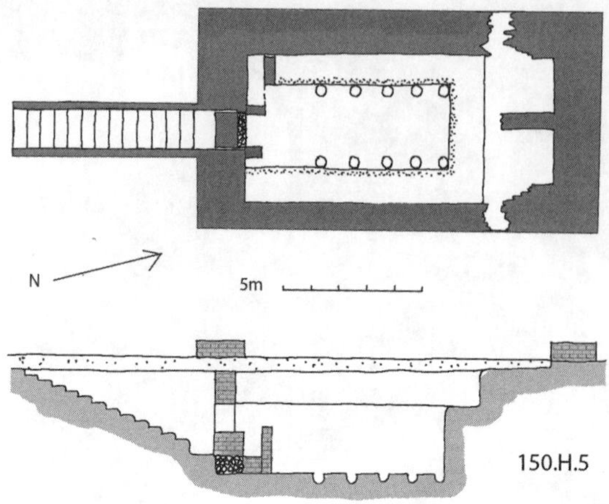

Figure 67. The unlined tomb 150.H.5 at Helwan, whose burial chamber's roof was set two meters below the surface.

As with the ordinary pit tombs at this site, there were other ways to obtain greater overhead and lateral protection in the unlined stairway tomb, for instance by increasing the depth of the roof, as in the mid-First Dynasty tomb 150.H.5 (Fig. 67). Unlike 1.H.4, its unlined stairway descended northward, and, in addition to the usual backfill, it was further closed by a mud-brick wall at its base. Within the burial chamber, gravel-cut ledges supported a two-meter-deep recessed roof and a deep backfill. On the surface, the remains of its overlying superstructure indicate that its walls were an impressive 0.9 to 1.5 m thick and that it provided its substructure with a defensive footprint overhang of around two meters.[156]

Many substructures in these stairway tombs at Helwan were also brick-lined, both to consolidate the surrounding geology and to provide lateral protection. In addition, various other architectural elements were introduced to improve security, some apparently more effective than others.

Tomb 407.H.4, for example, was approached at its extreme northern end by a simple gravel-cut stairway from the west, whose only significant blocking, apart from the usual stair backfill, was a mud-brick wall at the entrance to the pit. However, the substructure itself was better defended. It comprised a 5.9 m deep pit that was lined with 0.3 m thick mud-brick walls and wooden planks (Fig. 68).[157] Notably, this had a 3.9 m deep recessed roof that would have supported around 190 cubic meters of backfill, which would have weighed more than 300 tonnes,[158] offering the burial an unusually high level of protection from overhead and lateral attack. On the surface, it was presumably protected by a superstructure of some form, but no traces remained in situ.

Better defended aboveground was tomb 785.H.5 (Fig. 69). Entered from the west by a mud-brick reinforced stairway with a single portcullis at its base, its 5.5 m deep pit was lined with substantial mud-brick walls approximately 1.1 m thick. Inside at its northern end were two layers of magazines, and the whole substructure, according to Saad, was roofed with "huge blocks of timber" that secured the pit and supported the large superstructure. Surrounded by an enclosure wall, the mastaba's 0.75 to 3 m thick mud-brick walls enclosed fourteen internal magazines,[159] and would have provided a protective footprint overhang approximately three meters wide over the pit and its external stairway.

As with pit tombs, a few of these substructures had double roofs, for example tomb 355.H.4, whose mud-brick-lined stairway was closed at one

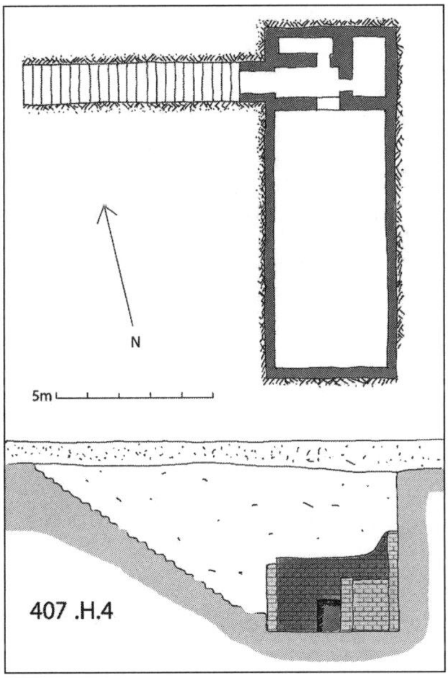

Figure 68. The mud-brick-lined tomb 407.H.4 at Helwan. Its 3.9 m deep burial chamber roof could support three hundred tonnes of backfill.

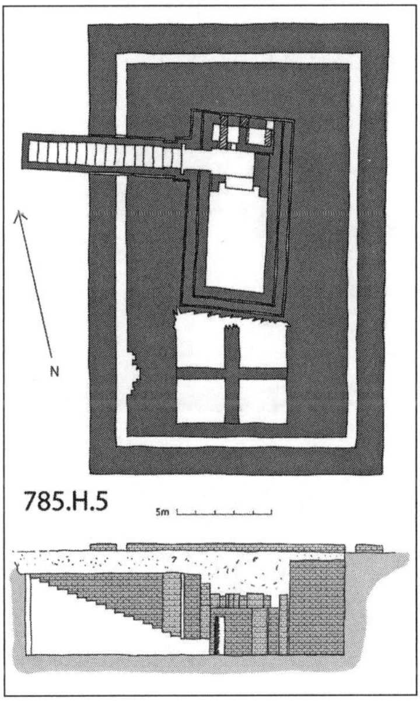

Figure 69. Tomb 785.H.5 at Helwan, whose roof contained "huge blocks of timber."

end with a portcullis and backfilled with rubble. Beyond it a 2.9 m deep lined pit had two layers of 0.3 m thick mud-brick liners to support roofing beams (Fig. 70), one set at 1.7 m from the floor, the other 0.7 m higher. The lower roof may have been packed with a layer of rubble or used for storage, and the upper may have supported a 0.5 m thick layer of roof and backfill,[160] presumably protected by a superstructure.

Like at Saqqara, some tombs at this site had stairways that changed direction during their descent, as in the case of two slightly later tombs from the end of the dynasty, 1371.H.2 and 1502.H.2 (Fig. 71). Both tombs were accessed by mud-brick-lined L-shaped descents, which were blocked internally with two portcullises, the second of these in 1371.H.2 weighing around 2.2 tonnes![161] Both tombs are also notable for the strength of their burial chambers' mud-brick liners, which in both cases were between 1 and 1.7 m thick.[162] In this vein, most unusually, the stairway of nearby tomb 553.H.2 descended south and then changed direction 180 degrees, via a half-landing, to head north to its burial chamber (Fig. 72).[163] These features lead one to the conclusion that in some cases the direction of descent was deliberately chosen either to conceal the location of the burial chamber from grave robbers[164] or perhaps more mundanely, to simply avoid another grave.[165]

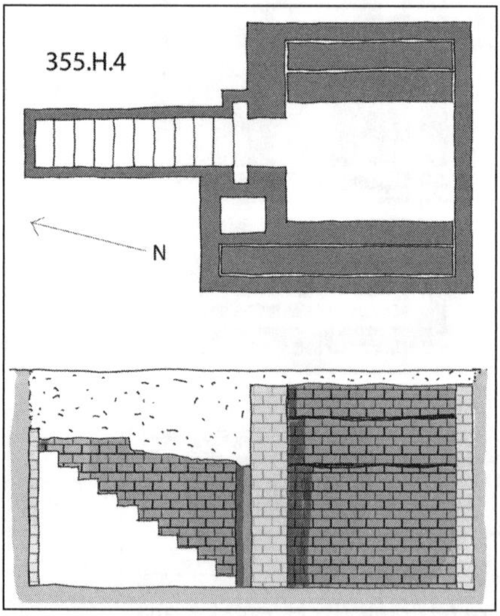

Figure 70. The double-roofed and twin-walled tomb 355.H.4 at Helwan.

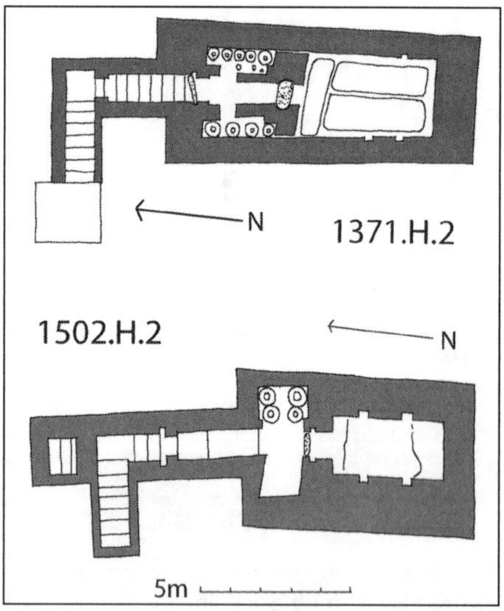

Figure 71. Tombs 1371.H.2 and 1502.H.2 at Helwan, which both had L-shaped stairways and twin portcullises.

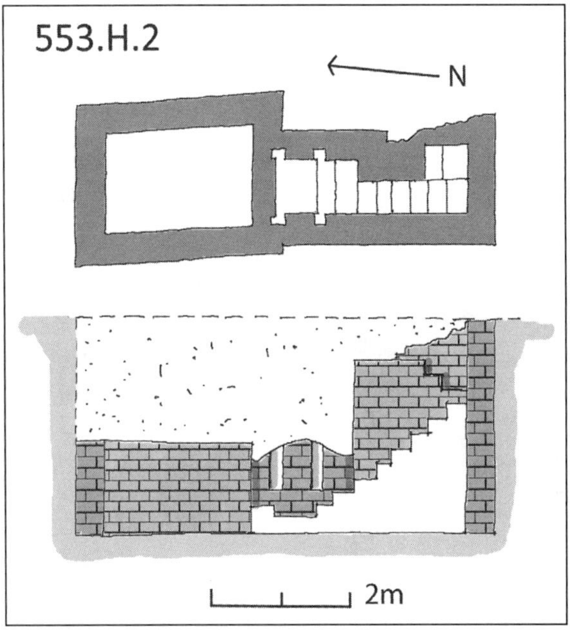

Figure 72. Tomb 553.H.2 at Helwan. Its stairway had a half-landing and doubled back on itself.

Many of the burial chambers of the stairway tombs at Helwan were reinforced with stone for additional security, like those at Tura al-Asmant. Among these, 385.H.4 is exceptional for the size of its defenses. In the tomb, a gravel-cut stairway, whose base was blocked by a substantial mud-brick wall, led to a pit that was internally divided at the stair end with mud-brick walls which formed magazines and flanked a second internal mud-brick stairway. At the base of these second stairs, within the 4.15 m deep pit, the remaining space in the chamber was lined with enormous limestone orthostats set on their longest edges (Fig. 73). These were four meters long, two meters wide, and 0.4 m thick at the narrow ends of the pit. Comparable slabs were used on the longer sides, with shorter sections to fill the gaps. Remarkably, the larger slabs would have weighed in the region of seven metric tonnes each.[166] A ledge high up on either side of the pit may have supported a stone slab roof, and the remainder was probably backfilled with around 1.8 m of rubble and leveled. Although there is no trace of a superstructure, it was presumably protected by one in the usual manner. Despite the enormous investment in these precautions, the tomb had still been robbed by means of a tunnel dug through the gravel, under the roof and through one of the stone slabs into the chamber.[167]

Figure 73. Interior of tomb 385.H.4 at Helwan, which was lined with forty-centimeter-thick orthostats. The robbers' tunnel is visible on the left.

One of the finest examples of the use of stone as 'armor' for a burial chamber is 40.H.3,[168] which has recently been re-excavated by Christiana Köhler (Fig. 74).[169] The entrance consists of an axial staircase four meters long, lined with stone and with stone steps, which descends south to a two-meter-long passageway, lined on each side with 0.2 m thick stone slabs. Beyond, in a pit dug into the surrounding strata of sand, gravel, clay, and silt, a shorter stone-walled corridor, closed by a portcullis at either end, led to a stone-lined anteroom before the burial chamber. The now broken portcullises were 0.3 m thick and bored to accept lowering ropes. Assuming they were originally about two meters high, they would both have weighed about 1.5 tonnes. In the rest of the pit, the cuts were lined with a 0.63 m thick layer of masonry on three sides,[170] which offered a first layer of lateral protection. Against these walls were leaned large stone slabs, the greatest of which is 1.45 m wide, 2.35 m high, and 0.26 m thick, and the entrance was fitted with enormous stone jambs 1 to 1.3 m wide, 2.6 m high, and 0.4 m thick. A stone roof may have closed the pit, but it is more likely to have been wooden beams covered with mats, mud-bricks, and around a hundred cubic meters of rubble backfill to support

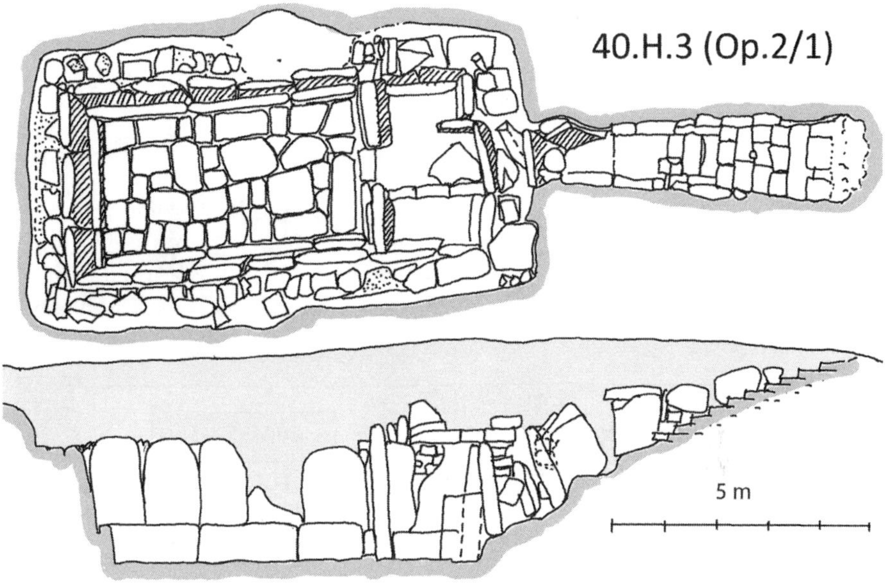

Figure 74. The complex stone lining of tomb 40.H.3 (Op. 2/1) at Helwan. Even the staircase was lined for protection.

the superstructure. Made of mud-brick, the latter may have been approximately twenty meters long and ten meters wide, and for extra security it may have covered both the stairway and the pit. The tomb was plundered despite these lavish defenses, and there is evidence that robbers may have gained entry to the antechamber through its stone walls.[171]

A similar stone-lined tomb, on a much larger scale but less well reported, was the enormous 1.H.3. Its mud-brick-lined stairway was internally clad with stone slabs, but it was L-shaped rather than straight like that of 40.H.3. Internally, the descent was secured by four portcullises of unknown dimensions, the largest number of blockings found at Helwan in a single tomb (Fig. 75). From the top of the staircase, after the ninety degree turn onto its straight descent, a portcullis blocked access to the passage beyond and its two flanking magazines. Further down, the remains of grooves in the wall suggest that an additional portcullis blocked the way. Another slab was found in situ a short distance further on, protecting two more magazines; its base drilled with four holes for lowering ropes. Lastly, a final portcullis slab barred the entrance to the burial chamber itself.

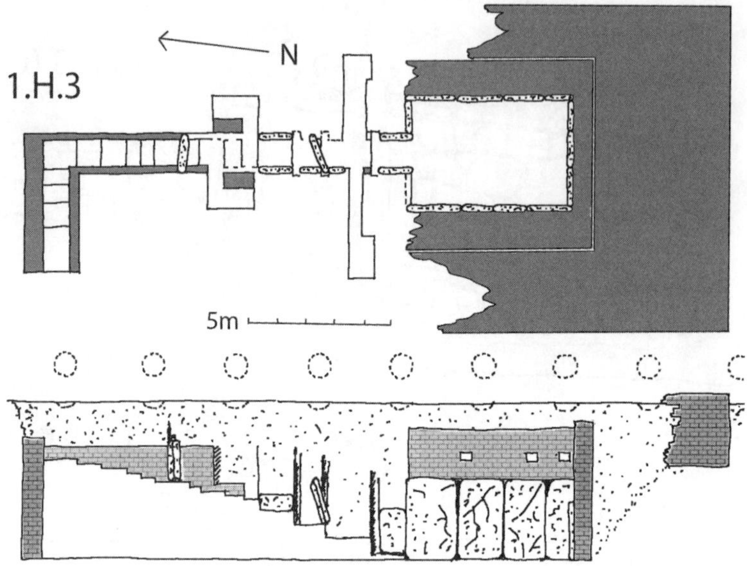

Figure 75. The stone-lined tomb 1.H.3 at Helwan. It was equipped with four portcullises in its L-shaped descent.

Inside its deep gravel-cut pit, the burial chamber, which was lined with 0.6 to 1.3 m thick mud-brick walls, was clad with stone slabs approximately 2.7 m high, 1.5 m wide, and 0.2 m thick. Just above these, large wooden beams supported a planked roof that held up approximately 1.7 m of gravel backfill and supported the tomb's superstructure.

Although the walls seem badly damaged, the plan of 1.H.3 shows that its substructure would have been protected from above by a substantial superstructure with a minimum footprint overhang of approximately three meters. Unsurprisingly, at some point these mighty defenses were overcome by tomb robbers, and Saad reported that the tomb had been set on fire, the intensity of the heat turning the mud-brick liners the color of fired red brick.[172]

That these stone-lined tombs sometimes also had stone roofs is confirmed by the excavation of tomb 60.H.1,[173] where it appears stone slabs 0.25 m thick were placed over the pit to create a roof, which offered the substructure a good level of protection and was strong enough to have supported a 0.4 m deep rubble backfill.[174]

Compared to the burial chambers of Saqqara, which benefited from the strength of the surrounding rock, the tombs at Helwan demonstrate a wider variety of security responses due to the weaker geology of the necropolis. The most popular measure seems to have been reinforcement of the chamber with thick mud-brick liners, or less frequently stone, to deter lateral penetration, together with a recessed roof to increase the depth of backfill, which made tunneling into the chamber more difficult from all directions. That said, there is less variety in the orientation of burial chambers in relation to their superstructures than at Saqqara, probably because of the tombs' generally smaller size. This left them more vulnerable to *sondages* by tomb robbers, who could more easily predict their location.

Tarkhan

South of Helwan at Tarkhan, pit tombs without external access routes and entrances remained in vogue and, like the adjacent Mastaba 1060 from the first half of the dynasty, also relied on the surrounding limestone geology to protect their burial chambers. There are two very similar examples, which date to the reign of Den (Fig. 76).[175] The unlined burial chamber of Mastaba 2050 was excavated in the gravel and rock to a depth of approximately 6.1 m, and although no remains were present, it was presumably roofed in wood. Aboveground, it was protected by its 35.8 m by 15.3 m superstructure, whose stout 3.8 m thick mud-brick palace façade walls[176] probably contained a sand or rubble core and provided a 4.5 m defensive footprint overhang.

Nearby, the burial chamber of Mastaba 2038 comprised a 5.58 m deep unlined burial pit into which an internal access slope descended halfway. Because the pit was unlined, Petrie suggested that a wooden shrine may have been installed to contain the burial, which could presumably have supported some sort of roofing. Overhead, the tomb's superstructure was also constructed of substantial mud-brick palace façade walls 3.37 to 3.9 m thick that surrounded an inner core of gravel and sand. Its footprint overhang was slightly smaller at approximately 4.5 m.[177]

Although the provision of external access seems not to have gained favor in these tombs at Tarkhan, it could be that we are seeing, in Mastaba 2038, a vestigial attempt to introduce some form of descent to access the burial, albeit one that would have been fully concealed by its mastaba. Moreover, it is apparent that these tombs' superstructures were, like Mastaba 1060, no longer being used for storage, as neither contained internal divisions for magazines.

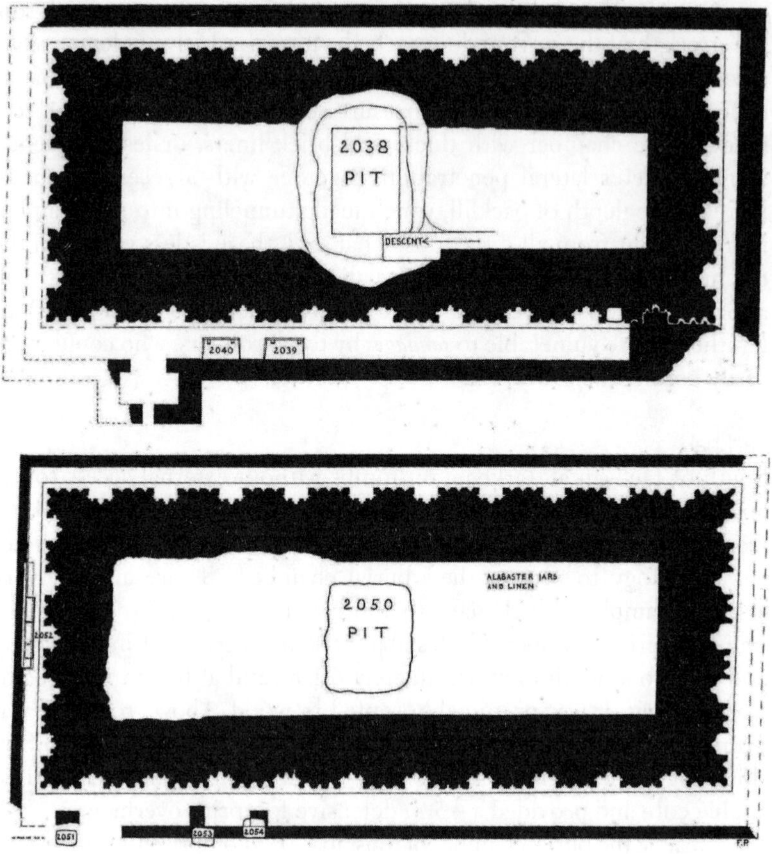

Figure 76. Tombs 2038 and 2050 at Tarkhan, with their palace façade superstructures.

Middle Egypt

Awlad al-Sheikh

In the last pit tomb in our analysis of the period, located in Awlad al-Sheikh in Middle Egypt, stone was used to defend the burial chamber of tomb III, which dates to the mid-First Dynasty.[178] It comprised a rectangular pit roughly 2.8 m deep (Fig. 77), within which a rectangular burial chamber was formed by large dressed limestone slabs, two meters high, 0.1 meters thick, and of varying widths. The gaps formed between the pit walls and these slabs were then backfilled with a thick layer of sand; beyond the slabs, a void was left at one end and four magazines created in it using mud-brick walls. The whole was roofed with wooden beams that rested on the stone slabs and supported a reed roof coated with mud

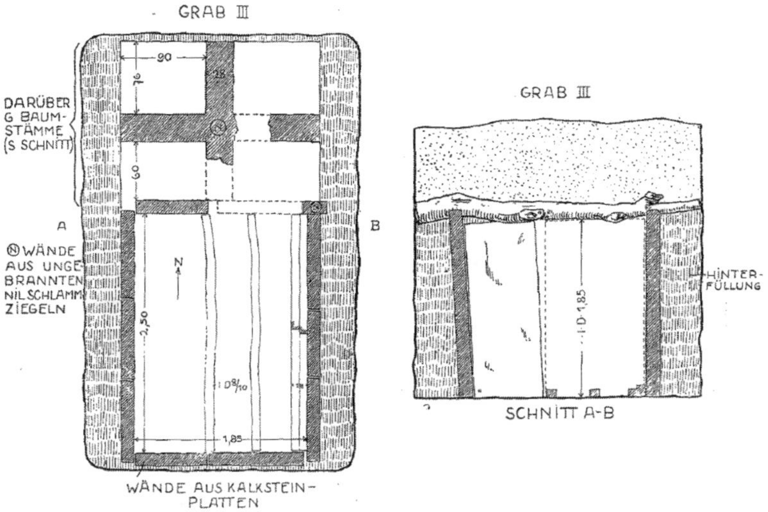

Figure 77. The stone-lined pit tomb III at Awlad al-Sheikh.

and sand cement, plus about a meter of backfill.[179] No trace was found of a superstructure. Despite these defenses, the tomb was looted by robbers, who had pulled down one of the slabs to enter the magazines that lay behind it. Interestingly, the robbers did not bother to penetrate beyond the first two magazines. This, Hermann Ranke suggested, is because they knew where the valuable grave goods had been placed—the untouched magazines at the back containing only wine jars and vessels.[180]

Upper Egypt

There are few published tombs from this period in Upper Egypt, save for a couple in Naga al-Deir and lone examples at Mahasna, Abydos, and al-Amra.

Naga al-Deir

Stone (albeit unquarried) played a part in the defense of the Naqada IIIC2–D[181] stairway tombs N 1512 and N 1581 in Cemetery 1500 at Naga al-Deir, where the underlying rock was exploited to secure their burial chambers. Both tombs were entered by gravel-cut and mud-brick-lined staircases that descended northeast for 5.4 m and 5.5 m, respectively, that of N 1581 being secured by a backfill of gravel and heavy boulders. There is no sign of their stairwells having been roofed,[182] probably because they were protected by their superstructures, which

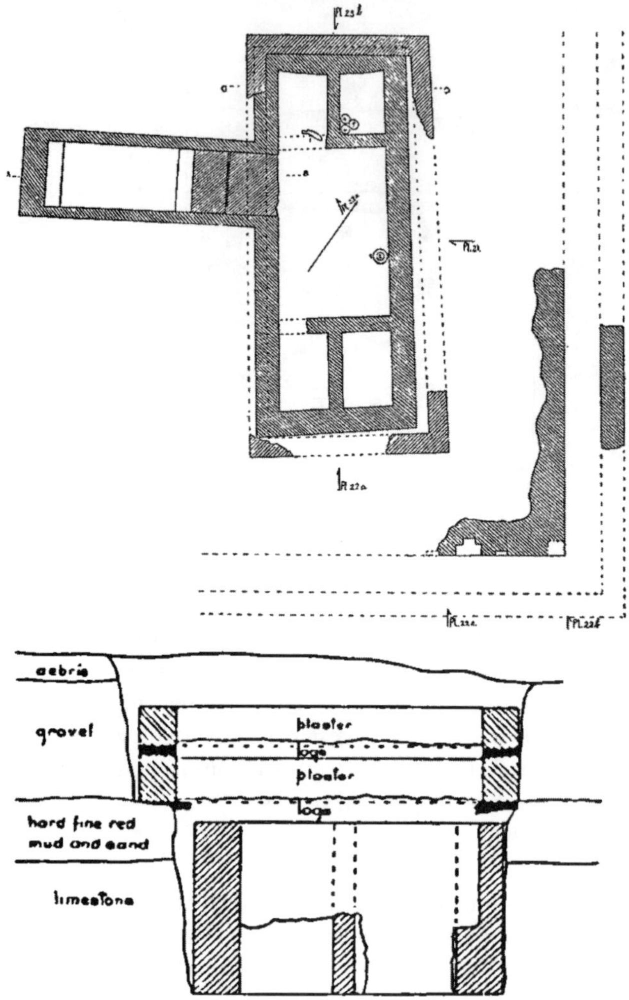

Figure 78. Tomb N 1581 at Cemetery 1500 at Naga al-Deir, whose substructure was cut into the bedrock for extra security.

we know unusually in the case of N 1581 was built *after* the interment had taken place.[183] As at Helwan, the use of the mud-brick liner in these stairways presumably demonstrates a need to consolidate the surrounding gravel and provide additional lateral protection.

At the end of the stairway in N 1581, a rectangular pit 3.5 m deep was excavated through the gravel layer into the limestone beneath (Fig. 78). Then, within the limestone layer, a mud-brick burial chamber and magazines were built and closed with a double roof formed of tree branches heavily plastered with mud.[184] Likewise according to Reisner, a similar arrangement would have been used in N 1512.[185]

While there is no trace of a superstructure for N 1512, the substructure and stairway of N 1581 were protected by a large mud-brick mastaba, whose one-meter-thick niched walls surrounded a core of gravel, limestone sherds, and "rubbish."[186] If we assume the substructure was centrally placed (75 percent of the mastaba was missing), it may be reasonable to suggest a footprint overhang of approximately two meters.[187] Therefore, with its burial chamber well protected by the rock, a robber would have had either to attack the tomb laterally via the thin mud and sand strata above the rock or to dig down through the superstructure and the twin roofs. Despite these measures both tombs were still looted. Indeed, sometime after it was robbed, N 1581 was completely covered by limestone spoil from the cutting of Middle and New Kingdom rock-cut tombs in the hill above, suggesting that the robbery occurred before or during their construction.[188]

Mahasna

At the beginning of the twentieth century, John Garstang recorded another rare example of a stairway tomb southeast of Naga al-Deir, on the west bank of the Nile at Mahasna, which probably dates to the reign of Den. The access route of tomb M1 consisted of a brick-lined axial staircase that led down to the burial chamber (Fig. 79). Although not much can be said about its construction, one can reasonably

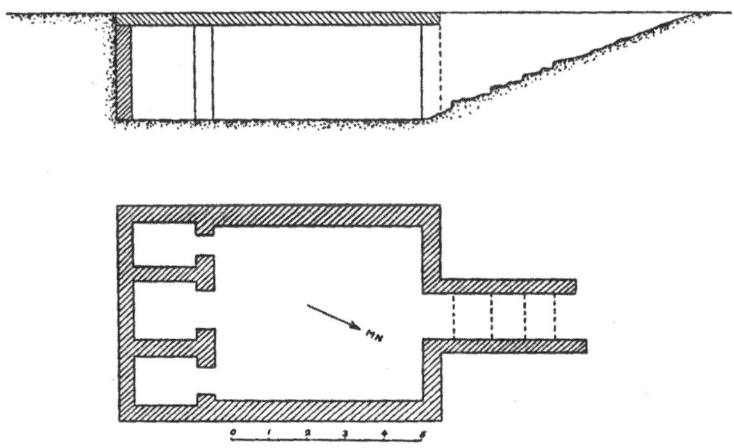

Figure 79. The shallow mud-brick-lined tomb M1 at Mahasna.

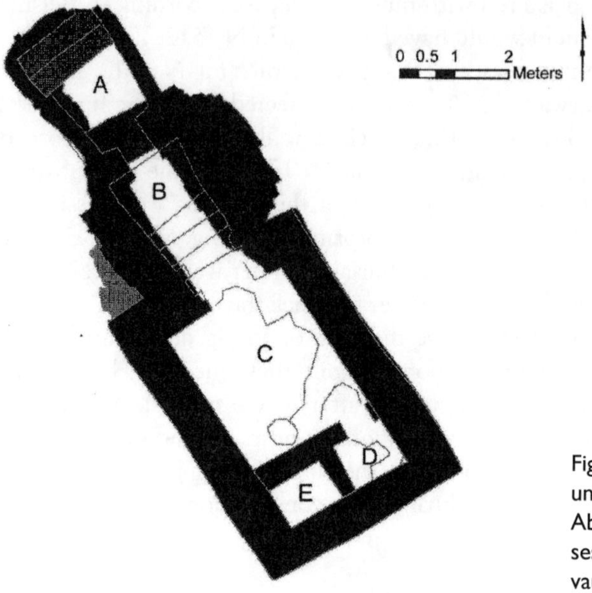

Figure 80. The unusual tomb I at Abydos, which possesses a mud-brick vaulted stairway.

assume from the tomb security point of view that its liners were necessary to reinforce the surrounding 'drift' sand and gravel. The burial chamber was built in a 2.5 m deep pit dug in the sand and gravel and lined with 0.4 m thick mud-brick walls for consolidation and protection. Although no traces were found of its roof, Garstang suggested it was probably built of wood and mud. No trace was found of a protective superstructure.[189]

Abydos

More recently, a stairway tomb has been excavated by the Supreme Council of Antiquities at Abydos in the newly discovered Early Dynastic cemetery. After an initial 'entrance vestibule,' its 3.5 m long mud-brick-lined stairway enters its substructure from the north in the usual manner (Fig. 80). Unusually, the stairway has a corbeled roof, which the tomb's excavator suggests might point to it being a "later addition."[190] At the base of the stairs, the burial chamber of tomb I is 2.8 m deep and lined with substantial mud-brick walls approximately 0.7 to 0.85 m thick, which would have consolidated the grave's sides and defended against lateral attack. To close the grave from above, a roof of wooden beams and planks was built,[191] which presumably was backfilled and brought level with the desert.

Al-Amra

As the last tomb in this chapter, we will look at a lone stairway tomb situated at al-Amra, just south of Abydos, which dates to the second half of the dynasty (Fig. 81). The 7.16 m long gravel-cut staircase of tomb b 91 was reinforced with mud-brick and accessed the pit laterally at the northern end of its western and longest side. The pit was 1.52 m deep and had a 0.4 m mud-brick liner that provided lateral protection and consolidation within the surrounding sand and hard gravel.[192] It was closed by a shallow roof built of tree branches and mud,[193] but aboveground it seems there was no trace of a protective superstructure. Nevertheless, the tomb's defenses seem to have worked, at least until the beginning of the twentieth century. When it was excavated by David Randall-MacIver in 1900, he noted that it had been recently robbed and observed, "The modern plunderers had done their work so carelessly that they had failed to discover the staircase."[194]

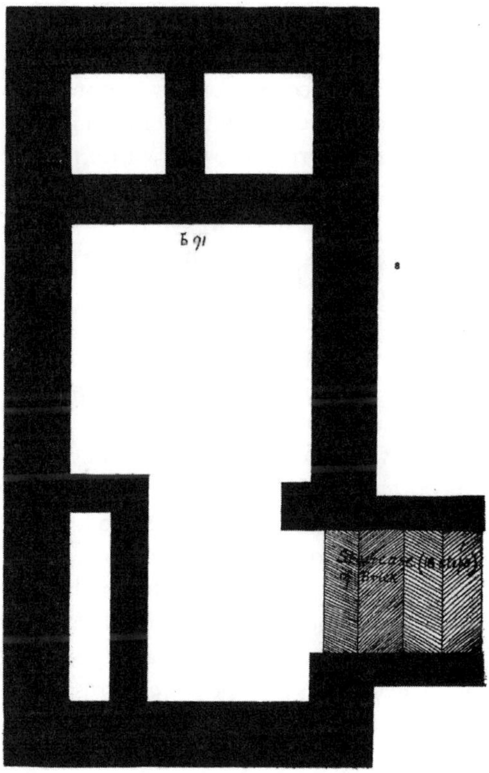

Figure 81. Tomb b 91 at al-Amra, whose defenses were unremarkable, but which remained untouched until the twentieth century.

Thematic Analysis: The Architecture and Security Features of Private Tombs in the Second Half of the First Dynasty

The second half of the First Dynasty saw the widespread use of an external entrance and access route in elite private tombs throughout Egypt, probably following royal precedent. However, there were a few exceptions at sites such as Minshat Abu Omar, Abu Rawash, Saqqara, Helwan, Tarkhan, and Awlad al-Sheikh, where simple pit tombs endured, largely unchanged save for some additional security measures where the geology demanded it. These included quarried stone linings in tombs at Tura al-Asmant, Helwan, and Awlad al-Sheikh, and double roofs and deeper pits with smaller and therefore harder to detect plans and cross sections in the limestones of Abu Rawash, Saqqara, and Tarkhan.

The use of an external access route in private stairway tombs flourished from the mid-First Dynasty onward, although in necropoleis with weak surrounding geology, such as Tura al-Asmant, Abu Ghurab, Helwan, and Naga al-Deir, access routes were often necessarily reinforced with more resistive materials such as wood, mud-brick, or stone. At Saqqara and Helwan, efforts were also made to conceal a tomb's entrance and access route by varying its placement, orientation, and direction of descent. And at some tombs in both locations, the entrance and descent were concealed within the superstructure itself to reduce the vulnerability of the access route still further.

A variety of blockings were developed to secure these new access routes. Loose aggregates in the form of sand, rubble, and soil were common fills, as well as built blockings of mud-brick to form a resistant barrier. Coinciding with its adoption in royal necropoleis, the portcullis became widespread in Lower Egypt among the stairway tombs of Abu Ghurab, Tura al-Asmant, Saqqara, and Helwan, and also in the curious subterranean tombs of Abu Rawash. Usually installed as a lone slab in the stairway before the burial chamber or within the substructure itself, the portcullis was occasionally deployed in twos, threes, and fours along the access route in large tombs at Saqqara and Helwan to provide additional protection within the descent.

As with ordinary pit tombs, the burial chambers of stairway tombs relied on various methods to reinforce their walls against lateral penetration, the choice of which was dependent on the surrounding geology of the necropolis and the material resources to hand. This is most notable in the gravels of Tura al-Asmant and Helwan, where use was made of thick mud-brick walls and, occasionally, linings of stone. At Helwan, however, an increase is seen in both the size of the orthostats used and the level of sophistication of their employment.

Meanwhile, the monumental tombs at Saqqara and Tarkhan still largely relied on the protection of the surrounding limestone as their primary defense. To reduce the risk from *sondages* still further, burial chambers at Saqqara were smaller and placed in varying locations and orientations under their mastabas, a luxury not possible among the smaller tombs at Helwan. For overhead protection, most tombs relied on wooden roofs and backfill to close their pits, but stone was used in some as reinforcement, as at Tura al-Asmant and Helwan. Finally, the introduction of entirely subterranean burial chambers in the limestones of Abu Rawash and Saqqara saw a new approach to security that discarded the roofed pit altogether and exploited the surrounding geology instead.

The architectural form of the superstructure of stairway tombs differed little from their pit tomb predecessors, insofar as the mass of the mud-brick mastaba protected the substructure from attack from above, while the footprint overhang defended it from the side. In most tombs, the superstructure now also partially covered any external stairways and concealed the portcullis emplacements. Moreover, with external access to the substructure, the stairway tombs could, unlike their pit tomb forebears, be largely completed during the lifetime of their owners,[195] thereby increasing the security and secrecy of the grave below. Initially, some mastabas at Saqqara and Helwan still retained internal magazines for grave goods. At Saqqara, some also contained deep gravel-filled shafts over their burial chambers for extra protection. However, by the reign of Adjib, among the elite tombs at Saqqara at least, the dual role of the superstructure as a storehouse declined in importance, its core now fully committed to defending the substructure, magazines, and access route that lay below.

Conclusion

During this period, various methods were used to improve the security of all types of pit tomb substructures—royal and private—through the strengthening of their linings and roofs. In the compact sand surrounding the royal tombs at Abydos, this usually took the form of massive mud-brick liners that supported thick wood and mud-brick roofs; whereas among private tombs, depending on the necropolis and its surrounding geology, the precautions could either take the latter form or, more rarely, include a double roof or incorporate stone.

While introducing an external means of access allowed a tomb to be completed early and remain less visible, it created problems of its own, as it formed a conduit to the heart of the tomb and needed securing. While varying the approach and orientation of a descent might temporarily misdirect a robber, the access route needed additional security in the shape of wooden or stone roofs and, in necropoleis with weak geology, liners built from mud-brick or, more rarely in private tombs, from stone.

Moreover, whatever the geology of the necropolis, a tomb's access route now needed to be sealed internally after the funeral with poured backfills, built blockings, or portcullises of wood or stone. Externally, its entrance also had to be concealed from view.

Aboveground, the high-status superstructure initially retained its dual function of defending the burial pit and serving as a storehouse for grave goods. But by the end of the dynasty its purpose was increasingly limited to defending the access route and burial chamber, grave goods being progressively confined to safer magazines in the substructure below.

Finally, in a new development, we see the introduction of entirely subterranean burial chambers in the self-supporting geologies of Abu Rawash and Saqqara, heralding their widespread adoption in the next dynasty, the full impact and implications of which are discussed in the next chapter.

BACKFILLS AND BLOCKINGS

The introduction of external access routes created the need for a secure means to close them. Although in many cases little evidence of these methods can be found today, it can be safely asserted that in the majority of tombs, both royal and private, some form of backfill or built blocking was employed, either singularly or in conjunction with another method. These differ from mechanisms like portcullises or plug-stones in that they can be made to fit any space, unlike the others which require moving parts and a comparatively high standard of stone engineering to work.

The simplest and most prevalent form of blocking used to secure a tomb's access route is a 'poured' backfill of some kind, which was widely used in stairways and shafts and required no building. However, it appears, judging by the lack of published information on the topic, that this was not of great interest to excavators in the past.[196] Although, we do know that a wide variety of materials were used, which includes sand, gravel, rubble, excavation waste, rough stone, *tafl*, and, more rarely, liquid mud—in fact, anything close to hand in some cases. Alternatively, built blockings could be used, usually at the entrances to burial chambers and the like, and these usually comprised mud-brick, drywall stone, or masonry, the latter sometimes mortared.

The limited number of royal tombs permits a definite pattern of development to be traced in the use of blockings. Perhaps in response to earlier robberies, it can be clearly seen that the selection of the backfill and blockings used to secure access routes evolved progressively from sand, wood, and mud-brick in the First and Second Dynasties to greater volumes of specially selected and increasingly resistant materials, such as rubble and masonry, in the Third Dynasty. But by the early Fourth Dynasty, improvements in stone technology seem to have led to a cessation of the use of rubble altogether and the wholesale adoption of masonry blockings, and of course plug-stones (discussed below).

The much larger number of private tombs presents a problem for the analysis of their blockings, as paradoxically, because of the lack of reporting there is statistically less evidence of the methods employed. Therefore, while there may be only one or two types of blocking reported in a necropolis, this does not necessarily mean that either was unique, or commonplace. However, it would be reasonable to assume that in the vast majority of private tombs in the First Dynasty, the principal closure of the tombs must have taken the form of a backfill, which was more or less resistant to penetration, depending on how 'diggable' the chosen material was, sand being easier to dig for instance than a rubble of large boulders.[197] This backfill could be used alone or in combination with another built blocking, such as mud-brick, masonry, or even a portcullis, which could either retain its position, act as a secondary closure, or provide additional security. As the use of stone architecture became more commonplace in the early Fourth Dynasty, so in high-status tombs the use of worked stone to provide a more solid in-depth secondary blocking became more frequent.

From an architectural viewpoint, the use of a backfill or in-depth blocking would seem not to have affected the design of a tomb or its access route, as its principal role was to act as a resistive space filler and fill the void that was available. Therefore, this is one of the few security measures that arguably had little or no direct effect on tomb architecture.

In the end, depending on the nature of their material, the majority of backfills or blockings in royal or private tombs could be either dug out or demolished. In the case of the most effective blockings, as is demonstrated by those stairs or shafts still closed by rubble or masonry, in many instances it was simply easier for robbers to bypass such an obstruction than to go through or remove it, they having worked out for themselves the least hazardous and most efficient plan of attack to reach their goal.

5

Subterranean Sepulchers: New Security Developments in the Second Dynasty

Royal Tombs

The Move to Saqqara

With the advent of the Second Dynasty the royal necropolis moved from Abydos in Upper Egypt to Saqqara in Lower Egypt, overlooking the capital of Memphis. The reason for the relocation is uncertain,[1] but the change of site and geology resulted in a radical redesign of the royal tombs of Kings Hotepsekhemwy/Raneb and Ninetjer,[2] which, unlike the desert-cut tombs of their predecessors at Umm al-Qa'b, were now excavated deep in the limestone strata of the Saqqara plateau and expanded in size enormously. Undoubtedly, this was done both to increase their security and to accommodate the ever-increasing quantities of funerary goods that were now required to accompany royal burials.[3] Located a kilometer south of the existing First Dynasty elite cemetery of North Saqqara, the site chosen for the royal tombs was virgin ground and may have been selected in order to create a *cordon sanitaire* between them and the latter.[4] Moreover, the hard limestone of North Saqqara would not have been suitable for the digging of the numerous underground passages and magazines required to house the vast quantity of grave goods securely, whereas the area selected, with its much softer layer of *tafl* under the rock,[5] was probably much easier to excavate.[6]

Hotepsekhemwy/Raneb

The earliest of these royal tombs at Saqqara has been identified from seals as the tomb of either Hotepsekhemwy or Raneb.[7] Probably built in five stages, which expanded outward from its original subterranean core, the whole substructure covers an area of over 5,850 square meters and is approximately 122 m long and 48 m wide (Fig. 82). Around 120 chambers have been identified to date.[8]

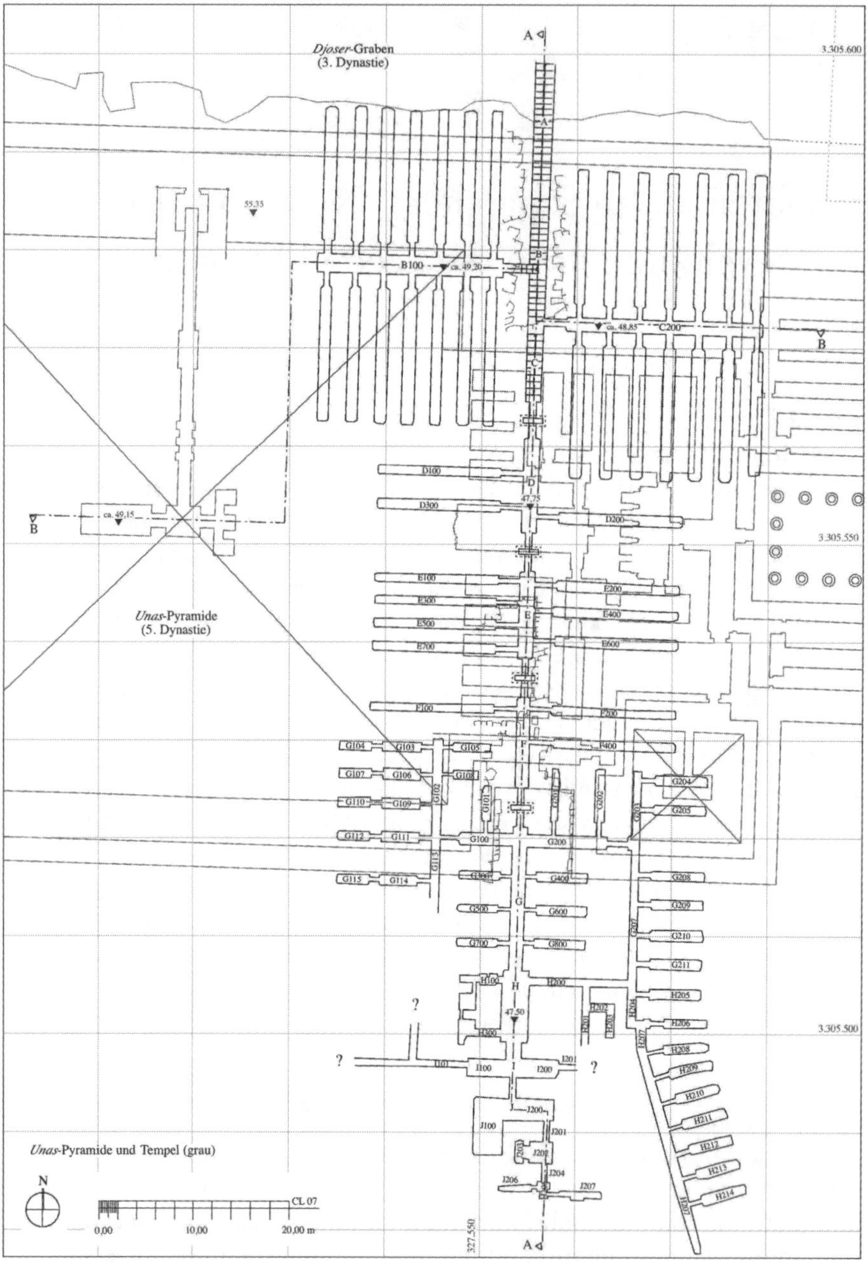

Figure 82. Plan of the enormous Second Dynasty rock-cut subterranean tomb of King Hotepsekhemwy/Raneb at Saqqara.

The entrance to the tomb lies in the courtyard just north of the pyramid temple of Unas and runs under both it and the eastern part of the pyramid itself.[9] It consists of a rock-cut open staircase comprising three flights of steps. From the middle steps, a doorway leads west to a subterranean passage from which symmetrical magazines branch like the teeth of a comb, an arrangement which is mirrored on the next landing in the eastern passage, before the final steps. At the bottom of these, after the first Tura limestone portcullis (sadly its dimensions are unknown, but according to Alessandro Barsanti it had been tunneled under by tomb robbers), a forty-meter-long 'cut and cover' passage was dug, which was probably then covered with stone beams and brought level with rubble to protect it from above (Fig. 83).[10] Further subdivided into three sections by two more portcullises, another thirteen magazines flank this passage before a fourth portcullis marks the entrance to the entirely subterranean part of the tomb, which contained the burial. This, the most secure part of the tomb, consists of a forty-meter-long, entirely tunneled subterranean complex whose main axial chambers are denoted 'G,' 'H,' 'I,' and 'J.' 'J100' may be the burial chamber. Labyrinthine passages and storage magazines lead from these chambers, many more of which may await discovery.[11] To protect the galleries, the builders took full advantage of the local geology by setting the floor level of the substructure 7.85 m below the surface. By excavating its internal passages between 2 and 2.2 m high, they created an extremely strong rock cover that would have averaged 5.65 to 5.85 m thick.[12]

Aboveground, the tomb was probably defended by a superstructure, but nothing remains of it today and it has been proposed that it may have been demolished during the construction of the Unas pyramid.[13] Details of its construction method and design are unknown, but Claudia Lacher-Raschdorff has studied the tomb closely and, while undecided as to the actual form, has proposed several plausible possibilities—most of which cover the bulk of the substructure, partially shelter the access stairway, and protect the portcullis shafts—based on parallels drawn from other contemporary tombs.[14] Whatever the design, as with most mastaba complexes, it would undoubtedly have offered its already well-defended substructure a considerable degree of extra protection.

Ninetjer

The labyrinthine rock-cut gallery tomb of the third king of the Second Dynasty, Ninetjer, lies 140 meters to the east of Hotepsekhemwy/Raneb and has been identified from jar seals. Covering an area of around 3,900

Figure 83. The stone roofing beams over the trench-cut stairway 'C' of the subterranean rock-cut tomb of Hotepsekhemwy/Raneb at Saqqara. The entrance to magazine C200 can be seen on the left.

square meters, about one-third smaller than its neighbor, it measures approximately 77 m by 50.5 m and comprises 192 separate passages and chambers (Fig. 84).[15]

The present entrance of the tomb commences under the southwest corner of the later mastaba of Nebkauhor Idu through an exposed portcullis shaft between the mastaba and the Unas causeway, which leads into the central north–south corridor of the tomb. This is not the original entrance. That was by means of an open cast rock-cut ramp and corridor some 24.5 m to the north, on the other side of the mastaba,[16] which ran south until it met with the portcullis stones that closed off the main corridor. Along the length of the original entrance ramp, magazines like those in the tomb of Hotepsekhemwy/Raneb branch from either side of the passage. It is not known if the new tomb entrance was visible when it was built, and a portion of it may, like its predecessor, have been protected by a superstructure, or simply filled with sand or limestone chips.[17]

At the southern end of the entrance ramp, two high-density limestone portcullises, each 3.4 m high, about 1.6 to 1.75 m wide, and 0.5 m

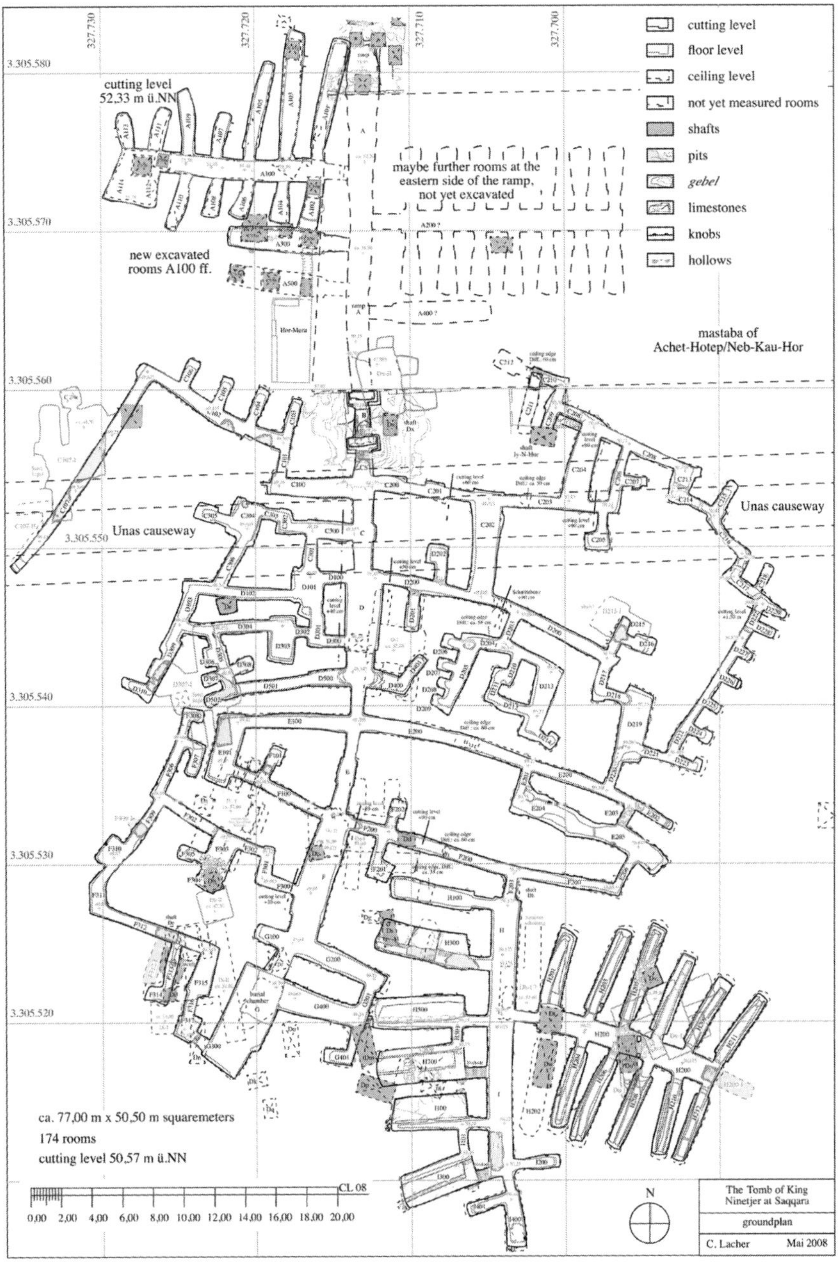

Figure 84. Plan of the rock-cut subterranean tomb of King Ninetjer at Saqqara, which lies partly under the causeway of the pyramid of Unas.

thick, possibly from the Tura or Mokkatam quarries, originally blocked access to the tomb at either end of the passage that forms the current entrance.[18] Both the passage and the emplacements that housed the portcullises are excavated deep in the rock and form a 'dumbbell' shape with the portcullis slots at either end. Each of the stones, being high-density limestone, would have weighed around eight tonnes, which combined with their substantial thickness would have provided the substructure with a considerable degree of security. From the remains of mud-brick walls adjacent to the portcullis emplacements, it has been suggested that these enormous slabs may have been lowered into position using escaping sand from a shaft formed by the walls, which was released by breaking the walls at the base when the time came to close the tomb.[19]

Beyond the tomb's entrance and portcullises, the main corridor between the portcullis slots and the royal burial chamber is approximately 33 m long and 2.5 m high. Branching off this corridor are fifteen side passages, which in turn lead to a maze-like warren of corridors and chambers. The burial chamber itself probably accommodated a wooden shrine, as in the royal tombs at Abydos. The natural rock cover that was formed by these chambers varied in depth from approximately three meters thick around the portcullis to around five meters thick above the burial chamber.[20]

Aboveground, it is assumed that the tomb had a superstructure similar to that of Hotepsekhemwy/Raneb, but no trace of it has been found. The northern part of it may have been demolished to make way for the causeway of Unas, and recent work by the German Archaeological Institute team has concluded that any remains were probably cleared away during construction on the site in the reign of Horemheb.[21] And, as with the tomb of Hotepsekhemwy/Raneb, Lacher-Raschdorff has suggested some possible designs for the missing structure.[22] Whatever the superstructure's form we can be certain, however, that it effectively deterred tunneling by would-be thieves and intrusive burials, based on the number of shafts that have penetrated the substructure since its removal, the earliest of which date to the Old Kingdom.[23]

Like their private counterparts in the First Dynasty, including the tombs at Cemetery M in Abu Rawash and S 3035, S 3120, and S 3121 at Saqqara,[24] both of these Saqqara royal tombs took advantage of the natural geology to gain the maximum protection, but on a greater scale. Now their substructures were protected from above by a solid limestone stratum more than five meters thick and laterally by the same rock to an unlimited degree. Furthermore, their internal layouts were invisible from above and thus offered a good degree of secrecy. With the absence of their protective superstructures, however, the numerous intrusive shafts that pierce their galleries[25] demonstrate that the enormous size of these complexes left them vulnerable to discovery, as without their superstructures there was a reasonable chance of a random *sondage* penetrating a chamber.

The Return to Abydos

Peribsen

It is not clear why Peribsen, the successor to Ninetjer, chose to return to Abydos to build his tomb.[26] What is certain, however, is that it reverted to a pit tomb in its design, like its First Dynasty predecessors (Fig. 85). This was probably due to the limitations of the surrounding geology and the available materials, although its small size and indications that it was built in a hurry may also imply a lack of time or resources.[27] Known as tomb 'P,'[28] access to its interior was by a roughly paved slope (presumably backfilled with sand after the burial, like all the stairway pit tombs at Umm al-Qa'b) from the desert level to a doorway in the southwestern corner. Recent excavations have shown that the main entrance was originally blocked with mud-brick, and many of the internal doorways were closed in the same manner.

The grave itself is built within a pit 3.5 to 4 m deep, and its internal mud-brick structure is formed of three concentric walls, the outer of which is approximately one meter thick. Within the bounds of the external wall a second structure was built, also with a doorway in its southwestern corner, thus forming a circulating corridor surrounding the inner core. Inside this final layer, projecting tongue walls on its longest sides created eight magazines, and the burial chamber was built from mud-brick within the space they formed and probably contained a wooden shrine. The roof, which was supported by wooden beams, was set 0.5 m below the present desert level and probably brought level with sand. On the surface, the grave, like earlier First Dynasty tombs at Umm al-Qa'b, was possibly covered with a brick-clad tumulus formed from the material excavated from its burial pit,[29] but there is no material evidence to confirm this.

In comparison to the monumental and more strongly built First Dynasty tombs of Djer, Djet, Den, and Qa'a, this tomb offered little in the way of security, although Petrie speculated that the outer enclosure corridor may have been a form of 'sand trap,'[30] rather like the passage surrounding Campbell's Tomb at Giza or Udjahorresnet's shaft tomb at Abusir,[31] which would have deterred lateral tunneling into the tomb. While

Figure 85. The mud-brick-lined pit tomb of King Peribsen at Umm al-Qa'b.

feasible, this hypothesis cannot be proven. It is true, however, that the one-meter-thick external walls would have provided a degree of resistance to lateral penetration, and if the intervening walls and chambers were filled with grave goods they too would have delayed progress into the burial chamber, leaving the putative wooden shrine as the last layer of defense.

Khasekhemwy

The last king of the dynasty, Khasekhemwy, was also buried at Umm al-Qa'b. Tomb V[32] was entered by an access ramp comprising a rough three-meter-wide slope that descended 7.5 m from the desert level in the northwest corner of the tomb to its northern entrance. This would almost certainly have been blocked with mud-brick, and indeed the doorways of the main southern corridor were sealed in just that way—a double-skinned blocking between chambers V53 and V54 remains intact today.

The main substructure is set in a pit whose floor is approximately 7.5 m below the desert level (Fig. 86). Built in three phases, its original

Figure 86. The mud-brick-lined gallery tomb of King Khasekhemwy at Umm al-Qa'b. The limestone-lined burial chamber was concealed under the floor of the substructure itself.

core layout was like that of Peribsen's tomb,[33] and the original plan was then enlarged by adding further magazines to accommodate more grave goods, perhaps reflecting a more successful reign with greater wealth to store. As a result of the enlargement, its final plan resembled the gallery tombs at Saqqara, which it was clearly designed to emulate.[34] It is roughly eighty-eight meters long and twenty meters wide and covers an area of 1,760 square meters, which is less than half that of Ninetjer's tomb and a third smaller than that of Hotepsekhemwy/Raneb. Most of the mud-brick substructure walls are approximately 2.35 m high and their upper edges finish at about five meters below the desert surface.[35] Projecting tongue walls subdivide the structure into fifty-eight chambers of varying lengths, which average 2.1 m wide. Approximately midway down the length of the substructure is the original core of the tomb, and within this small magazines surround a slightly off-center compartment where a stone-lined burial chamber has been fully sunk into the floor. This has been completely lined with limestone blocks 0.25 to 0.3 m thick, and traces of paint indicate that it originally contained a wooden shrine. It probably supported a protective stone slab roof that closed the chamber, which may have been concealed with a layer of Nile mud[36] to form a camouflaged layer of protection for the burial.

The entire tomb was covered with a huge roof consisting of wooden beams ten to twenty centimeters in diameter laid closely across the mud-brick walls. Unlike the First Dynasty tombs, these beams were not covered with layers of mud-brick but rather with reed matting and a coating of Nile mud. The tomb pit was then filled with a five-meter layer of excavated sand and gravel and brought level with the surface. Overhead, it was probably covered with a protective superstructure. Some anomalous dressed limestone blocks and the massive distortion of the mud-brick walls in the center of the substructure (probably caused by plastic deformation due to rainwater ingress) inspired Dreyer to suggest that the superstructure may have consisted of a sand-cored mud-brick mastaba approximately thirty-five meters long that was externally clad in dressed limestone, which would have protected about half the substructure. Indeed, load-bearing calculations have demonstrated that the beams of the substructure's roof could have supported a tumulus of this size approximately three meters high.[37]

Although smaller than its earlier Saqqara counterparts, a great deal of energy and materials was invested in the building of this tomb, which is the largest at Umm al-Qa'b. Unlike the Saqqara tombs, however, the surrounding geology was not solid rock. To obtain a decent standard of security, the answer was to create a deep substructure and protect it from above using the available local resources. Therefore, the tomb builders compensated for the unexceptional thickness of the mud-brick walls and roof covering by using around fourteen thousand metric tonnes of sand as a backfill.[38] Consequently, tunneling in this loose and shifting material was extremely hazardous. Within the tomb itself, the burial chamber's concealed position would have further hampered its discovery, and its limestone walls and internal wooden shrine would have provided a final inner layer of protection. Aboveground, the superstructure, as always, would have provided additional defense from overhead attack, although in this case, due to its size, some parts of the substructure were not as well shielded as its predecessors. Yet even with all this protection, there is still evidence of tomb-robbing. Robbers' holes exist in the separating wall between chambers 6 and 9 and the west walls of chambers 34 and 35, adjacent to the burial chamber. Chambers 56 and 57 were also broken into, and, interestingly, it appears from the size of the holes that the thieves may have employed children.[39]

Thematic Analysis: The Architecture and Security Features of Second Dynasty Royal Tombs

With the relocation of the royal necropolis to Saqqara, the entranceways of the huge subterranean tombs of Second Dynasty kings relied on the protection of the natural rock into which they were cut and may have been protected from above by a superstructure. Additionally, enormous portcullis slabs in rock-cut emplacements sealed their subterranean passageways and the vast quantities of grave goods stored within them. Yet, with the last tombs of the dynasty and the return to Abydos, the built entranceways of their nearby First Dynasty predecessors were eschewed in favor of a modest descending slope without portcullis blockings, which relied on the concealment and protection provided by sand.

The substructures of the tombs of the first three kings of the dynasty at Saqqara exploited the strength of the local limestone and geology to secure their enormous subterranean substructures. With the return to Abydos of the last two kings of the dynasty, the royal substructure necessarily reverted to the pit tomb format of its First Dynasty neighbors due to the local geology and the available resources. However, in the tomb of the final ruler of the dynasty, the royal substructure mirrored the numerous deep subterranean chambers and axial approach of its rock-cut predecessors at Saqqara, reinterpreted in mud-brick, stone, and sand.

Aboveground, though there is little physical evidence remaining, it is suggested that the royal tombs at Saqqara protected most of their substructures with a mud-brick superstructure of some form, and on a monumental scale. In contrast, we know that the superstructure of the last tomb of the dynasty was small in comparison to its substructure, but at least had its exterior built of stone.

Private Tombs

During the Second Dynasty, we once again see the design and security arrangements of the elite private tomb largely following the royal precedent, this time in the form of the subterranean stairway tomb. Although toward the end of the dynasty, the first stair-shaft and shaft-accessed tombs make their debut. However, there are a few exceptions in Upper Egypt, where several pit and stairway pit tombs are still being built that incorporate additional defensive architectural elements peculiar to the region.

Tomb Security in Lower Egypt

Abusir

The most northerly of the subterranean tombs from this period are to be found in the small necropolis of Second Dynasty subterranean tombs at Abusir.[40] Among these Hans Bonnet excavated several stairway tombs and a number of early shaft tombs,[41] cut in the compact mudstone matrix.[42]

One example, tomb 10B–4, was entered by a simple unlined staircase that descended southeast to a depth of 2.6 m, where the entrance to the burial chamber was blocked by a 0.4 m thick freestanding portcullis that would have weighed around 1.34 tonnes. The simple chamber beyond was around one meter high and would have been protected from above by about 1.6 m of mudstone cover (Fig. 87). A larger number of early subterranean shaft graves were found nearby, which averaged between three and five meters in depth, their substructures usually comprising a small chamber, sometimes with a recess.[43] Among these tombs was 12B–6, whose 3.2 m deep shaft was blocked at its base by a 0.3 m thick freestanding portcullis that would have weighed about 0.77 tonnes. This sealed off the small burial chamber beyond, which was protected from above by a roof approximately 2.1 m thick. The crudely cut chamber of nearby tomb 11D–2 was accessed by a brick-lined shaft approximately 5.1 m deep without any portcullis blocking, although in recompense it was defended by a roof nearly twice as thick. Deepest of the tombs at the

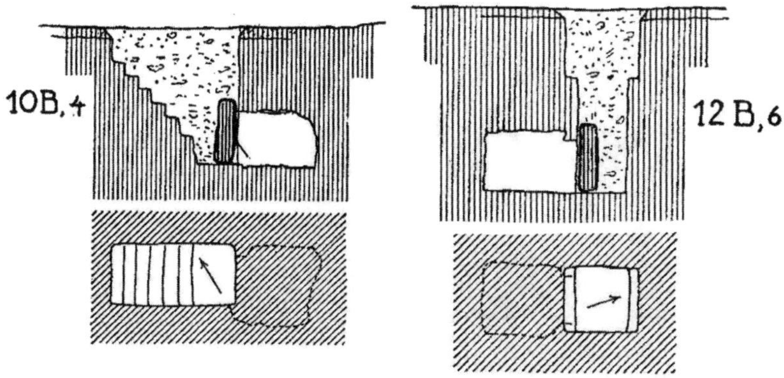

Figure 87. The subterranean stairway tomb 10B–4 and the shaft tomb 12B–6 at Abusir. Both were protected by portcullises.

site was 13B–5, which reached a depth of twelve meters,[44] but no details are available concerning its burial chamber. There were no traces of any superstructures found at this site, so quite how the entrances of these tombs were concealed remains open to question.

North Saqqara

Located on the eastern edge of the North Saqqara plateau, a large number of subterranean tombs dating to the Second and Third Dynasties sit behind the earlier First Dynasty tombs that dominate the escarpment.[45] Although many of these tombs remain unpublished,[46] a limited amount of material is available from Egyptologists such as Quibell and Emery that permits this discussion to take place. Their substructures are all excavated within the limestone and marl strata that are characteristic of this site,[47] which provided an excellent level of protection against tunneling by tomb robbers. Most of them were protected at ground level by their mud-brick superstructures, which are usually orientated on a north–south axis.

The entrances of a few early tombs at Saqqara were, like some of their nearby pit tomb predecessors, located externally, usually toward the northern end of the superstructure. This was the case with tomb S 3024, for example, which was accessed by an external rock-cut stairway that descended west before turning south to enter its burial chamber (Fig. 88). In addition to the overhead protection offered to the stairwell by the mud-brick superstructure, whose core fill consisted of rubble and sand, the stairwell's ceiling appears to have been further protected with

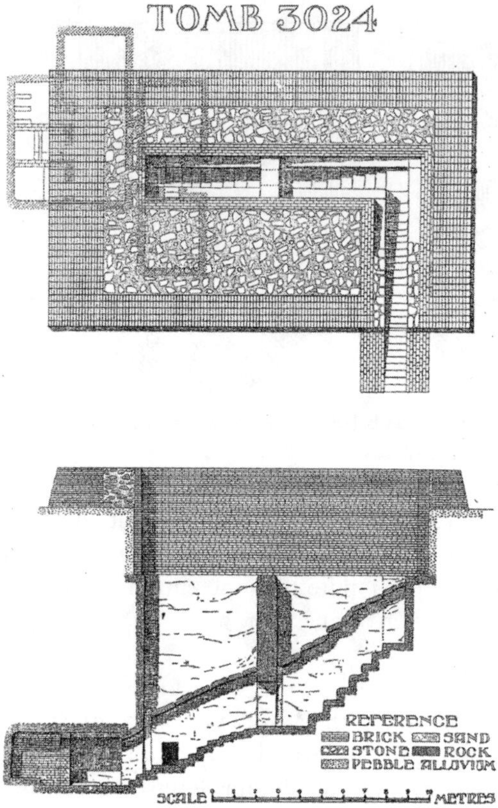

Figure 88. The rock-cut subterranean tomb S 3024 at Saqqara, which was accessed by an external stairway blocked internally by two portcullises.

stone slabs. To secure the stairway internally it was blocked on the first landing by a portcullis set in grooves. Past it, another flight of stairs led to a second landing flanked by two magazines, where a second portcullis rested in its emplacement and barred entrance to the burial chamber itself. Beyond, the floor of the 2.5 m high chamber was set approximately 12.5 m from the surface, leaving approximately 7.5 m of solid rock and 2.5 m of gravel by way of protective cover. And, like many of these chambers at the beginning of the dynasty, internally it was subdivided with mud-brick walls.[48]

However, by the mid-Second Dynasty the substructure layout in some of these elite tombs at Saqqara had changed to that of the 'house' type, with multiple chambers excavated separately in the rock (sometimes even including a dummy toilet[49]), which some believe resembled a contemporary dwelling. It could equally be argued, however, that the tombs of the elite were simply imitating the royal tombs of the period, or that they were being expanded to act as a more secure form of storage for grave goods, which in the First Dynasty had been previously stored in the superstructure.[50] A typical arrangement is portrayed in Emery's drawing of such an unidentified tomb (Fig. 89), where at the end of the stairwell, protected from above by 7.5 m of solid rock, the tomb's subterranean chambers branch from an axial corridor.[51] Similar examples of this type of substructure, but of unknown depth, are shown in Quibell's plans of tombs S 2171, S 2302, S 2307, S 2322, S 2337, S 2406, S 2429, and S 2498 (Fig. 90).[52] The largest of these substructures belonged to S 2302, whose twenty-three chambers covered an area of over ninety-two square meters and varied between 1.4 and 1.8 m in height (Fig. 91). These chambers were entered by means of an external stairway that descended west under the mastaba to meet an internal passage, which led south to the subterranean complex.[53] To the north and west of the passage were open magazines, but southward the route to the core was blocked by stone and a large portcullis.

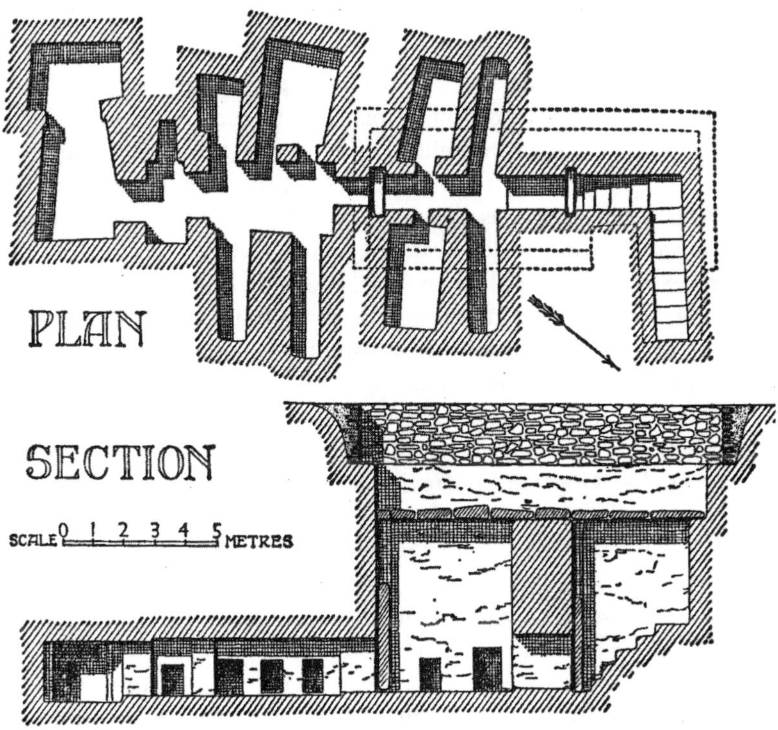

Figure 89. An unidentified 'house-type' subterranean stairway tomb at Saqqara.

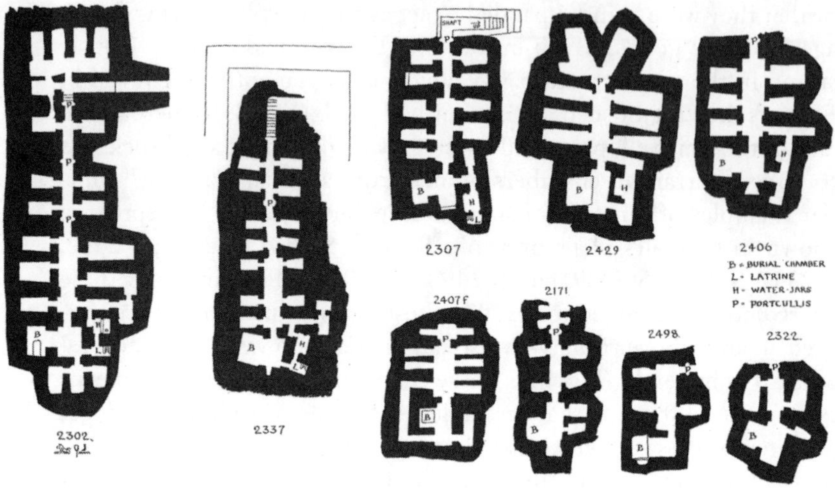

Figure 90. Assorted 'house-type' subterranean substructures at Saqqara, excavated by Quibell.

Further along the central passage, yet another portcullis prevented access to more flanking magazines, followed by what appears to be a third emplacement (marked on the plan but not mentioned by Quibell) that closed off the main complex. For additional protection, the stairwell had been roofed by stone slabs and was protected by the overlying superstructure's enormous inner core, which consisted of a gravel sublayer topped off by hardened liquid mud that was contained by the structure's three-meter-thick external mud-brick walls. Although the thickness of the substructure's rock cover was not recorded by Quibell, it is the only subterranean staircase tomb at Saqqara where we have the details of how it was robbed. Quibell reported that thieves had accessed the substructure by cutting two shafts through the overlying mastaba, penetrating the main corridor and from there tunneling around its blockings and portcullis to reach the interior.[54] This was not exceptional; indeed, a similar fate had befallen nearly every similar tomb in the necropolis. Quibell noted,

> It will not escape our notice that the robbers' shaft has been always sunk just at the point where it would drop down on the portcullis and we shall fairly draw the conclusion that the thieves who show so precise an acquaintance with the plan of a large and complicated tomb were not unconnected with its construction.[55]

It is clear in the substructure drawings that these 'house' tombs at Saqqara were orientated north–south, and, in some cases, such as S 3024 and Emery's unnamed tomb, the chambers projected beyond the protective footprint of the superstructure. This may be because unlike in a pit tomb, where the superstructure was vital to protect the burial chamber's wooden roof and backfill, the natural protection of the rock cover gave the tomb builders extra confidence. From the limited and anecdotal evidence available, this arrangement seems to have proved successful, even among the apparently more vulnerable larger multi-chambered tombs, as it appears that the preferred robbers' route at Saqqara was via the rock-cut shafts and entrances that these tombs necessarily possessed.

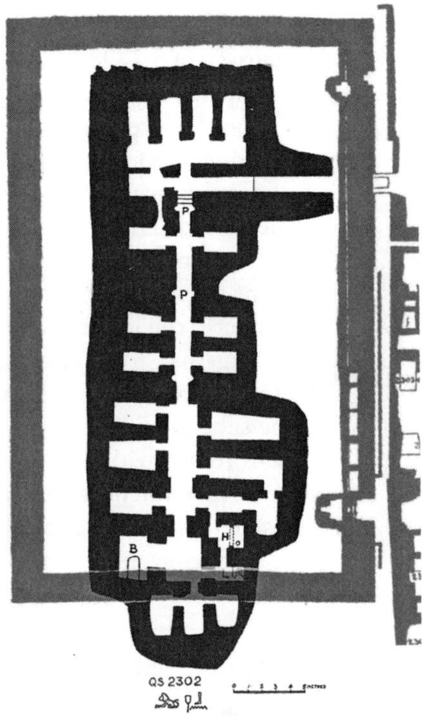

Figure 91. The enormous subterranean stairway tomb S 2302 at Saqqara, whose 'house-type' substructure was accessed by an external stairway.

Concerning these entrances, to deter robbers, many tombs at Saqqara had their entrances and stairways concealed in a variety of locations and orientations within the perimeter of their superstructure.[56] For example, in tomb S 2171, the stairway's unusual 'dogleg' descent began in the northeast quarter of its superstructure and descended south,[57] as did the straight staircase of S 2101.[58] The straight staircase of tomb S 2307, however, although still located in its superstructure's northern end, changed direction and descended west to meet its substructure.[59] Meanwhile, the straight stairway of S 2322 began farther south and continued its descent parallel to the inner western wall of its mastaba.[60] In contrast, the straight stairways of tombs S 2337 and S 2406 were axially placed within the northern end of the superstructure and descended south,[61] as did the descent of S 2452, which began farther south from the center of its superstructure.[62]

Some tombs had L-shaped staircases, such as S 2429, whose brick-lined stairway started in the northern end of its superstructure and descended west,[63] then turned south before it met its portcullis.[64] The stairway in S 2315 took the same approach.[65] On the other hand, the stairway of S 2498 started close against its eastern wall in the center of its superstructure and ran north before turning west to reach its destination.[66] Moreover, its stairwell had been roofed with stone slabs for additional protection and, besides the usual portcullis, also incorporated a most unusual form of blocking that is unique to this necropolis and the period. This consisted of flagstones set edge on and lengthways in the descent rather than across it, as might be expected, thus effectively increasing the depth of the blocking with the smallest amount of stone.[67] Similarly, the lower end of the rock-cut staircase of S 2171 was blocked by large flagstones running parallel to the passage, creating an impenetrable 1.5 m deep obstruction that barred access to the portcullis and the substructure beyond (Fig. 92).[68] This innovative measure provided both tombs with a highly effective in-depth blocking for a relatively small investment in materials and labor compared to that required to install masonry or a portcullis.

An even more complex descent is found in tomb S 3477, which dates to the end of the dynasty and which Emery discovered intact

Figure 92. The 'end-on' flagstones used to block the passage of tomb S 2171 at Saqqara.

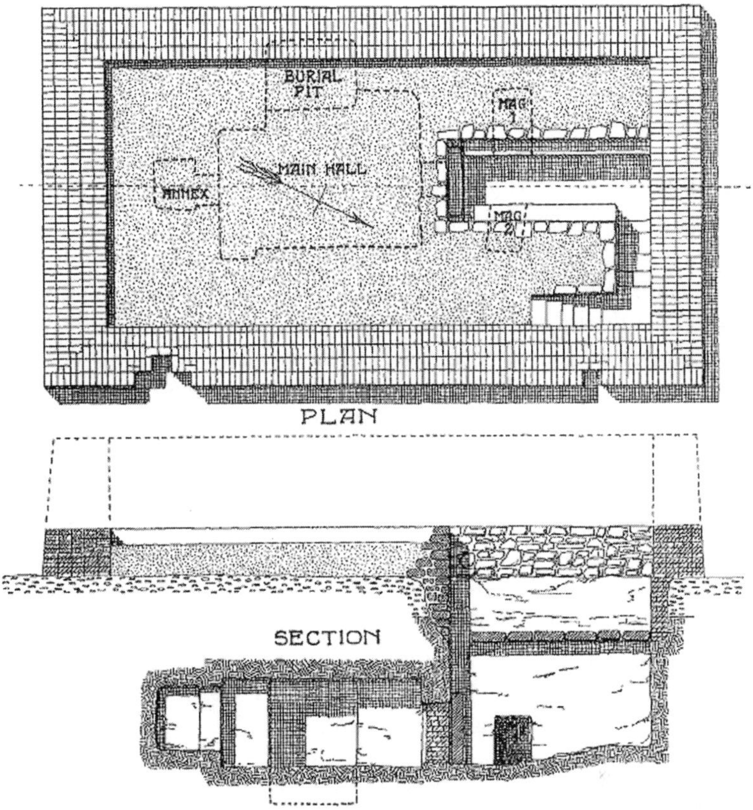

Figure 93. Tomb S 3477 at Saqqara, which was found intact by Emery. The stairway was completely concealed within the superstructure for security reasons.

(still containing the remains of the funerary feast). The substructure was accessed by a rock-cut stairway that began in the northeast corner of the superstructure, tight against its eastern wall, and, still following the wall, descended north (Fig. 93), then west. Reaching halfway, it turned south into a stone-roofed corridor that led to the tomb's flanking magazines and portcullis. The latter comprised a 1.8 m high and 0.3 m thick slab that weighed approximately 1.97 tonnes and was in a grooved emplacement.[69] Behind this monolith was a further blocking of mud-brick that acted as a secondary closure, and beyond that lay the burial chamber, which contained a recess and small annex. Internally, the chamber was approximately 2.2 m high and protected from overhead by natural rock cover around 1.5 m thick, plus a one-meter surface gravel layer. Protecting the whole aboveground was, of course, the superstructure, whose 1 to 1.6 m thick mud-brick walls contained an inner core of rubble and sand that would have concealed the stairway from view.[70]

Therefore, not only were the stairways of these tombs being placed in varied positions within the perimeter of their superstructurs to make them difficult to find, they were also protected and concealed from the *sondages* of tomb robbers by their inner core fills.

Quite when the backfilling of these cores took place is difficult to ascertain. Emery suggested that it took place after the funeral, while Quibell suggested that it may have been done before, leaving just a temporary gap to permit access to the stairway, which was then blocked and concealed. Tombs with smaller superstructures might have been built immediately after the funeral, perhaps on the same day.[71] The material used in these cores varied. In S 2101 and S 2315, for example, it consisted of limestone chips, which were presumably the spoil from the excavation of the substructure. In S 2307, S 2313, and S 2322, the fill comprised liquid mud that became hard as concrete when it dried. Tomb S 2171 was filled with gravel, which was difficult to dig, while the previously discussed tomb S 2302 combined both a gravel sub-layer and liquid mud for its enormous core, benefiting from the properties of both. Similarly, the core of S 2337 had three different layers of material: stone chips, followed by a 0.6 m layer of fired and green pottery, and finally a top coat of sand. Pottery also featured as a 0.5 m layer in the otherwise unidentified core of S 2452,[72] whereas the cores of the aforementioned S 3477 and S 3024 consisted of rubble and sand.[73]

The level of defense offered by these types of core fill can be demonstrated by taking one of the larger tomb superstructures, such as S 2171, as an example. If we assume its height was approximately five to six meters,[74] its core can be estimated to have contained as much as thirty-nine hundred cubic meters of gravel, which would weigh approximately 6,200 metric tonnes,[75] and thus presented a considerable obstacle and deterrent to a thief intent on locating the stairway. Moreover, it appears that in some larger tombs, such as S 2350, these cores may have been also roofed with mud-brick,[76] which would have caused additional hindrance to those intent on digging. Lastly, although largely superseded by extra storage underground and an increased reliance on the external offering place, a few superstructures at Saqqara still contained internal magazines (though not on the scale of their First Dynasty forerunners) and quantities of food, storage jars, and utensils,[77] and these too would have depended on the protection of the core fill.

Helwan

On the opposite bank of the Nile to Saqqara at Helwan, a wide variety of subterranean stairway tombs were dug in the gravel and mudstone matrix of the necropolis.[78] Many were excavated by Saad in his 1945 to 1947 campaigns and published in his *Royal Excavations* series and *Ceiling Stelae*,[79] but not all were accompanied with plans. More recently, however, Köhler added new tombs to the record.[80]

As at Saqqara, some tombs went deep underground in the search for security, as in the 10.5 m long substructure of 25.H.5, which was excavated to a depth of 7.8 m, and protected by a gravel roof up to 6.5 m thick (Fig. 94).[81] Entered by a straight, fifteen-meter-long gravel-cut staircase, the entrance to its burial chamber would have been blocked by a single portcullis.[82] Presumably due to its length, this tomb's stairway probably began outside its superstructure, its size, as with all stairways, dependent on the relationship between the desired depth of the substructure and achieving a safe descent. Although the tomb was robbed, unusually for a subterranean stairway tomb at Helwan there were no signs of a robbers' tunnel from above, which suggests that its thick gravel cover may have deterred an attack.

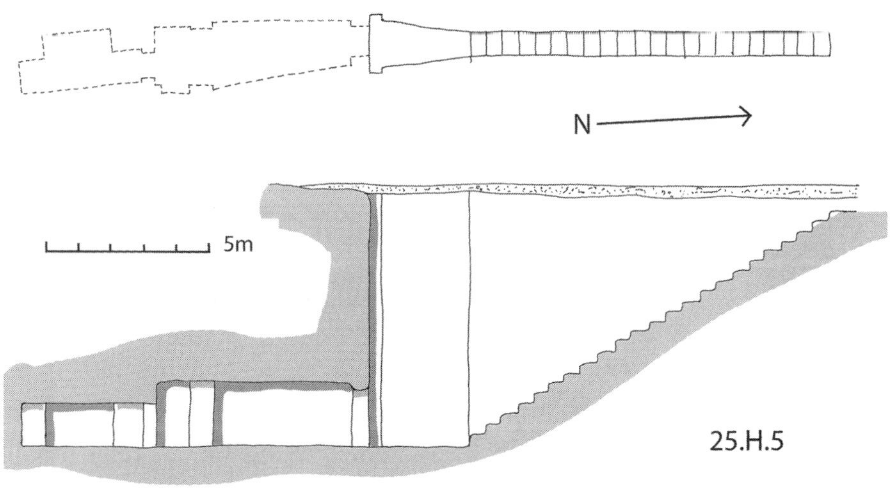

Figure 94. Tomb 25.H.5 at Helwan. A single portcullis would have blocked the entrance to the burial chamber.

In contrast, the burial chamber at the end of the multi-chambered substructure of 505.H.4 was only protected by a roof almost half the depth at 3.6 m thick (Fig. 95). Its L-shaped entrance stairway probably began outside its mastaba and was closed at its base by a massive two-meter-high stone portcullis in a typical grooved emplacement. But this was to no avail, as, like many of the stairway tombs at Helwan, its substructure had been penetrated by a robbers' tunnel from above that precisely targeted the complex below.[83]

Regarding portcullises and blockings in these stairway tombs at Helwan, although their access routes vary in their approach, generally the portcullis emplacements are very similar. In every case at Helwan in the Second Dynasty, where they are present,[84] there is only provision for one stone, albeit sometimes backed up with a secondary blocking of mud-brick or dry stone directly behind. The single emplacement's characteristic T-shaped slots are usually excavated directly in the gravel or rock by the entrance to the substructure, in contrast to their pit tomb predecessors at this site, which occasionally had several stones set in emplacements built into the stairway lining or the brickwork before the burial chamber.

In the interests of security, many other subterranean tombs at Helwan had their stairways concealed under their superstructures, but few traces of the latter remain. Among the few published examples is

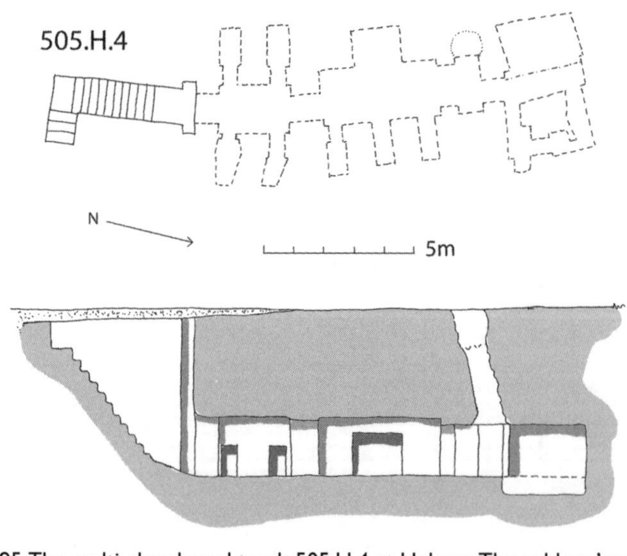

Figure 95. The multi-chambered tomb 505.H.4 at Helwan. The robbers' tunnel descended from the west straight into the substructure.

Op. 4/94, whose gravel-cut descent was completely protected from above by an eleven-meter-long superstructure (Fig. 96). At the base of its 6.2 m long stairway, a heap of large stones covered a portcullis in a grooved emplacement that lay directly in front of the entrance to the burial chamber, behind which was a secondary mud-brick blocking. Beyond, the chamber itself was protected by a gravel roof 2.6 m thick. But despite all this, the tomb had been robbed by means of a hole pierced through the blockings and a tunnel through its roof.[85] Similarly, the deeper five-meter stairway descent of Op. 4/4, whose mastaba was slightly shorter, was also completely protected by its superstructure (Fig. 97).[86] It too was closed by a stone portcullis with a thin secondary mud-brick wall behind, but, notably, the entire descent was also blocked with solid mud-brick rather than the usual backfill of gravel or other

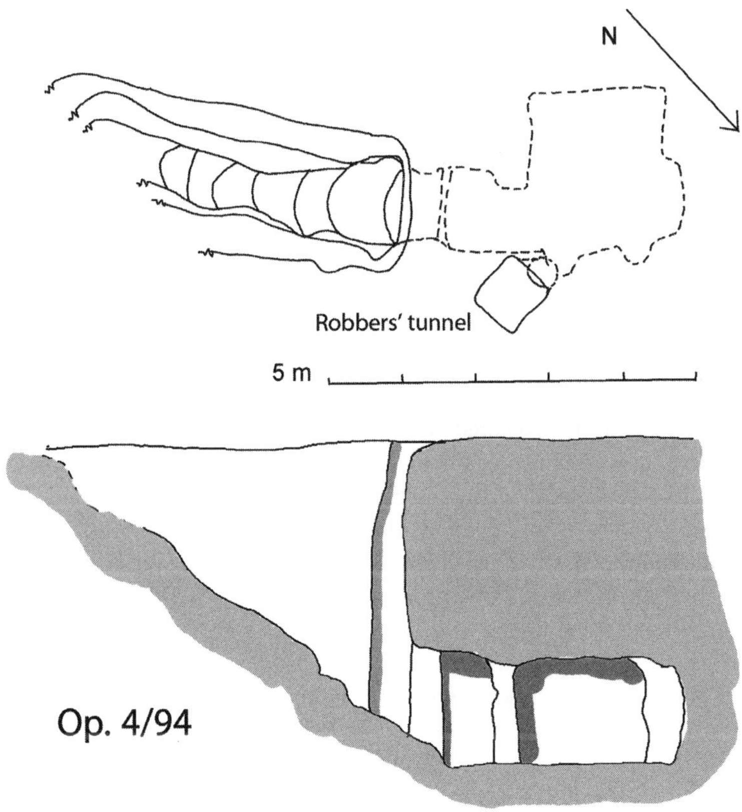

Figure 96. Tomb Op. 4/94 at Helwan. The robbers' tunnel began on the east and ran down into the burial chamber.

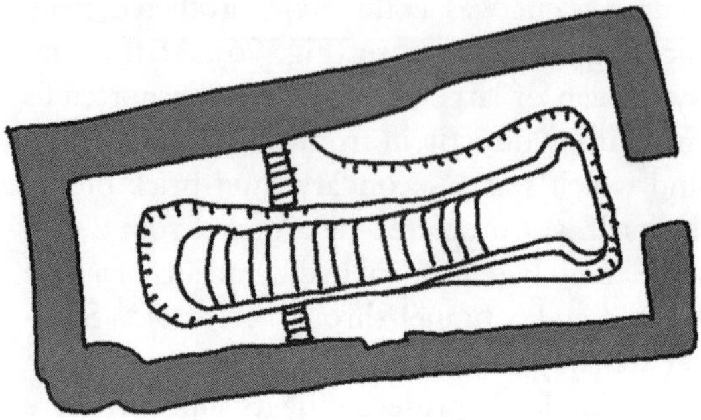

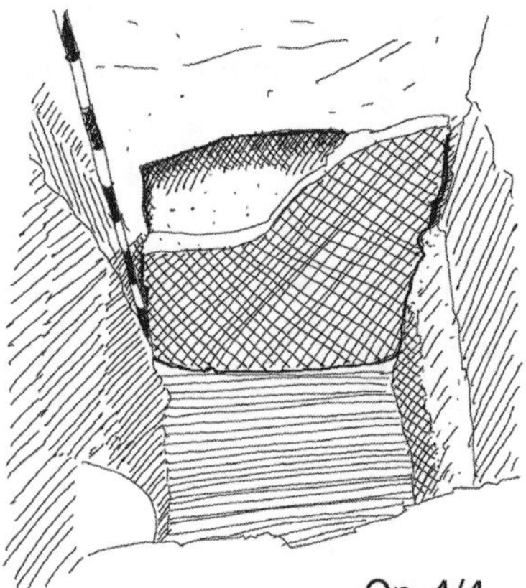

Op. 4/4

Figure 97. Plan of tomb Op. 4/4 at Helwan, whose stairway was entirely covered by its superstucture. The sketch shows the broken corner of the portcullis, where robbers entered the burial chamber.

detritus. In this instance, the tomb's burial chamber, which had a 3.4 m thick gravel roof, projected beyond the perimeter of the superstructure and so was unprotected by it. Not that this would have made a great deal of difference in this case, as here also the tomb had been robbed through a hole made in the top corner of its portcullis, which would have been made by digging down through the mastaba itself.[87] Nearby tomb Op. 4/123 was unusual insofar as it had an L-shaped or 'bent' gravel-cut staircase that initially ran east and then turned north and descended 3.76 m to the entrance of its burial chamber. Both staircase and burial chamber were entirely concealed and protected by a seven-meter-long mud-brick mastaba (Fig. 98). Like Op. 4/94, it was robbed by two routes: one through the mastaba and the mud-brick blocking to the burial chamber entrance, the other through a tunnel that began outside the northern end of the superstructure and ran down through 2.5 m of gravel cover into the burial chamber.[88]

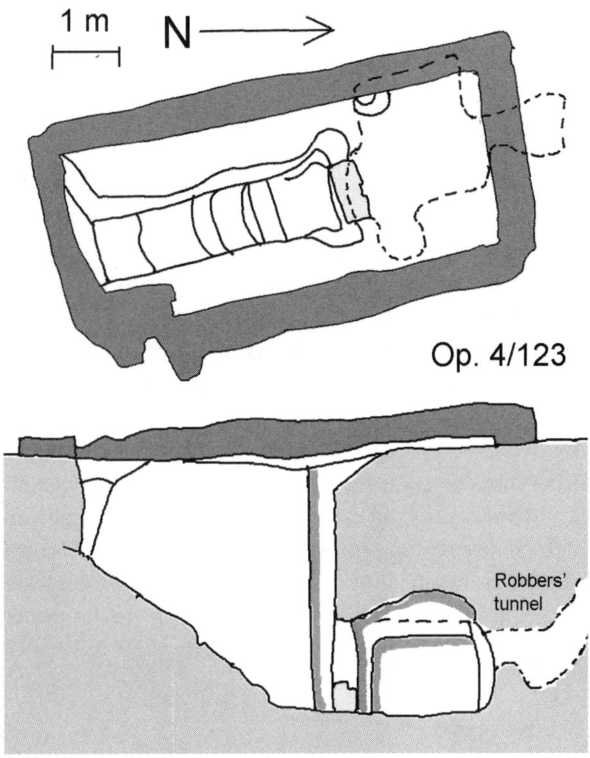

Figure 98. Tomb Op. 4/123 at Helwan, with its 'bent' stairway concealed under its superstructure. It was robbed through both the stairway and a robbers' tunnel from the north.

The comparison between Op. 4/94 and Op. 4/123, whose substructures had similar depths but quite different lengths, at eleven and seven meters, respectively, demonstrates that like at Saqqara, putting a turn in a descent meant that the stairway could reach a greater depth within the confines of a much shorter space. Unlike at Saqqara, however, the smaller size of the Helwan superstructures generally precluded them from varying the orientation and position of their stairways, which usually descend axially within the perimeter of the tomb. This meant their stairway locations were probably more easily located by *sondage* than those at Saqqara, and, due also to the less resistant geology at Helwan,[89] both they and their adjoining substructures were more prone to attack.

The latter part of the Second Dynasty saw the introduction of the 'deep stairway' subterranean tomb at Helwan, which may have been an attempt to improve the security of the tomb's access route by minimizing its plan and cross section. The theory is that by descending farther within a limited space, the deep staircase allowed both it and the burial chamber to be protected and concealed by a shorter mastaba than would have been needed with a traditional staircase. This would have been a distinct advantage in an already overcrowded necropolis.[90] In this type of descent, which seems to be limited mainly to Helwan and Naga al-Deir (although one example is known from Saqqara[91]), access to the substructure is made by a 'deep' staircase with two or three large steps, each as high as 1.5 m.[92] Of the five of this type that are known, a typical example is tomb Op. 4/148, whose 4.3 m gravel-cut descent was formed by two deep steps that led north to a portcullis, which blocked the entrance to the burial chamber (Fig. 99). This was protected by a gravel roof 2.85 m thick, which, like many subterranean tombs at Helwan, had been penetrated by a robbers' tunnel that began just outside the northeast corner of the superstructure, thereby avoiding the overlying seven- by four-meter mud-brick mastaba, whose footprint otherwise completely protected the deep stairway and burial chamber.[93]

Also toward the end of the dynasty, a few small subterranean tombs with shaft entrances make their appearance at Helwan.[94] With an even smaller footprint and cross section than the deep staircase, they were consequently harder to locate and able to be concealed by an even

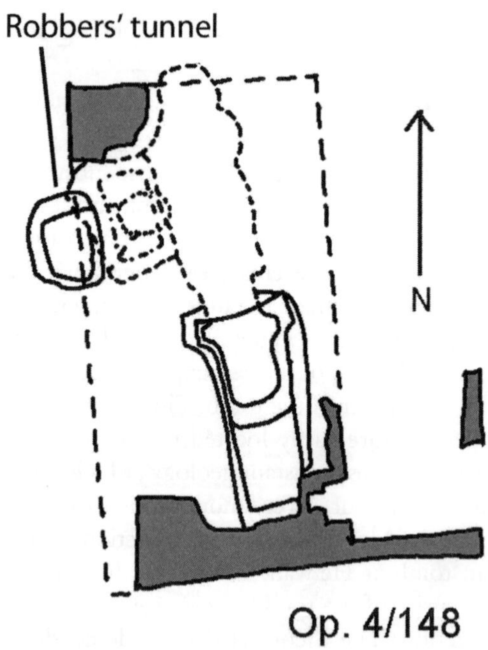

Figure 99. The 'deep staircase' tomb Op. 4/148 at Helwan. Despite being entirely protected by its mastaba, the substructure was still robbed through a tunnel from the west.

smaller superstructure. Their single burial chambers are usually small and occasionally include a recess. A typical example is 256.H.8, whose 1.3 m high burial chamber had its floor set 2.3 m below the surface, thus leaving it protected by a one-meter-thick gravel roof (Fig. 100).[95] Like most of the tombs in the group, it had been robbed by means of a tunnel dug through the gravel from above. Among the other recorded shaft tombs of this type in the same cemetery, the roofs vary from 0.6 to 2.1 m thick, but the deepest tomb of all was the unusual tomb 1.H.5, which was found intact and had two burial chambers at the base of its shaft at ninety degrees to each other, protected by gravel roofs 2.6 m and 2.7 m thick.[96]

Like the burial chambers of their staircase-accessed neighbors, these smaller tombs suffered from the systematic and remarkably accurate tunneling of tomb robbers, who were obviously cognizant of their layouts and aware of the ease with which they could penetrate the local geology. When we compare overall the methods used by tomb robbers at Helwan to those at Saqqara, it is apparent from the number of tunnels that penetrate the tombs in the weak geology of the Helwan necropolis that the roofs of the burial chambers were more vulnerable to attack than their entrances. In addition, from the accuracy of their

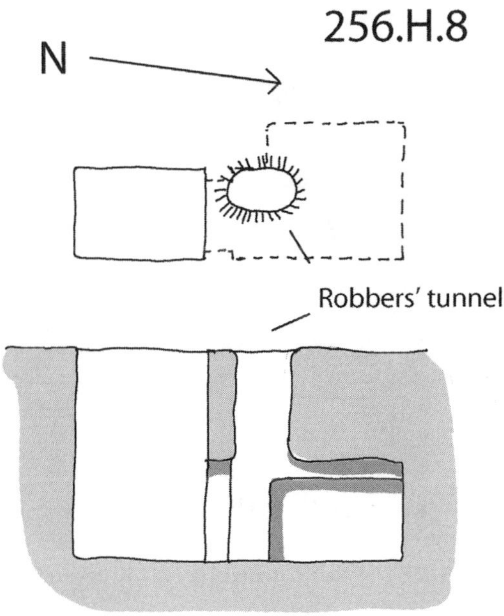

Figure 100. The shallow shaft tomb 256.H.8 at Helwan. As is usual in the gravel-cut subterranean tombs at Helwan, the tomb had been robbed through a tunnel from above.

tunneling, it is obvious that the perpetrators were familiar with the layouts of the tombs, which suggests that they were involved with either the building of the tomb or the subsequent funeral. Moreover, as with the large tombs at Saqqara, greater size and depth did not guarantee safety at Helwan either; in fact, it undoubtedly attracted attention.[97]

Tarkhan

Finally, there are two subterranean stairway tombs known from the necropolis at Tarkhan (or Kafr Amar, as Petrie called the site of later tombs in this area). Both have a small, west-facing burial chamber, just large enough to contain a short wooden coffin for a contracted burial. In grave 240, rock-cut stairs descended 3.17 m to a freestanding stone portcullis 0.22 m thick that weighed approximately 0.6 tonnes, which blocked the entrance to the burial chamber (Fig. 101). This was protected from overhead attack by a rock roof approximately 2.3 m thick. The stairway of nearby grave 545 descended deeper to 4.57 m, but the entrance to its burial chamber was merely closed with small stones.

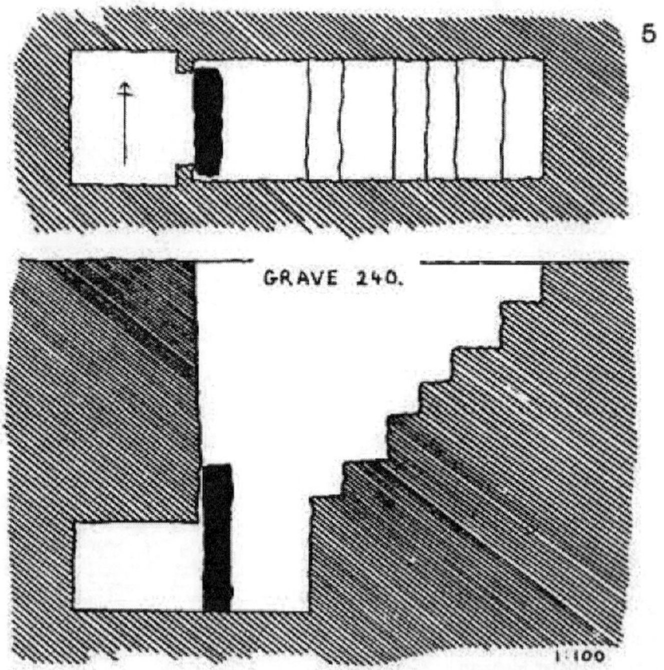

Figure 101. The rock-cut intact grave 240 at Tarkhan/Kafr Amar. The portcullis is marked in black.

By way of compensation, however, the rock cover above its chamber was greater than that of its neighbor, at 3.7 m thick. Although they seem to have lacked protective superstructures, both tombs were found intact.[98]

Tomb Security in Middle Egypt

Lahun

In the Bashkatib Cemetery at Lahun, near the entrance to the Fayum oasis, there are at least thirty subterranean staircase tombs that can be dated to the Second Dynasty, although their excavator Petrie placed them earlier. Their substructures often included a side recess and were carved in the soft marl below the upper limestone strata of the hill into which they were dug, which varied in thickness according to location.

One of the shallower examples is tomb 771, whose burial chamber floor was about 1.8 m from the surface and was protected by a limestone roof approximately 0.75 m thick (Fig. 102). It was entered by a

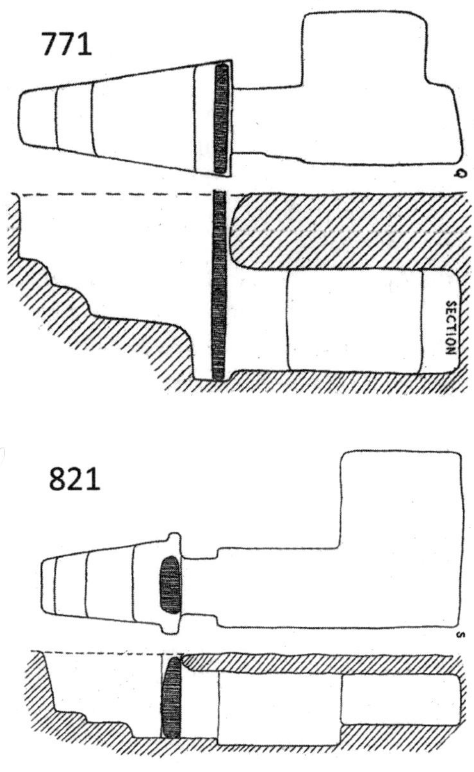

Figure 102. Graves 771 and 821 at the Bashkatib Cemetery, Lahun. The former was protected by a rock roof 0.75 m thick, while the roof of the latter was only 0.15 m thick.

tapering rock-cut staircase that was blocked at its base by 0.12 m thick, 0.56 tonne portcullis, which, as in many tombs at Bashkatib, rather than being inserted into grooves, seems to have relied on the wedge-shaped sides of its stairwell to create a loose emplacement against the burial chamber's entrance. However, the even shallower tomb 821, which only had 0.15 m of rock cover over its burial chamber (Fig. 102), did have portcullis grooves at the base of its stairway, although its 0.27 m thick, 0.7 tonne stone slab was not wide enough to fit them. Much deeper, and thus arguably better protected, was tomb 785. Its tapering staircase descended 3.75 m to a broken (by robbers?) free-standing portcullis in a wedge-shaped emplacement, beyond which its burial chamber was protected by a 2.74 m thick rock roof.[99] Devoid of superstructures and differing in their various orientations, there seems to be no evidence that the burial chambers of these tombs were penetrated by robbers' tunnels, which suggests that the limestone roofs successfully protected them from attack from above. Therefore, it is safe to suggest that the most vulnerable point of the tombs at Bashkatib must have been their entrances.

Sedment

Further south, and west of the ancient site of Herakleopolis, at the necropolis of Sedment, six stairway tombs published by Petrie and Brunton[100] were cut into the surrounding gravel and marl strata. They all had tapered entrance stairways, which perhaps formed a rudimentary portcullis emplacement at the base, like those at Lahun. Among these tombs, the intact grave 560 is the best reported (Fig. 103). It was entered from its northern end by a tapering combined slope and steep staircase that descended south and ended with another short slope at a depth of around 3.5 m. At its base stood a small, freestanding portcullis, oddly not as wide as the tomb's entrance, backed up by a secondary blocking in the form of a mud-brick wall. Beyond, the floor of its 1.37 m high substructure and recess was excavated to a depth of around 3.5 m, leaving a protective roof approximately 2.1 m thick.[101] The remaining tombs 526, 559, 568, and 569 are of a similar design, with roofs varying between 0.5 and 3.3 m thick. Exceptionally, the floor of the 2.13 m high burial chamber of tomb 94 was set at the considerable depth of 7.62 m, giving it approximately 5.5 m of cover.[102] Like the tombs at Lahun, there is no evidence that the tombs robbed at this site had been entered in any way other than by the stairway, nor are there any remains of protective superstructures.

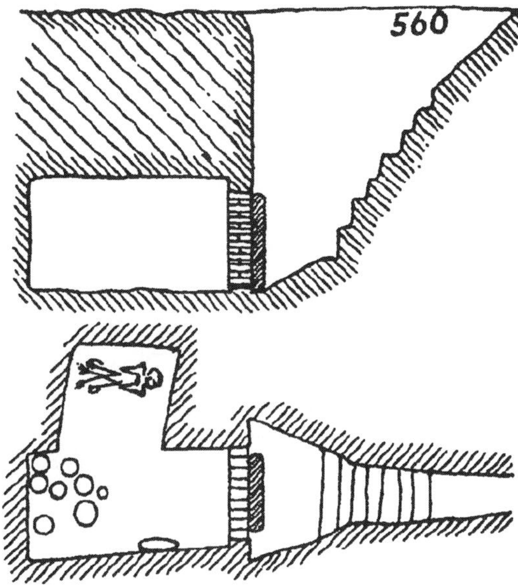

Figure 103. The intact tomb 560 at Sedment, showing its portcullis and secondary mud-brick blocking to the burial chamber entrance.

Qau and Badari

South of the Fayum, at Qaw al-Kebir, some forty-five kilometers from Asyut, there are four stairway tombs from this period cut in the gravel and marl of the Early Dynastic cemetery at Qau and one in the limestone detritus of Badari.[103]

At Cemetery 400 in Qau, some burial chambers were excavated to considerable depths in pursuit of security, such as that in the 8.63 m deep tomb 562, which was accessed by a gravel-cut stairway that was blocked at its base with limestone masonry and protected from overhead attack by a 6.48 m thick gravel roof (Fig 104). Slightly less well defended were the chambers of tombs 429 and 507, whose roofs were 4.5 and 5.35 m thick, respectively.[104]

However, farther afield at Spur 5 in Cemetery 3100 at Badari, the 4.72 m deep entrance staircase of tomb 3112 was cut in the local limestone debris (Fig. 105), which at the surface was surrounded by remains of a 15.29 m long and eight-meter-wide rectangular mud-brick wall. Despite Brunton's assertions to the contrary, this may well have been the remains of a mastaba that would have concealed and protected the tomb. At the base of the stairway, in contrast to the deeper tombs at Qau, its adjoining 1.6 m high burial chamber was only defended with a 3.12 m thick roof.[105]

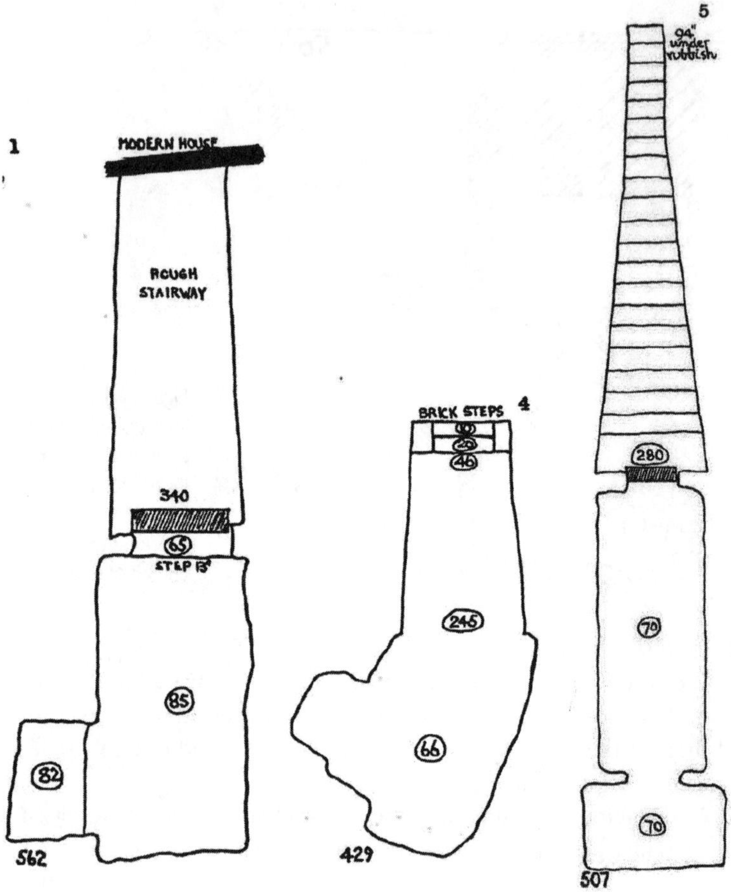

Figure 104. The deep gravel-cut tombs 562, 429, and 507 at Qau.

Here at Qau and Badari, the great depth of some of the tombs may have been the result of the search for strata solid enough to safely excavate a burial chamber. Equally, it could have compensated for the vulnerability of the local geology to tunneling. Without accurate information, it is difficult to be more precise.

Tomb Security in Upper Egypt

In Upper Egypt, while it appears that some tombs were being built with the new subterranean substructures, elsewhere at sites like Naga al-Deir, al-Siba'iya, al-Qara, and Masa'id the old pit substructure was retained, but it relied on other architectural features to provide security.

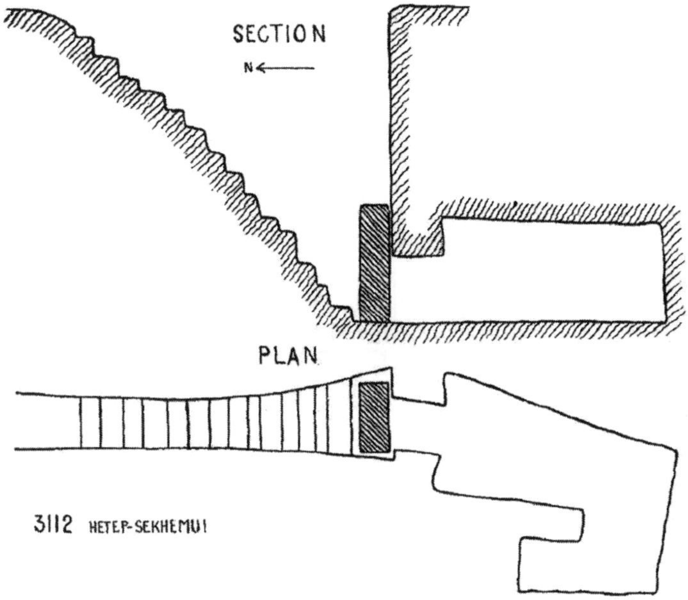

Figure 105. Tomb 3112 at Spur 5 in Cemetery 3100 at Badari.

Naga al-Deir

At Cemetery 1500 in Naga al-Deir, the old-style staircase pit tombs were still in vogue, but they were protected by a new form of closure: a roof made of corbeled mud-brick rather than the usual wood, as seen in tomb N 1586. Accessed by a brick entrance staircase that was backfilled with 'boulders' for its protection and blocked by a mud-brick wall at its base, the tomb's substructure comprised a mud-brick-lined pit sunk 3.25 m into the alluvium and subdivided into a main burial chamber with magazines at either end (Fig. 106). Rather than being covered in wood like most pit tombs, the roof of every chamber was built by stepping out each course of mud-brick to form a groined vault, which was then plastered internally. Externally, the main chamber roof was then roughly built up with mud and brick to be 0.5 m higher than that of the magazines, then brought level with the surface with about 0.75 m of backfill to support a protective superstructure.[106]

Reisner discussed the defensive benefits of the corbel roof and suggested that its great advantage over the wood and mud-brick variety was that it increased security[107] because it was not subject to the strain of bearing heavy mud-brick and the depredations of moisture.[108] This, of course, did not prevent corbel-roofed tombs from being robbed, and

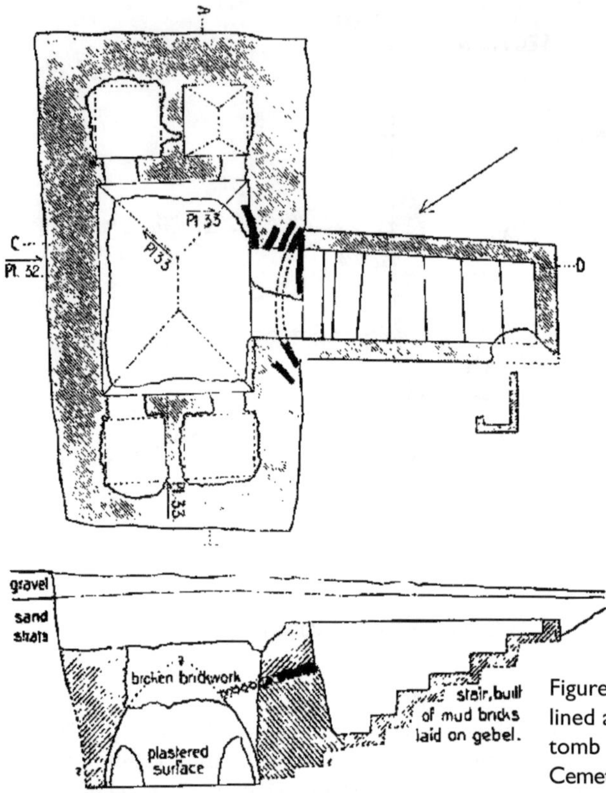

Figure 106. The mud-brick-lined and corbel-roofed pit tomb N 1586 from Cemetery 1500 at Naga al-Deir.

at least a couple of those that were plundered were found to have been entered by thieves smashing through the main vault.[109]

Armant

Further down the Nile at Armant, near modern-day Luxor, four of the newer-style subterranean staircase tombs are known from Cemetery 200. Their burial chambers take the usual form with a lateral recess and were presumably cut into the alternating layers of local gravels and fine-grained sedimentary rocks that make up the 'Armant formation.'[110] Typical is tomb 205, whose 1.8 m high burial chamber floor was set down 4.2 m from the surface and protected by a solid roof 2.4 m thick (Fig. 107). Similarly, the roofs of tombs 206, 207, and 208 were 2.8 m, 2.1 m, and 1.2 m thick, respectively. Unusually, three of these four tombs utilized a slope rather than a staircase (as in 207) to approach the substructure, and all varied in their orientation of approach, each

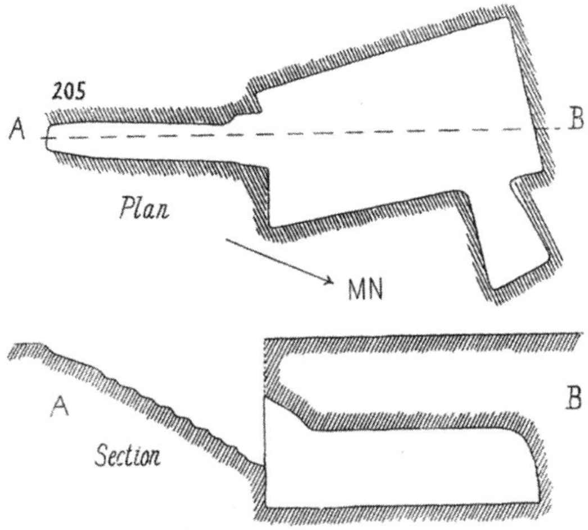

Figure 107. Tomb 205 from Cemetery 200 at Armant.

coming from a different point of the compass.[111] There is no evidence that there were protective superstructures above them, but, as elsewhere, this does not mean that they did not originally exist.

Al-Kab

Upstream at al-Kab, two smaller intact stairway tombs were also found cut into the surrounding Nile silts that form the 'al-Kab formation.'[112] Tomb St. 2 was excavated by Quibell and is described by him as "the smallest tomb of the kind that I have seen." Apparently, its stairway descended for one meter to the entrance of the burial chamber, to which "a large stone slab had been placed as a door." Beyond lay a burial chamber roughly one meter square with a very shallow roof, whose meager defenses Quibell succinctly described: "A robber had only to pierce 20 cm. of soil to get into the chamber through the roof."[113]

Better defended was the more recently excavated grave 64, discovered among the earlier tombs of the Naqada IIIA periods in Cemetery 24 (Fig. 108).[114] Approached by a slope, the entrance to its burial chamber was closed by a sandstone portcullis slotted into two specially cut grooves in the sides of its descent—it was 0.12 m thick and would have weighed approximately 0.15 tonnes.[115] The burial chamber's floor was set 1.3 m below the surface and protected by a roof approximately 0.7 m thick. No evidence was found of any defensive superstructures over these tombs, and although at first glance their limited defenses and shallow depths would suggest higher vulnerability to robbery, in fact it may have been their very small size and insignificance that eventually saved them.

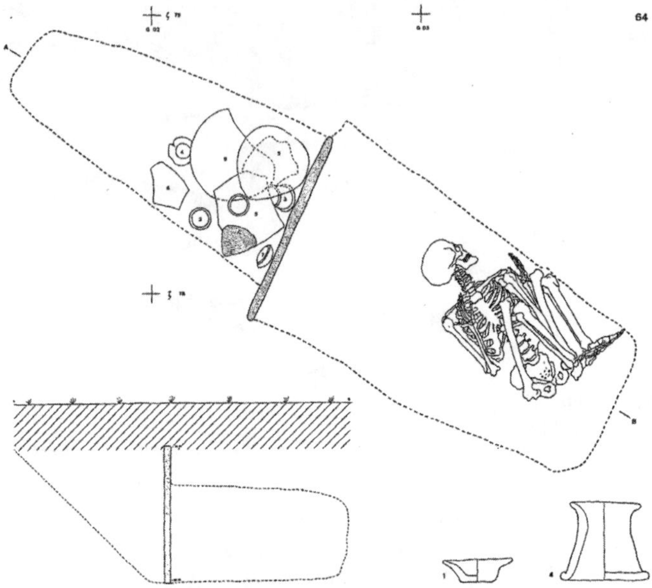

Figure 108. The intact grave 64 in Cemetery 24 at al-Kab.

Further south, beyond Esna, it seems that the mud-brick-lined pit tomb retained its popularity, but to make it more secure, stone seems to have been used as a regional specialty to bolster a tomb's defenses.

Al-Siba'iya

Twenty kilometers southeast of Esna, at al-Siba'iya East, de Morgan described finding a large pit tomb roofed with stone slabs, which is loosely dated to the Second or Third Dynasty.[116] Its 5.48 m long substructure had a brick liner 0.22 m thick that was partly covered with stone slabs for about 60 percent of its length. One of these measured an impressive 2.32 m long, 1.23 m wide, and 0.32 m thick, and the success of this 1.75 tonne monolith as a security measure can be judged by the fact that de Morgan was forced to resort to dynamite to open up the grave.[117]

Al-Qara

Further south, a pit tomb that employed stone for both its liners and roof was found seven kilometers north of Edfu at al-Qara. It is loosely dated to the Early Dynastic Period,[118] but stylistically similar to Second Dynasty structures.[119] Tomb 2 comprised a large gravel-cut pit in which a mud-brick-lined burial chamber was constructed (Fig. 109). This was in turn lined with stone slabs approximately 0.15 m thick to deter lateral tunneling. A massive stone roof closed the grave, which comprised three separate slabs approximately 0.25 m thick—the largest of which would have weighed around a tonne[120]—and then covered with a gravel or sand backfill approximately 1.2 m deep. Therefore, not only was this tomb undoubtedly well concealed, but belowground it was 'armored' with stone on its top and sides, as well.

Al-Masa'id

Finally, south of al-Qara and north of Jebel al-Silsila, five more tombs with stone slabs were found by de Morgan at al-Masa'id, among ninety-one tombs broadly dated to Naqada III. The only one described in detail was the intact Burial 28. It comprised a 1.8 m deep gravel-cut pit into which a backfill had been poured. The first 0.8 m of this fill comprised a "compacted mass of cemented pebbles" that formed "a

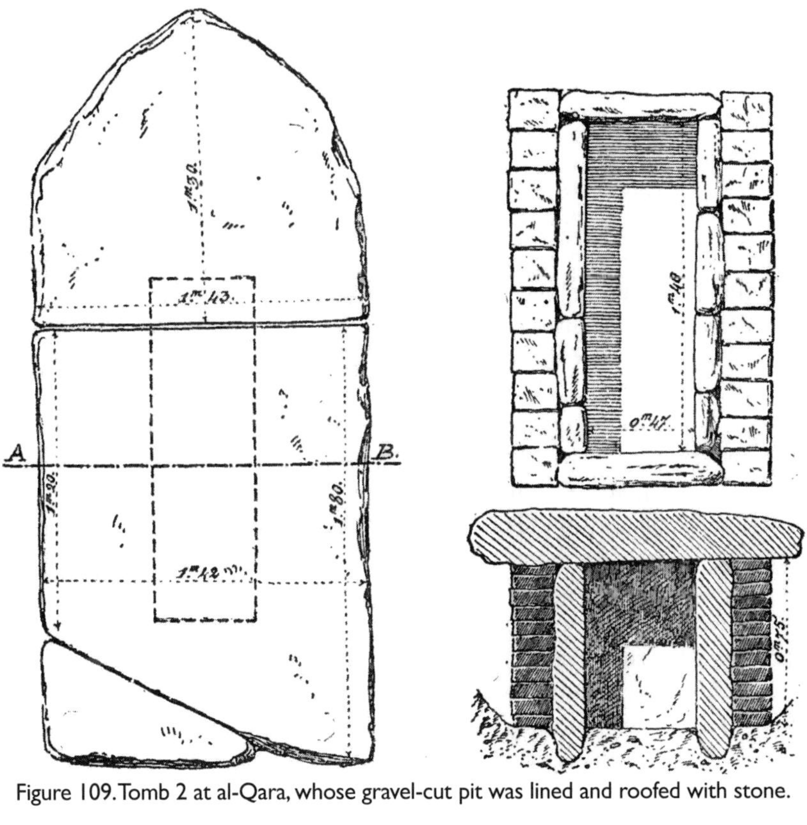

Figure 109. Tomb 2 at al-Qara, whose gravel-cut pit was lined and roofed with stone.

natural concrete as hard as a breccia," over which two large 1.6 m long, 0.6 m wide, and 0.15 m thick sandstone slabs were placed, each about 0.28 tonnes, creating a virtually impenetrable cover just over one meter thick.[121]

Thematic Analysis: The Architecture and Security Features of Second Dynasty Private Tombs

Initially, the security features of many early Second Dynasty subterranean tomb stairways hardly changed: their external stairwells often differed little from those of their First Dynasty predecessors, and they were thus liable to discovery and attack in much the same way. However, by moving the stairway entirely within the protective body of the tomb's superstructure, the level of protection was improved, and, by varying its position and orientation, the likelihood of detection greatly reduced. Moreover, in some larger tombs, where tomb builders sought to place the substructure farther belowground, changing the direction of the descent permitted it to go much deeper. Bigger stairwells were more vulnerable to robbers' *sondages*, but this problem was resolved by the end of the dynasty with the introduction of more easily concealed stair-shafts and shafts.

An assortment of poured backfills and built blockings was used to secure the stairways. The backfills usually consisted of sand, soil, or rubble and the built blockings of mud-brick, masonry, or sometimes quarried stone. These were frequently used in combination with just a single portcullis, and more rarely, in the larger tombs of Saqqara, with as many as two or three.

The defense of the subterranean substructure now entirely relied on the geology into which it was cut, being largely dependent on the resistance of its matrix to tunneling and the depth to which it was sunk. Moreover, the size of a substructure would in theory also affect the ease with which it might be located by *sondage*. These vulnerabilities were most evident in the multiple robbers' tunnels piercing the gravel-cut tombs at Helwan and notably absent in the harder limestones of Saqqara, Tarkhan, Lahun, and Sedment.

The defensive role of the superstructure changed, too, with the advent of the subterranean tomb. Now, rather than protecting a wooden-roofed or backfilled pit, the superstructure's mass and footprint protected the substructure's overlying geological cover instead. In addition, the interior of the superstructure increasingly concealed and defended the tomb's entrance, access route, and portcullis emplacements. These were often now contained entirely within its perimeter walls, whose mud-brick ramparts retained protective inner cores of gravel, sand, rubble, brick, and liquid mud, sometimes singly, more rarely in combination.

Lastly, in Upper Egypt, subterranean tombs were slow to catch on and the pit tomb still reigned supreme, relying on reinforced liners and closures of corbeled mud-brick or solid stone for better security.

Conclusion

The open pits and roofed substructures of the royal and private tombs of the previous dynasty were now largely superseded by subterranean substructures dug deep within their surrounding geology. The effectiveness of the substructure's protective cover now depended on the depth to which it was dug and the resistance of the adjacent geology, rather than on a wooden roof. Because it was hidden from prying eyes during construction, a substructure's disposition was now largely secret and therefore more secure. In addition, in those necropoleis with resistant geology, the tomb's access route was, for all intents and purposes, now the only practical way in.

To protect the vulnerable entrances and access routes of these tombs, they were increasingly brought within the bounds of the superstructure's footprint and located in various positions to avoid detection by *sondage*. But internally, they still relied on backfills, blockings, and portcullises of stone.

Aboveground, though the superstructure was once essential for the defense of a pit tomb, the substructure of a subterranean tomb was less dependent on it for defense, and so its role subtly began to change. No longer needed as a storehouse for grave goods, the superstructure's main defensive function became to conceal and protect the access route and its entrance from grave diggers.

But as these new subterranean substructures went ever deeper for greater security, the descents of their access routes grew both longer and larger and at the same time increasingly vulnerable to the attentions of tomb robbers. And it is the various solutions to this problem that are examined in the next chapter.

6

A Parting of the Ways: Step Pyramids and Mastabas in the Third Dynasty

As we have seen in the previous chapters, the design and security arrangements of royal and private tombs during the First and Second Dynasties largely had similar formats, with private tombs usually following the royal example. However, with the dawn of the Third Dynasty and the reign of King Djoser, royal and private tombs developed along distinctly separate paths, establishing a precedent for the remainder of the dynasty and those to come.

Royal Tombs
The Return to Saqqara

The Step Pyramid

With the reign of Horus Netjerykhet Djoser the site of the royal necropolis returned to Saqqara, and the tomb complex of the first king of the dynasty was built just north of the tombs of Hotepsekhemwy/Raneb and Ninetjer.

The Step Pyramid of Djoser represents a landmark in the design of royal tombs, not only for its architectural innovations and widespread use of stone but also for the efforts taken to protect the burial of its occupant. Many years after its construction, credit for its design was given to Imhotep, one of the high officials of the king.[1] Built in several stages, the tomb was initially designed as a mastaba surrounded by an enclosure wall, and the original route to the substructure began in the north as a twenty-meter-long descending stairway in an open trench, which then continued for a further thirty meters underground until it met the main shaft of the tomb, approximately twenty-five meters from the surface (Fig. 110).[2] This created a deep subterranean stairwell in the rock with a rock ceiling approximately seven meters thick, thus offering

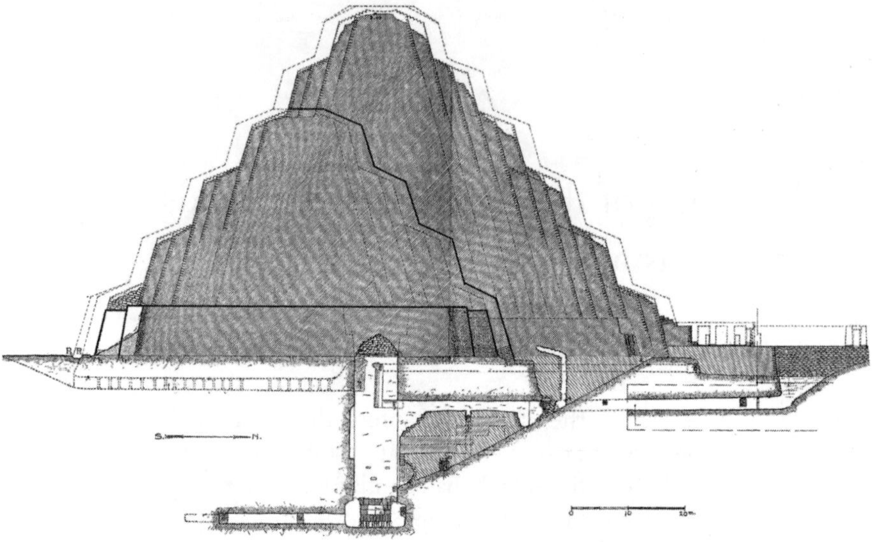

Figure 110. Cross-section of the Step Pyramid facing west, showing the substructure and stages of the superstructure's development.

it a considerable degree of both lateral and overhead protection. At the end of the stairwell, the tomb's enormous seven meter square by twenty-eight-meter deep main 'shaft' (or more accurately 'construction pit,' as it was never intended to function as an access route, but rather to facilitate the excavation of the substructure) was cut into the surrounding rock and its mouth topped with retaining walls that extended it into the body of the superstructure, permitting the latter to be erected around its open aperture.[3] It has been suggested that, originally, a burial chamber made of decorated limestone blocks may have been built at the base of the shaft to house the body of the king. Surrounding this chamber were four exits, one in each wall of the shaft, with passages leading to a complex of underground galleries that comprised magazines on three sides and, to the east, a tiled model 'palace' for the king's use in the afterlife (Fig 111).[4]

Aboveground, initially the superstructure took the usual form of a large protective mastaba over the royal burial, but this was revolutionary as it was constructed entirely of stone. It was built in six stages, the first three in the form of a mastaba and the final three being added toward the end of the tomb's development (Fig. 112). The first mastaba (M1) consisted of a Tura limestone-clad core of limestone rubble bonded with clay mortar that was 62.9 m long, 62.9 m wide, and 8 m high. In the second

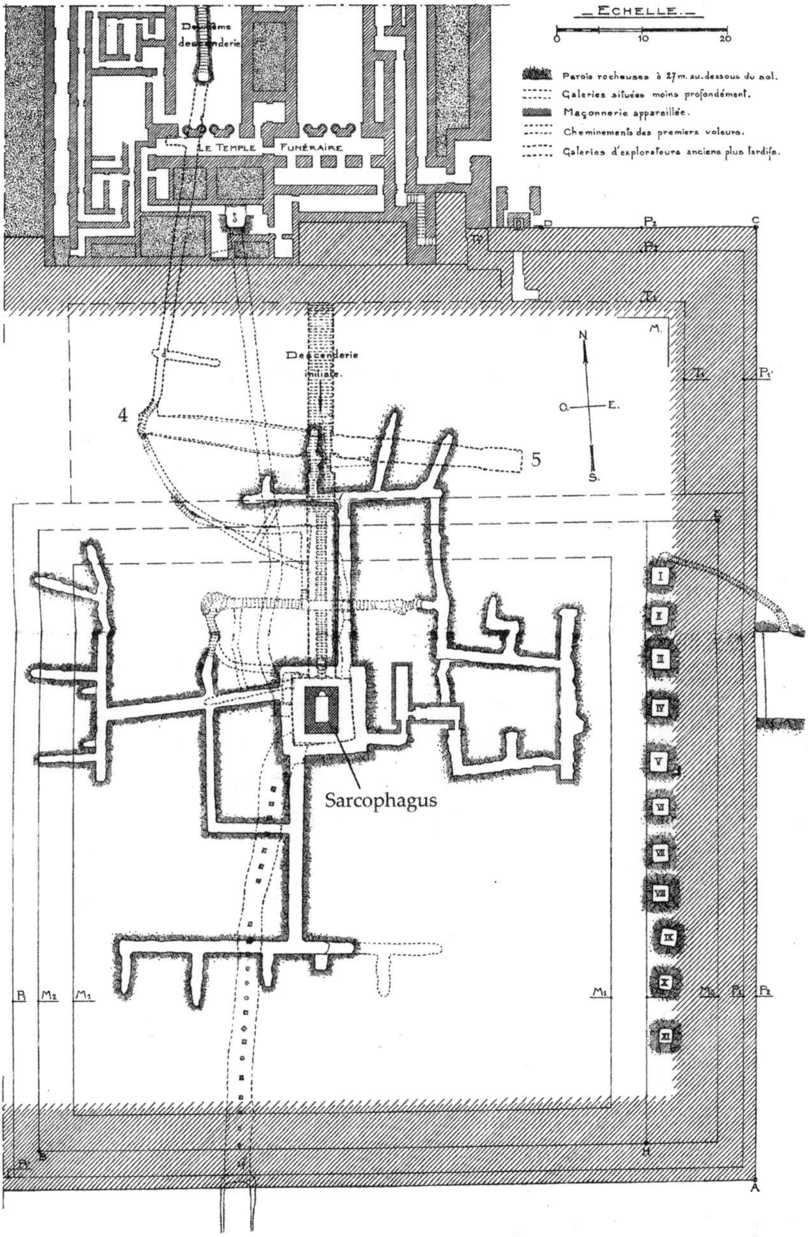

Figure 111. Plan of the Step Pyramid and its complex substructure of passages and robbers' tunnels. The deep shafts on the right lead to the burials of the royal family and magazines.

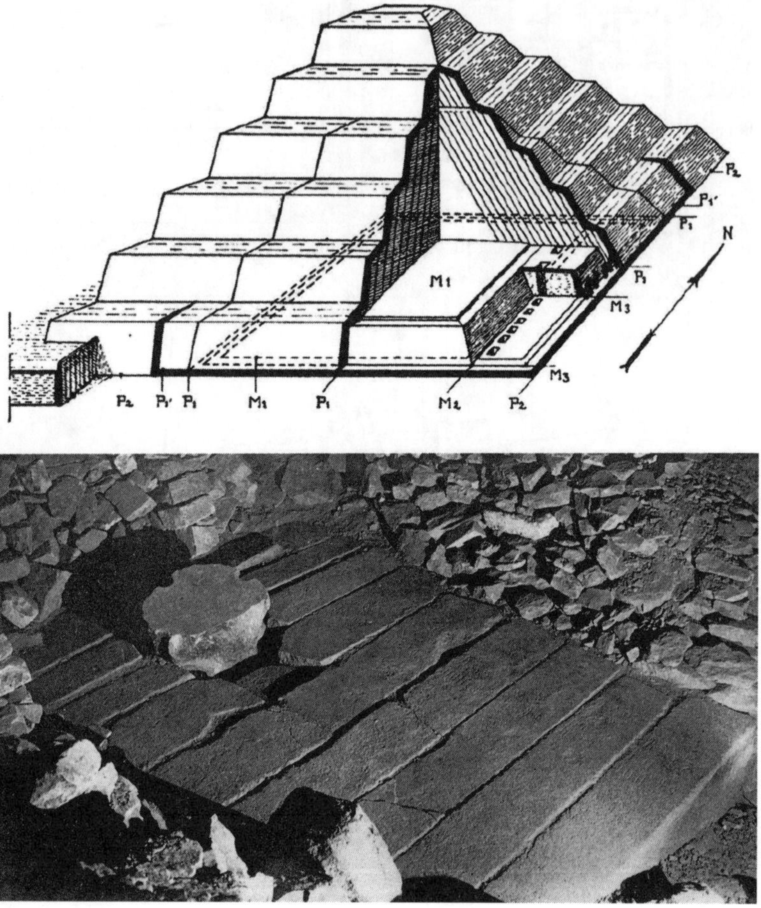

Figure 112. Axonometric view of the Step Pyramid's stages of development and view of the granite vault with its three-tonne plug in place.

stage (M2), it retained its square plan but was increased in size to 71.5 m by 71.5 m. In the third stage (M3), an 8.4 m thick layer of masonry was added on the eastern side, which covered the eastern tomb shafts of the royal family (see below) and created a rectangular structure. Therefore, at this stage a large stone mastaba protected the royal substructure, and although the original access shaft that extended up through the mastaba during its construction had been filled in,[5] in theory the shaft below remained vulnerable to overhead attack.

However, at some point the decision was made to turn the mastaba into a step pyramid and concomitantly improve the protection of the royal burial. The reasons behind this change are still the subject of much debate,[6] but it may be that the frequent experience of tomb robbery in royal sepulchers soon after the burials were made drove a desire to provide greater protection to the substructure than a mastaba could provide.[7]

Now built with inclined accretion layers of coursed stonework two to three meters thick for stability, the first stage of the Step Pyramid (P1) consisted of four steps, which increased the plan of the mastaba (M3) by 5.76 m overall on two sides and its overall height to approximately forty-two meters.[8] Perhaps unsatisfied by the uneven depth of cover offered by this lopsided arrangement, the tomb's architect increased the footprint and volume of the four-tiered pyramid enormously in the next stage (P1') by extending the structure on its northern and western sides and adding another two steps. Finally, a further layer was added (P2) to protect the original entrance stairway and its flanking cruciform passage, which resulted in the structure seen today: 121 m long, 109 m wide, and 60 m high and a hitherto unparalled 330,400 cubic meters in volume.[9]

This new shape, I suggest, was the most economical method, in terms of materials and the available technology, of providing what can be described as an impregnable 'carapace' of protection over the tomb's vulnerable shaft and galleries. This is because there is no advantage in just building a much taller mastaba: the protection offered vertically from the highest point and horizontally from the widest point are the minimum distances that would need to be tunneled to penetrate the substructure by this route, the upper external edges of such a structure being effectively superfluous. Therefore, the most efficient degree of cover could be achieved by building a roughly hemispherical or mound-like shape, as geometrically any point on a hemisphere's surface is the same distance from the center of its base. By using the technology available at the time, a rough approximation of that shape could be provided by building a step pyramid, which concomitantly saved an enormous amount of both labor and materials.

As a result, rather than being vulnerable to attack from above like the mastabas of the previous dynasties, drawing an imaginary straight line through the pyramid's section shows that an overhead assault from any direction would have to penetrate at least thirty-five meters of stone before reaching the top of the tomb's shaft. In addition, any attempt at lateral tunneling beneath the pyramid's enormous 13,189 square-meter footprint was unfeasible from a robber's point of view,[10] as it was more than forty-seven meters from its outside edge to the top of the main shaft. Moreover, the distance from the superstructure's perimeter through the bedrock to the burial chamber was even greater, at about fifty-three meters. Compared to any previous Egyptian tomb, therefore, the world's first pyramid offered its substructure an unrivalled degree of protection.

To provide the expanded pyramid with a foundation, the open part of the original exposed entrance stairwell had been filled in, and the underground section, which was fifteen meters high and three meters wide where it met the shaft, was carefully packed with large stone blocks and smaller coursed masonry to create a reduced passageway to the burial chamber, presumably making it easier to seal after the funeral. This meant that the original entrance stairway was now completely hidden under the pyramid and blocked, and that an entirely fresh entrance was needed. This was created within the floor of the western court of the newly built funerary temple, which now abutted the pyramid's north face. It took the form of a concealed staircase and shaft that descended eight meters from the temple pavement and led southward through a forty-meter-long passage with a roughly seven-meter-thick rock roof. This joined with a cruciform gallery (marked 4–5 on the plan, Fig. 111), which rejoined the original, but reduced, stairway to the burial shaft approximately two-thirds of the way down.[11]

At the base of the new stairway in the main shaft, it has been suggested the putative limestone vault was replaced with the granite one that remains to this day (Figs. 112–13). Its sides were built from two layers of enormous granite blocks 1.1 to 1.2 m thick and roofed and floored with horizontal ashlars of similar dimensions. Its entrance was through a hole in its roof closed by a two-meter-long tapered granite plug, one meter in diameter, which weighed 3.5 tonnes. Grooves in the top of the plug indicate that it was originally lowered into place by ropes. To permit this operation and the insertion of the king's body, Jean-Philippe Lauer suggested a limestone 'maneuvering' chamber was built over the vault. Once the burial had been made, this was paved internally with a 1.5 m thick schist floor overlying a layer of limestone sherds to conceal the vault below, above which a filling of limestone blocks may have been installed to seal the chamber, as in the nearby 'South Tomb' (discussed below).[12] The remainder of the shaft above was then backfilled to a depth of around twenty-five meters with about 1,225 cubic meters of rubble consisting of large stones and clay.

Therefore, like its royal Second Dynasty predecessors at Saqqara, the main substructure in the Step Pyramid took advantage of the natural protection offered by the surrounding geology. Compared to the

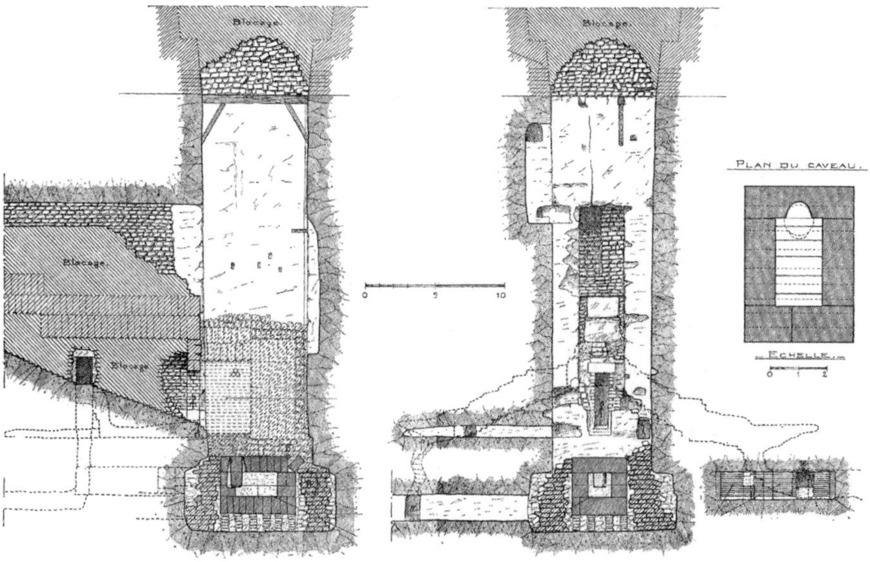

Figure 113. Sections through the shaft of the Step Pyramid showing details of the blocking in the descending passage and the granite vault.

tombs of Hotepsekhemwy/Raneb and Ninetjer, however, the level of protection was at least four times greater, with twenty-five meters of rock cover over its subterranean galleries. At its core, a further layer of defense for the king's body was provided by the revolutionary granite vault and its limestone maneuvering chamber, made more inaccessible after the burial by a filling of masonry. The overlying shaft itself was secured with around nineteen hundred tonnes of virtually impassable stone and clay backfill.

This, however, was not the full extent of the tomb's subterranean arrangements. Under the pyramid's eastern edge there are eleven thirty-three-meter-deep shafts that connect with horizontal galleries, some of which housed the burials of the royal family while others provided storage for a vast number of stone vessels (Fig. 110). Numbered I–XI, they are the first use of the shaft as an access route in a royal tomb and introduced a new level of security for their associated substructures, because of their inaccessibility and their capacity to contain a large volume of backfill. The entrances to these shafts were all concealed and covered by the pyramid, but there is what Lauer described as an auxiliary access route, which leads to shaft 'I' and whose exact purpose is unknown, although it could have been intended to permit later access to the shafts for carrying out the burials of the royal family. The horizontal galleries connected to the shafts run approximately thirty meters west and are protected from above by solid rock approximately thirty-one to thirty-three meters thick. Galleries I–V were paneled with wood and functioned as the tombs of the royal family,[13] whereas VI to XI consisted of unlined magazine storage, of which VI and VII were notable for containing the remains of around forty thousand assorted stone vessels.[14]

To close these shafts, an assortment of blocking methods were used whose complexity demonstrates the considerable thought that went into making them secure. In the upper part of shaft I, which may have been used partly as an entrance shaft, the remains of its backfill (two-thirds of which is still in situ) comprised clay, pebbles, and limestone waste,[15] as did the backfill of shaft IV, where the same material was used to protect a gallery containing sarcophagi. However, other shafts leading to further burials of the royal family were better protected. Shaft II, for example, was filled with a rubble of large stones that also blocked its horizontal gallery for approximately five meters, beyond which the remains of sarcophagi and funerary furniture were found. Shaft III and its gallery were blocked in the same manner, protecting the remnants of sarcophagi and funerary equipment. Shaft V contained an earth fill despite leading to a burial, while shaft VI was blocked with "clayey soil." The choice of a less resistant and more 'diggable' backfill in shaft VI may have been because its associated gallery, along with gallery VII, contained only stone vessels that were perhaps thought less needy of protection. By way of confirmation, shafts VIII to XI and their galleries, which were probably general purpose magazines, were similarly backfilled with compacted earth.[16] Besides backfill and rubble, other closures were employed for extra protection. Shafts IV and V, where less resistant materials were used as backfill than in the shafts that led to burials, were, by way of compensation, each provided with 2.6 m high, two-tonne freestanding limestone portcullises, intended to block the entrances to their adjoining galleries. Despite their size, both had been tipped askew by tomb robbers, who had bypassed them by tunneling between the two galleries. Additionally, beyond these slabs for extra protection, both galleries had one-meter-thick fine limestone masonry blockings that prevented access to the sarcophagi beyond.[17]

Finally, at the southern end of the pyramid complex, a 'South Tomb' was built within and under the enclosure wall whose purpose is still the subject of much debate (Fig. 114).[18] Aboveground, the South Tomb's superstructure was much simpler than the pyramid and provided far less protection. Built as a rectangular mastaba 81.25 m long and 9.85 to 10.5 m wide, it finished approximately four meters above the upper terrace of the southern enclosure wall, where, clad in white limestone, its core was made of accretion layers like those of the pyramid.[19] This protected the South Tomb's underlying substructure to an extent, but its footprint, while lying over the access stairway and shaft, did not quite cover the most northerly and easterly of the lower galleries, nor did it provide a great deal of lateral protection for the shaft on its northern and southern edges.

Access to the substructure mirrored the original design of the pyramid access, except it was orientated east–west to permit it to be concealed within the enclosure wall. A thirty-meter-long open stairway descended between two battered retaining limestone walls until it entered the bedrock. At 3.7 m below the rock layer, a doorway opened onto an entirely rock-cut stairwell, within which the stairs descended for another twenty meters before meeting the burial shaft. To close off the access route after the burial had been installed, the internal

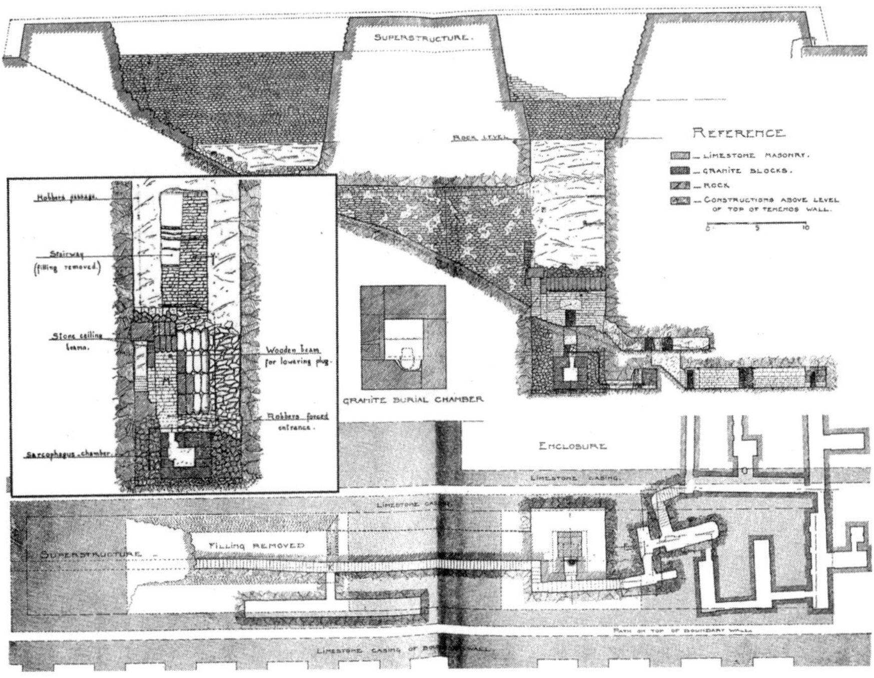

Figure 114. Plan and cross-section of the Step Pyramid South Tomb.

staircase, already two-thirds closed with stone rubble and clay during its construction, was filled and sealed with more of the same, and the preceding open stairwell backfilled with rubble.[20]

At the base of the internal stairway is a shaft arrangement comparable to that of the main pyramid, which has almost identical dimensions. At its base is a similar but smaller granite vault, built of four courses of blocks between 0.9 and 1.25 m wide, whose floor and roof were 0.85 m and 1 m thick, respectively. Too small to house a body,[21] the vault's likely contents and purpose are, like the 'tomb' itself, the subject of much debate. Its entrance was, like that of its larger neighbor, sealed with a granite stopper, but rather than being in one piece, it comprised eight or nine interlocking segments in the manner of a 'Chinese puzzle.'[22] Once closed, it too was probably covered by a 1.5 m layer of alabaster spoil and a hard stone pavement. Above this was then built a 'maneuvering' chamber in limestone to enable the lowering of the plug. Roofed with two layers of thick limestone beams 1.1 m and 0.9 m thick,[23] the chamber's east and west walls were constructed of coursed limestone masonry. However, the north wall was made of four courses of limestone monoliths 2.5 m long, 1.4 m high, and 0.6 m thick, built four layers deep to create a defensive wall 2.4 m wide. Their purpose, Lauer suggested, may have been to mislead potential tomb robbers into believing the vault was concealed within.

Following the putative 'burial,' the maneuvering chamber above the granite vault was entirely filled with limestone masonry bound with clay mortar (found in situ during the excavation of the tomb) to prevent access to the granite plug in the vault underneath.[24] Lastly, to secure the chamber from above, the whole shaft was, like the shaft in the pyramid, backfilled with very large stones (some as big as a man, if not larger) and clay mortar, creating a significant obstruction that would have been extremely difficult to remove.[25] Sadly, this still failed to prevent the tomb from being robbed, as grave robbers, having attempted without success to get through the stairway blocking, circumvented it entirely and instead tunneled down into the shaft to get to the substructure.[26] From there they burrowed beneath the protective pavement in the maneuvering chamber to gain access to the roof of the vault[27] and removed the plug, parts of which were found in later years lying by the pyramid of Unas. Moreover, in the passages beyond the vault, which were also blocked with coursed masonry and led to the connecting underground apartments, the robbers' tunnels avoided the blockings entirely and ran instead through the surrounding rock.[28]

The long history of the Step Pyramid complex and the multiple explorations of its various substructures by thieves[29] means it is difficult to assess the success of its security overall. Nevertheless, we have seen that efforts were made aboveground to conceal and protect the entrance and substructure using the tomb's innovative stone architecture. Equally, at the subterranean level, full use was made of the rock-cutting skills learned during the Second Dynasty to exploit the surrounding rock geology for protection.

Pyramid of Sekhemkhet

Approximately a hundred and forty-four meters southwest of the Step Pyramid, Djoser's successor, King Sekhemkhet, also built a step pyramid,[30] undoubtedly following his predecessor's example. A stone terrace, approximately five hundred and thirty-six meters long and a hundred and ninety-four meters wide, delineates the boundaries of the complex, which is orientated on a north–south axis (Fig. 115). Originally, it was only about two hundred and sixty meters long, its northernmost point now marked by the remains of a palace façade wall, but it was later enlarged to match the size of Djoser's complex.[31]

The entrance to the substructure was located just outside what may have been a funerary temple north of the pyramid. It was reached through a rock-cut trench lined with battered (sloping) coursed stone walls, which began 36.5 m from the northern face of the pyramid and descended southward. At the end of this slope, 10.7 m below the terrace level, a door in the rock face led to a corridor whose floor descended continuously along its length at a slope of approximately sixteen degrees, but at this point its rock roof was horizontal and 8.36 m thick.[32] After 13.4 m, stone jambs formed a portal and marked a change of levels for a horizontal rock ceiling about 11 m thick, which covered the remainder of the sloping well formed by the descent. The corridor then descended for a further 21.5 m until it reached a doorway in its western wall. This led to the tomb's magazine complex, which was accessed by a passage that ran 5.3 m west and then 42.1 m north to join an extensive U-shaped magazine complex. This contained a hundred and thirty-two unused two-meter-high storage chambers set out on either side of an ambulatory corridor in a staggered arrangement resembling the teeth of a comb. These were protected from above by a roof about seventeen meters thick, comprising the natural rock and the pyramid enclosure's terrace.[33] However, unlike the burial chamber, they were not accorded the protection of the superstructure's footprint.

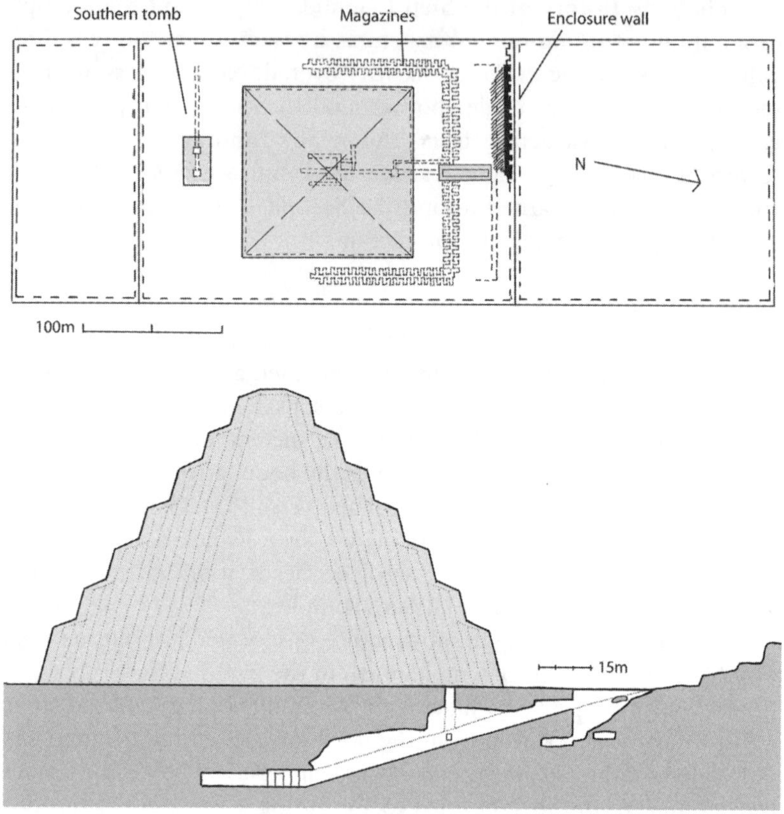

Figure 115. Plan and cross-section of the Pyramid of Sekhemkhet.

Immediately above the doorway in the corridor leading to the magazines, a 2.7 m square shaft, originally 12.6 m deep, led to the surface. Its purpose is not entirely clear,[34] but it would have been covered by the pyramid and presumably concealed entirely from view. Beyond this, the corridor continued to descend until it reached the entrance to the burial chamber, 80.6 m from the entrance, its floor some 32.18 m beneath the terrace of the temple.[35]

To secure the descent and access to the magazines and substructure after the burial, a variety of methods were used. To close the open trench that led to the entrance, it was filled with substantial masonry blocks and any remaining gaps blocked up with loose stones. At the end of the trench, both the rock-cut doorway and the corridor beyond were sealed with an eight-meter-deep stone blocking (found intact), which was constructed in two halves, on the east carefully laid coursed stone that initially closed the passage, and on the west a more hurriedly built blocking that finally sealed the tomb.[36] Farther down the passage, above the doorway that led to the tomb's magazine complex, large limestone blocks and rubble had been thrown down the shaft to seal both the shaft and the corridor, creating a formidable ten-meter-thick blockage from floor to ceiling that would have been extremely dangerous for anyone to remove. Indeed, the effectiveness of this method as a security feature due to the hazards it presented to anyone attempting to clear the blocking is graphically illustrated by the unfortunate death of one of Zakaria Goneim's excavation team, who was injured with two colleagues when some of the shaft's rubble and stone blocking collapsed into the corridor below.[37]

Farther down the corridor, seventy-two meters from its entrance, what appeared to be a solid wall of rock led Goneim to believe the passage had ended and been abandoned by the tomb's builders. As he described it, "ahead of us lay a seemingly impervious mass of rock which at first baffled and depressed us because the corridor led nowhere and there was no burial chamber." Undeterred, they began to clear the passage, which took several weeks but finally revealed a doorway to the burial chamber beyond. Its concealment by this "mass of rock," which was in fact *tafl*, suggests that *tafl* was chosen deliberately to camouflage the entrance,[38] providing both a highly resistant blocking and an element of misdirection.

This, however, was not the end of the story, as the now exposed rock-cut doorway was found to be closed by a 4.72 m deep "massive blocking" of dry stone masonry, which sealed the passage leading to the burial chamber.[39] Once cleared, this revealed a trident-shaped complex of crudely cut rooms, and within its central 'prong' was found an intact alabaster sarcophagus covered by a funerary wreath (Fig. 116). At this point, the roof of the chamber was protected by approximately twenty-three meters of solid rock cover, which lay below the center of the overlying pyramid. The fine alabaster sarcophagus was closed by a 227 kilogram T-shaped sliding panel in one end, apparently sealed in antiquity. Sadly, when it was finally opened in front of senior members of the Department of Antiquities it was found to be completely empty.[40]

At the surface, the substructure was intended to be protected by a step pyramid that was never finished. Its seven-meter-high and approximately 120 square-meter first stage was discovered by Goneim

Figure 116. Exposed corner of the first stage of the unfinished pyramid of Sekhemkhet and the unopened alabaster sarcophagus.

during his excavations (Fig. 116).[41] Built of fourteen sloping limestone accretion layers, bound with clay much like the latter stages of the Step Pyramid, it would—if completed—have reached a height of around seventy meters in seven steps, making it some ten meters higher than its predecessor. The pyramid's 14,400 square-meter footprint was more or less centered over the burial chamber and overlapped the substructure's vertical shaft by 13.2 m, thus concealing and protecting both these and a large part of the descending passage but still leaving most of its subterranean magazines unprotected. Its footprint and mass offered the substructure a considerable degree of cover, as a thief would have to dig at least sixty-three meters to access the burial chamber directly from the pyramid's perimeter.[42]

Like Djoser's complex, the pyramid also possessed a 'South Tomb,' whose original entrance seems to have been via a sloping corridor, the entrance of which, despite Lauer's best efforts, has never been found. This descended east–west at an angle of thirty degrees until it reached a stairwell and then leveled out and met a vertical shaft approximately twenty-nine meters deep. Beyond the shaft, the corridor continued for approximately fourteen meters to join with the burial chamber, which at this point would have been protected by a rock ceiling about twenty-four meters thick,[43] the overlying terrace, and of course laterally by the surrounding geology.[44] Unlike in Djoser's South Tomb, the chamber may have actually been used, as in the adjacent passage remains of a wooden sarcophagus decorated with gold leaf were found containing the skeleton of a small child, whom Lauer assumed to be royal.[45]

Finally, on the terrace above, the substructure was protected by an east–west oriented mastaba approximately thirty-two meters long and sixteen meters wide. This originally encompassed the underlying shaft and sheltered the final few meters of the entrance passage and burial chamber with its protective footprint, presumably leaving the majority of its (still unexcavated) access passage unprotected to the west.[46]

Although aboveground the pyramid was unfinished, when excavated its substructure was found undisturbed.[47] Therefore, the tomb's subterranean defenses had worked perfectly, despite the lower level of protection offered by the incomplete superstructure. It could be argued that this is due more to the pyramid's unfinished state than better security, as it would have attracted less attention from tomb robbers than the nearby Step Pyramid. On the other hand, despite the main tomb being intact, we know the pyramid complex itself was undoubtedly subject to the attentions of tomb robbers, as there is evidence that the South Tomb's sloping entrance passage had been entered by plunderers, who gained access by an undetermined route.[48] Finally, the question still remains, that despite the undeniable success of the pyramid's complex security measures, as the king's body was seemingly never interred in the tomb,[49] why was all this time and energy devoted to protecting it?

The Move to Zawiyat al-Aryan and Abu Rawash

The Layer Pyramid

The next monarch chose Zawiyat al-Aryan as the site for his tomb, where it is located on the edge of an escarpment that leads down to the floodplain. Attributed to Khaba, like that of Sekhemkhet, its pyramid, substructure, and cult installations were never completed.[50] Some scholars have suggested that its location may have been chosen due to a lack of room at Saqqara, or the desire to start anew with a site solely dedicated to its owner. Others have noted that remains found at the desert's edge suggest a possible valley temple and causeway for the pyramid, and may indicate that a less sophisticated arrangement for the king's cult was intended, thus signaling a watershed in the layout of the pyramid complex itself (Fig. 117).[51]

The substructure, according to Barsanti,[52] was accessed by a steep rock-cut staircase that led to a descending passage thirty-six meters long, which, unlike that of Sekhemkhet, ran in an east–west direction from the northeast corner of the pyramid, parallel with its north face. At its end, lining up centrally with the north axis of the pyramid and about ten meters from its edge, a 1.4 square-meter shaft descended to the substructure below. A short distance down the shaft, an opening led to a seventeen-meter-long blind corridor, which ran north–south. Farther down the shaft, an additional two passages cut on the same level ran independently north and south. The southern passage proceeded for twenty meters, where it divided in two at a stairwell. From it an upper corridor ran straight on and ended in another cul-de-sac, but at the base of the stairwell the lower corridor continued and ended in an empty rock-cut burial chamber three meters high, right under the center of the pyramid, whose floor would have been twenty-four meters below the surface.[53] Returning to the main shaft, the northern corridor, which was on the same level as the southern corridor, led directly to a U-shaped magazine complex,[54] similar to that found in Sekhemkhet's substructure, which also lay outside the protective footprint of the pyramid.[55] At the surface, the remains of the unfinished pyramid (which gains its name from the exposed layers of its internal structure that can be seen on its north face) consist of around fourteen angled accretion layers of stone against an inner core of masonry, which were bonded with a *tafl* mortar. If completed, they would have created a square structure 78.45 by 78.45 m across the base, which may have reached a height of 42 to 45 m in five steps.[56]

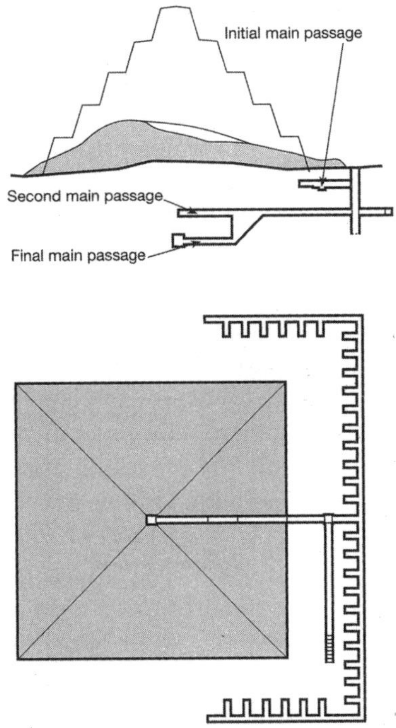

Figure 117. Plan and section of the Layer Pyramid at Zawiyat al-Aryan, according to Dodson.

Like the descending corridors of its predecessors, the access routes in this pyramid relied on the protection offered by the surrounding rock. On this occasion, however, its entrance and corridor were orientated east–west, and this may have been to conceal their true whereabouts for security reasons, bearing in mind its antecedents, whose descending passages were both in the north.[57] In addition, by introducing a shaft, other security benefits may have been gained. One of these was its increased inaccessibility. Another was the relative ease with which it could be blocked. Quite how the various shafts, passages, and chambers would have been secured is not known, but presumably blockings similar to those in Djoser's and Sekhemkhet's tombs would have been used. Aboveground, like its forebears, the pyramid's footprint of 1,154 square meters and its mass would have provided protection for the substructure from attack from above, though arguably less successfully than its predecessors owing to its smaller size. It can be estimated that the distance that one would have had to tunnel from the edge of the pyramid to the burial chamber would have been in the region of forty-three meters by the shortest route. It thus did not provide quite as much cover as its predecessors. However, due to their outlying positions, both the substructure's entrance shaft and the subterranean magazines were beyond the pyramid's protection and thus would have remained vulnerable to tunneling.

The Brick Pyramid

The final royal tomb of the dynasty was built eight kilometers north of Giza at Abu Rawash, where it has been suggested that King Huni built his Brick Pyramid, also known as Lepsius' pyramid no. 1.[58] The pyramid was first mentioned by Howard Vyse, who initially noted the ruined brickwork, and later noticed "upon a projecting knoll" a "building of considerable magnitude and solidity."[59] Subsequently, it was recorded by Carl Richard Lepsius in 1842–43, who reported the colossal remains of a pyramid of black Nile mud-brick built around a core of rock, and noted that a shaft and limestone sarcophagus were still to be seen within its rock core.[60] Although later second-hand reports exist,[61] the pyramid was finally published by the late Nabil Swelim,[62] who produced the only in-depth report of the monument. Largely denuded of its brickwork by *sebbakhin*,[63] the site is situated near to the floodplain, where its location would have permitted handy access to the raw materials for its construction.[64]

At the heart of the tomb is a limestone rock knoll (Fig. 118), which is more or less elliptical in plan and approximately 150 m long, sixty-five to a hundred meters wide, and twenty to twenty-five meters high. Its geology is "of thin layer bedding." It has been cut into various ramps, slopes, terraces, and trenches, which are oriented north. The most important of these is the second terrace, which lies in the center of the knoll's northern face and in which the entrance to the descending corridor is cut.[65] At the corridor's end, it briefly levels out and then drops two meters into an offset five-meter-high burial chamber whose middle is located in what would be the center of the pyramid's plan.[66] Unlike the pyramids of Djoser, Sekhemkhet, and Khaba, however, the burial chamber was not in the usual location twenty to thirty meters below ground level and linked to accessible subterranean magazines, but set so its floor was level with the floodplain, thirteen to fourteen meters above sea level,[67] and cocooned within the solid rock core of the projecting knoll. This predated the later incorporation of natural rock formations found under the pyramids of Khufu, Djedefre, Khafre, and Senwosret II, which also took advantage of geological features to improve their security.[68]

Although the roof of the burial chamber was only theoretically five meters above the ground level surrounding the pyramid, about twenty-two meters of rock still lay between it and the slope of the knoll at its narrowest point. This probably increased to around thirty meters at the knoll's summit,[69] and, due to the knoll's elliptical shape, was much greater elsewhere. This meant that the burial chamber was not only protected by an equivalent thickness of rock cover compared to that of its predecessors, but was also in the perfect position for its innovative descending corridor to enter it at a reasonable and safe angle. This was 1.8 meters square and was also cut into the knoll. Working from the tomb's burial chamber outward, the corridor runs north horizontally for 3.3 m, then ascends at an angle of twenty-five degrees for 19.5 m, where it exits the rock. It would then have run up through the mud-brick superstructure of the pyramid that was built over the knoll, and would have been lined internally with dressed stone. Its total length was possibly seventy meters, and it would have exited the pyramid's face twenty-five meters up from the pyramid's base,[70] thus creating the first raised entrance in a pyramid, and predating the better known example in the pyramid of Meidum.

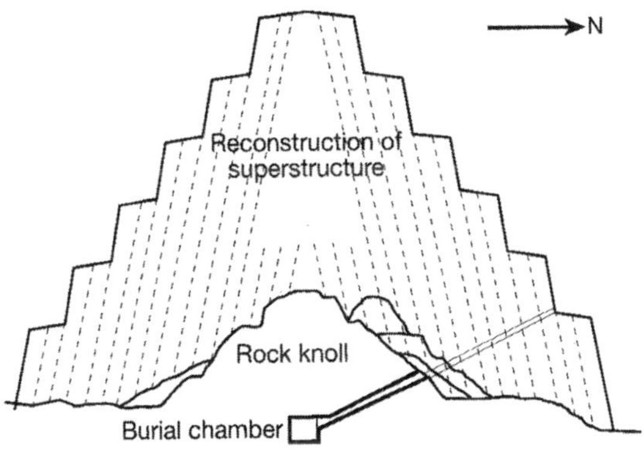

Figure 118. The remains of the Brick Pyramid at Abu Rawash as seen by Lepsius in 1842, and a reconstructed section from the west showing the rocky knoll, core, and conjectural brick superstructure of the pyramid.

Aboveground, according to Swelim, a mud-brick pyramid was built over the whole of the rocky knoll, probably in the form of accretion layers constructed over terraces cut in the limestone. This structure was observed by Lepsius in 1842, who noted that its shape and form were quite clear and that seventeen-meter-high remnants of mud-brick walls from its original structure were still to be seen. He considered it to be the largest of all the brick pyramids and estimated it to be a hundred and forty-five meters across its base and around a third bigger than the northern brick pyramid at Dahshur.[71] Although possibly unfinished, Swelim suggested that the pyramid's inner core may have comprised a rectangular brick structure 150 meters long, a hundred meters wide, and twenty-five to thirty meters high, on top of which a nucleus was constructed against which the rest of the pyramid was built. He noted that it was probably a step pyramid and calculated that the sides of its base may have been about 215 meters and its height anywhere between 107.5 and 150.5 m—comparable in size to the later pyramids of Sneferu and Khafre. This would have made it the largest pyramid constructed to date and probably the fourth largest ever built.[72]

Therefore, with a footprint in the region of 46,225 square meters, it would have offered its substructure a considerable degree of protection from lateral tunneling. In this case it can be estimated that a tunnel would have had to penetrate approximately a hundred and five meters through the structure, of which about thirty meters would have been the limestone knoll and the balance mud-brick, with an even greater proportion of rock on its east–west axis. Moreover, the pyramid's descending corridor would have been well protected from external attack along its length by a combination of the surrounding solid rock of the knoll, a stone liner, and the brick pyramid itself. In addition, the concept of locating its entrance high up in the latter's face was revolutionary, as until then all pyramid entrances were situated at ground level, and, in the case of the pyramids of Saqqara, protected by their funerary temples. This innovation brought several advantages. First, it raised the entrance out of harm's way and made it difficult to find and inaccessible. Second, its new position would have misdirected tomb robbers, who usually would expect an entrance somewhere at ground level. Third, the small cross section of its passage would have made it difficult to locate by *sondage* in any direction. Lastly, attempts to enter the pyramid at this raised level would have been visible and liable to detection.

It should be mentioned at this point that some scholars believe that the sloping corridor in a pyramid functioned as a route toward the circumpolar stars,[73] through which the king could either ascend to the northern sky or alternatively descend to the netherworld.[74] But, as the slope of the corridor was also used to aid with the insertion of plug-stones (at least in later pyramids), it may be that its origins were more practical and that it only had magical functions ascribed to it at later times.[75] Indeed, other scholars have confirmed that the angle of slope is more likely to aid the descent of plug-stones than to point at a particular star, which we shall discuss in the next chapter.[76]

Thematic Analysis: The Architecture and Security Features of Third Dynasty Royal Tombs

With the return of the royal necropolis to the Memphite region in the Third Dynasty, the builders of the first pyramids once again relied on the natural rock geology and their overlying superstructures for the defense of their access routes, together with their new funerary complexes, which now concealed their entrances. Internally, these passageways and shafts, rather than being backfilled with soil and detritus, were now sealed with selected and increasingly resistant materials, such as rubble and dressed masonry, chosen specifically for their defensive properties, and, more rarely, a portcullis. But, by the end of the Third Dynasty the relocation of the royal tomb's entrance to high up in the face of the pyramid signaled a complete change in approach. Now the access route to the royal burial chamber was protected by the mass of the superstructure, its inaccessibility, its blocking and the small cross section of its passage—a basic format that would be retained until the middle of the Fourth Dynasty, and then with variations beyond into the Middle Kingdom.[77]

To secure their substructures from tunneling, the builders of the first three pyramids of the dynasty went much deeper underground than their Second Dynasty forebears to take advantage of the local geology, but each in a different way. Whereas the Step Pyramid relied on a limestone chamber and a deep rubble-filled shaft to protect its tough granite burial vault, in Sekhemkhet's tomb more reliance was placed on the thickness of the living rock, and its sarcophagus became less defensive and more decorative. Similarly, at the Layer Pyramid, the emphasis was still on going deep underground. But, with the Brick Pyramid, the natural mound formed by the underlying rock knoll was exploited to provide a similar level of protection for a burial chamber now set at ground level, which concomitantly also permitted the introduction of the tomb's innovative raised entrance and sloping corridor, and greatly increased the access route's security.

Aboveground, the introduction of stone rather than mud-brick as the principal material for the royal superstructure during the reign of Djoser was undoubtedly a major step forward in improving the security of the underlying substructure. However, the conversion of Djoser's still-vulnerable stone mastaba into a step pyramid increased its defensive capability enormously. Now the depth of cover provided, which was previously limited by the height of the superstructure, rather than its footprint, could be defined instead by the 'hemisphere' of material that could be theoretically formed within it. This economic use of materials to provide the maximum degree of cover in all directions was emulated by Djoser's successors at Saqqara and Zawiyat al-Aryan, who built their step pyramids in a similar fashion. On an even greater scale, the Brick Pyramid at Abu Rawash, although now additionally protecting its innovative descending passage, essentially performed the same function, albeit that much of it was constructed in less resilient mud-brick.

Private Tombs

As mentioned earlier, during the Third Dynasty the design of elite private tombs no longer follows the royal precedent. Pyramid superstructures are now the monopoly of kings, while private tombs still retain their mastaba format. However, while the subterranean burial chamber continued to predominate as the most secure way of protecting the body, the method of accessing it begins to change, and for security reasons we see the stairway being gradually superseded by the stair-shaft and shaft, providing an increased level of protection for the substructure below. As in the previous chapters, we examine only the most noteworthy tombs from the period, which incorporate the most interesting defensive architecture.

Tomb Security in the Delta

Quesna

There are almost no sufficiently published Third Dynasty elite private tombs north of the Memphite Necropolis, with the sole exception of a recently discovered tomb in the central Delta at Quesna, which is dated from a seal impression to the reign of Khaba. Unlike most tombs elsewhere from this period, due to it being constructed on a sand *gezira* (a sandy mound of 'turtleback' elevated above the floodplain),[78] its substructure seems to be that of a pit tomb that may have once possessed a stairway (erosion, alterations and damage by tomb robbers make it difficult to be certain), rather than the subterranean tomb one might ordinarily expect. Aboveground, its substructure was protected by a 14.1 by 6.1 m mud-brick superstructure, which may have had a gravel or sand core.[79] As mentioned above, the tomb had been thoroughly robbed, with evidence at the site pointing to some of the robbing occurring during the Ptolemaic Period.[80]

Tomb Security in Lower Egypt

Giza

The remains of an enormous mastaba known as Covington's Tomb are found on the southerly slopes of the Giza plateau, approximately 1.2 kilometers south of the pyramid of Khufu.[81] It is remarkable both for its size and for its substructure's complex security arrangements, which were accessed via a new type of descent known as a 'stair-shaft,' whose design is considered a 'transitional' stage between the traditional stairway descent and the entirely vertical shaft (Fig. 119).[82] The advantage of this innovation was that it combined the space-saving progressive descent of an abbreviated stairway with the increased depth of a shaft. This was advantageous because with the desire to locate the subterranean burial chamber at ever greater depths to increase its protection, the stair-shaft permitted the substructure to be accessed over a shorter horizontal distance within the protective cover of its superstructure than the descent of a conventional stairway would permit.[83]

Thus, in Covington's Tomb, at the northern end of its large solid mud-brick superstructure, a short eastern descent of four steps took a ninety-degree turn and descended south as a 12.5 m long stairway, which passed through the mud-brick of the mastaba and into the marly limestone strata beneath. It met the southern wall of its adjoining shaft, which was 2.3 m long, 1.26 m wide, and 11 m deep, at a point about 7 m up from the latter's base.[84] To protect the descent and shaft once the burial had been made, it was backfilled with an "immense mass of heavy debris," which so daunted Lorenzo Dow Covington, the tomb's excavator, that rather than clear it he dug a trench to access the stair-shaft from the side. The material used comprised "heavy stones in soiled and caked sand" and "was a constant menace to those using the shaft." Indeed, Covington's drawing of the tomb shows that this rubble ran down into the shaft itself, and thus it is rational to suggest that the remainder of the shaft was similarly filled.

Meanwhile at the base of the shaft, progress into the substructure was barred by an enormous white limestone portcullis set in a large grooved emplacement. Rather than a rectangular block, the monolith

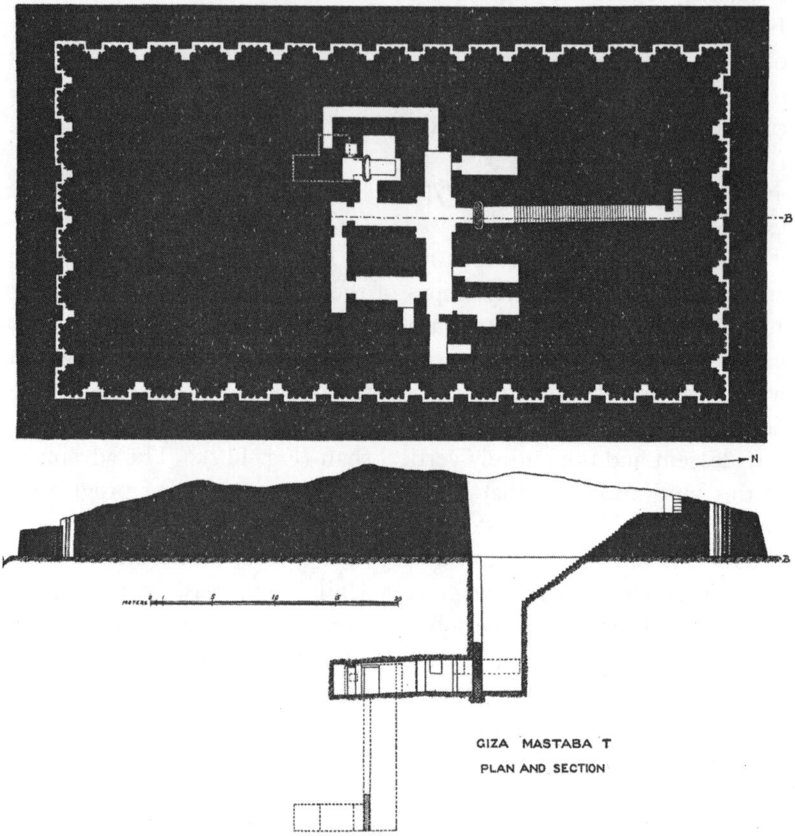

Figure 119. Plan and section of Covington's Tomb at Giza, showing its stair-shaft, solid mud-brick superstructure, and enclosure wall.

was oval in shape with slightly rounded faces, and its top, sides, and base were semi-circular in profile. It was a noteworthy 4.5 m high, 1.92 m wide, and 0.28 m thick and would have weighed around 5.2 tonnes. It was found embedded a half-meter down in the "clay" at the base of the shaft, its top overlapping the entrance door by 1.4 m. Beyond, the substructure consisted of two levels excavated deep into the surrounding "sand stone" and "clay" strata that lie beneath an upper layer of red sand at the surface.[85] The uppermost level leading from the shaft comprised a multi-chambered complex whose ceiling was approximately eight meters below ground level.[86] In one of the western chambers that branched off the north–south axial corridor, a further shaft descended

10.5 m and was filled with a "debris of clay" (*tafl*?), which according to Covington was so solid that it could be cut into and worked under without fear of collapse. At the shaft's base a second portcullis of fine quality limestone, which at 2.33 tonnes was smaller than its predecessor, sat in a grooved emplacement. Beyond it, a short corridor led to a small burial chamber that was 2 m high,[87] whose floor was now approximately 23.5 m from the surface, and which would have been extremely well protected by a roof of marly limestone strata roughly 21.5 m thick.

Aboveground, the enormous solid mud-brick superstructure was 54.97 m long, 27.99 m wide, and decorated on all four sides with a palace façade.[88] It was surrounded by an enclosure wall 3 m thick that was possibly 2.7 m high, but did not permit access to the corridor beyond, which was only 0.25 m wide and thus inaccessible, except for the void formed by the niches.[89] As we mentioned earlier, the entrance stair-shaft was partially built within the brickwork of the inner mastaba, which was at least seven meters high, and possibly as much as ten meters high,[90] and once backfilled was presumably bricked over and concealed. Positioned like a fortress on a hill, the enormous fifteen hundred and thirty-eight square-meter footprint of the structure and its enclosure wall would have offered its substructure excellent protection from tunneling, and its bulk would have made its concealed stair-shaft difficult to find. Even with these precautions, as with many of its contemporaries, it was the tomb's access route, once discovered, that proved to be its downfall. Despite the great depths to which they sank, the tomb was robbed via its shafts in antiquity, thieves having tunneled through the soft rock around both its portcullises.[91]

North Saqqara

While there are a few Third Dynasty private tombs in nearby Abusir,[92] better reported are those from North Saqqara, where there is a greater variety of elite subterranean tombs, variously accessed by stairways, stair-shafts, and shafts.

The first example is S 2405 (Hesyra),[93] which at first glance bears a remarkable resemblance to Covington's Tomb at Giza (Fig. 120). A mud-brick straight staircase descended south from the northeastern quarter of the solid brick superstructure, through its brick mass and a layer of gravel into the rock below, until it met with its five-meter-long by two-meter-wide shaft at a distance of about eight meters from the surface. From this shaft, access could be gained to the first of the substructure's three levels. At this point, a 0.3 m thick portcullis set in a grooved emplacement

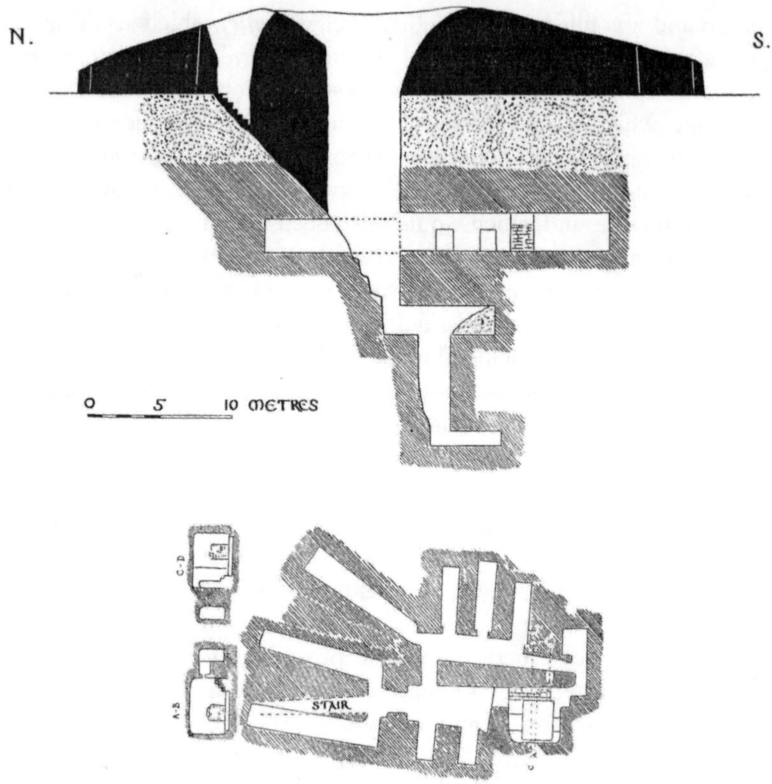

Figure 120. The stair-shaft tomb of Hesyra at Saqqara with its differing substructure levels and solid mud-brick superstructure.

would have blocked access to the first level, but it was damaged and displaced by tomb robbers in antiquity (remarkably, even the remains of the slab can still be estimated to weigh around 1.25 tonnes). Beyond it was a multi-chambered complex that contained the burial chamber, which originally was concealed behind a masonry-blocked doorway.[94] Its floor was set 10.4 m down from the surface and it was protected by a rock and gravel roof 7.9 to 8.2 m thick. From this level, the shaft's south face then descended vertically to the second and third levels, which may also have been burial chambers, or possibly later intrusive additions.[95] These were set at 16 and 23.4 m from the surface, respectively, and would have in turn been protected by roofs 14.1 and 22.5 m thick (similar depths to those reached in Covington's Tomb).[96]

The protective superstructure was equally complex. Built in three phases that probably matched its substructure's expansion, it was initially developed from a simple mastaba with a cruciform chapel that was walled up in the second phase, and provided with a larger chapel with a palace façade. In the chapel, wooden panels depicted Hesyra. More importantly from the tomb security point of view, on the opposite wall painted offering lists provided 'magical' supplies for the benefit of the deceased,[97] which replaced the costly real items[98] and would have been of no interest to tomb robbers. They suggest an underlying reason for the popularity of decorated tomb chapels in later periods: graphic renderings of provisions for the afterlife were effectively unstealable and hence in the long term infinitely more durable.[99] Finally, the chapel was then further extended to create yet another corridor and a statue serdab. Now at over five meters high and approximately forty-three meters long and twenty-three meters wide, the large footprint of the inner superstructure covered most of the tomb's substructure. Its mass protected the stair-shaft that descended through its body, which once sealed (with mud-brick in this case), like its contemporaries at Giza and Beit Khallaf, would have been difficult to find. Despite these mighty defenses and the great depths of the substructure, evidence of continuous exploration throughout the rest of the tomb, and little damage elsewhere, points to the blockings themselves actually being its weakest point.[100]

The next example is S 3050, which was a 'twin mastaba' (a single tomb with two separate offering places, burial chambers, and entrances, usually for the owner and a spouse[101]) from the early part of the dynasty. It incorporated both a stairway and a stair-shaft entrance, located in slightly unusual positions for increased security. In the center of the sixty-meter by by twenty-five-meter superstructure, a stairway led to a single main burial chamber that was carved into the hard limestone (Fig. 121). Its floor was set at nine meters from the surface and was well protected by a rock roof approximately seven meters thick. The second burial chamber was accessed via a stair-shaft located in the northeastern corner of the superstructure, close to the latter's perimeter wall. It was less well defended by a rock cover only around five meters thick. To protect the access routes to the burial chambers, both descents had grooved emplacements at their bases to hold portcullis stones (now missing) and would have had their external entrances concealed by the enormous volume of the sand and rubble core contained within the 4.5 m thick mud-brick walls of its mastaba.[102] But, as is usual in tombs of this type at Saqqara, in spite of all these complex precautions both burial chambers had been plundered in ancient times.

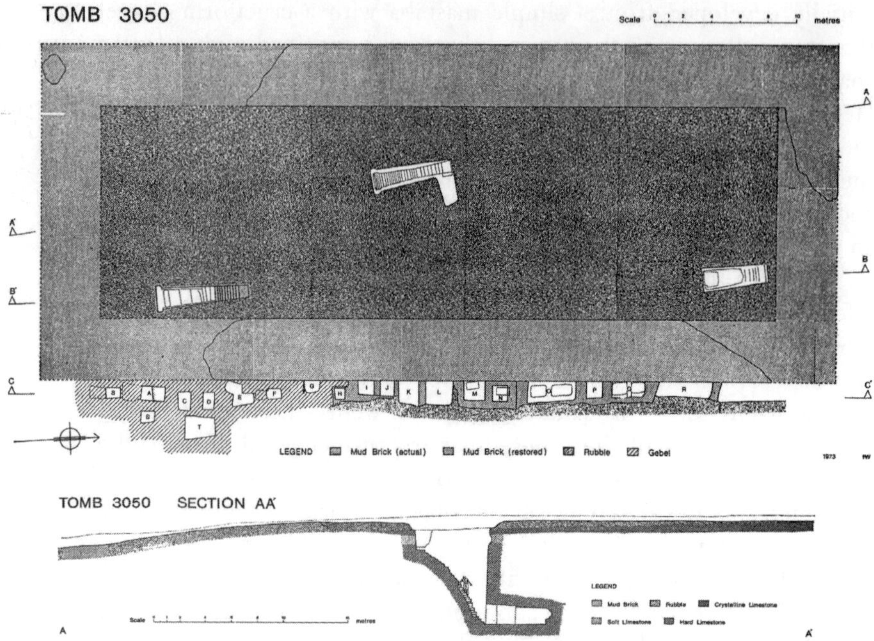

Figure 121. The 'twin mastaba' tomb S 3050 at Saqqara, showing the stairway descent and associated burial chamber in section (N.B. the section drawing is reversed by the draughtsman).

The next tomb, S 3070, is also a 'twin mastaba,' but it lacked stairway access to its substructures. Instead it had a stair-shaft and a shaft to reach its burial chambers, which permits discussion of the security benefits of the shaft as compared to the other two types of access route with regard to concealment from detection and *sondages*. This can be done by comparing the area of the mouth of the 15.1 m deep southern shaft to that of the stairwell plan of its nearby 10.5 m deep stair-shaft (Fig. 122).[103] Although axially placed near the cruciform offering niche, leaving it vulnerable in some respects, the shaft's mouth was just 0.18 percent of the area of the tomb's superstructure in comparison to the plan of the stair-shaft's stairwell, which at 1.95 percent was over ten times bigger![104] This provides a graphic illustration of how once a shaft was concealed under its superstructure's rubble core, it would have been far harder to locate than a stair-shaft.

The benefits did not stop there, as, of course, the cross section of the shaft would also be much smaller, making it harder to find by lateral exploration too. Moreover, its smaller volume would require less backfill to secure it, which was an advantage from the tomb-builders' point of view. On the other hand, for tomb robbers the shaft and its backfill were undoubtedly problematic, as there was always danger of the backfill collapsing when tunneling into it. To overcome that hazard, they would have had either to shore it up or to completely excavate it, which would have been an arduous task. Indeed, Jeffrey Spencer gives us an idea of how much time it might take to clear a shaft. Employing a

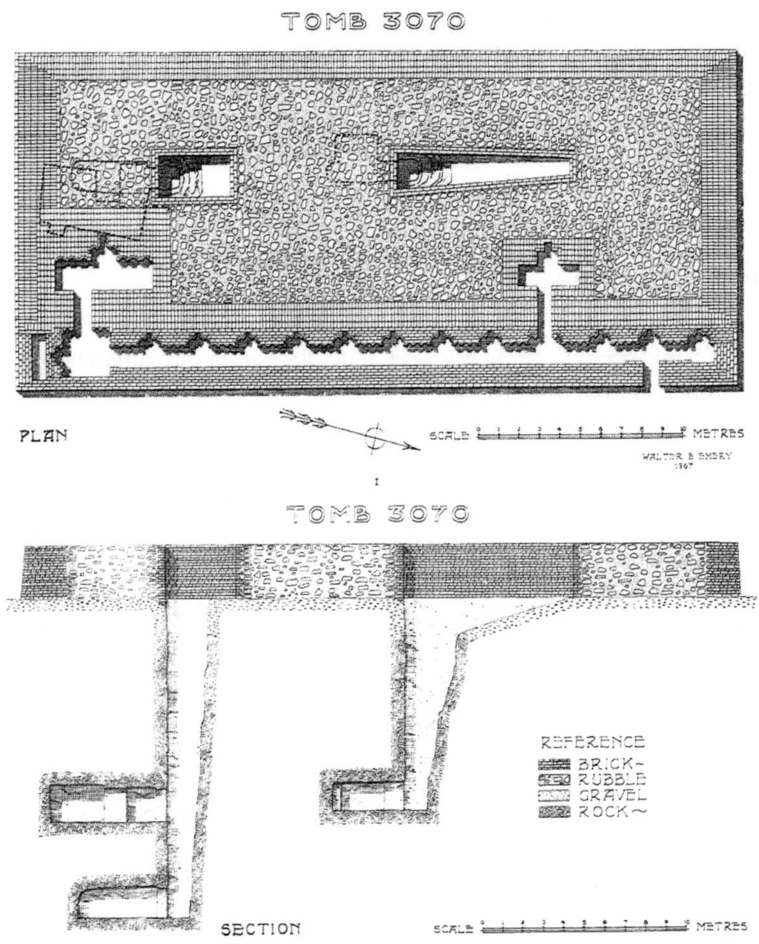

Figure 122. The 'twin mastaba' tomb S 3070 at Saqqara, showing the southern shaft with burial chambers on two levels on the left and the northern stair-shaft on the right with its single chamber.

team of half a dozen laborers to excavate a tomb, it would in his experience take at least a week of hard labor using ropes and baskets to empty a two-meter-square by eight-meter-deep shaft of its fill, and a further few days to tackle the burial chamber itself.[105] Thus it was not a task that could be undertaken lightly, or be easily hidden from view, which implies that it was either done at night or with the collusion or acceptance of whoever was in charge of the necropolis at the time. That notwithstanding, once the shaft was emptied, returning to the surface would be equally difficult, as there would have been little to gain a purchase on, and ropes and ladders may have been required. The overall reduction in the size of the tomb's subterranean entrance in the form of the shaft may have also had other long-term implications. Now, with more room available in the superstructure, which was previously taken up with concealing stairways, there was extra space for offering niches and chapels, the final developments of which, I propose, can be seen in the multi-roomed mastabas of the Fifth and Sixth Dynasties.[106]

Returning to tomb S 3070, below ground, the northern stair-shaft led to a single burial chamber set 10.5 m from the surface, which was protected from above by a gravel and rock roof approximately 8.7 m thick. But better defended from the cover point of view was the lower burial chamber of the two, which ran from the southern shaft. This was protected by a gravel and rock roof 13.5 m thick, although its adjacent upper chamber was somewhat less well secured with only 8.75 m of cover.

The tomb, of course, had been robbed, and judging by the lack of any robbers' tunnels in the excavation drawings, like the majority of rock-cut subterranean tombs at Saqqara, we can be reasonably sure it was plundered via its access route.

On a slightly smaller scale was tomb S 3518, which some suggest belonged to Imhotep, the putative architect of the Step Pyramid, who was later venerated and deified.[107] It was also a 'twin mastaba,' but this time its burial chambers were accessed only by shafts. These were offset west from the superstructure's central north–south axis and just within its perimeter wall. The 9.3 m deep southern shaft was set in about twenty-three meters from its end, presumably to avoid the mastaba's internal offering niche and chapel complex, and the 10.6 m deep northern shaft was approximately 13 m from its respective end (Fig. 123). At the latter's base stood a 2.5 m high, 0.3 m thick, and 2.4 tonne freestanding portcullis that would have blocked the way to the burial chamber. It, in turn, was defended by a nine-meter-thick roof. However, details of

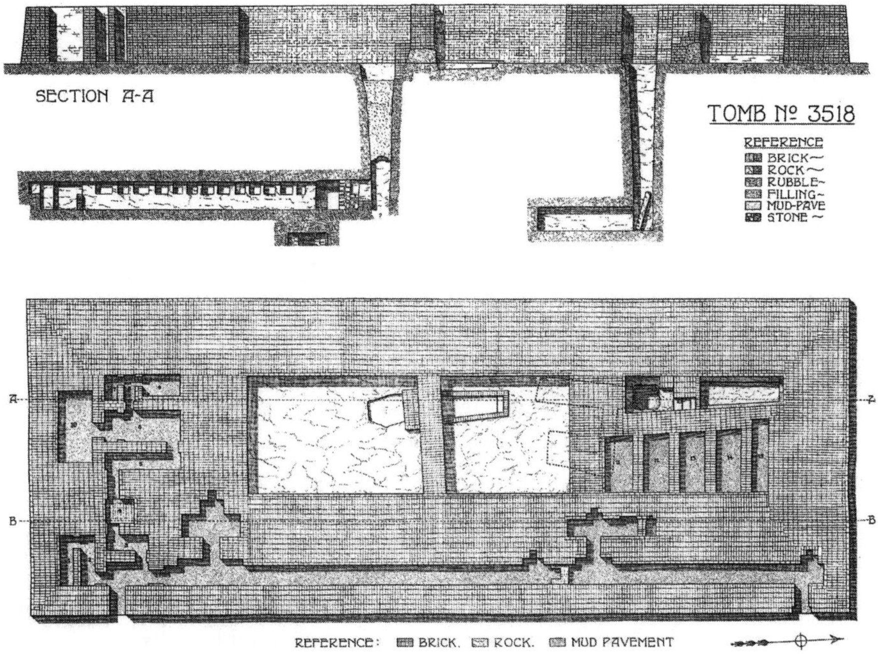

Figure 123. The 'twin mastaba' shaft tomb S 3518 (Imhotep?) at Saqqara. The southern shaft is now part of the baboon galleries.

the arrangement of the southern burial chamber(s) are unknown, as the shaft was interrupted by an intrusive baboon gallery in later times and discovered by Emery to be filled with the original rubble blocking:

> There were indications of the existence of burial chambers leading from the shaft, but these were full of debris which could not be removed because of the overhang of the shaft filling which appeared to be original. Any attempt to dislodge this filling might well have been fatal.[108]

Protecting the whole was the superstructure, which was fifty-two meters long by nineteen meters wide and possibly the best defended example of this type in the necropolis. Its main 4.5 to 5 m thick mud-brick walls created a central subdivided void that contained its 'southern' shaft and at its northern end purpose built magazines and the other shaft. These were all presumably concealed and protected with rubble or gravel, and with the shafts' entrances occupying just 0.54 percent and 0.26 percent, respectively, of the total superstructure area,[109] they would have been difficult to find. Despite this and the perils presented by the shafts' backfill, the northern burial chamber had been plundered. The robbers tipped aside the portcullis, leaving it askew,[110] thus demonstrating the major weakness of the otherwise well defended rock-cut subterranean tombs at Saqqara—their access routes.

Helwan

On the opposite bank of the Nile at the Helwan necropolis, there are few published tombs from the period. One subterranean shaft tomb there does stand out, its notable defenses reflecting a specific response to the geology of the necropolis, and perhaps the wholesale plundering of its Second Dynasty predecessors. Aboveground, the fifty-six-meter-long and 27.4 m wide superstructure of tomb 287.H.6 was constructed of stone (Fig. 124), which is a material rarely used in a private context until the early Fourth Dynasty (see below). Built of small limestone blocks, its exposed eastern face was sloping, but its remaining walls were vertical and enclosed by a mud-brick wall between 3.2 and 6 m thick, whose exterior was further protected by "larger boulders and unshaped stones." Although it is difficult to establish the nature of its inner core, we can be certain that its shaft and substructure would have been well protected from lateral attack by its large footprint, and that the former's entrance would have been difficult to find, as the mouth of the shaft was centrally located within the superstructure and amounted to only 1.17 percent of its area.[111]

Even with a small plan and cross section that made it difficult to locate, once discovered a tomb's shaft could still be vulnerable to attack by robbers in weak geology like that at Helwan, especially when that attack came from within rather than without. In response to this problem, the builders of tomb 287.H.6 lined the eleven-meter-deep shaft with stone blocks on three sides to defend it from attempts to mount a lateral attack through the surrounding gravel. For additional insurance and to prevent the burial chamber from being tunneled into from within the shaft, huge 4.5 m long, 1.1 m high, and 0.3 m thick orthostats were used to reinforce the shaft's entire southern wall (Fig. 124). At the base of the shaft, a 1.5 m high antechamber led to a small burial chamber and two magazines, built entirely out of stone and roofed completely with enormous ashlars a meter thick. These were protected by a further 8.5 m of overlying 'gravel' cover, making it by far the deepest substructure in the Helwan necropolis. Notwithstanding this high level

Figure 124. Plan and section of the stone-lined shaft tomb 287.H.6 at Helwan, with a view of the massive stone blocks that lined the shaft.

of security, Saad reported that the burial chamber had been robbed via its western magazine after several previously unsuccessful attempts to enter via the southern wall.[112]

Tomb Security in Middle Egypt

Lahun

The rock-cut subterranean tombs of the Bashkatib cemetery in Lahun continued into the Third Dynasty, but on the west and north of the cemetery thicker layers of limestone and marl strata permitted shafts to be cut to a more secure depth of 2.4 to 4.6 m.[113] Some of these shafts had multiple burial chambers running from them, such as the intact tomb 769, whose shaft descended to 3.45 m. The two small burial chambers running from the shaft, one blocked off with mud-brick and set at ninety degrees to the other, would have been protected by roofs 2.35 and 2.73 m thick, respectively (Fig. 125). Similarly, the horizontally opposed chambers of the robbed tomb 735 were accessed by a 2.84 m deep trapezoidal shaft and protected by 1.85 m and 1.91 m of cover, although in this instance no blockings were found.[114] As with the earlier

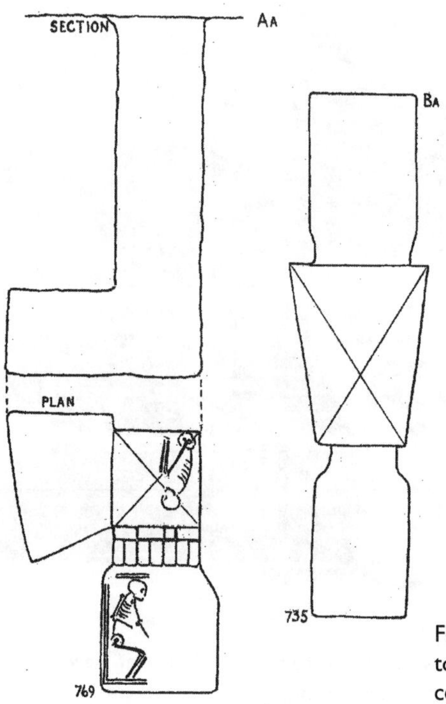

Figure 125. The Third Dynasty shaft tombs 769 and 735 at Bashkatib cemetery in Lahun.

stairway tombs at this site, there is no indication of how the entrances to these shaft tombs were concealed, or whether they were provided with protective superstructures.

Badari

Subterranean stairway tombs were still in vogue in the limestone detritus of Badari Cemetery 3200 at Spur 6, where there are three tombs accessed by long staircases.[115] The descents of tombs 3228 and 3229 were cut in the limestone detritus to a depth of 5.94 m and 6.09 m, respectively (Fig. 126). The former unusually had two burial chambers set one above the other. The floor of the lowest chamber was 5.94 m from the surface and that of the upper was 3.6 m below, leaving the higher chamber protected by a 2.23 m thick roof, and the lower by only the 0.92 m thick dividing layer between them. The upper burial was undisturbed, but the lower had been plundered via a tunnel from the neighboring tomb 3229, whose own robbed burial chamber only had a 4.44 m thick solid roof. But the most notable of these tombs was nearby 3227, whose staircase reached the great depth of

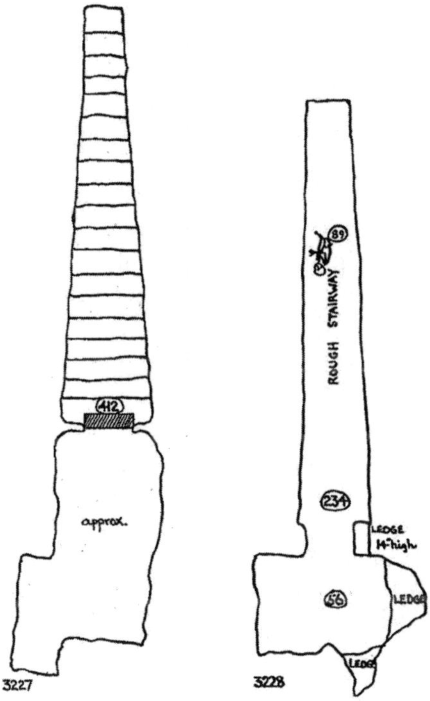

Figure 126. Two of the three Third Dynasty Type IIA tombs at Badari: tombs 3227 and 3228.

10.46 m.[116] Although little is known about the burial chamber beyond, if we assume that its height was similar to that of its neighbors, it could possibly have been the best protected of all, with a roof approximately nine meters thick. Moreover, unlike the other two, at the surface it was surrounded by the remains of a rectangular brick wall 22.25 m long, which Brunton, the tomb's excavator, suggested was an enclosure wall due to its size, rather than the side of a mastaba.[117] However, if these dimensions are considered along with the known sizes of many of the other superstructures in this book, they seem hardly exceptional and may point to a monumental mud-brick superstructure after all. Like its neighbors, tomb 3227 had been robbed, and like 3228 apparently via its stairway, although vestiges of a later intrusive burial suggest that this was not in modern times.

Tomb Security in Upper Egypt

In Upper Egypt, subterranean tombs had finally become the norm for high-status burials during this period, and while their occurence can hardly be considered widespread, there are some notable examples in the Thinite region with remarkable security measures, and some less noteworthy examples besides.

Naga al-Deir

At Naga al-Deir there are examples of both stairway and stair-shaft descents in the gravel-cut subterranean tombs of Cemetery 500-900. As we shall see, these provincial tombs incorporated the very latest security features of the time, but on a smaller scale, albeit not always successfully due to limitations of size and the local geology.

The tapering gravel-cut stairways of tombs N 574 and N 599 descended southeast to a depth of 6 and 4.4 m, respectively, and were both fully concealed and protected by their gravel-cored mud-brick superstructures (Fig. 127). Unlike their burial chambers, which although protected by gravel roofs 4.5 and 3.5 m thick, respectively, were only partially covered by their mastabas at the surface. While there is no evidence of any blockings for N 574 at the base of its stairway, the entrance to the burial chamber of N 599 was blocked by a free-standing 0.35 m thick, 1.1-tonne stone slab backed up by a secondary mud-brick wall.[118] The portcullis was probably secured in place by the wedge-shaped emplacement formed by the stairway. Both tombs had been robbed, but with no evidence of tunneling we can safely assume that entrance was gained via their superstructures and stairways.

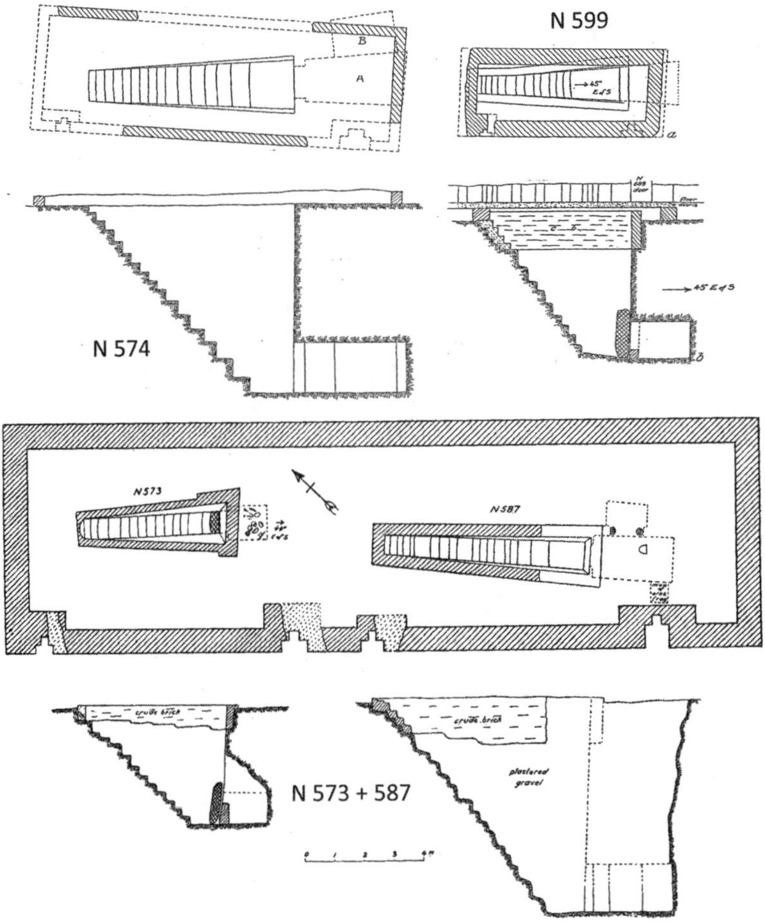

Figure 127. Stairway tombs N 574, N 599, and N 573 + 587 in Cemetery 500-900 at Naga al-Deir.

Better protected was the 'twin mastaba' tomb N 573 + 587, which housed two burials. The smaller of the tomb's two gravel-cut staircases on the southern end (N 573) descended southeast to a depth of 3.85 m, where progress was barred by a freestanding stone portcullis and secondary mud-brick blocking. At the northern end the larger staircase (N 587) reached a depth of 7.1 m, but it was unprotected by blockings at its base (Fig. 127). The small northern burial chamber (N 573) was protected by a gravel roof approximately 2.75 m thick, whereas the larger south chamber (N 587), which can be attributed to the tomb's principal owner, was better defended by 5.1 m of cover. Aboveground, both sets of stairways and substructures were reasonably well shielded by the footprint of their 25.8 m long and 5.6 m wide superstructure, whose 0.8 m thick mud-brick walls contained a gravel core. Both graves were still robbed, and there is evidence that the burial chamber of N 573 was entered by breaking through its roof over the portcullis via the stairwell.[119]

Stair-shafts were also used as access routes in some subterranean tombs in Cemetery 500-900, among which N 593 is probably the best example (Fig. 128). A 3.6 m long crude gravel slope led to a step that joined with a shaft whose base sat at 3.4 m from ground level. Here, a freestanding 0.9 tonne portcullis, found in situ, secured the entrance to the burial chamber, backed up by a secondary mud-brick blocking. The

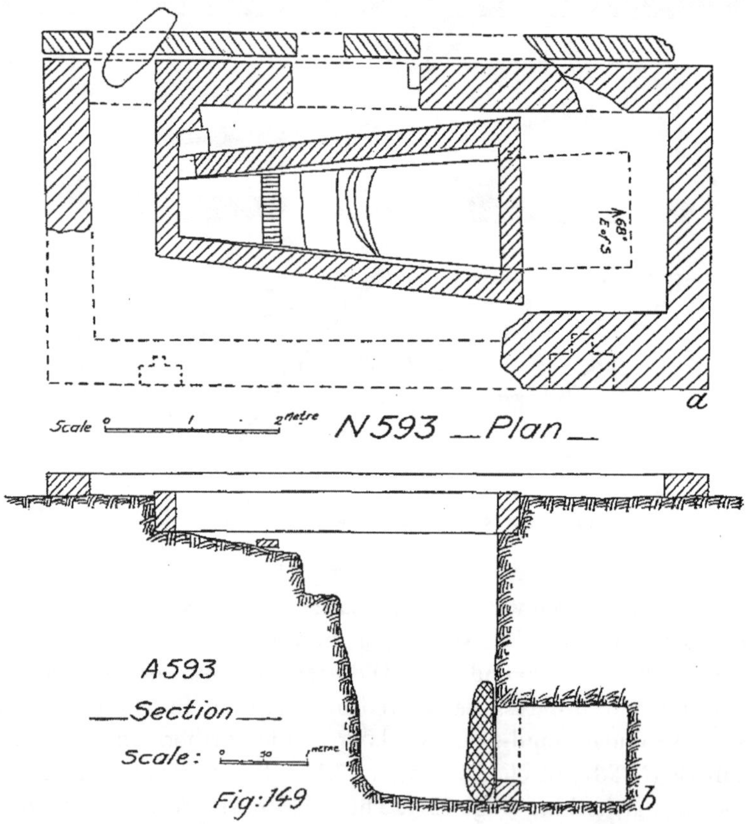

Figure 128. Tomb N 593 in Cemetery 500-900 at Naga al-Deir, with its stair-shaft descent.

chamber was protected from above by around 2.3 m of gravel cover and, unlike some of the stairway tombs discussed above, was entirely protected by the footprint of its mud-brick superstructure, which was 7.6 m long, 3.6 m wide, and contained an unknown core.[120]

In this tomb we can see the theoretical benefits of the stair-shaft in comparison to the stairway, as it enabled the descent and the burial chamber to be completely protected by a comparatively small superstructure. In reality, however, given the modest size of the tomb and its vulnerability to attack due to the comparatively small difference between the size of the mouth of its stair-shaft and its mastaba's plan, the stair-shaft would not have made a great deal of difference. The real security advantages of the stair-shaft were best realized in much larger and deeper tombs, like those we have seen at Saqqara and Giza.

Reqaqnah

Some thirty kilometers south of Sohag on the western bank of the Nile is the necropolis of Reqaqnah, where there are several subterranean stairway tombs that are contemporary with nearby tombs at Beit Khallaf (discussed below).[121] Their multi-chambered substructures are substantially larger than those in Naga al-Deir and are excavated in the compact gravel strata that underlie the loose surface gravel.

Of the two examples we will look at here, the largest is tomb R1, whose substructure was accessed by a combined mud-brick slope and steep staircase that started at the northern end of the substructure and descended south to a depth of 7.95 m. Due to the loose nature of the surrounding desert gravel, the stairwell cutting had sloping sides, which were brick-lined and shored up with thick mud-brick cross-walls that formed barrel vaults over the stairs. This created three 'shafts,' perhaps intended for portcullises and also providing a foundation for the superstructure (Fig. 129). Slightly smaller, but very similar, was nearby tomb R40, whose 8.4 m deep stairway was similarly designed, oriented, and protected.[122]

At the base of their stairways, both tombs were fitted with single portcullises (despite there apparently being provision for more). The largest was that in R1, whose crudely cut 3.2 tonne freestanding stone was around 0.6 m thick, whereas in R40 a deep bottom step formed a rather more supporting emplacement for a slightly smaller 0.5 m thick, 3 tonne stone. Behind their portcullises, the substructures of R1 and R40 varied slightly. The floors of the three chambers of R1 were set at about eight meters from the surface and protected by a gravel roof

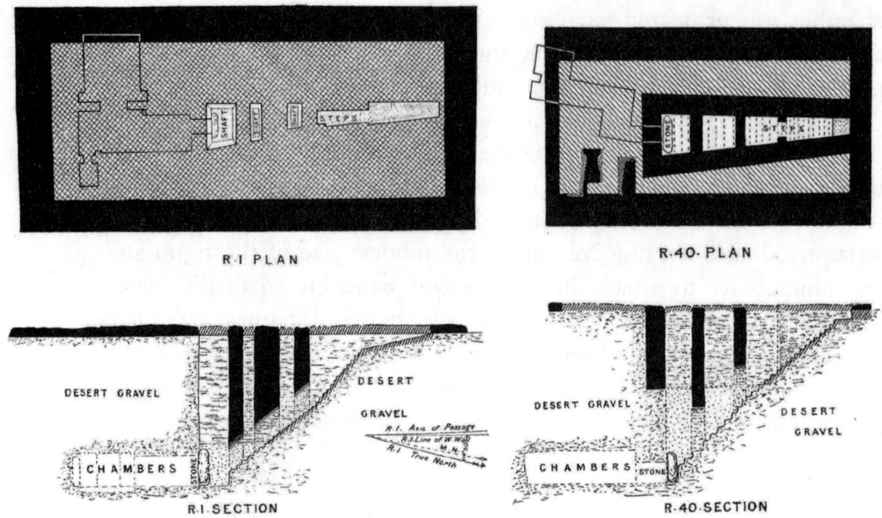

Figure 129. The multi-chambered stairway tombs R1 and R40 at Reqaqnah.

approximately 6.2 m thick, whereas the 'dogleg' chambers of R40 were set at 9 m below the surface and protected by approximately 7.2 m of gravel cover.[123]

Aboveground, Garstang found few extant remains of the tombs' superstructures. However, according to Reisner, they were conventionally constructed, with external mud-brick retaining walls and "filled," presumably with the surrounding desert gravel? What can be ascertained from the plans is that the 1.75 m thick walls of R1 surrounded a core that entirely covered its substructure and stairway, but the 1 to 1.75 m thick walls of R40, and its core, left its underlying burial chamber partially exposed at its southern end. We can speculate that this may have been the reason that Garstang found the burial chamber already entered via a "hole" from above when he excavated the tomb.[124] Indeed, Garstang's description of removing the portcullis from nearby tomb R2 confirms that this was a typical method of attack for robbers in the gravel geology of the necropolis:

> After pulling back the great slab of stone which served as usual for a door a serious subsidence occurred, necessitating the excavation to be renewed from above by removing all the superimposed weight of gravel. It was then found that a plunderer's hole had already been in the same direction.[125]

Garstang's comments both illustrate a typical tomb robber's technique for bypassing such an obstruction and suggest the underlying reasons for the choice of an alternative route.

Beit Khallaf

Roughly 2.5 kilometers south of Reqaqnah and ten kilometers west of Girga lies the necropolis of Beit Khallaf. Among the five published tombs found at this site by Garstang, two are exceptional both for their size and for the complex steps taken to secure them, the remainder being more conventional stairway tombs.[126]

The larger of the two tombs is K1, which stands out for the sheer size of its enormous mud-brick superstructure, which is eighty-five meters long, forty-five meters wide, and eight meters high. Access to the substructure was through the top of this mastaba, via a fifty-seven-meter-long U-shaped staircase built within its mud-brick core,[127] whose entrance was originally probably concealed from view with mud-bricks (Fig. 130). Excavated "somewhat laboriously" by Garstang and his team, it was found to be filled with "hardened Nile-mud," into which were embedded numerous alabaster artefacts.[128] The effectiveness of this type of blocking can be gathered from Garstang:[129]

> The original filling of the stairway had to be hewn out with pick and crowbar. The clearing of the steps was done carefully by hand, but all the more fragile vessels had perished anciently with the throwing in of the tenacious mud filling.[130]

The stairway itself began in the northeastern corner of the mastaba and descended north, then west, until it reached desert level, where a large 0.45 m thick, 4.8 tonne stone portcullis was intended to block further progress into the tomb. With only a single groove for support in its emplacement, the portcullis had fallen askew into the stairway. Beyond it, the stairway descended at thirty degrees south into the gravel beneath and was blocked by a further five increasingly large portcullises slotted into grooves, the first of which was some 0.2 m thicker than its fallen predecessor. The shafts that accommodated them were both built into the mastaba itself and cut through the gravel below. Garstang noted that the width of the grooves and the depth of the threshold cut to accommodate the portcullises ensured that tunneling around or under them would not only be problematic but also invite the collapse of the surrounding gravel matrix. Although the dimensions of the intervening

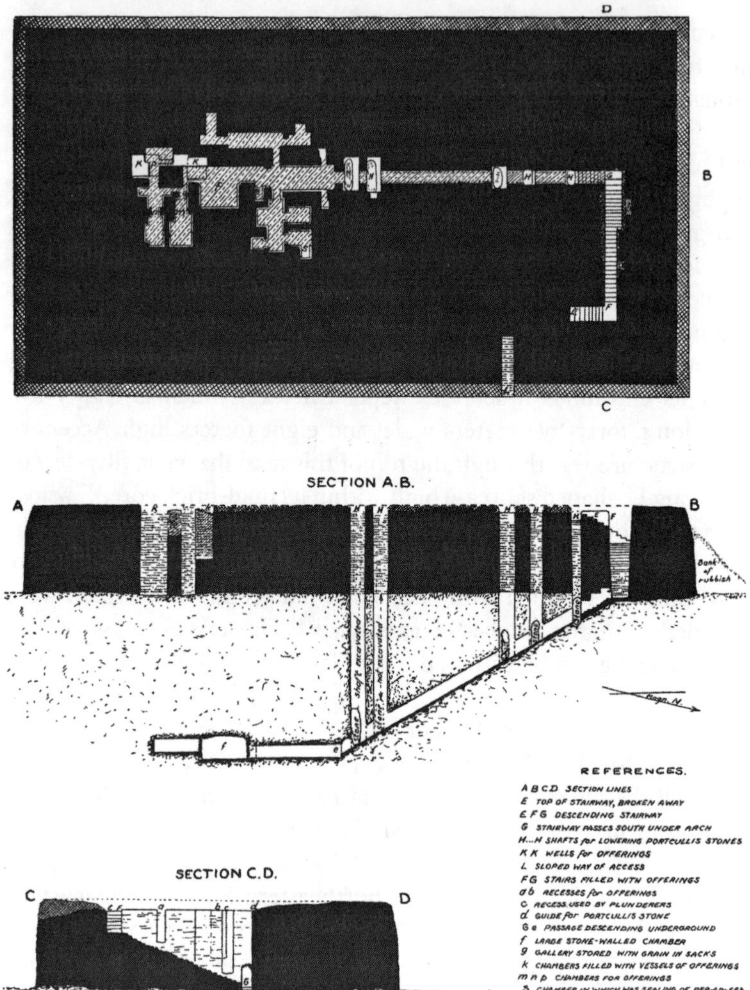

Figure 130. The enormous tomb K1 at Beit Khallaf with its U-shaped stairway, six portcullises, and stone-lined burial chamber.

three stones are not available, at the base of the stairs the final portcullis was a remarkable 5 m high, 3 m wide, and 0.45 to 0.6 m thick. It is estimated to have weighed around 19.5 tonnes,[131] the equivalent of two London double-decker buses.[132] As an added security measure, once these stones were lowered, it seems their "wells" were filled with Nile mud and their openings bricked over,[133] literally cementing them into position and making their removal virtually impossible.

At the end of the stairway's descent, the substructure consisted of an eighteen-chambered complex in excess of a hundred and thirty-seven square meters that stretched for twenty-five meters south of its entrance. Cut into the desert gravel, the floor of its main burial chamber was set at 19.7 m from the surface and would have been protected by a gravel roof approximately 16.7 m thick.[134] Exceptionally for this necropolis, its walls were lined with large blocks of stone, which it could be argued were there to provide protection against lateral tunneling, but were more likely there for aesthetic reasons, as the roof and remainder of the substructure were not similarly lined and remained vulnerable.

Therefore, the substructure of K1 was extremely well defended belowground, and also well protected aboveground by the considerable three thousand eight hundred and twenty-five-square-meter footprint of its thirty thousand six hundred cubic meter mud-brick '*massif*' (a mountainous plateau-like structure) superstructure. Indeed, an idea of the strength of its defenses can be gained from Garstang's description of the excavation:

> A stone pyramid could hardly have been more deceptive or difficult to enter than this great tomb, which, though it had been once previously opened, at this the second attempt, with a gang of sixty men, for seven weeks defied an entrance.[135]

Despite all of this, the team found the burial chamber plundered, as Garstang described:

> After making trial attempts in every likely place, these, most skilful of all tomb-robbers, had descended by means of a hole so small that the workmen had declared it to be the work of a jackal.[136]

What is more, the discovery of two Roman amphorae among the smashed remains, points to the likely date of the deed.

Nearby, the 'twin mastaba' tomb K2 is slightly smaller and contained two staircases within its superstructure (Fig. 131). The northernmost, as in K1, descended in an 18.25 m long U-shape from the top of the northeastern corner of the superstructure, entering the desert gravel on its westward descent, and then proceeded south under a protective 'barrel roofed' mud-brick arch to a depth of 13.4 m from the surface. Here progress would have been barred by a single portcullis, but it had never been lowered, remaining supported by "slender walls

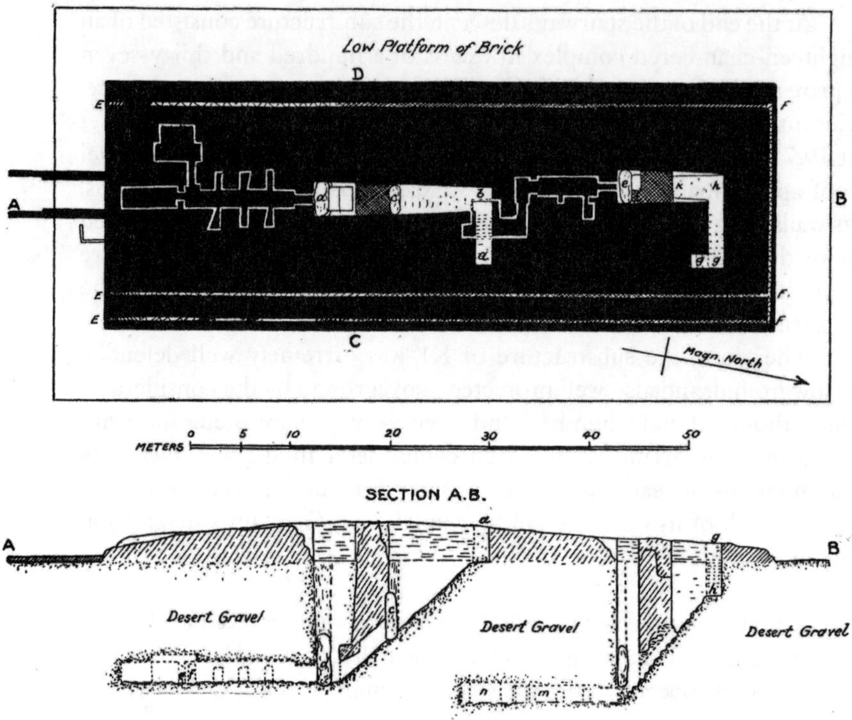

Figure 131. Plan and section of the huge 'twin mastaba' tomb K2 at Beit Khallaf.

of brick" that were intended to be removed to lower it. Beyond the slab, the 'dogleg' shaped burial chamber complex was protected by a twelve-meter-thick gravel roof. The southern stairway entrance, meanwhile, was a simpler L-shape and started midway in the superstructure, descending west and then south through the gravel. It too was partially protected on its descent by a mud-brick vault and obstructed halfway by a portcullis of unrecorded dimensions. Further down, at a depth of 11.5 m, a second large portcullis blocked the entrance to the subterranean complex beyond. At 5.18 m high, 2.43 to 2.74 m wide, and 0.61 m thick, it rivaled that of the largest stone from tomb K1 and would have weighed around 18.5 tonnes.[137]

The burial chamber complex itself was protected by a gravel roof 9.5 m thick, which curiously was less than that of its northern counterpart, and was in turn protected by the 1,531 square-meter footprint of the 64.9 m long by 23.6 m wide mud-brick superstructure. Although the latter was severely denuded, Garstang suggested that as in tomb

K1, liquid mud and mud-brick was used to seal its stairways and portcullis shafts. While it appears the northern complex was never used, the southern contained a burial. However, when Garstang burrowed under the base of its enormous portcullis to gain admittance, he discovered that it had already been robbed in antiquity—the bones and coffin fragments of its owner scattered around the burial chamber, along with a few high-status grave goods. [138]

Al-Kab

Quibell excavated a dozen or so Third Dynasty subterranean stairway tombs at al-Kab,[139] but there are no tomb plans and most were poorly recorded, with the exception of some sketches of the entrance and stairway of an unspecified tomb by Annie Pirie (later Mrs. Annie Quibell) (Fig. 132).[140] Quibell did report that two examples, St. 9 and St. 12, had portcullises. While little detail is available, interestingly from the tomb security point of view, he described the methods used by tomb robbers to defeat the blocking of St. 9:

FROM BELOW LOOKING NORTH   FROM BELOW LOOKING SOUTH

Figure 132. Sketch drawings of the descent and entrance of an unidentified Third Dynasty stairway tomb at al-Kab, whose entrance was originally blocked by a portcullis.

> The stone door of the burial chamber was still standing, the robbers having apparently found it easier to force their way through the comparatively soft earth above the great slab. We were frequently able to trace their mode of entrance, and found that they sank their shafts at the deep end of the stairway, never clearing the long flight of steps.[141]

There is one further example of an elite tomb at al-Kab whose location and architecture are remarkable for Upper Egypt. The superstructure of tomb 274 sits on the summit of the fifty-meter-high Rock necropolis at al-Kab, in a position without precedent in any other Egyptian necropolis (Fig. 133). Its 0.9 to 1.4 m thick mud-brick walls are decorated with a palace façade and an offering niche on its northeastern face, and it is divided internally into two compartments. One functioned as a magazine and was found filled with beer jars, whereas the other enclosed the tomb's stair-shaft.[142] This consists of an L-shaped rock-cut stairway that descends to a depth of ten meters before joining with its 1.75 m square shaft, which descends a further 14.5 m to reach the remarkable depth of 24.5 m. At its base, the comparatively small two-meter-high burial chamber of this tomb was crudely carved in the poor quality sandstone,[143] and is protected by a rock roof approximately 22.5 m thick, which probably makes it the deepest private subterranean burial chamber of the period in all of Egypt (if we accept that Hesyra's lower chamber at Saqqara was a later addition).[144] Although nothing is known about the original rubble backfill that must have filled the shaft,[145] an indication of the quantity of material that would have to be cleared by robbers to gain admittance to the tomb can be gleaned from the three weeks it took the tomb's modern excavators to empty the ten-meter stairwell—before it joined with its shaft! Even so, when finally cleared, intrusive burials indicated that the tomb had been usurped several times, and the excavated backfill was found to be filled with several thousand Old Kingdom vase fragments in assorted stones that were probably the original funerary goods.[146]

Thematic Analysis: The Architecture and Security Features of Third Dynasty Private Tombs

In the Third Dynasty we see a transitional period, during which different types of access routes were introduced in the quest for greater security. While the stairway was retained in Middle and Upper Egypt, indeed perhaps reaching its zenith in the mud-brick *massifs* of the mighty tombs at

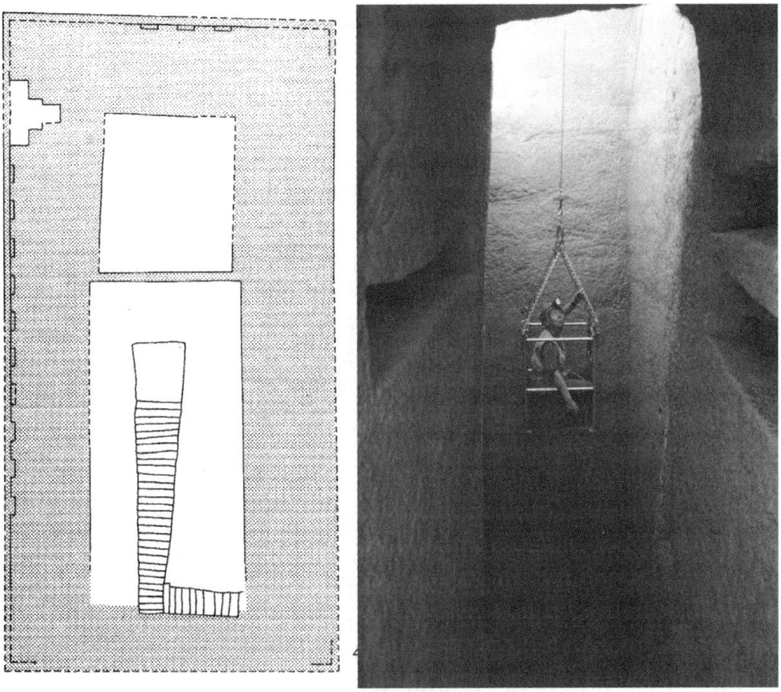

Figure 133. Plan of the superstructure of tomb 274 at the rock necropolis at al-Kab, together with an internal view of the shaft during the tomb's excavation.

Beit Khallaf, the stair-shaft was being experimented with elsewhere. Its design permitted the substructure to be accessed over a shorter horizontal distance within the superstructure than the descent of a conventional stairway would permit.[147] This brought the further benefit that it was smaller and less liable to be discovered by *sondage* than a full-length staircase, which was a desirable feature, better exploited by the simultaneous introduction of the true shaft. The precipitous nature of the latter undoubtedly made tomb robbers' already difficult task of plundering a tomb's substructure far more hazardous than negotiating a stairway. But the real security advantage of the shaft was its reduced plan and cross section, at least in larger tombs. Its smaller mouth was more difficult to locate by *sondage*, especially when concealed by a superstructure, and its smaller cross section was far harder to find by lateral tunneling.

To secure these access routes, the tomb builders still relied on poured aggregates such as soil, gravel, rubble, and detritus, usually in conjunction with man-made blockings such as mud-brick, masonry, and stone portcullises, some of these in enormous quantities or scale. But, other materials were also successfully employed, like the in-depth mud-brick in Hesyra's descent at Saqqara, or the liquid mud in the stairways and portcullis shafts at Beit Khallaf.

The burial chambers of these 'transitional' stair-shaft tombs generally do not seem to have been constructed in weak geology, with the exception of the anomalous examples from the lower status tombs at Naga al-Deir. As the rock-cut examples from Giza, Saqqara, and al-Kab demonstrate, the great depth and resistant nature of the rock geology made tunneling unfeasible. The success of this strategy is apparent, as in those tombs that have been robbed, it is the access route that was usually used to gain admittance. In sites with weaker geology, such as Helwan, Badari, and Beit Khallaf, a burial chamber's protection could be greatly improved by excavating it at greater depths, and on rare occasions lining it with stone.

The superstructures of most Third Dynasty subterranean tombs protected and concealed their substructures and access routes like their Second Dynasty predecessors, with an assortment of sand, gravel, mud-brick, and liquid mud cores, retained and protected by their stout external mud-brick walls. But the high-status tombs at Giza, Saqqara, and Beit Khallaf were often protected by solid mud-brick *massif* mastabas that not only defended their substructures but also sheltered and housed their access routes, which were backfilled and concealed from view. Lastly, at Helwan, for extra protection in the soft geology, we see the introduction of the first stone mastaba in a private context, foreshadowing further developments in the dynasties yet to come.

Concomitant with these changes, a noticeable increase in the space allocated to cult purposes becomes discernible at Saqqara, perhaps reflecting a change in an aspect of the superstructure's role, from part secure storehouse for grave goods to part chapel for the reception of offerings.[148] Moreover, these changes may have introduced further security benefits in themselves, as the magical offerings painted in these chapels would have been unstealable, unlike the treasures previously stored deep within the tomb and indeed sometimes in the superstructure itself.[149]

Conclusion

In response to the wholesale plunder that took place in previous dynasties, several important new security features were introduced during the Third Dynasty that fundamentally altered the design of the Egyptian royal tomb and significantly improved the security of its private counterpart.

At the beginning of the dynasty, the royal burial chamber was set deeper underground than ever before, to better exploit the defensive properties of the surrounding geology. Aboveground, for improved overhead protection, its protective mastaba was built for the first time in solid stone. To improve matters further, the royal superstructure was next transformed from a mastaba into a step pyramid, whose enormous mass and footprint gave a much higher level of protection for its substructure against overhead and lateral attack. Moreover, the tomb's vulnerable access route was now hidden in the pyramid's funerary temple, rather than being exposed and accessible as before. But, by the end of the dynasty, the royal substructure was no longer set deep underground; its burial chamber now being raised up to the surface and sheltered within a protective rock knoll. This enabled a further innovation: so as to increase the protection of the tomb's vulnerable access route, it now took the form of a narrow sloping corridor with a small entrance placed high up in the façade of the pyramid—making the opening, and its passageway, both undetectable and inaccessible.

Among private tombs, security improvements took different forms depending on their owner's status and the necropolis location. Many subterranean substructures, like those of their royal counterparts, were dug deeper to increase their protection, and the surrounding geology provided resistance to attack. Where that proved inadequate, extra reinforcement was occasionally provided internally with stone. More secure access routes were introduced in the form of the stair-shaft, whose reduced plan and cross section was less detectable and enabled it to gain greater depth in a shorter space, as well as the shaft, whose smaller profile and opening was even harder to locate, and indeed more difficult to negotiate.

Aboveground, while many private tomb superstructures retained their recognizable Second Dynasty characteristics, and protected their underlying access routes and burial chambers with mud-brick walls and various inner cores as before, in the weak geology at Helwan, a lone example went 'one better' and for the first time did the same in stone. The tomb builders at some other high-status sites opted for mud-brick *massifs*, which enveloped and secured much of the access route aboveground, their enormous footprints still providing defense for the remainder of the substructure below.

The Third Dynasty therefore saw a seminal change and division in the design of royal and private tombs, which now took completely separate paths of development architecturally. Many increasingly explored and exploited new technologies, such as mud-brick in volume and the working of stone. These innovations were to be refined and improved on in the following dynasty, the application of which is fully explored in the next chapter.

PORTCULLISES

Although the architecture of the external access route in tombs from the mid-First Dynasty until the early Fourth Dynasty evolved progressively from stairway to shaft, it is evident that in the majority of cases the basic design of the portcullis and its emplacement remained largely unchanged. Usually made of limestone, which was the material of choice for all stone portcullises, royal and private, right up until the reign of Khufu,[150] the mechanics of its use remained essentially the same within stairway or shaft, insofar as gravity lowered it into place and a close fit was needed to follow the stone's profile and ensure a tight and secure seal. This in turn governed the design of the tomb's access route to a certain degree, as its architecture would need to cater both for the portcullis stone and its direction of travel. In addition, the side walls of a passageway, stairwell, or shaft often formed or housed a portcullis' emplacement, and needed to be able to accommodate it. Moreover, when a slab was placed before a substructure's entrance, the wall above needed to be in the vertical plane to allow the slab to slide down or be laid against it. Indeed, long after the use of the portcullis was discontinued, some of these architectural elements remained a feature of access route design, the original reasons for their inclusion having perhaps been forgotten over time.

From the security point of view, the inclusion of a portcullis in a tomb's entrance passage, stair, or shaft offered several benefits. The first, and probably the most important, was that it permitted secure closure of the substructure immediately after the burial, thus preventing interference with its contents before the access route was closed with an in-depth static backfill or blocking. Second, in the event that the backfill was compromised, it formed an additional layer of protection, which in terms of its resistance to penetration and removal was a far more robust defense than a mud-brick or masonry wall. But the strength of its defense was always dependent on other factors:

the portcullis' weight, which prevented it from being easily moved out of position; the slab's thickness and density, which affected how easily it could be penetrated or broken; and the sturdiness of its surrounding emplacement and geology, which were often the alternative subject of a robber's attack when the portcullis proved too heavy or strong to overcome.

The Lowering of Portcullises

Throughout the book, wherever possible, I have discussed the methods used to lower portcullises, but they are worth summarizing. Whether a stone was lowered before a tomb's superstructure was built remains unclear, although some have suggested that large slabs would have been too heavy to maneuver over a mud-brick mastaba.[151] On the other hand, we know that mud-brick ramps were perfectly capable of supporting large loads, as they were used in the construction of some pyramids and such mighty structures as the first pylon at Karnak.[152]

Either way, the portcullis had to be lowered into position somehow, and to enable this to happen it would appear from the cemeteries of Abu Rawash, Dahshur, Saqqara, Helwan, and Meidum that some portcullises were drilled or grooved to accept lowering ropes. Judging by the hole and groove sizes in these stones, the ropes would have been of sizeable dimensions, and as an ancient rope of 5.7 cm in diameter could carry 6 to 7 tonnes of weight, with a breaking point of 20 tonnes,[153] it is evident that the majority of the portcullises in the discussion could have been easily lowered by just a single rope. The position of the holes at the top or bottom of the stone seems to have varied, presumably at the whim of the tomb's architect, as for example in tombs X and S 3500 at Saqqara, whose stones were drilled at the top and bottom, respectively.[154] However, as we have seen, some portcullises had several holes and/or grooves, which suggests that more than one rope was used on many occasions. In the case of larger stones or those in awkward situations, multiple ropes were presumably employed. Among those stones that lacked anchor points, it must be assumed that they were bound in some form of harness or noose, such as in the Helwan tomb 809.H.3, which had notches carved for lowering ropes in its upper half and base.[155]

In either case, as the stones needed to move in the vertical plane and the workforce would be hauling on the horizontal plane, this implies that some type of framework or fulcrum must have been employed over which these ropes could pass and change direction. This may have taken the form of a wooden framework built over the shaft,[156] or perhaps a bearing stone such as the basalt example found by Selim Hassan at Giza.[157]

An alternative method of lowering a portcullis was by removing stone or mud-brick packings placed under it, such as those found at Beit Khallaf and Meidum (although they equally could have been used to raise it[158]). The stone would initially have been manually placed in position, or lowered by ropes, onto the packing material. Presumably in those staircase tombs that lacked grooved emplacements in which to slide the stones, the slab could just be carried down the stairway and placed in position on top of the packings. Once the slab was in position the packings most probably would have been removed one by one to permit a controlled closure. However, it could just be that the packings were used to bear the weight of the stone and relieve the tension on any lowering ropes until the final moment of closing, in a similar manner to the wooden beams found in the private tombs at Dahshur. Another method that may have been used to lower the slab in a shaft, or a mud-brick 'well' built for the purpose, was to place it on a bed of sand and then slowly release the latter to lower the stone into its emplacement,[159] which it has been suggested was the method used in the tomb of King Ninetjer.[160]

The Importance of the Portcullis Emplacement

The most secure portcullis emplacements over the period we have discussed were the grooved type. These were formed on either side of the passage, stairway, or shaft that the stone was intended to block and performed two functions. They provided a channel for the stone to slide in, which ensured that it went where it was intended and was close up against the entrance it was blocking, forming a tight seal. They also prevented the stone being tipped askew by tomb robbers. However, their success at preventing this kind of attack would have been limited by the strength of the geology into which they were cut, or the material of which they were built. A similar function can be ascribed to those subterranean tombs with tapering staircases, especially at Helwan and Lahun, where their wedge-like shape probably provided both the stone's guide and its support, again within the limitations of the surrounding geology. Least secure of all would be those tombs where the stone was entirely free-standing, as all that kept the stone in place would be its weight and the surrounding backfill. Once dug away, as is evident in some tombs at Abusir, Saqqara, and Meidum, this allowed the slabs to be easily dislodged by tomb robbers.

7

Pyramids and Plug-Stones: Security Innovations in the Early Fourth Dynasty

In the previous chapter we saw how the architecture and security arrangements of the royal tomb in the Third Dynasty took a different path of development to those of the private tomb, the step pyramid providing the king's burial with both an unsurpassed level of protection and an exclusive and distinctive monument. The private tomb retained its external mastaba form, albeit sometimes on a massive scale, but benefited from deeper subterranean substructures entered by less detectable and therefore more secure access routes.

In this penultimate chapter we shall discuss how in the early Fourth Dynasty the need to protect the royal sepulcher in new necropoleis with weaker geologies drove much of the architectural development of the royal pyramid, and how correspondingly the builders of private tombs in the associated nucleus cemeteries of these pyramids developed ever more complex security measures in response to similar problems.

Royal Tombs

The Pyramid of Meidum

With the accession of King Sneferu, once again the royal necropolis was relocated, this time to Meidum at the entrance to the Fayum oasis, where work began on the king's new pyramid[1]—the first of three built for him.

The pyramid of Meidum was built in several stages on a leveled rock base. A north–south oriented trench was dug in this base to house the lower end of a descending access corridor and horizontal passage whose entrance began high up on the façade of the pyramid, like that of the earlier Brick Pyramid at Abu Rawash (Fig. 134).[2] The pyramid itself initially comprised seven steps constructed from an inner core of mortared limestone masonry and six sloping accretion layers (E1). This

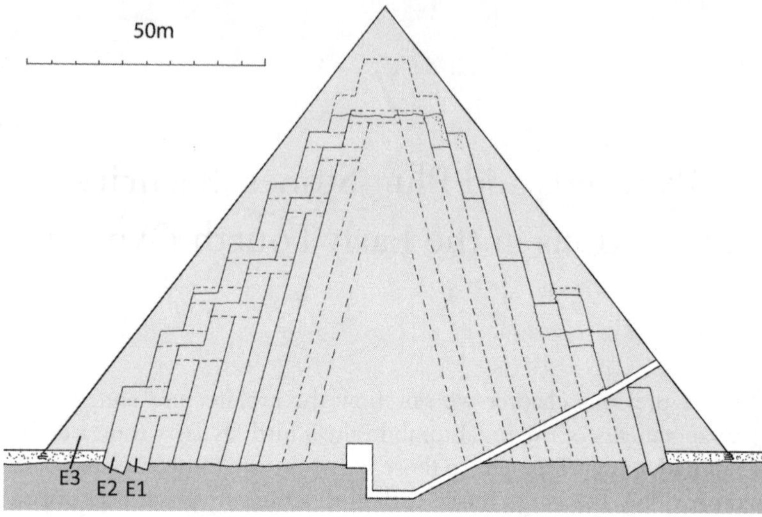

Figure 134. Section of the pyramid of Meidum looking west, showing the internal layers before it was converted into a 'true' pyramid.

was later expanded by adding another layer to form an eight-stepped pyramid (E2). Both were intended to be finished structures in their own right. In a final construction phase undertaken while the pyramid's replacement was being constructed at Dahshur (see below),[3] these steps were filled in and covered with limestone cladding that formed the first 'true' pyramid (E3),[4] the exterior of which has long since collapsed,[5] and whose shape is still the subject of much scholarly debate.[6] It can certainly be argued that its new smooth faces would have made it more difficult for robbers to scale and attack.

To gain admittance to the interior, the pyramid was entered high on its northern face, 18.5 m up from the pyramid's pavement.[7] The funerary temples that once covered its predecessors' low-level entrances at Saqqara were now completely relocated to the pyramid's eastern side (Fig. 135).[8] To disguise its whereabouts, the mouth of the 1.58 m high and 0.81 to 0.87 m wide entrance was cleverly concealed by plug-stones that were shaped to appear part of the stone cladding of the pyramid. This was achieved by tapering the lower two layers of the three courses of stone blocks that flanked the internal edges of the doorway, so that similarly shaped plug-stones would then wedge tightly into the corridor and be prevented from slipping within.[9] Additionally, to protect the latter and its adjoining descending corridor

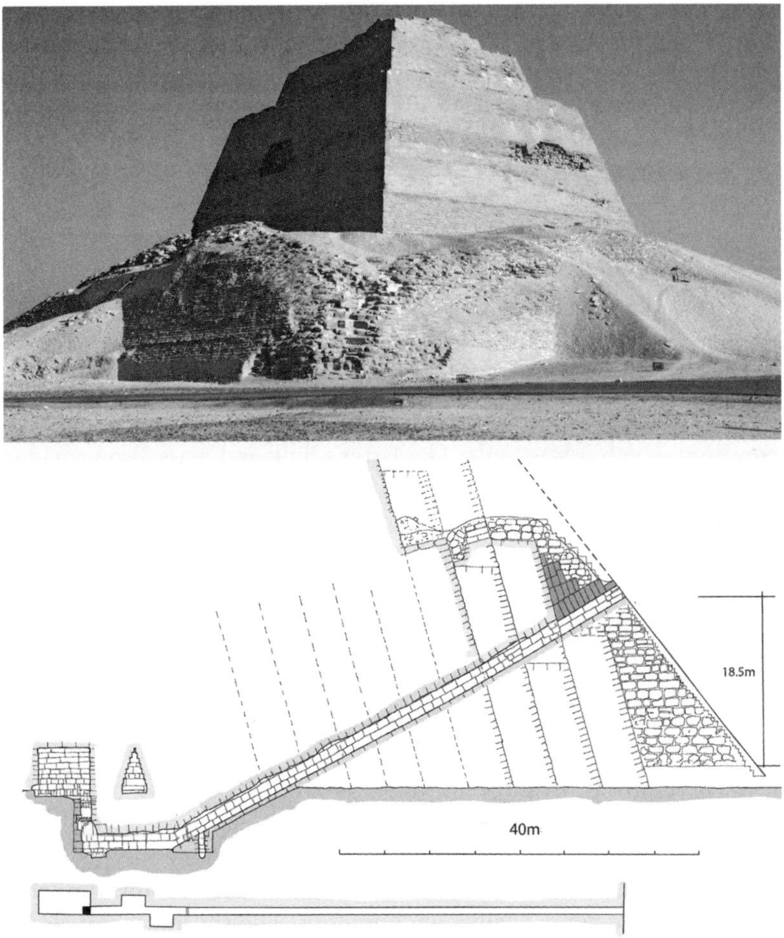

Figure 135. Photograph of the pyramid of Meidum in recent times and close-up section of its substructure, descending corridor, and raised burial chamber looking west. The large reinforcing stones over the entrance are marked in dark grey.

from external attack, the roof from the entrance down to the outer edge of the last stage of the original step pyramid (E2) was reinforced by nine 2.1 m high stone lintels, which were further reinforced by four layers of similar stones that reduced in thickness as they rose in height.

The masonry-lined corridor, which at around 1.6 m high and 0.85 m wide[10] was smaller in section than that of the Brick Pyramid, and probably designed to accept plug-stones,[11] descended at between twenty-seven degrees thirty-six minutes and thirty degrees twenty-three minutes to enable the latter's safe installation in a controlled descent.[12] It runs 58.75 m down into a trench excavated in the rock, until it levels out and proceeds horizontally for another 9.2 m until its end. Protected from attack by its 0.5 m thick stone floor and one-meter-thick walls, the horizontal passage is flanked by two niches that once contained blocking stones, which probably filled the whole space and obstructed access to the vertical shaft which lies at the end. This ascends 6.65 m into the floor of the limestone burial chamber, which was set at ground level,[13] making it difficult for robbers to detect by exploratory tunneling through the underlying soft rock (see below).

For the first time in an Egyptian tomb, the burial chamber's roof was corbeled to relieve the superincumbent pressure from the pyramid core into which it was built. The latter's bulk and mass also provided the chamber with its main defense from aboveground attack.[14] Thus, the core effectively formed the man-made equivalent of the Brick Pyramid's rocky knoll, but built in stone, which coincidentally also sheltered the majority of the descending corridor in a similar manner. This was necessary because, as we shall see in the remainder of the chapter, unlike the limestone geology of the earlier royal necropoleis of Saqqara, Zawiyat al-Aryan, and Abu Rawash, the soft nature of the crumbly underlying rock at Meidum made tombs built in it vulnerable to tunneling and undermining.[15]

Therefore, at Meidum the king's burial (if it had been completed) would have been protected by its 144.3 m long, 144.3 m wide, and 94.5 m high pyramid,[16] which was effectively a 638,733 cubic meter 'mountain' of solid limestone,[17] whose 20,592 square-meter footprint offered it exceptional defense against undermining. The shortest point to the burial chamber from the edge of the pyramid's base was approximately sixty-seven meters.[18] Indeed, confirmation of the success of these defenses is that no robbers' tunnels are evident either within or under the structure. That notwithstanding, despite lacking a burial (there was no sarcophagus[19]) the pyramid was plundered in ancient times via the usual route in pyramids, its descending corridor, but of course only after its plug-stones and blockings had first been laboriously removed.[20]

The 'Bent' or Southern Pyramid at Dahshur

Abandoning Meidum,[21] Sneferu relocated the royal necropolis at Dahshur and began work on a second pyramid.[22] Built on an even larger scale than its forerunner at Meidum, the pyramid was also designed to protect

Figure 136. The Bent Pyramid at Dahshur (photograph by the author).

its aboveground burial chamber and descending corridors by enshrouding them in stone. Its footprint was also intended to prevent undermining in the soft shale of the necropolis (Fig. 136). Externally, the pyramid's smooth sloping sides comprised of layers of inclined stones built at a comparable angle to those of the refaced pyramid of Meidum, making it hard to climb and its entrance more difficult to detect. However, the poor quality of the underlying shale led to cracking and subsidence in the substructure during construction, which was aggravated by its inner core of rough stone blocks that were loosely bonded with debris and *tafl* mortar. To remedy these problems an extra layer of masonry was used to girdle the outer section of the existing structure. The angle of slope of the upper half of the structure was also decreased in an attempt to stabilize it,[23] which resulted in the pyramid's characteristic appearance. Moreover, to gain further strength and stability, rather than being inclined its stone courses were now laid horizontally.

Internally, the tomb seems to possess two apparently separate substructure systems set at different levels and orientations, each of which are entered by independent access routes.[24] But this is not the original layout, which was planned to be similar to that at Meidum. Initially the main entrance was set 11.8 m up in the northern face of the pyramid, from which a 1.1 m high, 1.06 m wide, and 79.53 m long corridor descended at an angle of twenty-five degrees twenty-four minutes[25] to the tomb's lower substructure. Once the pyramid was sealed, this corridor was probably blocked with plug-stones and its entrance concealed from view (Fig. 137).[26]

At the base of the corridor, the lower substructure was built below ground level in a 22.4 m deep trench dug in the easily cut shale deposits that lay under the thin layer of sand and gravel at the site.[27] A narrow corbeled antechamber ('A') sat at the bottom of the trench and permitted

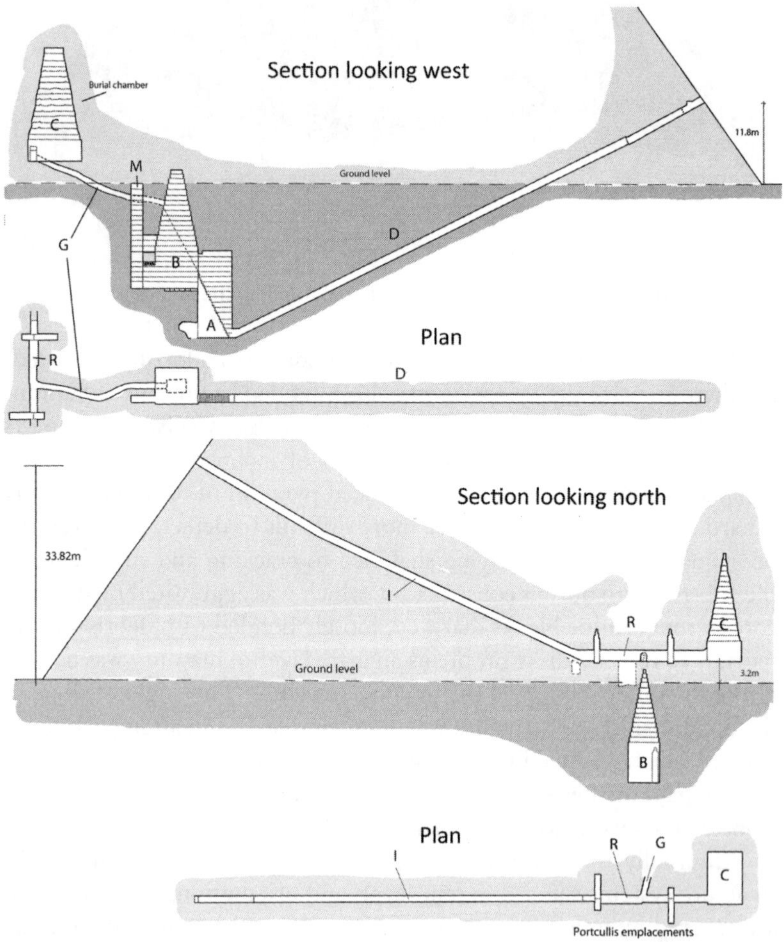

Figure 137. Plans and sections of the two substructure systems in the Bent Pyramid. Above: The northern descending corridor and its antechambers. Below: The western descending corridor and the burial chamber.

access via a stone block staircase to the 17.3 m high north–south oriented lower chamber 'B,' whose roof, which projects just a couple of meters above ground level, was corbeled on all four sides to relieve the pressure from the surrounding rock and the overlying superstructure.[28] At the lower chamber's southern end, and exactly at the central axis of the pyramid, is a fifteen-meter-high unfinished blind ascending shaft 'M,' which like the vertical shaft in the pyramid of Meidum stops at ground level and was perhaps intended to link to the upper chamber 'C,'[29] thus possibly making both chambers 'A' and 'B' antechambers to chamber 'C' rather than a separate system.[30] Structural problems encountered during construction perhaps brought the connection of 'B' to 'C' via shaft 'M' to a halt. Instead, both chambers 'B' and 'C' were linked at a later date via a tunneled passage 'G' that was created within the solid masonry after the original structure was finished.[31] This runs between the apex of the upper part of the lower chamber 'B' and the horizontal corridor 'R,' which leads to the upper chamber 'C.' Its purpose is unknown, but it could have been to act as a substitute for the aforementioned unfinished shaft 'M,' which may have been intended to connect the chambers but was never finished. It could also have been an escape route for the tomb's builders, like that in the later pyramid of Khufu.[32]

The upper chamber 'C,' which was presumably intended to be the burial chamber due to its better defenses, is built and oriented in a similar manner entirely within the body of the superstructure. As in the pyramid of Meidum, however, it is set much higher, with its floor above ground level, about a meter higher than the apex of the lower chamber. It is 16.5 m high and corbeled like the lower chamber.[33] Internally it was found filled with masonry blocks reinforced with cedar beams that may have formed part of the burial chamber's security, similar to the limestone blocks that protected the sarcophagus in the maneuvering chamber in the South Tomb at the Step Pyramid,[34] but no coffin or sarcophagus were found among them.[35]

However, other arrangements had already been made to install the royal burial via a new and even more secure access route from the western face of the pyramid. Its entrance sits at an impressive 33.32 m from the pyramid's base and 13.7 m off center; its opening concealed in the face of the pyramid by a casing block that rendered it undetectable from the outside.[36] From there, a 1.05 m wide, 1.1 m high, and 67.66 m long stone-lined corridor descends at an angle of thirty degrees four minutes. Smaller in section than the corridor in the pyramid at Meidum, it was originally completely blocked with plug-stones, which had been plastered individually as they were inserted from outside.[37] The plaster was probably used both as lubrication to aid the stones' descent and as a mortar to secure them in place. At its end, where the passage levels out, the corridor proceeds for a further 2.4 m until the tomb's first enormous portcullis bars the way. This was housed in an unusual corbeled emplacement (Fig. 138) that incorporates a thirty-five degree internal ramp, down which the massive limestone slab was designed to slide. When originally closed, the slab was plastered on both sides and presented the appearance of a solid wall viewed from the approaching passage, but it was broken through at the top by tomb robbers in antiquity. Beyond this, a twenty-meter passage led to a second portcullis and emplacement whose ramp sloped in the opposite direction, perhaps to confuse robbers. For unknown reasons, its stone was never lowered and remains in situ, propped up with a piece of timber.[38] Both portcullises were 0.75 m thick and would have weighed about 5.4 tonnes apiece.[39] Although the original passage floor between the portcullises is now missing, a discolored line left on the closed portcullis marks its original level and indicates that it would have concealed the base of the stone, which would have made it extremely difficult to lever the stone from its emplacement.

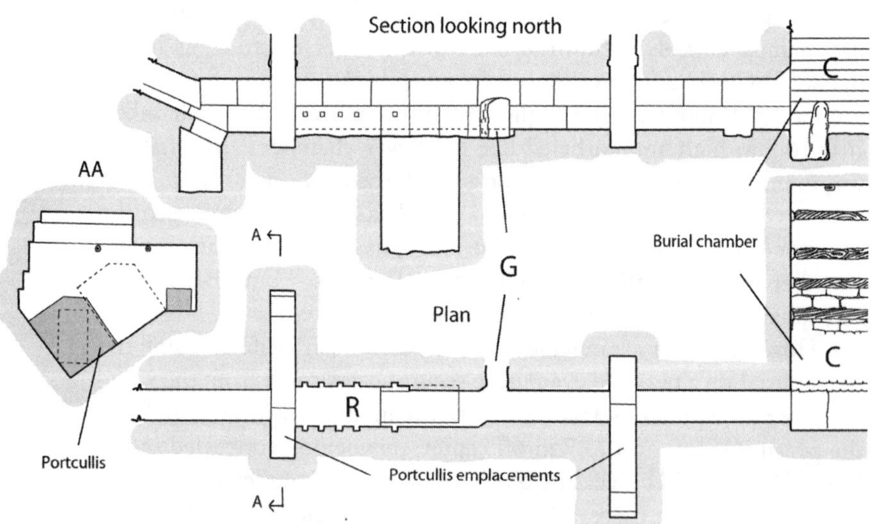

Figure 138. Close-up plan and section of the portcullis arrangements in the Bent Pyramid, which run from the western descending corridor and lead to the burial chamber.

Approximately 189.5 m long, 189.5 m wide, and 104.7 m high, the Bent Pyramid directly protected its upper burial chamber and western descending corridor with 1,237,040 cubic meters of stone, which is nearly double the volume of its predecessor at Meidum.[40] From the southern upper slope of the pyramid, it would have required a robbers' tunnel around fifty-two meters in length at its shortest point to penetrate the burial chamber. In addition, its enormous 35,910 square-meter footprint would have sheltered the subterranean elements of its northern descending corridor and antechambers from lateral tunneling, as it was now a minimum of around 85 m from the substructure to the pyramid's outer edge, which is approximately 25 percent further than in the pyramid of Meidum. Regardless of these defenses, the tomb was entered in antiquity and thoroughly searched. As is usual in pyramids, this was done via its access route, the broken remains of plug-stones being found by John Shae Perring in the northern descending corridor in 1837.[41] Indeed, during his later excavations Ahmed Fakhry found a mummified bat dated to the Ptolemaic Period buried in the tomb's western descending corridor, which provides a *terminus post quem* (earliest date at which a find can be accurately dated) for such intrusions.[42]

South of the main pyramid, a satellite pyramid was built, which is of note because it contains a falling plug-stone system that predates the one in the grand gallery of the Great Pyramid. The structure was entered by a descending passage whose entrance was probably closed and concealed with a casing block (Fig. 139). From its base, an ascending passage rose that led to the pyramid's 'burial chamber,' which had its floor set 2.4 m above ground level and a corbeled roof. It was thus protected by the mass of its superstructure in a similar fashion to the main pyramid. To secure the chamber, within the upper half of the ascending passage four plug-stones were retained by two wooden props attached to ropes leading outside the pyramid. When the time came, the ropes were pulled so that the blocks could descend under their own weight to the bottom of the passage. Ingenious as this mechanism was, in the event only two blocks arrived in their intended positions, the upper two having jammed halfway down during their descent, probably as a result of the angle of inclination being too shallow or a lack of lubrication.[43]

The Red or Northern Pyramid

Presumably unhappy with the problems experienced at the Bent Pyramid, Sneferu decided to build a third pyramid at Dahshur, which is thought to be the final burial place of the king.[44] To avoid the structural

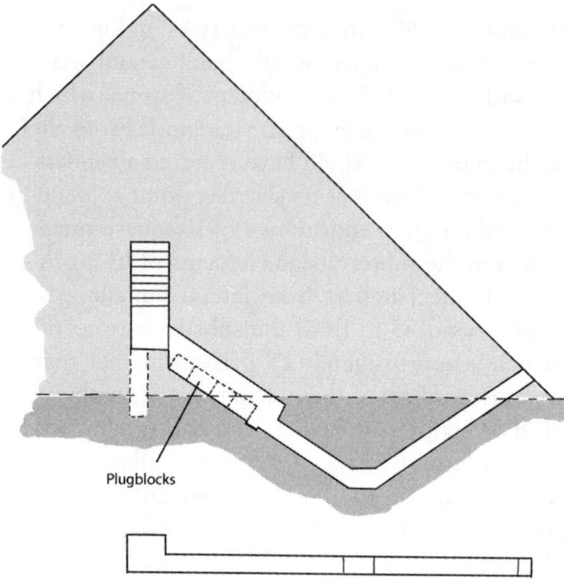

Figure 139. Section view of the Bent Pyramid's satellite pyramid showing the 'falling block' plug-stone system.

problems experienced previously, the Red Pyramid was built on firmer ground four kilometers to the north that consisted of silicified sand and gravel layers. In addition, for stability the structure was built with a shallower slope similar to that of the upper half of the Bent Pyramid, and its masonry was laid in horizontal courses. Although it was of a similar height to its predecessor, as a result of the gentler incline the pyramid had a much larger footprint, which spread the superincumbent load and relieved pressure on the underlying geology. The tomb's descending corridor and antechambers, rather than being set below ground level as at Meidum and South Dahshur, were set further up in the fabric of the pyramid, along with the burial chamber, which concomitantly enabled its swifter construction.[45]

The substructure was accessed by a single descending corridor from the north, whose entrance was 3.81 m east of the center of the pyramid and 28.65 m up from its base (Fig. 140). From it the 1.05 m wide, 1.2 m high corridor, which was lined and paved with stone, descended at an angle of twenty-seven degrees fifty-six minutes for 62.63 m, where at its end a 7.41 m horizontal passage led to the first of the tomb's three internal chambers.[46] To secure the descending corridor after the king's interment, it would probably have been blocked with plug-stones, like those in the Bent Pyramid, and its entrance suitably camouflaged to conceal it from view.[47]

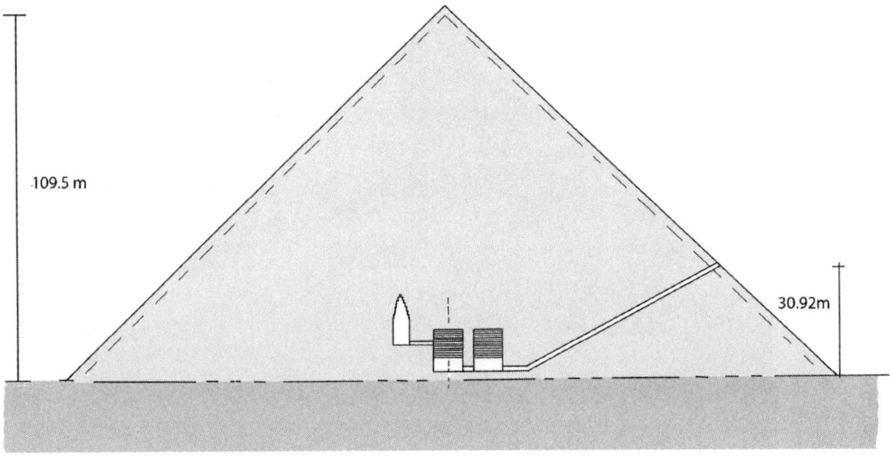

Figure 140. Section through the Red Pyramid at Dahshur looking west.

The horizontal passage leads to two north–south oriented antechambers in tandem, whose 1.3 m thick stone floors are both set a few meters above ground level (Fig. 141). Their roofs, as in the burial chamber at Meidum, are corbeled inward on their longest sides. The first of the antechambers 'A' is 12.3 m high and connected to the second chamber 'B' via a passage 'P.' The second chamber is a similar size, and is centrally located under the apex of the pyramid. From it, passage 'S,' whose entrance presumably was intended to be concealed from view, and at a height inaccessible to robbers, begins 8.6 m up in its southern wall and leads to the 14.65 m high east–west oriented burial chamber, which was corbeled like its immediate neighbors. The floor was set 11.3 m above ground level and may have once concealed the king's masonry sarcophagus under its pavement, which has now largely been removed by treasure hunters.[48]

Protecting the burial chamber and its associated corridors and substructures was 1,694,000 cubic meters of the limestone that surrounded the pyramid,[49] which was a 37 percent increase in volume compared to its predecessor. Approximately 219 m by 219 m across its base and originally 109.5 m high,[50] in this new pyramid the minimum distance that a robber attacking via its sloping face would have to tunnel to reach the burial chamber can be estimated at around 50 m. However, its 47,961 square-meter footprint, although a third larger than that of the Bent Pyramid, did not have quite the same effect on its lateral protection, as due to its different internal design, the distance to

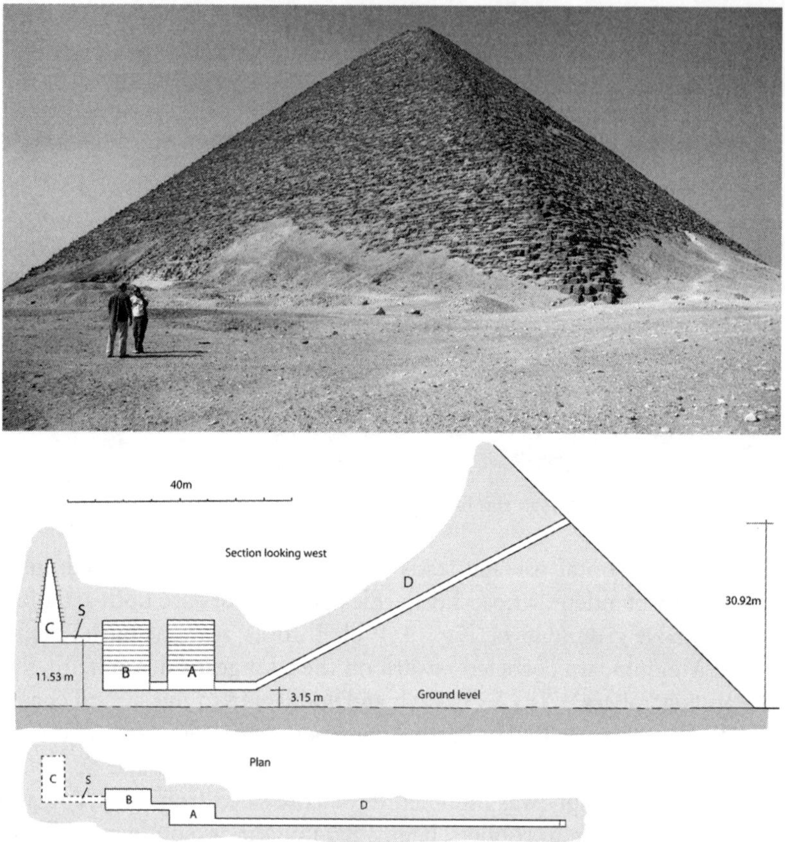

Figure 141. View of the Red Pyramid and close-up plan and section showing the substructure, which lies above ground level.

its substructure (if of course it could be located as it was aboveground) was only about 9 percent greater at approximately 93 m.

Although already well protected by the pyramid that enveloped them, the placing of the two antechambers above ground level made them inherently less vulnerable to undermining and lateral tunneling under the pyramid's base than those in the lower system of the Bent Pyramid, which were set in a trench. Moreover, by raising the burial chamber high up within the pyramid's superstructure, it was protected from the remote possibility of attack from below. Predictably, however, the pyramid was entered by its weakest point: its descending corridor. The culprits, having removed the latter's plug-stones, found the concealed passage high up within the second antechamber, cleared its blockings, and plundered the burial chamber, leaving only what is assumed to be the remains of the sarcophagus and the king's mummy for posterity.[51]

Thematic Analysis: The Architecture and Security of Early Fourth Dynasty Royal Tombs

The raised entrance and descending corridor first introduced in the late Third Dynasty at Abu Rawash were retained in the royal pyramids of the early Fourth Dynasty, which benefited from the increased security offered by this type of inaccessible and hard to find access route. However, their design was further refined in Sneferu's pyramids by the incorporation of smaller and thus less easily detectable corridors and entrances. Moreover, the use of high quality masonry, combined with the exploitation of the laws of physics and the forces of gravity, enabled these corridors to be blocked with plug-stones—a method that proved so successful for securing royal pyramid access routes that it endured, with variations, well into the Old and Middle Kingdoms.

The new raised position of the burial chamber was retained within the protective bulk of the superstructure of Sneferu's first pyramid at Meidum, the inner core of which substituted for the former's rocky knoll. Now necessarily built of masonry, and corbeled to cope with the pyramid's superincumbent load, the chamber's position permitted both the innovative raised entrance and sloping access route to be retained, and more importantly reduced its exposure to undermining in the friable rock of the pyramid's foundations. However, the implementation of this successful arrangement on a much larger scale at Sneferu's next pyramid at Dahshur brought unanticipated structural problems, caused by deep excavations and the soft geology. These bedeviled the satisfactory completion of its antechambers and access routes and forced the creation of a second higher western entrance and corridor. The lessons learned from this compromise are reflected in the design of the final tomb of Sneferu's reign, where raised antechambers were now set aboveground for security and a much higher burial chamber brought up into the core of the pyramid, offering the royal burial greater protection from undermining and tunneling within the protective mantle of the pyramid itself.

Aboveground, the architects of the royal tombs created progressively larger superstructures whose external designs changed as a response both to new concepts of kingship in the royal tomb and to the structural and security problems that these demands placed on the nascent stone technology of the time and the royal necropoleis' doubtful foundations. Thus, the pyramids at Meidum and Dahshur reflect an evolving material technology that was coping with changing concepts of royal monumentality while being built on unsound geology. Its basic function, however, despite differences in size, architecture, and significance, was, like the original tumuli of the kings at Umm al-Qa'b, essentially to protect the royal burial.

Private Tombs

As in preceding dynasties, the distribution and importance of elite cemeteries in Egypt varied in the early Fourth Dynasty. While some declined in importance, such as North Saqqara, others were on the ascent, such as Abusir. While the designs and security measures of tombs at the older, established necropoleis largely followed the pattern of their Third Dynasty predecessors, among the tombs of the newer cemeteries associated with Sneferu's pyramid complexes, such as Meidum and Dahshur, we see new security features and tomb designs appearing.

Tomb Security in Lower Egypt

Abusir

The most northerly tombs from this period are those found in Abusir, where there are several subterranean 'transitional type' stair-shaft and shaft tombs. The first two examples are located on the western ridge of the North Saqqara plateau, and the largest of these externally is tomb AS 33, whose mud-brick superstructure is 53.53 m long and 23.25 m wide (Fig. 142). Its substructure is accessed by a stair-shaft consisting of three 'deep' steps located centrally and slightly off the tomb's main axis, which descends southward 5.5 m to meet its 9.8 m shaft. At the bottom of the shaft, an enormous 4.3 tonne freestanding portcullis, 3.9 m high, 1.3 m wide, and 0.3 to 0.4 m thick, obstructed the entrance to the tomb's underground complex, and behind this lay what the excavator described as a "massive wall built of local limestone chips and irregular blocks" that acted as a secondary blocking. Beyond the wall, a complex of eleven rooms leads to the burial chamber (Room IX), which is protected by a limestone bedrock roof approximately thirteen meters thick.

Aboveground, the superstructure is severely denuded today. Its original height is unknown, although there are sufficient remains to identify a full-length corridor on its eastern elevation that enclosed a cruciform chapel and a cult niche. As with all large superstructures,

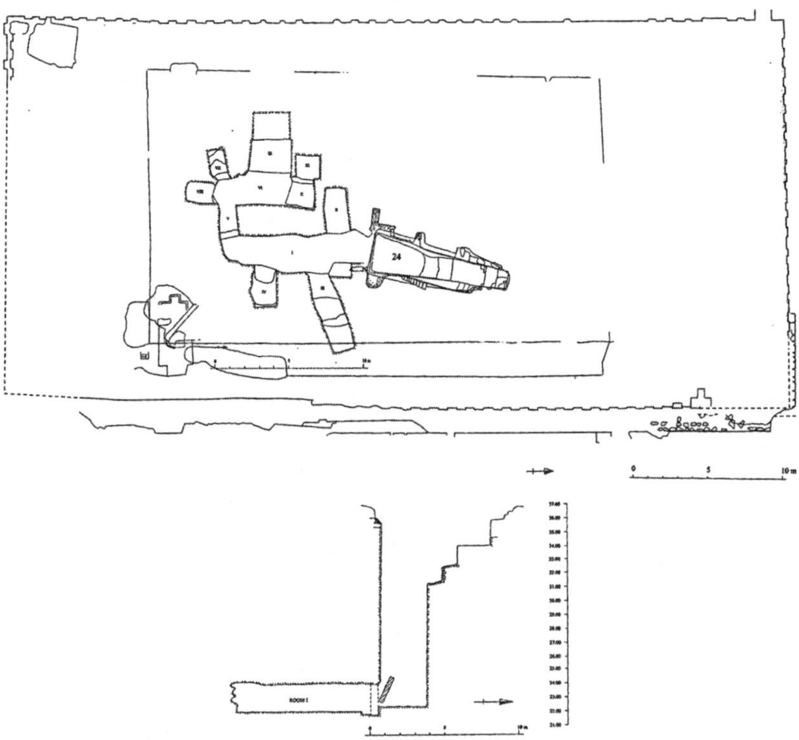

Figure 142. Plan and section of the stair-shaft tomb AS 33 at Abusir, with its multi-chambered substructure.

its huge area would have helped hide the location of the stair-shaft's entrance, which was presumably concealed by being bricked over in the usual fashion. Sadly, this did not prevent the tomb from being plundered via this route (the easiest way considering its depth and geology), as the tomb's excavator found its mighty portcullis tipped out of position, presumably by robbers, who must have cleared the shaft's backfill to do it.[52]

Nearby and on a slightly smaller scale is the 'twin mastaba' stair-shaft tomb AS 20, the tomb of Hetepi, whose superstructure was constructed in an unusual manner (Fig. 143). Externally, it was built with normal 1 to 1.6 m thick mud-brick walls. Within these, two independently accessed corridors were built in the eastern face: the southern one serviced a stone-lined cruciform chapel, while the northern one led to a small rectangular chapel and a separate offering niche. Behind these, and enclosed by the outer mud-brick walls on the south, west, and north, is an inner wall of limestone 1 to 1.2 m thick, which offered the mastaba's interior extra lateral protection from *sondages*. This in turn surrounded the core's fill of limestone chips, sherds, and sand, which was intended to protect and conceal the tomb's stair-shafts. The stair-shafts have a very unusual form, as rather than going straight down or changing direction, their stairways descend in a single direction but take a 'meandering' approach. The southernmost begins about halfway down the center of the superstructure and descends to a depth of four meters through the mastaba's core to join with its 10.75 m deep shaft. Its northern counterpart starts about five meters in from the north on the same axis and descends for five meters, where it meets a shallower 6.8 m shaft. Both would have been well protected laterally by the *tafl* into which they were cut, and from above by the mastaba's inner core.[53] Curiously, unlike stairways with half and quarter landings that descend in an L- or U-shape, this type of stairway does not save much space as far as the length of the descent goes, because most of the treads are in the same direction, even though the stairway 'meanders.' It is possible that the idea was to prevent the mastaba's loose inner core from slipping

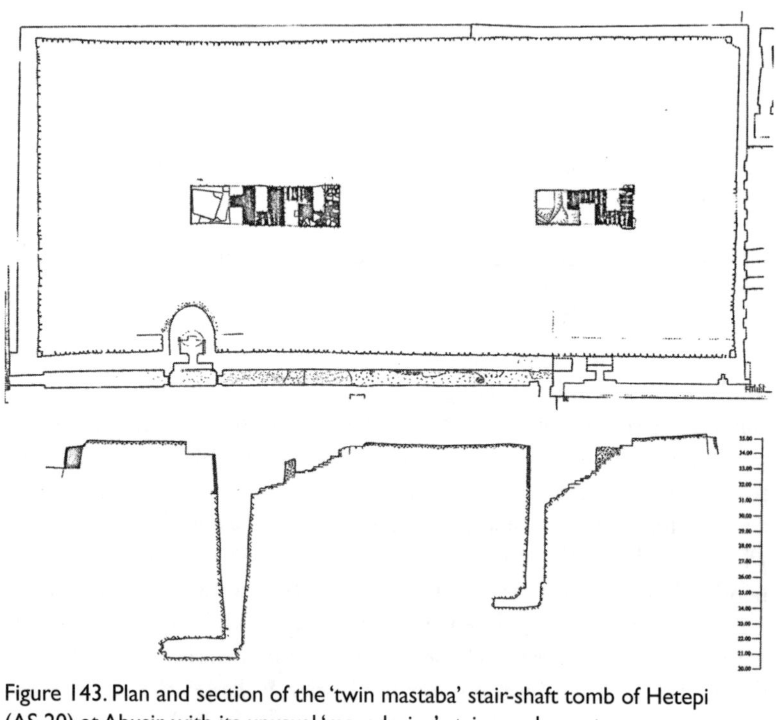

Figure 143. Plan and section of the 'twin mastaba' stair-shaft tomb of Hetepi (AS 20) at Abusir, with its unusual 'meandering' stairway descents.

down toward its shafts during the inevitable settlement of the limestone chip and sand fill, and thus give away the position of the entrances. Alternatively, they may have been a method of compensating for too steep a rake in the steps, as the many half landings would have made them safer to descend. As for the substructures that led from them, the floor of the 1.4 m high southern burial chamber was excavated into the *tafl* bedrock 14.75 m from the surface and protected by a roof 13.35 m thick. Its shallower northern counterpart had a simple rectangular chamber only 0.6 m high, set at 11.8 m from the surface and defended by a roof 10.6 m thick. Miroslav Bárta's recent excavations revealed that the southern chamber had been wrecked by robbers, as fragments of the coffin, mummy, and an offering table were all that was left. The northern chamber was empty. With no sign of robbers' tunnels in the tomb, it may be safe to assume that both were robbed via their stair-shafts,[54] which, as with tomb AS 33, demonstrates both the vulnerability of the tomb's access routes, despite its stone-reinforced mastaba, and the solidity of the geology surrounding the burial chambers.

Finally, there is a single subterranean shaft tomb from the period, known as the 'Lake of Abusir' tomb 1, which is situated near the causeway of the later pyramid of Niussera (Fig. 144).[55] Its 25.65 m long by 13.1 m wide superstructure, rather than being made of solid mud-brick like that of AS 33, was constructed of mud-brick like its earlier neighbors in North Saqqara. Its 1.5 m thick walls surrounded a fill of sand and rubble that protected the tomb's shaft, over which a skin of mud-brick may have been used to form a convex roof. Externally, a corridor was built on its eastern elevation that led to a cruciform chapel in the southeastern body of the superstructure. At the latter's extreme southeastern end, adjacent to its cruciform cult chapel, a 1.6 meter square shaft (which was only 0.75 percent of its mastaba's area) descends 8.5 m into the surrounding *tafl* bedrock to meet with a short passage that leads to its burial chamber on the north. Rather than a portcullis, the substructure relied for its access route's defense on the shaft's *tafl* backfill, which was presumably the spoil from the substructure's excavation, and a single-thickness mud-brick wall that blocked the entrance to the burial chamber. This consisted of a 1.7 m high vaulted burial chamber excavated in the *tafl* that was entirely lined with a single course of mud-bricks. These presumably provided a certain degree of support and reinforcement in addition to the approximately 6.8 m thick layer of *tafl* cover that protected the burial chamber above. Like its neighbors, the tomb had been robbed, and via the usual route at Abusir. Robbers

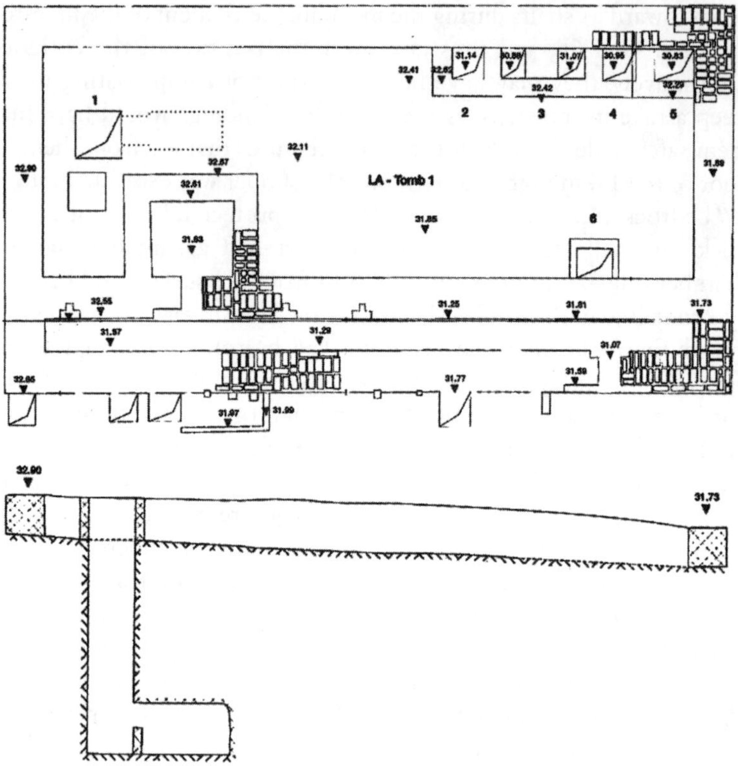

Figure 144. Plan and section of the 'Lake of Abusir' tomb 1. Its deep shaft leads to a vaulted mud-brick burial chamber.

having tunneled down through the shaft's northeast corner to gain access to the burial.[56] Their chosen route suggests a certain stability in the *tafl* backfill once it was settled that may be attributable to its clay-like properties and moisture content.[57]

It is clear in these tombs at Abusir, therefore, that, like at Saqqara, when robbers were confronted by deep substructures and resistant geology, they took the easier option (laborious and hazardous as it may have been) of locating a tomb's well-hidden entrance and gaining admission via its descent rather than tunneling through solid rock.

Dahshur

Accompanying Sneferu's two pyramids at the Dahshur necropolis were the tombs of nobles and officials, many of which, like their predecessors at Meidum, incorporated special security architecture to deal with the friable nature of the surrounding soil and *tafl* strata.[58] (The reader may wish to read the section on Meidum first if interested in the sequential development.)

The first three examples are associated with the Bent Pyramid and are spread between opposite ends of the necropolis. Most northerly is tomb no. 1, which is located just south of the pyramid of Senwosret III among de Morgan's "*mastabas du sud*" and is dated to the early Fourth Dynasty.[59] Devoid of a protective superstructure (whether by omission or erosion is unknown), the subterranean substructure was entered by a T-shaped shaft that reached a depth of eleven meters, which was brick-lined for the first three meters of its descent and stone-lined for the remainder (Fig. 145). At its base, in an emplacement formed by the full-depth slots created by the shaft's characteristic T-shape, stood a large portcullis approximately 2 m high, 1.8 m wide, and 0.4 m thick that would have weighed around 3.1 tonnes. Excavated within what de Morgan described as "*grès argileux*" (sandstone clay), the burial chamber beyond was reached by a short passage and built of Tura limestone slabs. It was protected by a corbeled roof of stone, which, if the drawings are accurate, would have been approximately 1.25 m thick at its apex. Allowing for a burial chamber around 4.5 m high, this means that the protective cover over the chamber's roof at its highest point would have been approximately 6.75 m thick.[60]

At the southern end of the necropolis, south of the pyramid of Amenemhat III, some nine hundred meters from the Bent Pyramid,

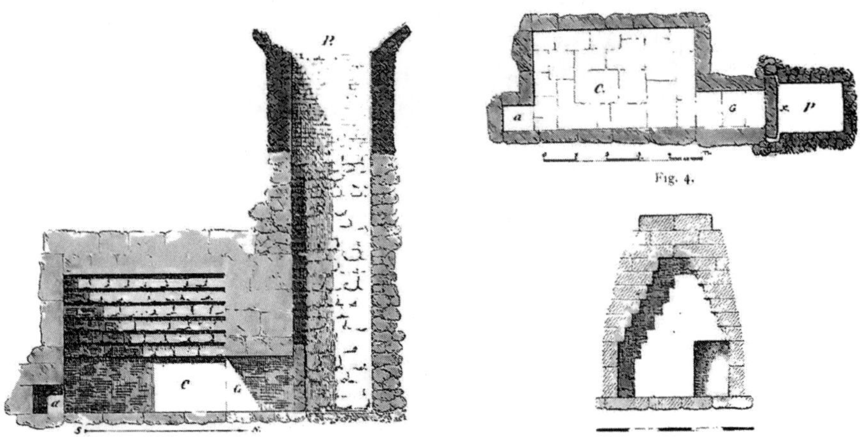

Figure 145. The substructure of the stone-lined tomb no. 1 at Dahshur, with its unusual corbeled burial chamber.

lie tombs DAS 9 (Ipy) and DAS 32-4 (Iinefer).[61] Within the protective inner limestone core of the former's 26.5 m long and 12.25 m wide superstructure,[62] the centrally positioned shaft leading to the tomb's burial chamber is 7.75 m deep and initially stone-lined, until it descends into the strata of limestone and shale into which the rest of the substructure is dug (Fig. 146). At its base, apparently unprotected by a portcullis or blockings, a six-meter-long horizontal rock-cut passage leads to the burial chamber, which is 1.95 m high and lined with blocks of Tura limestone on its four walls and floor. It is protected by a roof approximately 5.8 m thick, formed from the overlying limestone stratum. This was undoubtedly considered sufficient protection from above, as it can be clearly seen in the section drawing that the stone walls and flooring were only necessary to protect the chamber in the lower, softer shale layer. Even with these defenses, it is evident that the tomb was entered on many occasions,[63] and since there is no sign of robbers' tunnels elsewhere, presumably this was done via the shaft.

A similar but even deeper substructure arrangement is seen in Barsanti's drawing of nearby tomb DAS 32-4 (Iinefer), where it seems (if

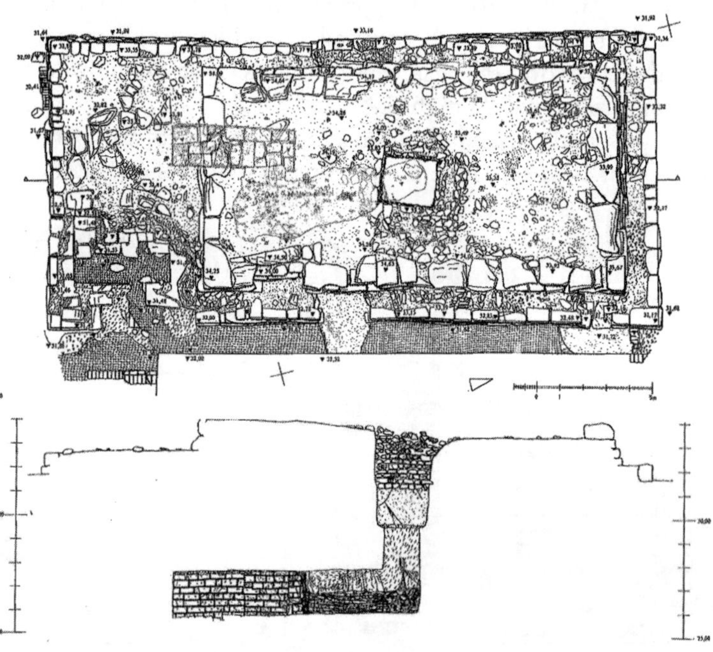

Figure 146. Plan and section of the shaft tomb DAS 9 (Ipy) at Dahshur, whose burial chamber was stone-lined and set beneath the overlying limestone stratum.

the drawing can be relied on) that the burial chamber floor was set at approximately nineteen meters from the surface (Fig. 147). Approached by a stone-lined shaft and passage, the burial chamber's walls and floor were masonry-lined. Instead of a corbeled roof, it had an early saddle roof, which presumably offered better protection because it directed the thrust of the superincumbent weight down and into the side walls of the structure.[64] Moreover, above the roof was an additional fourteen meters of *tafl* cover, making it the best protected and deepest burial chamber in the necropolis. During his excavations, however, Barsanti deduced from the disturbed nature of the shaft's backfill that the tomb had been entered before via the shaft.[65]

The final tomb is from the 'Lepsius' mastaba field southeast of the Red Pyramid, which is contemporary with and associated with the royal sepulcher.[66] These tombs, like their neighbors and predecessors, relied on a great deal of stone in their construction for added security in the weak geology. Indeed, excavations have revealed that the burial chambers of at least two of them were built at the end of sloping construction trenches, which were necessary in order to handle the masonry used to

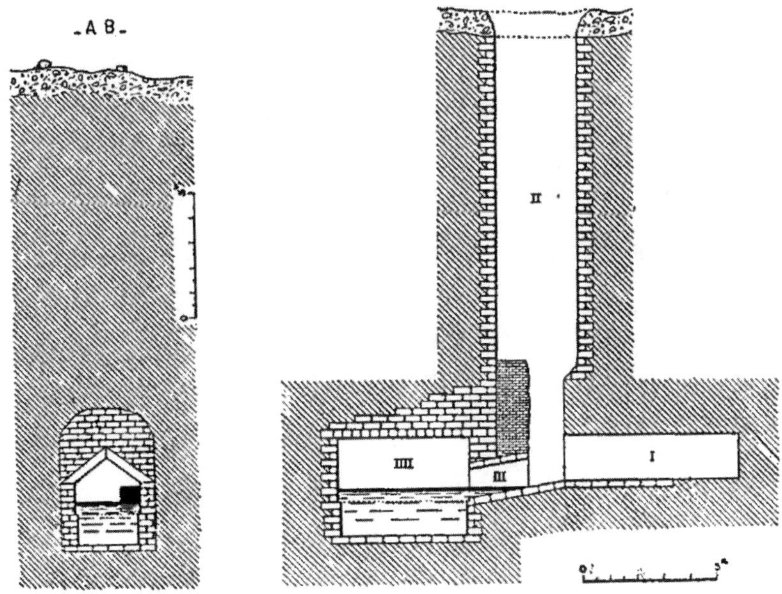

Fig. 5. Fig. 6.

Figure 147. Section through the deep stone-lined substructure of DAS 32-4 (Iinefer) at Dahshur, whose burial chamber was protected by an early 'saddle roof.'

line their burial chambers and shaft within the soft *tafl*.[67] A number of these tombs have been published in recent years, and have very similar layouts.[68] Probably the best reported is Mastaba II/1, the tomb of Netjer-Aperef, which was published by the late Nicole Alexanian.

On the surface, the stone-clad superstructure of Mastaba II/1 was 35.1 m long, 18.9 m wide, and about 4.5 m high.[69] Its approximately 5.5 m thick battered outer walls were constructed of concentric layers of first Tura and then local limestone bonded with clay mortar (Fig. 148). Within them, an inner core consisting of limestone chips, gravel, clay, and soil concealed and protected the mouth of the tomb's axially positioned shaft, which lay just south of the mastaba's center. Originally

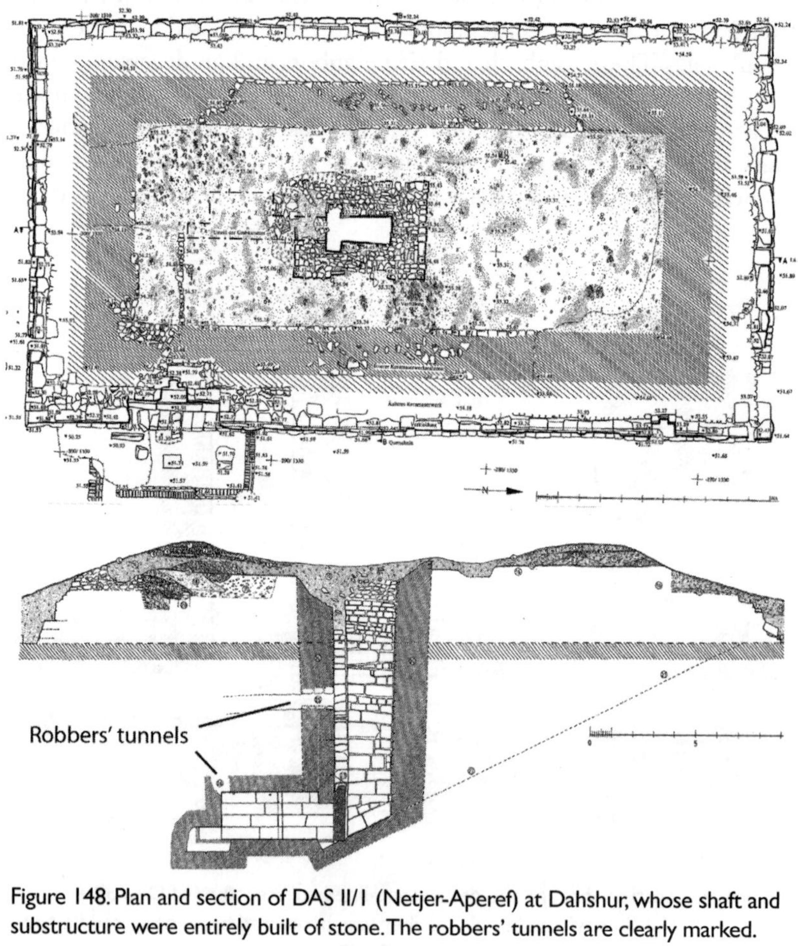

Figure 148. Plan and section of DAS II/1 (Netjer-Aperef) at Dahshur, whose shaft and substructure were entirely built of stone. The robbers' tunnels are clearly marked.

constructed in a backfilled sloping trench, the shaft was 9.1 m deep and lined with masonry walls that varied in thickness between 1 and 1.75 m. It increased in block size as it went deeper, its characteristic T-shape providing the grooves and emplacement to accommodate its portcullis. On the shaft's south side, three wide slabs filled its entire width to a height of 4.35 m above the burial chamber entrance to prevent tunneling over the portcullis. The bottom slab formed the lintel to the entrance. In the grooved emplacement at the base of the shaft, a 4.5 tonne,[70] 2.41 m high, 1.68 m wide, and 0.52 m thick portcullis was found that had been carved with three 0.16 m wide and 0.8 m deep channels at its base to accommodate lowering ropes. Rectangular recesses in the shaft's walls suggest that a wooden beam was used to support the stone before it was closed. Presumably, after taking the strain on the portcullis' lowering ropes, it could then have been cut away just before it was lowered into position.[71] Beyond the portcullis lay a short stone-lined access corridor leading to a 2.18 m high burial chamber (Fig. 149), whose walls were constructed of large, tightly jointed limestone blocks that were roofed and floored with full-width slabs of the same material. Combined with the *tafl* above, this provided the chamber with a total of 6.9 m of overhead cover. At the southern end of the chamber was a small canopic recess that may have been concealed with thinner slabs, and investigations in this area have demonstrated that the burial chamber walls were up to two meters thick!

Despite the great lengths gone to by the tomb's architects to make sure it was well protected, unsurprisingly it was robbed. To avoid the substantial obstacle of the shaft's stone blocking, tomb robbers dug into the face of the shaft wall and tunneled directly down through the *tafl* to the southeast corner of the burial chamber below, thus bypassing both the blocking and the portcullis, both of which it would appear were attacked again on subsequent occasions.[72] In particular, robbers breached the portcullis at some point, using fire to assist with the shattering of the stone.[73]

Undoubtedly because of the innate vulnerability of the friable underlying geology, the architects of these private tombs at Dahshur incorporated a considerable amount of stone to protect their substructures from robbery. It would appear that the stone-reinforced superstructures and protective footprints of these tombs did their job, as there appear to have been few incursions into their shafts or substructures from undermining or lateral tunneling. Unfortunately, in almost every case, once the entrance to the tomb shaft itself had been discovered, its associated access route inadvertently led the plunderers toward

Figure 149. Interior view of the stone-lined burial chamber of DAS II/1 (Netjer-Aperef) at Dahshur. The breach in the portcullis was made by using fire and water to shatter the stone.

their goal, and they inevitably, given enough time, found ways to bypass even the most complex of blockings and stone defenses.

Tomb Security in Middle Egypt

Meidum

The private tombs surrounding King Sneferu's first pyramid are a mixed bag. There are extraordinarily high-status tombs of an enormous size with innovative security measures not seen elsewhere in Egypt, and there are subterranean shaft tombs that might be found in any of the necropoleis that we have discussed in this book. Moreover, in a few instances we see new substructure and access route designs being experimented with for the first time in a private context. Many of these innovations are direct responses to the problematic friable geology of the necropolis and, of course, the threat of tomb robbery. To set the scene, we will first discuss three subterranean shaft tombs that largely follow the pattern seen elsewhere in Egypt, then look at some of the more extraordinary tombs whose security measures and designs are unique to Meidum.

Located in the Northern Cemetery, the 'twin mastaba' tomb No. 6 of Rahotep and Nefert (famous for their crystal-eyed statues in the Cairo museum) aboveground comprised a large solid mud-brick mastaba built in four distinct phases.[74] The original inner mastaba was built of mud-brick reinforced with vertically placed logs 2.5 to 3 m long, which acted as wooden ties (Fig. 150).[75] Within it two descending shafts were formed that joined with their underlying rock-cut counterparts and led to their respective burial chambers. On its eastern face, a stone-lined cruciform chapel in the south was matched by a smaller offering niche in the north. An extension was added to this completed structure on the northern end, and over that a further two skins of brick on all four walls, which concealed and protected the cruciform chapel and its celebrated statues until their discovery in the nineteenth century.[76] In its final form it was an

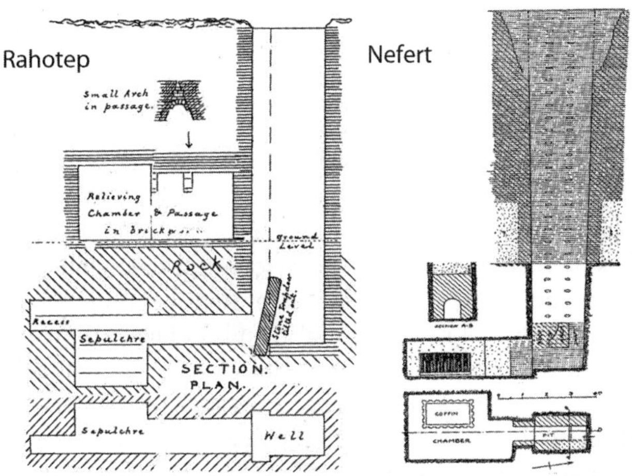

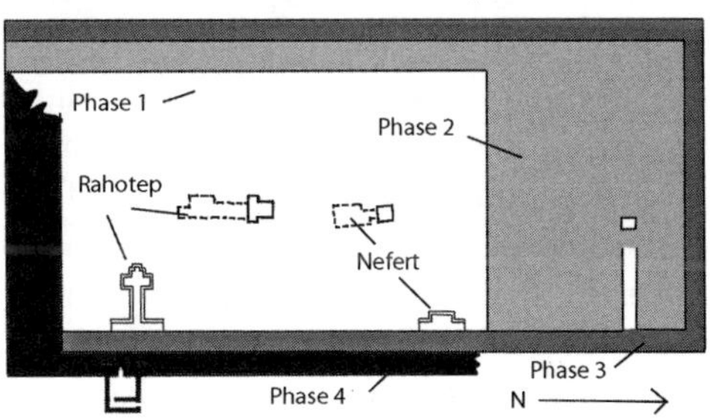

Figure 150. Plan and sections of the tomb of Rahotep and Nefert at Meidum, which was largely dependent on its enormous mud-brick *massif* superstructure for defense.

impressive 82.5 m long, 42 m wide, and possibly 9 to 10 m high (nearly as large as the *massif* of K1 at Beit Khallaf), and offered both its shafts, substructures, and chapels an exceptional level of concealment and protection. This is graphically illustrated by Petrie's comments on Auguste Mariette's early attempts to find the substructure:

> The central pit of the mastaba had been furiously searched for by Mariette's men; they dug vast holes in the brick body, but never cleared the top; and a trench of theirs cut away one side of the well, without their seeing it.[77]

Within this enormous superstructure, two axially placed shafts were built. That of Rahotep was located approximately a third of the way in from the mastaba's southern end and descended for 8.5 m through the latter's mud-brick body, before continuing 4.5 m into the rock. Nefert's shaft was centrally placed and plunged 12.5 m through the mud-brick, before descending a further five meters into the rock. As a result, both would have been well protected by the mastaba's mass and extremely difficult to locate due to their comparatively tiny shaft openings, which amounted to 0.11 and 0.09 percent, respectively, of the structure's area.[78]

Belowground, the closures and burial chambers of the two substructures differed greatly. At the bottom of Rahotep's shaft, a 6.6 tonne, 2.56 m high, and 0.45 m thick portcullis stone[79] originally sat in a T-shaped emplacement that was rebated at its base to prevent it from being levered up. Beyond it, a connecting passage, which was sealed with forty-one fifty-kilogram limestone blocks bonded together with mortar, led to the 3.4 m high burial chamber. This was excavated in the marl at what seems an unexpectedly shallow depth, as its rock cover was only about two meters thick. This is presumably because rather than rely on the friable rock, the tomb's builders intended to depend on the enormous bulk of the overlying brick mastaba to be the main defense. Indeed, evidence that the builders were concerned about the fragility of the rock strata is evident from the relieving chambers built within the mastaba directly above the burial chamber to allay the pressure from the superincumbent load.[80] Unlike that of her spouse, Nefert's shaft lacked a portcullis blocking. Mud impressions from her coffin demonstrate that the shaft was filled with liquid mud, which ran beyond the shaft and set hard inside the burial chamber.[81] Structurally, Nefert's burial chamber was set just below the base of the shaft, but it was arguably better protected than that of Rahotep by a 3.75 m thick layer of rock, plus a three-meter layer of "pebbles" and the huge mastaba.[82]

Both burial chambers were robbed in antiquity, and it would seem in this instance some time after the interments, as the liquid mud impressions in Nefert's shaft and chamber indicate that it had time to set before the deed was done.[83] Rahotep's portcullis was found tipped out of its emplacement despite the grooves and rebated base that housed it, and the shaft behind was strewn with the stone blocks that had once sealed the connecting passage to the burial chamber.

Similarly, the substructure of the nearby 'twin mastaba' No. 9 of Ranefer, which was also a subterranean shaft tomb, depended largely on the protection offered by its mud-brick superstructure. It was smaller at fifty-seven meters long and thirty-three meters wide, and possessed twin stone-lined offering niches on its eastern side.[84] Its internal descending shafts were also protected by at least seven meters of encompassing brickwork before they married with their rock-cut lower sections. In addition, the whole mastaba was covered by a 1.5 m layer of gravel on its roof that would have concealed the shafts' entrances, which occupied 0.28 and 0.22 percent of its area, respectively.[85]

Little is known about the shaft belonging to Ranefer, apart from that it was T-shaped to accommodate a portcullis and centrally placed in the superstructure (Fig. 151). We do know from Petrie's excavation report that it took his team two whole weeks to empty it, so it must have been of a considerable depth. At its base a portcullis stone sat in its T-shaped emplacement, behind which a connecting corridor that was blocked with solid masonry led to the burial chamber. Not much is known about the latter, save that from Petrie's sketch it appears to have been constructed of stone and corbeled, presumably to relieve the stresses placed on it from above. The shaft of Ranefer's spouse is better reported. It was located opposite the offering niche and descended through 10.5 m of mud-brick mastaba and gravel before penetrating the rock for a further 7.75 m. Internally, it took an unusual form, as the burial chamber's entrance was positioned three meters up from the shaft's base.[86] Whether it was protected by a portcullis is uncertain. Although in Alan Rowe's plan some notches are drawn and mentioned by Reisner,[87] they could also be postholes to accommodate a supporting beam. No mention is made of the presence of any stone.[88] The chamber itself is unremarkable, save that it was protected by three meters of rock cover and, of course, a further 10.5 m of the mud-brick of its mastaba.

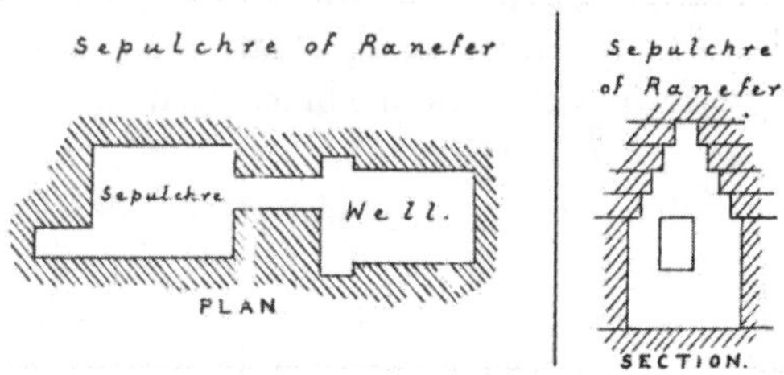

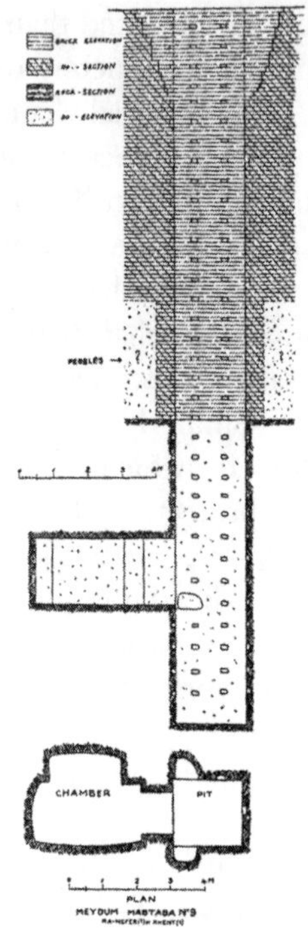

Figure 151. Substructure sections of the tomb of Ranefer and his spouse at Meidum. Ranefer's burial chamber seems to have been corbeled, while his spouse's was simply rock-cut. Like the tomb of Rahotep, both substructures relied on their huge mud-brick mastaba for protection.

When the shaft of Ranefer was finally exposed and excavated by Petrie, the portcullis was found in situ, which Petrie's men duly levered open, having cut away the sides of its grooved emplacement. The blockwork in the connecting passage was then removed. It was so hard that it had to be cut out with a hammer and chisel to permit access. Petrie's hopes of finding an intact burial were soon dashed, as he discovered a large robbers' tunnel in the chamber's floor, which originated from behind the false door in the southern chapel of Ranefer.[89] This demonstrates both the dangers of installing an accessible chapel within a mastaba and the apparent familiarity of the robbers with the tomb's layout! Ranefer's mutilated mummy was found propped up in the chamber. Sadly, after being donated to the Royal College of Surgeons, it was later destroyed in the London blitz in the Second World War.[90]

Not every shaft tomb at Meidum was as complex or as well defended as Rahotep's and Ranefer's examples. In the Far Western Cemetery, which is located four hundred meters west of the pyramid, Gerald Wainwright excavated thirty-five lower-status subterranean shaft tombs set out in rows. Most of them had T-shaped shafts that averaged 2.2 m by

1 m in plan, which were built to accommodate portcullises. Their depths varied between 4.11 and 11.8 meters. Their entrances were probably originally intended to be protected by superstructures, although none was found by the excavators.[91]

Unusually, twenty-nine of these tombs were found with portcullises in situ,[92] but within the individual shafts the portcullis stones frequently varied in size. Most unusually, the excavation report gives us many but not all of their dimensions.[93] The smallest portcullis was the 1.46 tonne example in tomb 68, which at 1.67 m high, 1.16 m wide, and 0.35 m thick barely covered the doorway behind it and certainly would not have been retained by its oversize portcullis grooves. The largest was that in tomb 63, which, unlike the one in tomb 68, appears to have been a close fit within its emplacement. It was 2.57 m high, 1.6 m wide, and 0.48 m thick, and it would have weighed approximately 4.24 tonnes.[94] With one or two exceptions, the majority of the slabs were 1.67 to 2.1 m high and 1.06 to 1.5 m wide, and had a volume of somewhere between 0.68 and 1.29 cubic m.

Although this in itself does not tell us much, it does suggest that overall there was an optimum average size for a portcullis slab in the cemetery. This assumption, if correct, indicated that the size was determined by several factors. Perhaps one of these was the ability of men physically to handle a certain size of stone and lower it into position. Another may be that the size was governed by the optimum size of slab that could be extracted by the local stone quarry. There may also have been a minimum weight and size that was judged to be best for defending a tomb's entrance, or an accepted standard size for a staircase or shaft in a particular cemetery, in the way we standardize windows and doors today. Perhaps rather than make a portcullis to fit the tomb, a prefabricated 'standard portcullis' slab would be obtained from the local quarry and the tomb entrance and emplacement would then be built to fit the portcullis?

Of particular note among these tombs is that in the majority of cases the portcullises were not closed but left raised up, supported by small pieces of stone,[95] in a similar manner to tomb K2 at Beit Khallaf.[96] Since they lack any holes or grooves for lowering ropes, it may be that the portcullises would have been closed by removing them one by one, perhaps after tilting the stones by levering, as has been suggested by Martin Isler.[97] Another possibility has been proposed by Wainwright: "Little or no effort would have been required to lower the portcullises, except to knock away the stone piles beneath them."[98]

Behind the portcullises, short connecting corridors led to rock-cut burial chambers. The majority of these were lined with masonry walls, which were roofed with wide limestone blocks and paved with stone floors 0.15 to 0.25 m thick. In addition to these linings, the burial chambers were protected by the strata of "loose rock" into which they were cut and a 3.3 m layer of gravel at the surface. The thickness of cover varied from seven meters at the shallowest to 10.8 m at the deepest, in tomb 51,[99] whose typical plan and section is included here (Fig. 152).

Predating the stone-lined tombs at Dahshur, the depth and stone linings of these burial chambers in the Far Western Cemetery suggest an alternative approach to providing security at Meidum that did not rely on a massive superstructure. It is impossible to be sure, as it seems the cemetery was abandoned, perhaps because the royal necropolis was relocated before the demise of its intended occupants and before the superstructures could be built.[100] However, it does at least present us with a fascinating 'snapshot' in time of an unfinished cemetery for court officials still awaiting burials, its 'mass-produced' portcullises poised ready in mid-air, waiting to be closed.[101]

Closer to the pyramid, there are examples of tombs with a completely different type of substructure and access route that is unique to Meidum. Entirely built in a trench cut in the soft rock, their stone-built

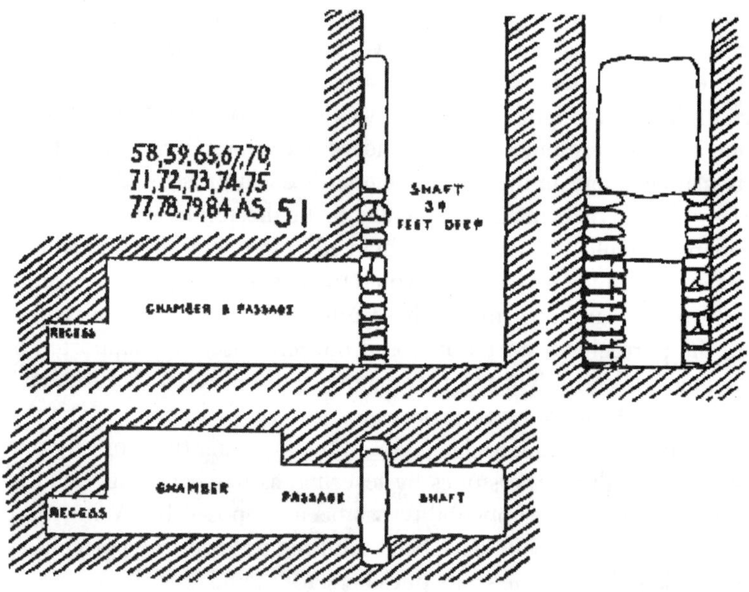

Figure 152. Sections through tomb 51 from the Far Western Cemetery at Meidum, showing the portcullis propped up on stones, still waiting to be lowered.

substructures are entered by sloping corridors, like that in the nearby pyramid, which coincidentally descend at similar inclines to permit the insertion of plug-stones. Like many of their lower-status contemporaries nearby, they seem to have lacked a protective superstructure.[102] A good example, and the best documented of these 'cut and cover' tombs with sloping corridors, is tomb 'A' from the Great Western Cemetery, which lies roughly a hundred and eighty meters west of the pyramid's enclosure (Fig. 153). A brick-lined shaft 6.04 m deep, which was probably a later intrusive addition as the adjacent identical tombs 'B' and 'C' are without it, leads to what was the original access route. This consists of a descending stone-lined corridor 1.39 m high, 1.04 m wide, and 4.92 m long that was undoubtedly intended to be obstructed by plug-stones, a discarded block having been found by the adjacent tomb 'C.' A raised step at the corridor's end provided a convenient stop for the blocks, preventing them from entering the burial chamber. The latter was entirely built of masonry at the base of a 10.5 m deep rock-cut trench, but for reasons unknown it was set off-center, leaving the block-work on its eastern side approximately 3.5 m thick, as opposed to 1.5 m on the western side. Internally, the chamber was 1.8 m high. Its floor

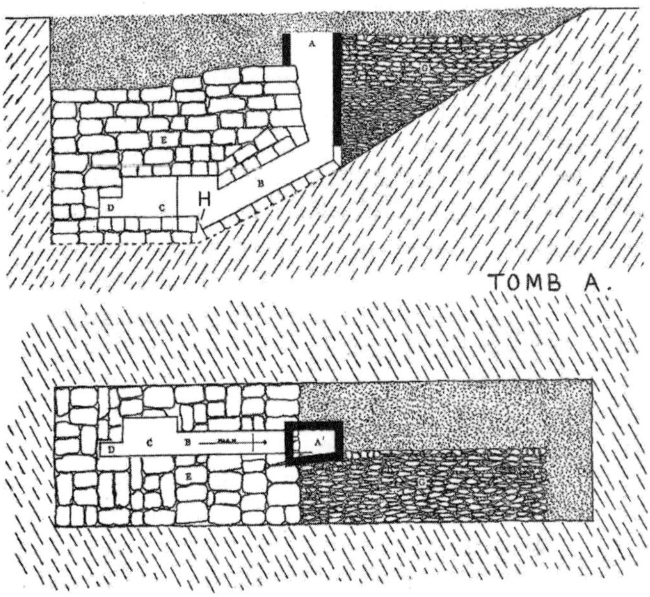

Figure 153. Petrie's plan and section of tomb A in the Great Western Cemetery at Meidum. Its substructure and descending corridor were entirely built of stone.

consisted of a couple of courses of stone and its four-meter-thick roof was made of large limestone blocks bedded in mortar.[103] The latter was doubtless covered with backfill, giving the chamber below about eight meters of cover in total.

The construction and dimensions of the access corridors of the remaining published tombs of this type at Meidum—'B,' 'C,' 202, 277, and 393—are remarkably similar.[104] Presumably they were all once blocked with plug-stones, although, as previously mentioned, only tomb C had direct evidence of this. While the structural details of the burial chambers of nearby tombs 'B' and 'C' are not recorded, those of tombs 202, 277, and 393 are virtually identical. While not much detail is available, the depths of their masonry roofs and backfill can be estimated at around 7.5 m, 7.4 m, and 8.1 m thick, respectively.[105]

The success of these tombs' stone architecture in deterring the serious threat of tunneling by robbers in the soft rock is undeniable, as it appears that none were attacked in this way.[106] Their descending corridors and blockings were, like those of most subterranean tombs, not so secure. As in the neighboring pyramid, tomb robbers discovered their entrances and smashed and removed their plug-stones.[107] Indeed, Rowe's discovery of a Roman coin and a contemporary body in the descending corridor of tomb 202 gives us at least one date for such an intrusion.[108]

Meanwhile, in the Southern Cemetery just northeast of the pyramid enclosure, a much larger tomb with a far more complex substructure had been built, probably soon after or during the construction of the pyramid,[109] which theoretically offered its occupant a much higher level of protection. Mastaba 17 is exceptional for the stone architecture of its burial chamber, which was built on a far greater scale and contained the largest stone ashlars used to that date in a private tomb in Egypt (Fig. 154).[110] Within a pit created to house its protective superstructure at bedrock level, another smaller pit was dug to accept the substructure, whose base was approximately eleven meters from the desert surface. Inside it, an unusual cruciform substructure was built. The side walls of the burial chamber were constructed of large dressed stone blocks, which at the rear of the sarcophagus were about a meter thick.[111] Over the top of these a roof was formed from enormous limestone orthostats laid vertically on edge, one of which Wainwright reported as 5.53 m long, 1.27 m thick, and 2.63 m high, which can be estimated to have weighed a remarkable 31 to 48 tonnes (Fig. 155).[112] Within the apex

Figure 154. View of Mastaba 17 today and section drawing, showing the mud-brick walls of the superstructure, which were built on the bedrock and then filled with a hundred thousand tonnes of gravel.

of the chamber itself, a granite sarcophagus (the earliest found in Egypt) was placed to await its occupant.[113]

To enter the burial chamber, a very unusual access route was constructed. Within the lower pit in which the substructure was built, just up from its floor and thus not accessible from the surface, a stone built corridor begins almost immediately and enters the substructure from the east (Fig. 155). Internally, approximately a meter square, it descended at an angle of eleven degrees for 4.65 m and was roofed and protected by large stone beams of around 1.2 by 0.5 m, laid edge on.[114] After the funeral had taken place, it was blocked with plug-stones, and only then were both it and the entire substructure in the pit covered by a gravel and marl backfill,[115] leaving the entrance entirely undetectable and unreachable.

Above the substructure's now backfilled pit was built the tomb's protective superstructure. It was constructed on the sloping bedrock base of the larger pit (the smaller inner one having been used for the substructure), which was then lined with a mud-brick retaining 'box' wall. This allowed the mud-brick walls of the 103.05 m long, 51.6 m wide superstructure to be erected within it directly on strong

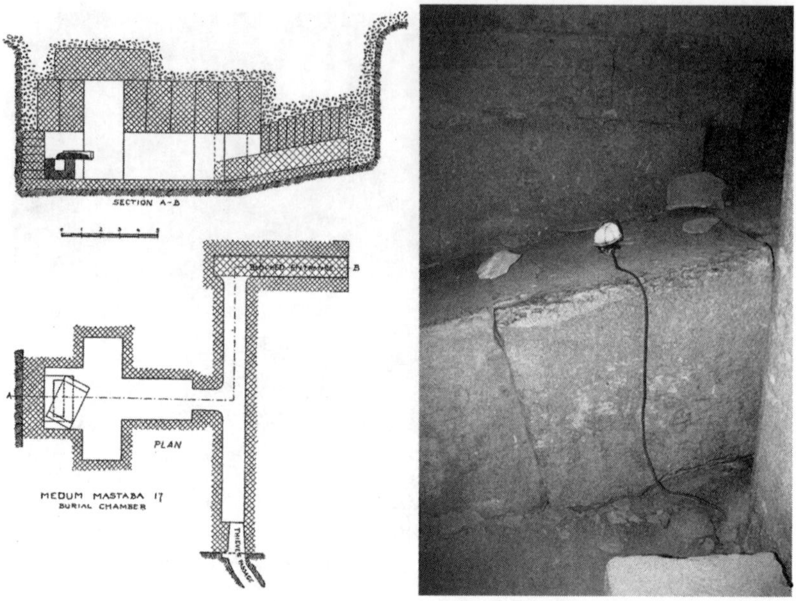

Figure 155. Close-up plan and section of the interior layout of Mastaba 17, and view of the plug-stones still in position.

foundations, and enabled its sloping sides to be built at the correct angle from an unlevel footing.[116] The inner core was then filled with layers of limestone chips and marl that were retained by a series of stone cross-walls to ensure stability.[117] This all formed an unstable and extremely formidable defense. Indeed, Petrie estimated that there was a hundred thousand tonnes of this material,[118] and its effectiveness at concealing its substructure was confirmed by his attempts to find it:

> I had already scraped off the surface of the mastaba on the top all along the middle, down to clean firm chips, to search for a well, but in vain. I then sank a large square pit with winding stairway, in the axis of the mastaba, reaching from about the middle to near the latitude of the N. end of the facade. This pit we carried down to 48 feet under the top—a considerable work; but we neither reached a central chamber, nor any passage leading to the chamber, as I had hoped we might have done.[119]

Eventually, Petrie discovered the location of the substructure by sinking a deep shaft behind the false door, but because of the danger posed by the enormous quantity of loose material, he could only proceed further by trenching through the east wall of the mastaba.[120] Wainwright summed up the hazards of the work in his report:

> It proved a hard and long job to open No. 17, for we had to dig the great pit shewn in pl. x, as it would have been dangerous for the men to work in any smaller space, owing to the continual fall of chips, which would have blocked a smaller pit.[121]

Having eventually gained admittance to the substructure, they found that the tomb had been robbed. The perpetrators, who were certainly cognizant of the tomb's layout, had avoided all of these complex defenses and tunneled directly through the soft bedrock from the south of the tomb to the end of the north–south passage wall. Then, using a charcoal fire, they had shattered part of the masonry to gain entry. Once inside, they had levered open the sarcophagus lid using an acacia branch and propped it up with a stonemason's mallet, further confirming the identity of the most likely culprits: the tomb builders themselves![122]

Finally, returning to the Northern Cemetery, there is an even larger tomb whose defenses, although different in nature, equal if not surpass those of Mastaba 17. At a hundred and twenty meters long, sixty-eight meters long, and possibly up to ten meters high,[123] the 'twin mastaba' No. 16 of Nefermaat and Atet is by far the largest private tomb in Old Kingdom Egypt (Fig. 156).[124] Its unique substructure combines elements of both the 'cut and cover' and subterranean shaft tomb architecture seen elsewhere at Meidum, but made secure in an unusual way.

At the base of a 4.57 m deep shaft or pit excavated in the soft rock, the 2.37 m high burial chamber of Nefermaat was built on a thick mud foundation and constructed of large masonry blocks.[125] It was one of the earliest private burial chambers to incorporate a stone corbeled roof, similar to that found in the adjacent pyramid. This was designed as a defensive barrier in itself, as well as to relieve the pressure from the mastaba above and the very unusual backfill that surrounded it in the shaft,[126] which was, according to Wainwright, "choked with great masses of roughly squared stones, each about 5 × 3 × 2 feet and all filled up solid with mud."[127] These ponderous limestone slabs, each weighing around 1.75 tonnes, had probably been set in the mud as it dried in layers.[128] This hardened conglomerate was intended to create serious difficulties for anyone trying to tunnel between the sides of the shaft and the chamber within.

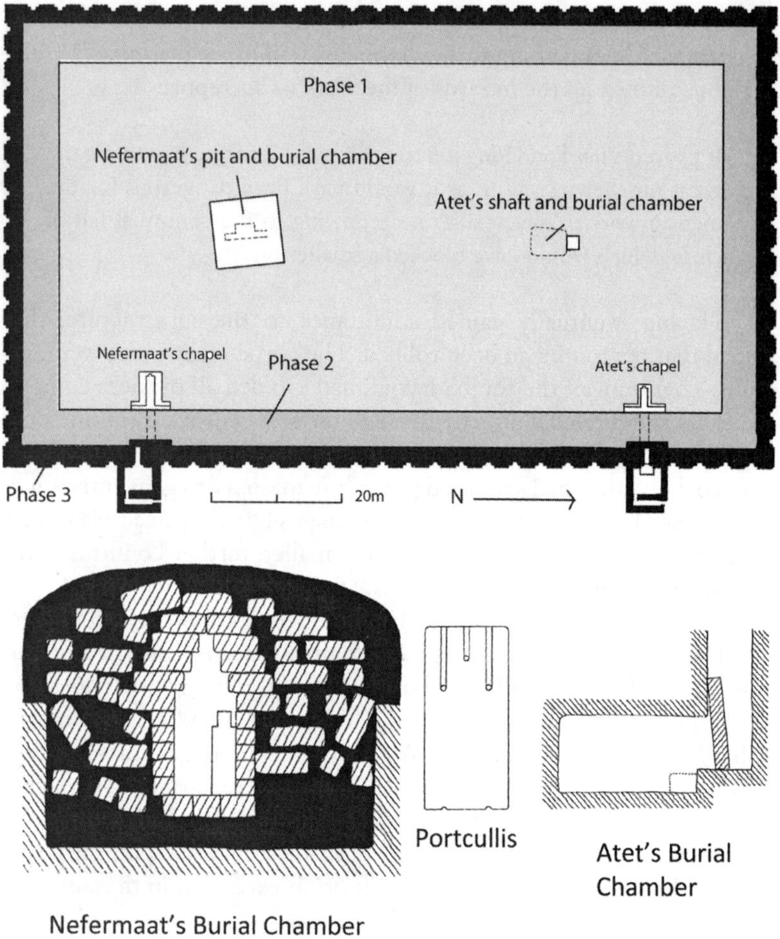

Figure 156. Plan and sections of burial chambers in Nefermaat and Atet's tomb at Meidum, together with a sketch of the portcullis showing the grooves and holes for lowering ropes.

The entrance to the burial chamber consisted of a stone-lined passage 3.24 m long that was found entirely blocked with "prepared stones," bonded with mortar.[129] At the corridor's end, the way was barred by a wooden door (probably the earliest extant wooden door found in Egypt[130]) made of two thick planks held together by cross-braces and locked in place with a thick beam across the door's wooden jambs, which was further secured by a layer of mortared stone blockwork across its top. The tomb's excavators went no further in their explorations, and the starting point of the access route has never been found,[131] leaving one to speculate that perhaps for security reasons its entrance stopped short in the pit, rather like that in Mastaba 17.

Much more is known about the details of the access route leading to Atet's burial chamber. This comprised a shaft, whose 1.75 to 1.82 m square entrance was axially placed about a third of the way in from the superstructure's north end, and, being only 0.04 percent of the latter's area, would have been extremely difficult to locate.[132] At the base of the shaft (whose depth is unrecorded), a 6.8 tonne, 3.5 m high, 0.55 m thick freestanding stone was found leaning against the south wall, its upper edge approximately 1.5 m above the burial chamber's entrance (Fig. 151). The stone had originally been lowered into position using ropes, which ran through three 0.1 m holes in its upper edge and were strung around a notched wooden beam. From the outer two holes, grooves ran down the slab's face that were designed to prevent the ropes from binding against the beam. Matching notches in the stone's base provided further anchor points and permitted the withdrawal of the ropes after the stone was in place. Once this had been done, the shaft was then filled with liquid mud, to seal the stone in place and block further access to the burial chamber. The latter was, unlike that of Atet's spouse, unremarkable; consisting of, as Wainwright put it, "a large chamber hewn out of the soft marl, without even a stone lining."[133]

Aboveground, the tomb's protective superstructure was built in several phases. The first stage consisted of a mud-brick-walled mastaba that protected the underlying substructures and access routes with an inner core consisting of millions of liters of liquid mud that had been poured over time in successive layers.[134] Once dried, these had set like concrete and provided an effective barrier against prospective tunnelers, as Petrie described:

> The material of hard dried mud was very difficult to examine, as it could scarcely be broken, and the included flints made it wear away chisels quicker than cutting limestone rock.[135]

Built into this mastaba's eastern face were two U-shaped chapels that were lined and faced with enormous orthostats,[136] the southernmost of which was formed from slabs that weighed between eight and thirty-three tonnes (to put these chapels into context, the famous 'Geese of Meidum' frieze originates from Atet's chapel). Although these decorated monoliths were undoubtedly a demonstration of the tomb owners' high status,[137] it is reasonable to suggest that they may also have had a defensive function, judging by the robbers' tunnels that led from both chapels into the tomb.[138] Indeed, during the mastaba's subsequent enlargement, external access to these chapels was first limited and then stopped altogether as the structure developed.[139] But whether this was for security reasons, it is difficult to be certain. When finally completed, the superstructure's roof was also covered with 1 to 1.5 m of sand and gravel, intended to soak up rain. Petrie's description of his search for the tomb's shafts demonstrates the effectiveness of the huge bulk of this superstructure at protecting its substructure:

> I endeavoured to find the well, or entrance to the chamber, during some weeks of work. The top coat of gravel was removed, and the mud body tested from end to end all along the axis; in the middle, around which Mariette's men had made some wide digging, I cut down to about 20 feet deep, and at the northern part in the axis, behind the north door, I also went down 20 feet deep. But only the same layers of Nile mud were found. I also cleared the N. end down to the ground, but found no trace of an entrance.[140]

In fact, the pit containing the burial of Nefermaat was only discovered in Petrie's second expedition at Meidum some nineteen years later, after around seven weeks of excavation by Wainwright, who had discovered the shaft of Atet a little earlier.[141] Their efforts revealed that despite the ample protection offered by this enormous mastaba, the burials had been robbed well before the latter's completion. Remains of the smashed body of Atet were found in her chamber, embedded in the liquid mud, which had seeped in during the sealing of the shaft. This demonstrates that the chamber was pillaged almost immediately after the burial, perhaps even before the shaft was sealed. Nefermaat's body and coffin were found in a similar condition, the mud slurry also having seeped into the burial chamber and surrounded his broken remains. The grim conclusion is that the robbery was yet another 'inside job' perpetrated by someone involved with either the construction of the tomb or the funeral arrangements.[142]

It is evident from the unusual and varied architecture of these large high-status tombs at Meidum that what we are seeing are direct responses to the security problems posed by the friable local geology, the nature of which, it is clear, the tomb builders at the site were all too well aware. Their defensive measures incorporated a variety of resistant materials, such as wood, stone, gravel, dried mud, and mud-brick, often in astounding quantities and sizes.

Tomb Security in Upper Egypt

There are very few well published tombs from the reign of Sneferu in Upper Egypt, though reports do exist for assorted stairway and shaft tombs in the necropoleis of Naga al-Deir, Reqaqnah, Abydos, Ballas, and al-Kab. The best examples, from the viewpoint of tomb security, are those from Naga al-Deir and al-Kab.

Naga al-Deir

Three examples of subterranean shaft tombs from the period were found at Cemetery 500-900 at Naga al-Deir, each with differing security arrangements. The first is tomb N 629. At the base of its approximately 1.1 m square, 3.7 m deep unlined shaft, a portcullis 1 m high, 0.95 m wide, and 0.2 m thick, weighing around 0.43 tonnes,[143] blocked the entrance to the burial chamber, which was cut in the gravel and protected by a roof 2.8 m thick.[144] Guarding the shaft and substructure aboveground was a mud-brick mastaba 7.2 m long and 3.9 m wide, with a gravel core. With an underlying shaft mouth that was around 4 percent of the latter's area, the tomb would have been easy to locate by *sondage* compared to much larger tombs. Indeed, robbers discovered the shaft at some point, dug through its fill, and tunneled over the top of the portcullis into the burial chamber's roof.

Nearby tomb N 739[145] and the 'twin mastaba' N 546 + N 604[146] were also accessed by shafts, but more unusually these were lined with mud-brick (Fig. 157). In N 739,[147] what Reisner referred to as "a rough construction stair" had been dug before a mud-brick shaft was formed within the rough descent (although it could originally have been a stairway tomb that had simply been updated?). Unusually, as backfill is rarely reported, Reisner noted that the shaft was backfilled with sand and gravel and capped with a layer of mud. At the shaft's base, the entrance to the burial chamber was blocked by a simple mud-brick wall. Beyond this, the chamber was protected by a gravel roof approximately 4.6 m thick, which had suffered a collapse. Overhead, the tomb's 10.35 m long, 6.3 m wide mastaba consisted of a 0.75 m thick mud-brick wall surrounding a gravel core, which reached a height of perhaps 1.5 m and had been roofed in brick. When the tomb was finally entered

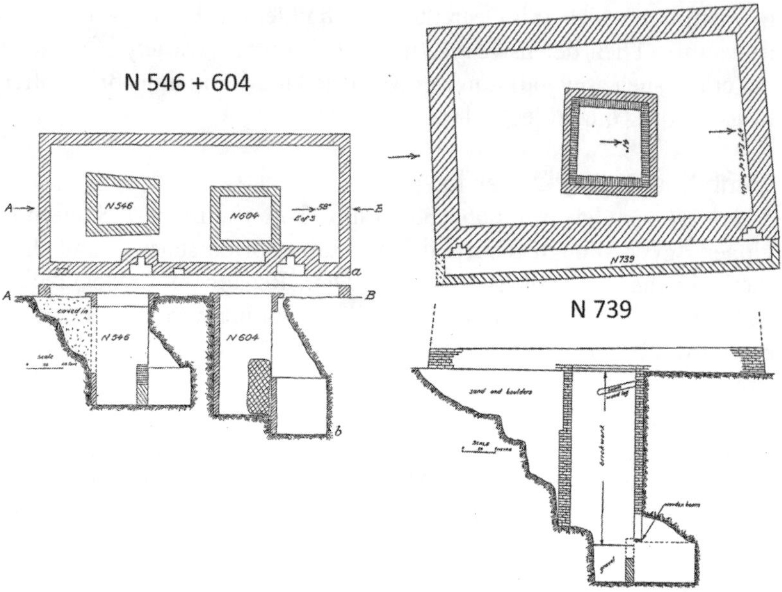

Figure 157. Shaft tombs N 546 + 604 and N 739 at Cemetery 500-900 at Naga al-Deir.

by Reisner, he found the body and grave goods broken and in disarray, not because of robbery but merely as a result of the partial collapse of the shaft and the burial chamber's ceiling.[148]

Lastly, the 'twin' mastaba N 546 + N 604 also used a so-called 'construction slope' in its southern shaft, the northernmost being a true shaft from the outset. Both were brick-lined. The southern shaft (N 546) was three meters deep and blocked at its base with a mud-brick wall, while the northern shaft (N 604) was 3.3 m deep and closed with a substantial 0.6 m thick, 2.2 tonne portcullis,[149] as well as a secondary mud-brick blocking. Internally, the burial chambers were protected by gravel roofs 2 m and 2.3 m thick, respectively. Overhead, the substructure and shafts were defended by an 8.95 m long, 3.5 m wide superstructure whose walls were only 0.3 m thick. Its core was filled with gravel like those of its neighbors, but bearing in mind its smaller size and larger number of shafts it would have offered less protection than that found in N 739. Indeed, tomb robbers had plundered both burials via their shafts, tunneling over their blockings and breaking through their burial chambers' roofs.[150] The large size of the tomb's shaft mouths in comparison to the mastaba's area (about 5 percent in each case), together with its shallow substructures, probably made it a comparatively easy target. That being said, the shaft opening of N 739, which was unrobbed, was 5.6 percent of its mastaba's area and therefore slightly larger![151]

These unremarkable tombs at Naga al-Deir incorporate all of the defensive features that a provincial tomb owner could have asked for—a shaft, portcullis, subterranean burial chamber, and protective mastaba—albeit on a smaller scale than their northern contemporaries in pyramid necropoleis. However, as we have seen with the three examples above, escaping the depredations of tomb robbers at this cemetery seems to have been more a matter of luck than the result of successful security features. The odds were not helped by the small size of the tombs, which would have increased the robbers' chances of locating their access routes and burial chambers.

Al-Kab

The last tomb that we shall look at is in al-Kab. Among the many subterranean shaft tombs from this period excavated by Quibell at this site, in only one are there enough details of its construction to permit discussion here. The 4.5 m deep shaft of Mastaba 'A,' the tomb of Kamena,[152] was centrally positioned under its superstructure. If Quibell's plan is accurate, its entrance was approximately four by three meters across, which is quite large for a tomb shaft, but may be accounted for by the need to introduce the constructional material used in its substructure. Aboveground, it was covered by a mud-brick mastaba with three-meter-thick walls. The mastaba was internally divided by cross-walls whose compartments were filled with what Quibell described as "brick earth," which presumably would have hidden and protected the shaft's entrance (Fig. 158). Once the burial was installed in the tomb, a freestanding sandstone portcullis approximately 7.5 cm thick was put in place that obstructed the burial chamber's entrance. The shaft was then backfilled with "thick, damp clay." Most unusually for a tomb at this site, when Quibell excavated the interior of the burial chamber it was found to be entirely lined with slabs of sandstone approximately 7.5 to 10 cm thick, with a roof of thinner sandstone sheets that had collapsed under the weight of the 3.5 m thick Nile sediments above.[153] Quibell also found the chamber "full of a very tenacious clay, much of which had to be cut away with a knife, for in so tough a substance a light blow with an adze has no effect."[154] Whether this clay fill was an intentional security measure or a result of flooding is unknown, but it certainly protected the tomb, as all the grave goods, and Kamena himself, albeit completely decomposed, were found still in situ.[155]

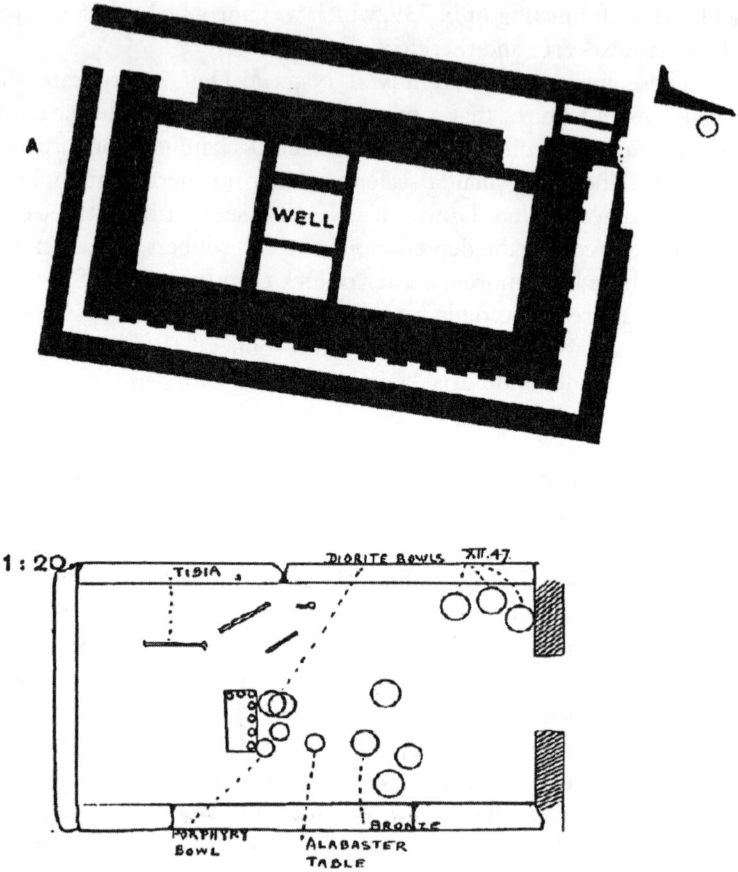

Figure 158. The superstructure and tomb plans of Kamena at al-Kab.

Thematic Analysis: The Architecture and Security of the Early Fourth Dynasty Private Tomb

During this period, although we see a new form of access route introduced at Meidum, some earlier types were still being used and others were in decline. Stair-shafts, for example, were only retained in the cemetery of Abusir, the shaft now becoming the predominant access route in the necropoleis of Dahshur, Meidum, Naga al-Deir, and al-Kab—its small plan and section still offering the best method of avoiding detection and the highest level of security. Where the local geology was weak, and a tomb owner's high status merited the investment, stone linings were now introduced to provide additional defense. This material was also an essential component of the new sloping corridors in the 'cut and cover' tombs of Meidum, forming the conduit within which their new plug-stone blockings could slide. Moreover, the entrances of some tombs at Meidum were now set deep belowground, their overlying backfill rendering them both unreachable and inviolable.

To secure the shaft and stair-shaft access routes of most of these tombs, the usual pourable backfills in the form of rubbles, *tafl*, detritus, and sand were used. At Meidum liquid mud proved very effective, although it seems it was used far too late in some cases. Portcullises, too, continued to play an important part, but despite their increasing size they were frequently tipped aside or tunneled over by tomb robbers. In addition, carefully built masonry blockings were used to seal some corridors at Abusir and Meidum and, more unusually, to fill shafts at Dahshur. While the new sloping corridors of the 'cut and cover' tombs at Meidum relied on plug-stones for closure, like those of their royal neighbor, once discovered by robbers they suffered a similar fate.

It is the entirely subterranean burial chamber accessed by shaft or stair-shaft that predominates during this period. New protective measures were introduced in those necropoleis with weak geology and royal connections, the deep-set rock-cut subterranean burial chambers at Abusir needing no further protection, and the poorer provincial tombs at Naga al-Deir relying on gravel alone. Stone linings provided additional defense in those burial chambers in the soft geologies of Meidum and the mastaba fields of Dahshur, as well as the Nile silts of al-Kab. Many of these were built using the new 'cut and cover' technique, with their masonry substructures constructed in a trench or pit. A few at Meidum were built on a massive scale, their pits backfilled with vast quantities of mud, gravel, and stone after the burial was complete.

Aboveground, the superstructures of the tombs at Naga al-Deir and al-Kab, like many of their predecessors elsewhere, were built of mud-brick with cores of gravel or soil, protecting their access routes and substructures in the usual way. The enormous solid mud-brick superstructures at Meidum imitated their forebears at Giza, Saqqara, and Beit Khallaf by housing their access routes within *massif* mastabas, trusting their bulk and footprints to compensate for the friable geology below. Exceptionally, Mastabas 16 and 17 depended on more unusual inner cores, with the former exploiting the resistant properties of oceans of hardened mud whose density hindered any digging, and the latter depending on the instability and impenetrability of vast quantities of free-flowing aggregate. Lastly, in the mastabas of Abusir and Dahshur, quarried stone featured extensively, both to increase their defensive properties and to aesthetically enhance their architecture.

Conclusion

The reign of Sneferu saw the builders and architects of the royal tomb face a 'steep learning curve' as they developed their skills in stone technology. This was reflected in the rapidly evolving security arrangements and architecture of the king's three pyramids. The lessons learned from the construction of these pyramids were frequently applied in the private tombs of the king's officials, but on a smaller scale.

Like its predecessor, the burial chamber in the king's first pyramid at Meidum was set above ground level, but within its own artificial 'knoll' of stone. This protected it from undermining in the soft geology and permitted access to it via a high-level entrance whose small sectioned sloping corridor was less detectable and whose incline facilitated its blocking with sliding plug-stones. Externally, the encompassing stone pyramid's enormous mass and footprint provided its internal arrangements with an unparalled level of protection. The substructure of the king's next tomb at Dahshur was built along the same lines, with a similar access route and closures, but for better protection its pyramid was on a much larger scale. Its faces were intentionally smooth from the beginning, making it harder to climb. However, the overly steep pyramid sides and weak geology resulted in structural failures. This caused the abandonment of the lower substructure and a change in the pyramid's incline, together with a new higher access route to the burial chamber, now further secured by two huge portcullises. Still unsatisfied, the king had his final pyramid made even larger, but by reducing its incline and expanding its footprint, his architects avoided its predecessor's fate. This brought benefits to its interior, which was now aboveground to avoid undermining; its burial chamber placed even higher up within the protective body of the king's final pyramid.

Meanwhile, private tombs in the various pyramid necropoleis were incorporating similar security features, which offered them extra protection in the soft geology, most notably at Meidum, where a few tombs were fitted with descending corridors and plug-stones like those in the adjacent pyramid. Additionally, stone-lined burial chambers were frequently installed in tombs at both Meidum and Dahshur, a few of them corbeled like those in the pyramids and a few others built on a cyclopean scale. Aboveground, while the bulk and footprints of enormous mud-brick *massif* mastabas protected some high-status tombs at Meidum, others used tonnes of gravel or vast quantities of mud for their defense instead. In some of the mastabas of Abusir and Dahshur, there was more use of stone, which, as in their royal counterparts, was exploited for its twofold architectural properties, both as an essential part of a tomb's fortification and for its beautification, setting the standard for the dynasties to come.

PLUG-STONES

From the early Fourth Dynasty, a new access route closure mechanism that suddenly appeared in conjunction with the raised pyramid entrance was the plug-stone.[156] This took the form of a rectangular cuboid stone blocking, used in numbers, which was specifically designed to closely fit within an inclined descending corridor of uniform section along its length. With its introduction in the pyramids of Sneferu, an in-depth form of rapid blocking had at last become available, whose level of protection, unlike a portcullis, was only limited by its corridor's length. However, its use was dependent on the surrounding architecture, as tailoring passages to specifically accommodate the blocks became essential. Therefore, factors such as ease of access, a uniform cross section, and the need for the incline to overcome the coefficient of friction, together with practical limits on the size of the stone, now had to be considered and incorporated in the design. Moreover, as we have seen in the Bent Pyramid, when the plug-stones were installed, they probably needed to be lubricated with mud or plaster both to aid their descent and to seal them in place. That notwithstanding, their apparent success and popularity as a blocking method is reflected in their continuous use right up until the end of the Middle Kingdom.[157] But, as we have seen throughout this book, once discovered, any number of plug-stones could be removed or bypassed by determined robbers, given sufficient time. And once removed, their surrounding corridors conveniently led directly to the heart of the tomb.

8
Conclusion

The aim of this book was to present an in-depth discussion of the architecture of tomb security in Egypt from the Predynastic Period until the end of the reign of King Sneferu, in order to review and establish the protective measures taken to defend the ancient Egyptian tomb. At the same time, I sought to discuss the influences these measures had on the design of royal and private tombs during the period concerned. These security features were examined chronologically from the Late Paleolithic until the end of the Predynastic Period, and a thematic analysis of the main architectural elements of the Egyptian tomb from the Early Dynastic Period onward was included at the end of each chapter. As a result, I hope I have demonstrated that many of the architectural features of the Egyptian tomb, while undoubtedly adapted over time to suit changing requirements, tastes, and ideologies, were originally the result of the need to protect the tomb and improve its defenses, rather than the initial consequence of religious or monumental considerations.

After an in-depth discussion of the funerary beliefs of the ancient Egyptians and the possible reasons why tombs needed to be made secure in Chapter 1, the book went on to look at the history of Egyptian tomb development, royal and private. It did this by discussing in separate chapters, from the tomb security point of view, all of the royal tombs from each dynasty, and then a broad selection of private tombs from the same period, thematically summarizing their relevant architectural and security features at the end of each chapter.

Early Responses to Tomb Robbery

The architecture of the earliest tombs was examined in Chapter 2 to assess if there was any evidence of efforts being made to defend them.

We saw that measures were taken to protect the grave from the earliest times and that there is evidence that tomb robbery was commonplace in Egypt from the Badarian Period onward, especially among higher-status burials. In response to these depredations, simple security measures were employed during the Badarian Period and Naqada I, which used vegetative materials, such as wood branches, twigs, reeds, and matting, to reinforce or support the backfill, and perhaps an ephemeral mound of soil over the whole to protect the underlying grave. Furthermore, by Naqada II, the desire for greater storage for funerary goods led to elite graves with deeper pits, whose sides were consolidated with mud-brick and supported wooden roofs for overhead protection. However, these roofs could often be tunneled under by tomb robbers, due to their lack of depth and weak surrounding geology. During Naqada IIIA, as a reaction to this problem and continued pillaging, it was suggested that the roofs of some high-status tombs were now made deeper to increase their overhead and lateral defenses. Alternatively, at a few sites, slabs of stone were used for better protection. To exploit the surrounding geology for defense, the first pit tombs with loculi were introduced, which provided natural overhead protection and concurrently heralded the introduction of the earliest stone blockings. This coincided with the emergence of more permanent aboveground defenses for the substructure, which in Egypt took the form of mud-brick superstructures, whose introduction anticipated developments in the dynasties to come. Thus it seems clear that many of the elements of early tomb architecture, which were incorporated in the tombs of the Early Dynastic Period and beyond, developed as a result of the search for improved security during the Predynastic Period, or even earlier.

Securing the Substructure

The discussion of the architecture and security of the burial chamber from Chapter 3 onward has illustrated that at the beginning of the Early Dynastic Period, like their Predynastic forerunners, the majority of both royal and private substructures were still lined and roofed pit tombs. In order to make them secure, a wide variety of architectural solutions was developed, which were usually contingent on the surrounding geology, the status of the owner, and the material resources available. They were typically reinforced with mud-brick of varying thickness, or less frequently liners of wood or stone, and were closed with a wooden roof or backfill that was either secure in its own right or capable of supporting a superstructure. It is evident from the numerous robberies in these tombs, however, that their substructures remained susceptible to overhead and lateral attack, the robberies still occurring despite sometimes complex reinforcements, or changes to the tombs' positions or axes, because of their shallow depths and vulnerable roofs.

In response to these threats, entirely subterranean substructures were introduced in the latter half of the First Dynasty, which were almost universally adopted from the Second Dynasty onward, in both royal and private tombs. No longer reliant on a built roof or backfill, the effectiveness of these unlined substructures was determined by the density of the surrounding geological matrix and the depths of their cover, which in royal pyramids of the early Third Dynasty was often tens of meters.

However, the many robbers' tunnels at sites like Helwan confirm that in areas with weak geology, alternative architectural solutions were needed. An answer to this problem was revealed by the analysis of the substructures of the Third and early Fourth Dynasties, where it was demonstrated that increased expertise in stone engineering meant there was no longer a need for tomb builders to rely on just the immediate surrounding geology for protection. This was evident both in the magnificent corbeled stone burial chambers of the tombs of King Sneferu, which instead of being set deep underground in the friable rock were raised up into the core of his pyramids, and in the subterranean burial chambers of the tombs of the private necropoleis that accompanied them, whose stone linings were designed to compensate for the weak surrounding ground. Moreover, although these developments progressively improved burial chambers' security, it was clear that their resulting impregnability often forced their plunderers to take a different approach, which was usually via the access route.

Protecting the Access Route

We saw from Chapter 4 onward that the introduction of external access routes in the First Dynasty permitted a tomb to be completed before its owner's demise, but brought concomitant problems, as these too required defending and concealment. To protect these new stairways, their positions and axes were frequently varied to avoid detection, and in weaker geologies they were often reinforced and roofed. Despite these measures, they remained vulnerable, and as a result, by the end of the dynasty, the stairways of a few private tombs were concealed under their superstructures to protect them from attack. Moreover, with the advent of the more secure subterranean substructure toward the end of the First Dynasty, the stairway's security became even more vital, as it was now the only practical way into the tomb.

During the Second and Third Dynasties, while the descents of some tombs remained external, for better protection many of them were brought within the perimeter of their superstructures. As substructures were dug deeper for greater security, their connecting stairways often grew longer and thus needed changes in direction to permit them to fit, which paradoxically made it easier to locate their positions by *sondage*. To solve this problem the stair-shaft was introduced, whose reduced profile and plan allowed even greater depths to be reached within the superstructure's span, thus increasing the substructure's protection.

Additionally, it was clear that to improve the access route's security even further, the vertical shaft was now widely used, because its small plan and cross section were not only harder to locate but also, once found, more difficult to negotiate. Indeed, the vertical shaft's success as a secure access route was confirmed by its extensive use in Egyptian private tombs for the next two millenia.

We also saw that by the Third Dynasty the access routes of royal tombs had taken a separate path of development and adopted the subterranean descending corridor, which was protected by its pyramid complex and entirely concealed from view. It was noted how in the tomb of the last king of the dynasty, in a change of approach to improve its security, the entrance was raised up in the face of the brick pyramid and made inaccessible, its descent protected by the pyramid's mass and a passage of stone. Furthermore, this approach was retained in the three pyramids of Sneferu that followed, whose concealed and unreachable entrances led to descending corridors completely enshrouded in stone. Their cross sections becoming progressively smaller for greater security, and their architecture and gradients specifically designed to accommodate plug-stones. The effectiveness of this feature, I proposed, was signaled by its widespread adoption in the majority of royal tombs, and less frequently in private examples, throughout both the Old and Middle Kingdoms.

Securing the Access Route

The creation of an access route meant that it needed to be secured, and in Chapters 4 to 7 we looked at the static and mechanical methods used to seal the access routes in royal and private tombs from the mid-First Dynasty onward. The static forms consisted of a wide variety of blockings that were either loose aggregates or built obstructions, the majority of which were used as void fillers. Their effectiveness depended in all cases on their volume and bulk density. Moreover, it was highlighted that from the Third Dynasty onward, in a search of greater security, more specialized backfills and increasingly resistant closures were chosen for use in royal and high-status tombs. While effective as blockings, none of these methods dictated the shape of their surrounding architecture, as they could all be made to fill any zone. The discussion also demonstrated that some blockings, such as portcullises and plug-stones, rather than being static, were simple mechanisms that could speedily and effectively secure a tomb. Moreover, we saw that special architecture was needed for the installation of the stones, and that this in part governed the access route's design. The results of these requirements, it was suggested, were visible in the architecture of the access routes and sloping corridors of private and royal tombs of the period, and right up into the Old and Middle Kingdoms.

The Protective Role of the Superstructure

Throughout the book, the defensive aspects of the superstructure were discussed. From its earliest initial appearances in the Predynastic Period, it was suggested that from the reign of Hor-Aha onward the substructures of royal and private pit tombs were probably protected by a superstructure of some form. Whether in early royal tombs this took the form of a sand tumulus or a mastaba of mud-brick, like those of their private contemporaries, remains open to question. However, it is certain from the evidence gathered from the excavations of private tombs that the mass and footprint of a superstructure became the standard method for defending a pit tomb's roof and substructure from overhead and lateral attack, and concomitantly, acted both as a monument and the focus for the celebration and maintenance of the tomb-owner's cult. Additionally, it appears that in some high-status private tombs, a superstructure could also function as a secure storehouse for its owner's grave goods and, with the introduction of external access routes in the mid-First Dynasty, provide protection for some, or all, of the stairway and portcullis shaft as well. With the adoption of entirely subterranean substructures at the end of the dynasty, I suggested that this role became increasingly important, as although no roofs or backfills required protection, access stairways in the Second Dynasty were now often concealed within the mastaba and were thus the only way in. While the architects of royal tombs now relied on the architecture of the pyramid complex for the protection of the royal access route, the shrinking size and improved security of access route entrances among the private tombs of the period permitted a greater architectural exploitation of the internal space within their superstructures. The chapels created were used for the maintenance of the tomb owner's cult, and saw the introduction of magical offerings in the form of wall decorations, which replaced hitherto stealable grave goods and thus improved the tomb's security. Additionally, the continued construction of mud-brick *massifs* during this period demonstrated that a huge footprint and the ability to totally conceal an access route were still considered to be key elements of a tomb's defense, especially in necropoleis with weak geology. It was acknowledged that in the latter circumstances, and concomitant with its use in royal pyramids, stone was also increasingly used to provide similar protection on a smaller scale, thus auguring its widespread adoption in the mastaba fields of Giza and elsewhere in the dynasties to come.

The analysis of the superstructures of royal tombs from Chapter 6 onward established that a desire for greater security and an increased engineering ability was marked in the Third Dynasty by Djoser's mastaba at Saqqara, which was the first to be built of solid stone. Despite this new material, its effectiveness against attack was, like those of its private contemporaries, still limited by its low profile. This problem was resolved by adding further layers of masonry, which increased its mass and footprint immensely and protected its substructure omnidirectionally, with the first step pyramid made of stone. The success of the new royal superstructure's form as both protector and monument was then made manifest by its adoption by the kings of the remainder of the dynasty, using both mud-brick and stone. By the early Fourth Dynasty, advances in stone technology meant that the royal superstructure could now offer its substructure even greater protection, despite the latter's security being compromised by friable ground. This seems to have been achieved in Sneferu's new tombs by drawing their burial chambers up within the body of their superstructures, whose enormous bulk and footprints compensated for their necropoleis' weak geologies, and whose concomitant change in external profile now expressed new concepts of kingship, in the form of the first true pyramids.

An Evolving Architectural Response to Tomb Robbery

We have seen that, from the earliest times, a variety of security measures were used to protect the grave in Egypt as a direct response to the constant threat of tomb robbery. These architectural elements, rather than following a smooth and progressive timeline, were subject to empirical development and adaptation in the light of experience. Furthermore, their developments were usually interdependent on each other and formed a symbiotic relationship, each new measure having an effect on another in turn. It is also clear from the changes in tomb design that took place over time in different necropoleis with varying geologies that this evolution was inexorably linked to advances in materials, engineering, and mining technology, which together with human ingenuity were used to either exploit or compensate for the tomb's surrounding geology to make it secure.

The effects of these defensive measures are evident in the changing architectural elements of the Egyptian tomb and were certainly the major driving force behind many of them. However, it is undeniable that during this process some components, such as burial chambers and mastabas, were also modified to suit changing requirements, fashions, and beliefs. Despite the many alterations, the fundamental physical purpose of many of these structures, which I suggest was to protect the burial, remained largely unchanged.

Securing the Eternal Afterlife in the Egyptian Tomb

We have established that in ancient Egypt, the tomb, far from being just a convenient way to dispose of the dead, was in fact a multi-purpose structure. At its most basic, as in any culture, it provided a salubrious method of disposing of a body. But taking the funerary beliefs of the ancient Egyptians into account, we can see that it also provided a vehicle by which those beliefs could be realized and a successful afterlife attained and subsequently maintained. The tomb first provided physical protection for the body, which needed to remain intact in order that its other spiritual forms, the *ba* and the *ka*, which had been part of it in life and had separated from it in death, could successfully reunite with the body on a daily basis to become an 'effective' being, or *akh*, in the afterlife. Second, it provided a dwelling for the aforementioned entities to inhabit, throughout a perpetual and cyclical process of renewal. Third, it acted as a repository for those valuables and personal accoutrements that accompanied the deceased for use in the afterlife. Finally, it provided a visible monument to the deceased, whose offering place was a liminal zone, a portal, by which the aforementioned spiritual entities could access the outside world and partake of offerings supplied by the living, and through which the living could interact and communicate with the dead. In order for all these vital functions to continue undisturbed, the tomb needed to remain intact and its contents secure. But from early on, its visibility meant that it was subject to the constant depredations of tomb robbers, vandals, and the fortunes of war, which meant that structural measures had to be introduced to improve its security.

This book has established that many aspects of the architecture of the ancient Egyptian tomb originate from those security measures that were initially introduced to defend it from robbers. As these security features evolved, during what can best be described as an ongoing 'arms race' between tomb builders and tomb robbers (although it seems these were often one and the same), they were widely adopted and absorbed into the general corpus of mortuary architecture. As a result, many of these innovations go largely unnoticed today. What is often forgotten is that when they were introduced, they were 'cutting edge' security measures that in combination with the tomb itself, and its funerary cult, were intended to ensure the tomb owner's enjoyment of the afterlife for all eternity.

Chronology

LE = Lower Egypt; ME = Middle Egypt; UE = Upper Egypt.
All dates are approximate and theoretical until 690 BC.

Prehistory	
Middle Paleolithic	175,000–40,000 BC
Upper Paleolithic	40,000–35,000 BC
Late Paleolithic	21,000–12,000 BC
Epi-Paleolithic	12,000–7000 BC

Neolithic and Predynastic Periods, c. 5000–2950 BC	
Fayum Culture (ME)	5000 BC
Merimde Beni Salama (LE)	5000–4200 BC
Al-Omari Culture (LE)	4000 BC
Maadi Culture (LE)	4000–3400 BC
Badarian Culture (ME & UE)	5000–4000 BC
Naqada I	3900–3650 BC
Naqada II	3650–3300 BC
Naqada IIIA	3300–3150 BC
Naqada IIIB (Dynasty '0')	3150–2950 BC

Early Dynastic Period, c. 2950–2670 BC	
First Dynasty	2950–2800 BC
King Narmer	
Hor-Aha	
Djer	
Merneith	

Den	
Adjib	
Semerkhet	
Qa'a	
Second Dynasty	2800–2670 BC
Hotepsekhemwy	
Raneb	
Ninetjer	
Peribsen	
Khasekhemwy	

Old Kingdom, 2670–2195 BC

Third Dynasty	2670–2600 BC
Djoser	
Sekhemkhet	
Khaba	
Huni	
Fourth Dynasty	2600–2470 BC
Sneferu	
Khufu (Cheops)	
Djedefre	
Khafre	
Menkaure	
Shepseskaf	
Fifth Dynasty	2470–2360 BC
Sixth Dynasty	2360–2195 BC

First Intermediate Period, c. 2195–1540 BC

Seventh and Eighth Dynasties	2195–2160 BC
Ninth and Tenth Dynasties (LE)	2160–2040 BC
Eleventh Dynasty (a) (UE)	2160–2065 BC

Middle Kingdom, c. 2065–1540 BC

Eleventh Dynasty (b)	2065–1995 BC
Twelfth Dynasty	1995–1780 BC
Thirteenth Dynasty	1780–1650 BC
Fourteenth Dynasty (NE Delta)	1700–1650 BC

Fifteenth Dynasty (LE)	1650–1535 BC
Sixteenth Dynasty (UE)	1660–1590 BC
Seventeenth Dynasty (UE)	1585–1540 BC

New Kingdom, c.1540–664 BC

Eighteenth Dynasty	1540–1278 BC
Nineteenth Dynasty	1278–1176 BC
Twentieth Dynasty	1178–1078 BC
Twenty-first Dynasty	1078–941 BC
Twenty-second Dynasty	943–736 BC
Twenty-third Dynasty	736–666 BC
Twenty-fourth Dynasty (LE)	734–721 BC
Twenty-fifth Dynasty	713–664 BC

Saite Period, 664–525 BC

Twenty-sixth Dynasty	664–525 BC

Late Period, 525–332 BC

Twenty-seventh Dynasty (Persians)	525–405 BC
Twenty-eighth Dynasty	404–399 BC
Twenty-ninth Dynasty	399–380 BC
Thirtieth Dynasty	380–339 BC
Thirty-first Dynasty (Persians)	339–332 BC

Hellenistic Period, 332 BC–AD 395

Dynasty of Macedon	332–310 BC
Ptolemaic Dynasty	310–30 BC
Roman Period	30 BC–AD 395

I am indebted to Dr. Aidan Dodson for providing me with a copy of his *The Royal Tombs of Ancient Egypt* (2016) chronology, from which I have extrapolated the above from the Early Dynastic Period onward. The remainder is drawn together from various sources, including the preferred chronology for contributors to the UCLA Encyclopedia of Egyptology (https://uee.cdh.ucla.edu/chronology).

Notes

Epigraph

1 Strudwick 2005, 219.
2 Porter and Moss 1974–81, 626.

Notes to Preface

1 Spencer 1982, 74–111.
2 Arnold 1991, 218–31.

Notes to Introduction

1 Reisner, 1908, 11.
2 Those seeking that level of detail should perhaps consider reading my published thesis (Clark 2016) or Reisner's *The Development of the Egyptian Tomb Down to the Accession of Cheops* (1936).

Notes to Chapter 1

1 Snape 2011, 8–10.
2 Spencer 1993, 47. The earliest reported cases of tomb robbery date from the Badarian Period (Brunton and Caton-Thompson 1928, 9; Hoffman 1990, 143; Anderson 1992, 60–61).
3 Tombs 852 and 1845 at Tarkhan, which date to Naqada IIIA (Hendrickx 2001, 100), discovered by Petrie (1914, 2–3) are perhaps the earliest extant examples of superstructures with offering chapels.
4 Ikram and Dodson 1998, 15; Assmann 2005, 10–11; Taylor 2010, preface.
5 Bárta 2011b, 29–30; Snape 2011, 12–13, and 21.
6 For example, the First Dynasty monumental mastaba tombs at Saqqara North, such as S 3504 (Emery 1954, 5–13; Porter and Moss 1974–81, 445) and S 3035 (Emery 1938; Porter and Moss 1974–81, 440–42).

7 These beliefs and their relationship to the tomb are only briefly summarized here. They were constantly refined, revised, and added to over the three millennia of dynastic rule and thus form an extremely complex topic in themselves, which space does not permit to be fully explored in this book. For in-depth analyses of these beliefs throughout the history of Pharaonic Egypt, see Lloyd 1989; Assmann 2005; Taylor 2010.

8 The earliest textual sources concerning Egyptian beliefs about the afterlife are those found in the Pyramid Texts from the latter end of the Old Kingdom, the first examples occurring in the pyramid of Unas (Hays 2012, 1). For the Pyramid Texts also see Allen (2005).

9 Žabkar 1968, 60–61; Bolshakov 1997, 284; Assmann 2005, 87–90 and 96–97. See Lloyd (1989, 118–19) for a succinct summary of the nature of the *ba* and the *ka*.

10 Reisner 1936, 1; Assmann 2005, 122; Dodson and Ikram 2008, 14; Snape 2011, 21–23.

11 Kanawati 2001, 20 and 24; Taylor 2001, 20–21; 2010, 13, 89, and 104–105. Until the Fifth Dynasty however, Allen (2006, 10) suggests that the afterlife of the private person was considered to be largely restricted to the confines of the tomb.

12 Taylor 2001, 21, 31–32, and 46; Pinch 2002, 93; Allen 2005, 7–8; Assmann 2005, 101–102; Dodson and Ikram 2008, 16.

13 Hays 2009, 195.

14 In the event that the body was damaged, a representation of the deceased in the form of a statue or relief, or even just the inscribed name itself, could substitute for it instead (Bolshakov 1997, 210–12; Ikram and Dodson 1998, 15; Taylor 2001, 23–24).

15 Snape 2011, 2.

16 Stevenson 2011, 65–92.

17 Emery 1961, 214–35; Taylor 2001, 107–11; Grajetzki 2003, 7–10.

18 Although there is little documentary evidence concerning the motivations of tomb robbers, one can reasonably assume that they were stealing for personal gain. In the late Twentieth Dynasty, for example, it appears from the large number of "traders in every house" listed in the famous Tomb Robbery Papyri, BM 10068, that the items stolen by the accused necropolis workers (in this case gold, silver, and cloth) were frequently bartered with merchants for more mundane goods (Peet 1930, 90–91, n. 18). Moreover, in the contemporary papyrus BM10052, it was reported that the gold and silver booty belonging to one of the accused was used to obtain land, oxen, a slave, spelt, honey, and wine (Peet 1930,

144–45). For an in-depth discussion on tomb robbers and their loot, see Phillips (1992).

19 Phillips 1992, 163–64.

20 Taylor 2001, 95; 2010, 104. The Egyptians frequently supplemented or replaced real items in these situations with models or images, with the intention that should the regular maintenance of the offering cult cease for any reason, they would magically ensure a continuous supply (Spencer 1982, 63–67; Tooley 1995, 8–10). By the Old Kingdom this substitution had become the usual practice, and the supply of fresh foodstuffs continued to decline until the custom was revived in the New Kingdom (Taylor 2001, 93–95).

21 Anderson 2000, 129; Dodson and Ikram 2008, 16–17; Taylor 2010, 23.

22 For example, in addition to communicating with the dead, requests could be made for them to intercede on a relative's behalf with worldly problems, such as an illness or dispute, or pleas could be made for them not to haunt the living (Baines 1991, 152–53; Ritner 1993, 180–83; Taylor 2001, 95). For examples of letters to the dead dating from the Old to the New Kingdom, see Gardiner and Sethe (1928) and Wente (1990, 210–19).

23 Lloyd 1989, 129; Assmann 2005, 13 and 181.

24 Committing an act of vandalism against someone's tomb by damaging it, or erasing their name, image, or inscriptions in an act of *damnatio memoriae*, was considered to be as serious as damaging the body itself, and would result in the destruction of the tomb owner's afterlife (Dodson and Ikram 2008, 77; Ritner 2012, 396–69; Eyre 2013, 335).

25 For example, textual sources, such as the "Instruction of Merikare," suggest that the robbing and burning of the First and Second Dynasty royal tombs at Abydos may have occurred during the upheavals and chaos of the First Intermediate Period (Dreyer 2003b, 69; Snape 2011, 114). Moreover, it has been suggested that the plundering of some Middle Kingdom royal pyramids, such as those of Senwosrets II and III and Amenemhat III, could have taken place during the conquests by the Hyksos in the Fifteenth Dynasty, who may also have been responsible for the destruction of the tombs of the Sixteenth Dynasty kings at Thebes and Abydos (Ryholt 1997, 143–48).

Notes to Chapter 2

1 Vermeersch et al. 1998, 475–78.

2 Wendorf and Close 2005, 12–14.

3 Midant-Reynes 2000, 63–64.

4 Wendorf 1968, 954–57.
5 Geus 1991, 57; Bard 2007, 78.
6 Dodson and Ikram 2008, 31.
7 Butzer 1976, 9.
8 Arkell 1975, 146; Wenke 1989, 136.
9 Grajetzki 2003, 1.
10 Kemp 1968, 22–33; Midant-Reynes 2000, 116.
11 Lacovera 1988, 20; Wenke 1989, 137.
12 Reisner 1936, 1–3; Badawy 1954, 26; Adams 1988, 17; Dodson and Ikram 2008, 31.
13 Reisner 1936, 245 and 367.
14 Dupras et al. 2006, 109.
15 Personal communication by John Clarke of Brookwood Cemeteries Ltd. (March 17, 2009).
16 Connor 2007, 109.
17 Reisner 1936, 1–3; Badawy 1954, 26; Dodson and Ikram 2008, 31.
18 O'Connor 2009, 153.
19 Hoffman 1990, 143.
20 Brunton and Caton-Thompson 1928, 9.
21 Anderson 1992, 57–61.
22 Brunton and Caton-Thompson 1928, 18 and 20.
23 Connor 2007, 86.
24 Hoffman 1990, 192; Mortenson 2005, 717.
25 Debono and Mortensen 1990, 72–75.
26 See Klasens 1957, 64–65, plates 8.1–2 and 9.1.
27 Rizkana and Seeher 1990, 97–98; Seeher 1992, 226–28; Seeher 1999, 455.
28 Wengrow 2006, 36.
29 Hassan 1988, 138; Bard 2005a, 31.
30 Castillos 1982, 173–78; Hoffman 1990, 146.
31 Petrie and Quibell 1896, 18.
32 Midant-Reynes 2000, 187.
33 Friedman 1997, 2; 1998, 5.
34 Friedman 2008a, 20.
35 Ayrton and Loat 1911, 8; Reisner 1936, 1; Baumgartel 1960, 125.
36 Midant-Reynes 2000, 187; Wengrow 2006, 122.
37 Podzorski 2008, 98.
38 La Loggia 2009, 183.
39 Spencer 1982, 33; Brewer 2005, 95.
40 Bard 1994a, 112.
41 Kemp 1973, 41–42.

42 Petrie and Mace 1901, 33; Dreyer et al. 1996, 15–21; Görsdorf, Dreyer, and Hartung 1998, 643.
43 Spencer 1982, 34.
44 Adams 2004, 47–50; Friedman 2005, 4–5; 2006a, 7; 2008a, 14–18 and 26.
45 That Cemetery HK6 probably remained the focus of ongoing ancestor veneration and cult for a considerable time is evident from beer jars found at the site that date to at least the Third Dynasty (Friedman 2008c, 11).
46 Friedman 2008b, 1178–79.
47 Reisner 1936, 5.
48 Friedman 2008a, 18; Friedman, van Neer, and Linseele 2011, 187.
49 Porter and Moss 1937, 199; Kemp 1973, 43; Figueiredeo 2004, 19.
50 Quibell and Green 1902, 20–22.
51 Friedman 2006b, 11–12; 2008a, 22; 2008b, 1189 and n. 33.
52 Personal communication by Renée Friedman (May 7, 2009).
53 Williams 1994, 278.
54 Hassan 1988, 138.
55 Lacovera 1988, 20; Jánosi 1999, 27; Grajetzki 2003, 4; Dodson and Ikram 2008, 31.
56 Adams 1996, 13, fig. 6.
57 The tomb originally dated to Naqada IC–IIA, but had a newer brick-lined tomb inserted within its old structure (Friedman, van Neer, and Linseele 2011, 159).
58 Adams 2004, 41–42.
59 Friedman, van Neer, and Linseele 2011, 160. Recently discovered postholes suggest that it may originally have been flanked by an aboveground offering chapel dated to Naqada IC–IIA (Friedman 2011, 4–5).
60 Dreyer 1992, 295–96; 1998, 4–9, 17, and 19.
61 Wengrow 2006, 154.
62 Hendrickx and van Rossum 1994, 149 and 151.
63 Hendrickx and van Rossum 1994, 186, 194, and 215.
64 The use of stone to form a protective roof is more common during the First and Second Dynasties. For example, there are small pit tombs with stone roofs from Abu Rawash dating to Naqada IIIB–C1, such as tombs 363, 393, and 394 in Cemetery 300 (Klasens 1959, 34, plate 19.1) and the slightly later Naqada IIID tombs 820 and 836 from Cemetery 800 (Klasens 1960, 72). From the Second Dynasty there are numerous examples in Upper Egypt, for example, the stone-roofed tombs from al-Siba‘iya, al-Qara, and al-Masa‘id, and

tombs 4370, 4774, and 4379 from Cemetery 3500 at Naga al-Deir (Mace 1909, 20–21, 59–60, and 65). Additionally, there are two small, stone-roofed graves at al-Kab, nos. 76 and 78 (Hendrickx and van Rossum 1994, 208–209, 214, plates 58 and 61), which date to Naqada IIIC1.

65 Hendrickx and van Rossum 1994, 151–52.

66 Smith 1994, 361 and 372; Porter and Moss 1995, 52.

67 Firth 1927, 201.

68 Firth 1927, 207–208; Smith 1994, 363.

69 Firth 1927, 213.

70 Stevenson 2012, 230–41.

71 Williams 1986, 1–2 and 176–79; Smith 1994, 376; Wilkinson 1999, 48.

72 Seele 1974, 29.

73 Williams 1986, 176 and 229–358.

74 Wilkinson 1999, 48.

75 Seele 1974, 35; Williams 1986, 14–20 and 344.

76 Needler 1984, 111. Among the finds were wavy-handled Naqada IIIA jars and an A-Group bowl (Williams 1987, 19, n. 38).

77 De Morgan 1909, 271–72.

78 Williams 1980, 15. The A-Group cultures' earlier ceramic assemblages (typical pottery boxes found in funerary contexts) demonstrate historically strong associations with Upper Egypt. This is seen in the characteristic types of northern Early A-Group pottery that are found in many of the cemetery and habitation sites at Hierakonpolis (Gatto 2003, 15).

79 Wegner (1996, 98–100) writes: "The Lower Nubian A-Group was closely tied to the emerging Predynastic kingdoms of Southern Egypt, probably competitively as well as through trade and other modes of interaction." Additionally, Gatto (2006, 70–71) suggests that the pottery assemblages, together with the Late A-Groups' adoption of similar animal burial practices and side-chambered tomb designs, such as those at Hierakonpolis, points to either a mixed population or possibly a regional culture that shared common beliefs or a close relationship.

80 Birrell 2000, 18; Friedman 2008a, 26.

81 Hendrickx, Van Neer, Linseele, and Friedman 2004, 117.

82 Hoffman 1982, 48; Adams 1996, 2; 2000, 23.

83 Köhler 2004, 307; Smythe 2004, 328.

84 Petrie 1914, 2–3; Hendrickx 2001, 100; Mawdsley 2012, 229, n. 48.

85 Snape 2011, 11–13.

86 Hoffman 1982, 146.

Notes to Chapter 3

1 The progression of the Early Dynastic Period followed in this book is that suggested by Kahl (2006, 94–95), in which the Abydos-based kings Iry-Hor and Ka of 'Dynasty 0' are the predecessors of Narmer, who is regarded as the founding monarch of the First Dynasty.

2 This historical period can also be described in 'relative chronology' terms as Naqada IIIB–IIIC2. For a discussion of this method of dating, which is based on archaeological finds and is intended to compensate for the absence of a written historical record due to the lack of a writing system in Egypt during this period, see Hendrickx (2011, 15–16).

3 Dreyer 2003b, 64.

4 Porter and Moss 1937, 87; Kaiser and Dreyer 1982, 235; Hendrickx 2006, 88–89.

5 Kaiser and Dreyer 1982, 225; Dreyer et al. 1996, 49, fig. 1. Originally intended to be a two-chambered tomb, chamber '0,' which was found filled with wine jars, was only added later (Dreyer 2007b, 193–94).

6 Kaiser and Dreyer 1982, 220. Although only traces of the roof remain, Kaiser and Dreyer (1982, 224–25) have suggested that it was structurally similar to that found in nearby tombs B16–8/9b and Chamber 'x.' Moreover, in several tombs at Umm al-Qa'b the wooden roof beams overlap the brick lining of the tomb chamber itself, but this is within the tomb pit (below desert level), which is usually somewhat larger at the top than at the bottom (personal communication by Günter Dreyer, November 21, 2009).

7 Petrie 1901, 7, plate 59; Porter and Moss 1937, 87; Kaiser and Dreyer 1982, 221–22; Dreyer et al. 2003, 86.

8 Personal communication by Günter Dreyer (November 21, 2009).

9 Porter and Moss 1937, 88; Kaiser 1964, 100.

10 Kaiser and Dreyer 1982, 220–21, fig. 12.

11 Kaiser and Grossmann 1979, n. 10. This was in the twentieth century. Whether the ground was quite as firm in the third millennium BC is, of course, open to question.

12 La Loggia (2009, 175) describes the engineering principles behind the design of successful earth-retaining walls in Egyptian pit tombs: "The design of gravity-retaining earth structures is based on the theory of mass; that is, the greater the thickness of the wall (i.e., the heavier the wall is), the higher the lateral earth pressures that can be resisted by the wall, and the higher it can be built. Furthermore, when the wall is built with a lean-back, the lateral earth distribution on the wall is reduced, allowing it to be built higher with a reduced thickness."

13 Dodson and Ikram 2008, 134; Engel 2008, 35; O'Connor 2009, 153.

14 Dreyer 2003b, 64.

15 The possible existence of superstructures at this site is still the subject of some debate. For an overview of the current thinking on this topic, see O'Connor 2009, 151–56.

16 Porter and Moss 1937, 88; Kaiser 1964, 100; Kaiser and Grossmann 1979, 160.

17 Spencer 1996, 76. Most of the occupants of these graves were under twenty-five years old and had probably been sacrificed in order to accompany the king into the afterlife. In addition, accompanying them were seven lions for the king's hunt in the next world (Dreyer 2007b, 195). For further reading on subsidiary burials and their possible purposes, see Morris (2007a, 15–38) and van Dijk (2007, 135–55).

18 Petrie 1901, 7; Kaiser and Dreyer 1982, 213–15 and 218. Kaiser (1981, 247–54) suggested that these shrines were possibly intended to act as a model palace or chapel for the king's use in the hereafter. Alternatively, they may have been intended to protect their contents from the gaze of profane eyes and the likelihood of damage during construction. This may have been necessary due to the increased time now needed to close the tomb securely with the stronger roofing after the installation of the burial (Kaiser and Dreyer 1982, 248). Thus, they may have both protected the contents from interference by the tomb's builders and acted, once the tomb was closed, as a final bastion of defense against tomb robbers.

19 Kaiser and Dreyer 1982, 214–17.

20 Kaiser and Grossmann 1979, 159. Dreyer (2007b, 195) suggests that a sand tumulus protected the grave.

21 La Loggia (2009, 178) has recently studied fifteen First Dynasty tombs at Saqqara and comes to the conclusion that the primary function of the thick mud-brick walls of the burial chambers at that site was connected with security: "The thickening of these walls did not make them impregnable, but it would have made the task of tunnelling through them more arduous and risky for the tomb robber."

22 Amélineau 1899b, 90; Kaiser and Dreyer 1982, 217; Dreyer 2007b, n. 1.

23 From now on, this dimension will be referred to as the 'footprint overhang' and is taken as the shortest distance from the outside of the superstructure to the edge of the void of the pit or substructure (usually along its longest edge).

24 Petrie 1901, 14; Porter and Moss 1937, 78–81; Dreyer 2003b, 67; 2009b, 18; Dreyer et al. 2011, 58.

25 Dreyer 2003b, 67. Their unplastered ends and impressions in their mortar of the wood grain from the shrine indicate they were built after the chamber was constructed (Petrie 1901, 8). These chambers when excavated by Amélineau (1904, 156–84) contained numerous remains of funerary goods, including many stone vases.

26 Dreyer 2010, 21; Dreyer et al. 2011, 58–60. Dreyer (1991, 100) suggested that from photographs of a low wall seen in Amélineau's (1899a, plates 1/3, 2/5, 3/9, and 12) excavation report, and attributed by him to tomb robbers, this may be a retaining wall for a low tumulus, due to its similarity to the example found in the tomb of Djet.

27 Dreyer 1991, 100; 2010, 21.

28 Petrie 1901, 16–18, plate 1 (Cairo CG 52008–11). Petrie suggested the robbery may have taken place during the New Kingdom when the grave was being cleared for reuse as the "shrine of Osiris." But of course it may have been much earlier (see note 29 below).

29 This was adjacent to a staircase added later, which dates from the Middle Kingdom, as by the Thirteenth Dynasty the tomb had come to be regarded as the tomb of Osiris (Dodson 1997, 45). Moreover, a reclining basalt figure of the god on a bier (Cairo JE32090) was discovered in the tomb in January 1898 (Amélineau 1904, 187–97) that may originally have been installed during the Second Intermediate Period by King Khendjer of the Thirteenth Dynasty (Leahy 1977, 433–34).

30 Petrie 1900, 9–10 and 16; Porter and Moss 1937, 82–83; Dreyer 1991, 96; Bestock 2009, 37.

31 Dreyer 1991, 96, fig. 6; 2009a, 19, fig. 27.

32 The function of this mound, Dreyer (2007c, 198–99) has suggested, was as a form of 'back-up' tumulus, buried beneath the surface for theological reasons and forming a kind of hidden 'primeval mound' to magically ensure the king's rebirth in the next world. This claim is not necessarily supported by other scholars. For a discussion of this topic, see O'Connor 2009, 152–53.

33 Kaiser (2008, 364) has suggested that its purpose may have been simply to provide a temporary secure closure, after the burial and before the tomb was complete.

34 Petrie 1900, 9; Dreyer 1991, 96–99.

35 Dreyer 1991, 97–99 and 102; 1993, 11.

36 Petrie 1900, 10–11; Porter and Moss 1937, 82; Dodson and Hilton 2004, 46; Kahl 2006, 97.

37 Dreyer 1991, 100.

38 Dreyer 2007b, 193.

39 Reisner 1936, 345. The vast majority of burials of the non-elite throughout Egyptian history would have been in simple graves such as this (Jánosi 1999, 27; Dodson and Ikram 2008, 31).
40 Spencer 1979, 10.
41 La Loggia 2009, 176–96.
42 Dębowska-Ludwin 2010, 5 and 13.
43 Dębowska-Ludwin 2009, 462–63; 2011, 259–60.
44 Abłamowicz, Dębowska, and Jucha 2004, 413. Dębowska 2008, 1111–12; Dębowska-Ludwin 2009, 461; 2010, 7.
45 Dębowska-Ludwin 2011a, 30; 2011b, 266.
46 Dębowska-Ludwin 2011a, 33; 2012, 65.
47 Joanna Dębowska-Ludwin (personal communication, March 7, 2011) suggests that the physical protective properties of the mud covering may not have been its only function, as some offering vessels in later burials found elsewhere at the site were also found filled with pure mud for presumably magical reasons. In addition, the body in tomb 99 was covered with a fine layer of sand and red ochre, which also had apotropaic functions.
48 Chłodnicki and Ciałowicz 2009, 6–9; Dębowska-Ludwin et al. 2010, 25; Dębowska-Ludwin 2011a, 33; Ciałowicz and Dębowska-Ludwin 2013, 158.
49 Haarlem 1996, 7–9, 12; Tassie and van Wetering 2003a, 501–502.
50 Hassan 2000, 38–39; Tassie and van Wetering 2003a, 133; 2003b, 500–501; Tassie et al. 2008, 205.
51 Klasens 1959, 35; Porter and Moss 1974–81, 8; Tristant 2008b, 328.
52 There are many scholarly interpretations of the meaning of the palace façade decoration on superstructures. See Clark (2016, n. 2122) for a summary of the current thinking. For a comprehensive list of superstructures that are decorated with palace façades, see Hendrickx (2001, 87–89).
53 Daressy 1905, throughout; Petrie 1907, 2–7, plate 2; Porter and Moss 1974–81, 312; Jeffreys and Tavares 1994, 145; Martin 1997, 283.
54 Jeffreys and Tavares 1994, 146; Radwan 2000, 509–13.
55 The others being Abu Ghurab and Abusir (Jeffreys and Tavares 1994, 146–47), which are discussed above and in the following chapters.
56 Jeffreys and Tavares 1994, 147; Lehner 1997, 79; Mathieson et al. 1999, 23. The depth of the gravel layer varies from 0.75 to 4 m over the underlying rock (Emery 1958, 4; Dreyer 2003b, 71; Hendrickx 2008, 82).
57 Porter and Moss 1974–81, 443–44; Hendrickx 1999, 77; 2008, 73.

58 Emery 1939, 10–17.
59 Emery 1949, 13; Porter and Moss 1974–81, 444.
60 Emery 1949, 16–17.
61 Quibell 1923, 5–6, 15–16; Emery 1949, 3; Porter and Moss 1974–81, 437.
62 Emery 1954, 5, 7–13, 18–19; Porter and Moss 1974–81, 445.
63 See Morris (2007b, 174–77) for a discussion of the contents of this tomb and their significance.
64 The exact function of these bovine heads is unknown. See Clark (2016, n. 2151) for a summary of the current scholarly thinking on these unusual motifs.
65 Emery 1954, 5–6.
66 Emery 1954, 128–38; Porter and Moss 1974–81, 444–45; Hendrickx 2008, 74.
67 Emery 1954, 139–40.
68 Snape 2011, 14–15.
69 Jeffreys and Tavares 1994, 152; Köhler 2005, 1–2; Lacher-Raschdorff 2014, 47.
70 The matrix comprises a gravel and sand mixture interspersed with pebbles and boulders that lies over a compact desert clay stratum about 1.3 m below the surface, a further 0.5 m below which is a soft mudstone layer (Jeffreys and Tavares 1994, 152–53).
71 See Saad 1947, plans 2 and 3; 1951, plates 1–3.
72 Saad 1951, 7, plan 5.
73 Saad 1951, 7–8, plan 6.
74 Köhler 2008b, 122.
75 Petrie et al. 1913, 13–15, 18; Porter and Moss 1934, 86; Reisner 1936, 31; Hendrickx 1996, 60.
76 Ranke 1926, 8–9, 12 and n. 9, fig. 3–4.
77 Reisner 1908, 27–33; 1936, 35.
78 Reisner 1908, 33–34; 1936, 36–37; Podzorski 2008, 99.
79 Reisner 1908, 4–7 and 34.
80 Reisner 1908, 30 and 34.
81 Hussein 2011, 269.
82 Hussein 2011, 275–78.
83 Dodson and Hilton 2004, 46.
84 To the southwest of the 'Royal Tomb,' de Morgan (1897, 159, fig. 513) mentioned finding another large tomb. See Kemp (1967, 24–25) for a description of this structure.
85 Porter and Moss 1937, 118–19; Spencer 1979, 15; 1993, 61–62; Wilkinson 1999, 6, 37, and 70.

86 Borchardt 1898, 87–90; Reisner 1936, 27; Kaiser 1985, 26–27.
87 Dodson and Ikram 2008, 136; Spencer 1982, 46–47.
88 Mond and Myers 1937, 16–20.
89 Mond and Myers 1937, 16. There is a robbers' tunnel marked on the plan of tomb 1208 in its western corner (Mond and Myers 1937, plate 5).

Notes to Chapter 4

1 Reisner 1936, 57.
2 Porter and Moss 1937, 83–85; Dreyer 1990, 72.
3 Dreyer 2003b, 68.
4 Petrie 1901, 11.
5 The desert sand surrounding the nearby tomb of Narmer is described as having the consistency of soft sandstone (Kaiser and Grossmann 1979, n. 10).
6 Engel 2003, 44.
7 Dreyer 1990, 73–74; Dreyer et al. 1998, 141–42.
8 Personal communication by Günter Dreyer (October 3, 2011).
9 Dreyer 1990, 73.
10 For example: Reisner 1936, 185 and 353; Seidlmayer 1998, 31; Wilkinson 1999, 203; Birrell 2000, 19; Dodson and Ikram 2008, 137; Tristant 2008b, 346; Bárta 2011b, 70.
11 Dreyer et al. 1998, 141. Although it could be argued that if this was the case it may have been a later replacement. See my comments below regarding the blockings in the tombs of Adjib, Semerkhet, and Qa'a.
12 Petrie 1901, 12, plates 65 and 66. Outside the main substructure, within the much smaller southwest annex, which may have been intended to hold a *ka* statue of the king (Dreyer 2007c, 200–203), there is also provision for an arrangement similar to that in the tomb of Adjib. This, it has been suggested, consisted of wooden planks housed in a vertical portcullis-style slot and backed with a wall of mud-bricks (Petrie 1901, 10; Dreyer 1990, 76).
13 Dreyer 1991, 100; Dreyer et al. 1998, 141–42.
14 Petrie 1901, 10–11, plate 56A 1.
15 Kaiser 1981, 250.
16 Dreyer, Hartung, and Pumpenmeier 1993, 60.
17 A corner of the tomb has been restored by the German Archaeological Institute (DAI) to give an impression of the structural details. In it, two 0.3 m square section timber baulks have been placed to indicate the position of the beams used to support the shrine.

Similarly, three beams 0.3 m in diameter mark the position of the roof supports, over which layers of mat and brick form a base for the tumulus. Surrounding this, further brickwork has been used to create a suggested section of the tumulus retaining wall, which may have projected 26.2 cm (approximately half a cubit) over the chamber walls but sat below the desert surface itself (Dreyer et al. 2003, 88, plate 17b).

18 Dreyer 1990, 76–78, fig. 7 and 8; 2003b, 68.

19 Dreyer 1991, 102, n. 23; Dreyer et al. 1998, 142.

20 Reisner 1936, 60; Porter and Moss 1937, 82.

21 Petrie 1900, 12–13 and 17.

22 Dreyer 1991, 100.

23 Porter and Moss 1937, 85–86.

24 Engel 2008, 39.

25 Leaving a gap in the southwest corner, as in the other tombs at Umm al-Qa‘b, presumably for the king's *ka* to exit toward the wadi (Dreyer 2007c, 200).

26 Dreyer 2005, 15.

27 Dreyer (2008, 50) suggests that a stairway may have been intended but was never completed as the tomb was finished in a hurry.

28 Dreyer et al. 2000, 119; 2005, 13–14.

29 Petrie 1900, 13–14; Dreyer 2005, 14.

30 Leahy 1977, 424, n. 5; Snape 2011, 120–21. For in-depth discussions of these restorations in the Middle and New Kingdoms, see Dodson 1997, 44–46; Effland and Effland 2010, 127–58.

31 The burial chamber of Den is 15.2 m long by 8.9 m wide (Dreyer et al. 1998, 141–42), and that of Semerkhet is 16.65 m long by 7.4 m wide (Dreyer 2005, 13).

32 Dreyer 2005, 14.

33 Dreyer et al. 2006, 94.

34 Engel 2008, 8, n. 24.

35 Edwards 1971, 58; Emery 1961, 85; Wilkinson 1999, 80.
Although Reisner (1936, 62) suggested they were built against the superstructure.

36 Dreyer 2005, 15.

37 Porter and Moss 1937, 86–87.

38 At least eight phases of construction have been detected for this tomb, with additional magazines, subsidiary graves, and stairs being added as the structure was expanded to permit more storage (Dreyer et al. 1996, 58–61). For an exhaustive description of the construction phases, see Engel (2017).

39 Engel 1997, 5 and 27–28.
40 Dreyer et al. 1996, 62–64.
41 Engel (1997, 110) has described how the tomb was robbed from within the staircase rather than from the outside, so it could be argued that these structures had performed their security role successfully.
42 Engel 1997, 94.
43 Petrie 1900, 15. Also mentioned by Amélineau (1899b, 127), who thought the wall was built by tomb robbers.
44 This damage was probably done in the Middle or New Kingdoms to permit easy access to the tomb, when it was also bricked over (Engel 1997, 28 and n. 43).
45 Clark 2016, n. 1709–10.
46 Engel 1997, 8. These can be seen in Petrie's original excavation photographs (Petrie 1900, plate 66, no. 5).
47 Dreyer et al. 1996, 61 and fig. 19; Engel 1997, 5–6.
48 Engel 1997, 84–89.
49 Engel 1997, 6, 9, 16, 23, 25, and 44.
50 Dreyer 1991, 100; Engel 1997, 108.
51 Dreyer 2007c, 200–201.
52 Engel 2003, 43.
53 Engel 1997, 109–12.
54 Based on the bulk density of sand at 16 kN/m3 (Cobb 2004, 37).
55 Engel 1997, 110, fig. 70.
56 Kroeper 1992, 140.
57 Kroeper 1992, 133–34, 136, 138–39, 141, and 144; 2005, 638–39.
58 It is worth noting that both Kaiser and Dreyer (in Kroeper 1992, 144) opined that these graves would have been protected by a mound or superstructure of some sort, despite there being no physical evidence of any at the site.
59 Dębowska-Ludwin 2010, 5 and 13.
60 Dębowska-Ludwin 2009, 473–74.
61 Dębowska-Ludwin 2010, 14; 2012, 69–70.
62 Dębowska-Ludwin 2011b, 264–66.
63 Dębowska-Ludwin 2011a, 34.
64 This cemetery was probably built for the lesser elite of Memphis, with Saqqara acting as the main necropolis for the closest officials to the king or members of the royal family (Tristant 2008c, 9).
65 Tristant 2008a, 137.
66 Porter and Moss 1974–81, 7.
67 Hendrickx 1996, 60; Tristant 2008b, 329.
68 Klasens 1961, 108 and 110–11.

69 Tristant 2008b, 329.
70 Porter and Moss 1974–81, 5–6.
71 The term 'cover' is defined by the U.S. Bureau of Mines as the "total thickness of material overlying mine workings or an orebody" (Staff of the U.S. Bureau of Mines 1996).
72 Montet 1938, 18–20, plate 2; Tristant 2008a, 137–38.
73 Tristant 2008b, 330–31.
74 Montet 1938, 28–31, plate 2.
75 Montet 1938, 28–31.
76 See Montet 1938, 11–69; Porter and Moss 1974–81, 6–7.
77 Klasens 1961, 109.
78 Montet 1938, 19, 33, and 35.
79 Tristant 2008b, 331.
80 Montet 1938, 37–38.
81 Klasens 1961, 109.
82 Montet 1938, 50–52.
83 Klasens 1961, 109.
84 Jeffreys and Tavares 1994, 146.
85 Yacoub 1981, 160, plates 18, 14, and 17.
86 Yacoub 1981, 160, plate 20.
87 El-Khouli 1968, 75, plate 5.
88 Yacoub 1981, 160, plate 17.
89 Yacoub 1981, 160, plate 17.
90 Yacoub 1981, plate 14.
91 This can be dated to the reign of Qa'a on stylistic grounds due to the flanking magazines on the stairway. See Kaiser (1998, 78–82) for a discussion of the dating of Early Dynastic stairway pit tomb substructures.
92 Yacoub 1981, 160, plate 20.
93 Yacoub 1981, 160, plate 18.
94 El-Khouli 1968, 75, plate 5.
95 Porter and Moss 1974–81, 447.
96 The length of the pit of S 3507 was 5.25 m, whereas for example that in S 3503 was 14.25 m, S 3357 was 19.1 m, S 3504 was 22.6 m, and S 3471 was 30 m.
97 Kaiser 2008, 355 and 363.
98 The purpose of this hidden tumulus at Saqqara has been the subject of much scholarly debate. For further discussion on this topic, see Badawy 1956, 180–83; Edwards 1988, 24; Dreyer 1991, 101–102; O'Connor 1991, 6–9; Lehner 1997, 80; Kemp 2006, 103; Hendrickx 2008, 78; Kaiser 2008, 355.

99 Emery 1958, 75–80, plates 85–113.
100 Porter and Moss 1974–81, 446.
101 Emery 1958, 39–40 and 46.
102 Emery 1958, 38–44. Emery (1958, 41) also thought, from finds discovered later, that the substructure of the tomb may have been closed with an earth mound or stepped superstructure, as in tombs S 3507 and S 3038.
103 Emery 1958, 37 and 41–44.
104 Porter and Moss 1974–81, 440–42.
105 Emery 1938, 5–6. These sorts of grooves, according to Wainwright (Petrie et al. 1912, 26), would have ensured the stone's verticality, reduced friction on the ropes as they followed the stone into its emplacement, and aided their subsequent removal once the stone was in place.
106 It seems unlikely that this portcullis was originally placed in this position, as there is no evidence of any emplacement or structures to support it. That the portcullis was designed to be lowered is evident from the grooves and holes made in its surface to accept ropes. However, looking at Emery's drawings, the portcullis appears too narrow to have fitted in the slots on the main staircase, so it may not have originated from there either. Perhaps the row of holes on the descending slope that leads to the doorway held a timber framework, which would have supported the portcullis. Alternatively, it may have been brought in later from elsewhere to protect an intrusive burial in the rock-cut satellite magazine.
107 Emery 1938, 7–8.
108 Clark 2016, chart P1.
109 Emery 1938, plate 2.
110 Emery 1938, 6.
111 Emery (1938, 7) seemed undecided about the roofing arrangements of the pit and speculated whether wooden beams could be strong enough to support a span of 9.5 m plus the shaft of rubble reaching to the roof of the superstructure. Yet, the beams in tomb S 3506 spanned 11.7 m with no apparent difficulty (Emery 1958, 35–42), and the wooden beams in the tomb of Den at Abydos spanned 8.9 m and may have supported a hidden mound of sand and a superstructure as well (Dreyer et al. 1998, 141–45). Although no evidence remains of the roof's construction, the author sees no reason why either a double roof or a deep gravel fill should not have been used, as in the other tombs in the vicinity. As La Loggia (2009, 180–83) points out, unlike current building practice where the tolerance for

the deflection of beams is a concern for conservative modern structural engineers, the ancient Egyptians seemed to have been rather confident with the empirical selection and use of wooden beams to support enormous loads.

112 Emery 1938, 7–8.

113 Emery 1938, 6–7, plates 1 and 2.

114 Emery 1938, 3–4. These were in fact the only extant examples ever found of a wooden roof from a tomb of this style (Kaiser 1985, 37, n. 22) and could therefore reasonably be considered a model of the roofing method used in this type of superstructure.

115 Emery 1938, 7. The bulk density of loose gravel is approximately 16 kN/m^3 (Cobb 2004, 36).

116 Porter and Moss 1974–81, 442.

117 Emery 1949, 73–74.

118 See Clark (2016, 350) for the dimensions of portcullises in the stairway pit tombs at Saqqara.

119 Emery 1949, 71–75, plate 15.

120 Emery (1949, 75) reported that Cecil Mallaby Firth, the tomb's original excavator, had discovered a large quantity of burned wood during his work on the tomb in 1930.

121 Hendrickx 1996, 60; 2008, 67, tables 2 and 78.

122 Emery 1949, 107–109, plate 43.

123 Emery 1949, 125–27.

124 Clark 2016, chart P1.

125 Emery 1949, 125–27, plate 55.

126 Emery 1958, 5 and 103; Reisner 1936, 383.

127 The longest edge of a superstructure is normally the shortest distance to the burial chamber, as in many cases the ends are proportionally much farther from the pit than the sides.

128 Porter and Moss 1974–81, 444.

129 Emery 1958, 101; Clark 2016, chart P1.

130 Emery 1958, 99; plate 114.

131 Emery (1958, 98) suggested that the design of this mastaba marked the definitive changeover from the complex palace façade style of the First Dynasty to the plainer style of the Second Dynasty.

132 Emery 1958, 100–104, plate 114.

133 Porter and Moss 1974–81, 446.

134 Emery 1958, 5–7.

135 Emery (1958, 8–9) once again worried about the load-bearing capabilities of these beams, as discussed in relation to S 3035, the tomb of Hemaka.

136 Emery 1958, 7–8 and 10–11.
137 Quibell 1923, 19.
138 Reisner 1936, fig. 52.
139 Quibell 1923, 3.
140 Hendrickx 1996, 60.
141 Porter and Moss 1974–81, 443.
142 Emery 1949, 116–19, fig. 67.
143 Porter and Moss 1974–81, 443.
144 Emery 1949, 121–23, fig. 67a.
145 Emery 1949, 116–19 and 121–23.
146 Emery 1949, 121; 1961, 153.
147 Statistically they form less than 0.5 percent of the 10,285 tombs excavated by Saad, but the tombs at this necropolis are unrivaled in their use of stone in the Early Dynastic Period (La Loggia 2008, 76).
148 Saad 1969, 22–23, plates 11–13.
149 Saad 1947, Map 3; 1969, plate 16.
150 Saad 1969, 28; Köhler 2005, 28.
151 Köhler 2008b, 114.
152 This is because unlike at Saqqara, there is a limited number of associated burial assemblages (grave goods). However, more recent work by Köhler and Smythe (2004) and Smythe (2004) on establishing a ceramic corpus at Helwan is beginning to redress this situation. It is also possible to group the tombs roughly together on stylistic grounds. Thus, tombs with an entrance stairway at ninety degrees to the main longitudinal axis of the burial chamber may be attributed to the reigns of Adjib or Semerkhet (Wilkinson 1996, 339–43), and those with flanking magazine chambers on either side of the entrance route can loosely be ascribed to the reign of Qa'a (Kaiser 1998, 83; Köhler 2005, 26).
153 Köhler 2008b, 125, table 1. Köhler (2004, 300) adopts the term Naqada IIICD for tombs of an indeterminate date at Helwan. As she explains, "where no decision can be made on an earlier or later stage for tombs within this transitional phase, we refer to them as belonging to Group IIICD."
154 Saad 1947, 26–28; Jeffreys 2005, 440; Köhler 2008b, 122.
155 Saad 1951, 5–6, plan 3.
156 Saad 1951, 28–9, plan 15; Köhler 2005, 26. La Loggia (2009, 182) suggests, however, that rather than roof supports, the supporting posts may actually have been associated with the construction of wooden compartments of some kind.
157 Saad 1951, 11–12, plan 9.

158 Based on the assumption that this was just desert sand or loose gravel, bearing in mind the bulk density of either is around 16 kN/m3 (Cobb 2004, 36).
159 Saad 1969, 20–22, plate 9.
160 Saad 1951, 8–9, plan 7.
161 Clark 2016, chart P1.
162 Saad 1947, plates 38 and 40.
163 Saad 1947, 107, plate 36.
164 It should be mentioned that those tombs whose stairways were aligned on a north–south axis with the burial chamber would seem to have been particularly vulnerable to *sondages* on their northern and southern ends, as any digging there would likely have a good chance of hitting the stairway. From the point of view of tomb security, the alignment of most of these tombs on that axis may therefore have been somewhat counterproductive.
165 Although Köhler (2008b, 117) has suggested that the direction of descent of the stairways in these tombs "does not appear to follow a particular pattern other than accessibility to the site and to the tombs themselves."
166 This median figure is based upon limestone weighing 1.7 to 2.6 metric tonnes per cubic meter (Arnold 1991, 28).
167 Saad 1951, 9–11; 1969, 30.
168 For the original publication of the tomb, see Saad 1951, 164–66, plates 62 and 69–70.
169 Köhler 2005, 20–30. Köhler (2008b, 121) renumbers the tomb Op. 2/1 in her publication.
170 La Loggia 2008, table 3.
171 Saad 1951, 164–66; Köhler 1998, 69; 2005, 20–23 and 25.
172 Saad 1947, 163–64, plates 61 and 67–68.
173 Photographs of this tomb were taken at the time of the original excavation and have been published by Köhler (2008b, figs. 10–12).
174 Köhler 2008b, 120–21, figs. 11–12; La Loggia 2009, 180.
175 Hendrickx 1999, 79–80. Both Reisner (1936, 70–72) and Grajetzki (2008, 110) place Mastaba 2038 in the same period.
176 Petrie 1914, 3 and 6–7, plate 18.
177 Petrie 1914, 4–5, plate 18.
178 Köhler 2005, n. 134. Ranke (1926, 12–13) believed that this tomb dated from either the end of the Third or perhaps the beginning of the Fourth Dynasty, as the use of stone in a private grave before the Third Dynasty appeared to him inconceivable.
179 Ranke 1926, 10–12, fig. 6.

180 Ranke 1926, 12, n. 1.
181 Reisner 1908, 14.
182 Reisner 1908, 36–40; 1936, 130–31.
183 Reisner 1908, 6.
184 Reisner 1908, 36–38, figs. 65–67.
185 Reisner 1908, 38–40, figs. 68–70.
186 Reisner 1908, 36–38; 1936, 68–69.
187 Reisner 1936, fig. 51.
188 Reisner 1908, 37–38.
189 Garstang 1903, 28, plate 33; Reisner 1936, 67.
190 Hussein 2011, 271–73. Indeed, the author has not come across any stairway pit tombs with corbeled or arched stairways during his research, and they do not seem to be used until as late as the Third Dynasty in the subterranean stairway tombs at Beit Khallaf and Reqaqnah. See the discussion of these in Garstang 1904, 28–30. Perhaps the tomb was restored for reuse during the Third Dynasty or later and the existing stairway 'updated.' Alternatively, the entire stairway may have been added to an older pit tomb for similar reasons.
191 Hussein 2011, 271–73.
192 Nearby tomb B137 is described as enclosed by "hard gravel and sand" (Randall-MacIver and Mace 1902, 34).
193 Randall-MacIver and Mace 1902, 39.
194 Randall-MacIver and Mace 1902, 39, plates 3, 6 and 4, 8.
195 Reisner 1936, 57.
196 With perhaps the exception of Reisner (1942, 175–76), who discussed the backfill in the shafts of the Fourth Dynasty nucleus cemetery at Giza.
197 See Clark (2016, 208–28) for a complete discussion of this topic.

Notes to Chapter 5

1 Van Wetering 2004, 1075.
2 Porter and Moss 1974–81, 613.
3 During the First Dynasty, a progressive increase in the quantity of grave goods required to accompany the royal burial was already becoming apparent, and by the time of the Second Dynasty this amount had risen, resulting in enormous quantities of funerary equipment, furniture, and vessels that required secure storage (Stadelmann 1985b, 296). Kaiser (1994, 120), while agreeing with the architectural requirement for more storage, also suggests that the tomb's size may have been the result of an underlying desire of the kings to exceed and indeed surpass all of the other tombs at Saqqara in monumentality.

4 While the royal tombs would not have been visible from the cultivation at that time, unlike the elite private tombs to the north, it may be that they would have been equally—if not more—conspicuous to the local populace. This is particularly the case as the focus of attention may have been the Abusir wadi, which at this time was the main approach from the north, when the Saqqara plateau contained the cemetery for the city that was centered around the Abusir lake and valley (Mathieson and Tavares 1993, 26; Jeffreys and Tavares 1994, 150–51 and 158–59; Dodson 2010, 806–807).

5 At Saqqara the *tafl* layer is a soft marl that is the consistency of putty when damp and underlies the hard limestone strata at the surface (Martin 1981, 7–8).

6 Stadelmann 1985b, 296.

7 Barsanti 1901b, 250–52; 1902a, 183–84; Dreyer 2007a, 130. Wilkinson (1999, 84) suggests that Raneb may have either buried his predecessor in this tomb or usurped it. However, Lacher-Raschdorff (2014, 53) believes the tomb of Raneb lies elsewhere, probably somewhere between Hotepsekhemwy and Ninetjer.

8 Lacher 2008, 431, 441–47. The southern section of the substructure is not totally excavated, so there could be more chambers to be added to the plan. For the earliest drawing of the tomb, see Lauer (1936, fig. 2).

9 Lauer 1976, 143; Lacher 2008, 427.

10 Barsanti 1901b, 251. This is confirmed by Claudia Lacher-Raschdorff, who visited the tomb more recently (personal communication, October 12, 2010).

11 Lacher 2008, 431–33.

12 Calculated from levels marked on plans. See Lacher 2008, fig. 2.

13 Lauer 1976, 144.

14 Lacher 2008, 431; Lacher-Raschdorff 2014, 153–97.

15 Hassan 1938, 521; Lacher-Raschdorff 2014, 55.

16 Jeffreys and Tavares 1994, 150; Dreyer 2007a, 132.

17 Dreyer 2009a, 26; Lacher 2011, 217, 220; Lacher-Raschdorff 2014, 57–58. Among the finds within them were over a hundred wine jars with seals of Ninetjer in Gallery A500 and a number of flint knives in Gallery A300 (Lacher 2011, 218).

18 Dreyer 2007a, 132; Lacher-Raschdorff 2014, 58.

19 Lacher-Raschdorff 2014, 58–59.

20 Dreyer 2004, 19; 2007a, 133; Lacher 2011, 217. It is thought that when the tomb builders excavated these passages, they may have followed a layer of 0.4 m thick *tafl* to define their ceiling height, and

that the irregular geological formation of this stratum led to some of the passages being different in level to the rest of the tomb (Dreyer 2007d, 19).

21 Dreyer 2006, 19; 2007a, 135–36; Lacher 2011, 215.

22 Lacher-Raschdorff 2014, 153–97.

23 Lacher 2011, 217. See Lacher-Raschdorff (2011, 543–50) for an analysis of the tomb's reuse from the Old Kingdom onward.

24 Lacher 2008, 433.

25 Barsanti 1901b, 251–52; Dreyer 2007a, 132; Lacher 2011, 217–18.

26 Wilkinson (1999, 89) proposes that the choice of site may be an attempt to confer legitimacy on the king's reign. Likewise, van Wetering (2004, 1073) suggests that he wished to associate himself with the rulers of the First Dynasty after a period of political instability. O'Connor (2009, 156–57), in contrast, regards this sort of discussion as "too speculative" and notes that many later kings chose to be buried in preexisting royal necropoleis for reasons unconnected with politics. See Dodson (1996, 24–26) and Kahl (2006, 105) for summaries of the scholarship regarding Peribsen's reign.

27 Dreyer et al. 2006, 99–102; O'Connor 2009, 157.

28 Porter and Moss 1937, 81.

29 Dreyer 2003a, 13; Dreyer et al. 2006, 99–101, fig. 13.

30 Petrie 1901, 11. Also known as LG84, Campbell's Tomb, the Twenty-sixth Dynasty tomb of Pakap, was surrounded by a protective sand-filled channel, deeper than the burial chamber, which made it very awkward to tunnel under (Dodson and Ikram 2008, 287).

31 Vyse 1840a, 216–18; 1840b, 131–32, fig. 7; Bareš 1999, 63–64, figs. 2–4.

32 Porter and Moss 1937, 87.

33 Petrie 1901, 14; Dreyer et al. 1998, 165; 2003, 108, 111, fig. 15.

34 Kaiser 1994, 117; O'Connor 2009, 157.

35 Dreyer et al. 1998, 165; Dreyer 2007c, 203.

36 Dreyer et al. 2003, 108–10; Dreyer 2007c, 203.

37 Dreyer et al. 2000, 125; Dreyer et al. 2003, 110 and 112–14; 2006, 114.

38 This figure is calculated using the tomb's area and depth of backfill, which amounts to approximately 8,800 cubic meters and is based on sand's bulk density of 16 kN/m3, which equals approximately 1,600 kg/m3 (Cobb 2004, 37).

39 Dreyer et al. 1998, 165; 2003, 111; 2006, 110–11.

40 These lie west of Abusir village on the edge of the present cultivation (Jeffreys and Tavares 1994, 149).

41 Bonnet 1928, 4–6, plate 2; Bárta 2000, 338.
42 Mathieson and Tavares 1993, 24.
43 See Bonnet 1928, 1–5, plate 1.
44 Bonnet 1928, 2.
45 Jeffreys and Tavares 1994, 147. Quibell (1913, 1) described having "dug out" some five hundred of them in all during his campaigns.
46 A great deal of unpublished material belonging to Firth and Emery concerning these Saqqara mastabas is now in the possession of Professor Geoffrey Martin and is listed in his article on Firth and Emery's unpublished excavations (Martin 2007, 121–26). In it he estimates that there are approximately a hundred and seventy-nine mastabas described in this material, which consists of notes, notebooks, tomb plans, and photographs, from among which only twelve tombs were actually published by Emery.
47 The geology of the North Saqqara necropolis comprises a layer of hard limestone over a stratum of soft marl or *tafl* up to ten meters thick, which is easily cut with a chisel and thus excellent for quickly carving subterranean chambers (Martin 1981, 7–8).
48 Emery 1949, 11–12; 1961, 155.
49 These are in S 2302, S 2307, and S 2337 (Quibell 1923, 13, 29, and 31).
50 Quibell 1923, 12; Bolshakov 1997, 28–30; Tavares 2005, 857; Kanawati 1987, 59.
51 Emery 1961, fig. 96.
52 There is also evidence of high-status Type II private 'gallery' tombs one kilometer south of the North Saqqara Second Dynasty tombs, underneath the Eighteenth Dynasty tombs of Meryneith and Maya (Regulski 2011), which were usurped and considerably altered in antiquity. See, Raven et al. (2003, 91–109) and van Walsem (2003, 117–34) for the substructure under Meryneith. For that under Maya, see Raven et al. (2009, 17–20, fig. 10) and Regulski (2009).
53 Reisner 1936, 138; Emery 1961, 94, fig. 54; Porter and Moss 1974–81, 437.
54 Quibell 1923, 3, 12, 29–30.
55 Quibell 1923, vii–viii.
56 Quibell 1923, 3.
57 Quibell 1923, 7, 23, plates 15, 2; Porter and Moss 1974–81, 437.
58 Quibell 1923, 17; Reisner 1936, 146.
59 Quibell 1923, 31; Reisner 1936, 140.
60 Quibell 1923, 34; Reisner 1936, 141.
61 Quibell 1923, 35–36, 38; Reisner 1936, 141–43; Porter and Moss 1974–81, 437.

62 Quibell 1923, 42.
63 According to Quibell (1923, 40), the staircase of this tomb apparently had a ledge running along both sides of its length, which may suggest that it was roofed with wood or stone.
64 Quibell 1923, 40; Reisner 1936, 159–60; Porter and Moss 1974–81, 440.
65 Quibell 1923, 33; Reisner 1936, 143.
66 Quibell 1923, 44–45; Reisner 1936, 139–40; Porter and Moss 1974–81, 437.
67 Quibell 1923, 10 and 44, plate 24, 2.
68 Quibell 1923, 7, plates 5, 2; Porter and Moss 1974–81, 436; Birrell 2000, 22.
69 Clark 2016, chart P2.
70 Emery 1962, 4, plate 4; Porter and Moss 1974–81, 444.
71 Quibell 1923, vii; Emery 1961, 130.
72 Quibell 1923, 3, 17, 21, 23, 29, 33, 35–36, and 41.
73 Emery 1949, 12; 1962, 4.
74 Quibell 1923, vi.
75 This volume is based on the overall size of the superstructure at 41.7 m long and 18.3 m wide, less 2 m thick walls all around by 6 m height. The weight is based on loose gravel's bulk density of 16 kN/m^3 that equals approximately 1,600 kg/m3 (Cobb 2004, 36).
76 Quibell 1923, 37.
77 Quibell 1923, 1; Emery 1962, 2.
78 Half a meter below the 1.3 m of 'gravel' that forms the upper stratum at the site is a mudstone layer that is occasionally used as the 'roof' in these subterranean chambers (Jeffreys and Tavares 1994, 152–53). For an in-depth description of the geology of the cemetery, see Köhler (2005, 7–11).
79 Saad 1951; 1957.
80 Köhler 2003; 2004; 2005; 2008a; 2008b; 2009.
81 Saad 1951, 27, plan 13.
82 Saad 1951, 27.
83 Saad 1951, 15–17, plan 11.
84 This does not mean that all tombs at Helwan that lacked grooved emplacements also lacked portcullis stones. The evidence from other sites—for example, Sedment and Lahun—suggests that tombs could have a freestanding stone in position without a grooved emplacement. Indeed, the cemetery plans in Saad's publication (1951, plates 1–3) show many tapered staircases that may have provided 'wedge'-shaped portcullis emplacements. However, the presence of grooves

in an emplacement does at least mean there is a high probability that a portcullis was intended, even if none was present.

85 Köhler 2007, 192–94, fig. 2.

86 Although unlike Op. 4/94, its burial chamber projected beyond the footprint of its mastaba (Köhler 2000a, 39–40; 2000b, 89–90, fig. 5; 2003, 85).

87 Birrell 2000, 17; Köhler 2000b, 89–91.

88 Köhler 2008a, 172–73; 2008b, 122–23.

89 Most of the cemetery's geology consists of a mixture of gravel and sand interspersed with pebbles and small boulders over a stratum of clay 'bedrock' and mudstone (Jeffreys and Tavares 1994, 153).

90 Köhler (2008b, 126) notes that the numbers of both these and true shaft tombs seem to increase toward the latter part of the Second Dynasty. She suggests the reason for the rise may have been that they were being built at a time when the necropolis was becoming overcrowded and so there was less space for long staircases.

91 Quibell (1923, 41) describes the descent of S 2442 at Saqqara as a "stair of two large steps, 4 metres deep."

92 Köhler 2008b, 118.

93 Köhler 2009, 284.

94 Köhler 2008b, 126.

95 Saad 1957, 59, plan G.

96 Saad 1951, 23–26, fig. 7.

97 Köhler (2004, 297) suggests that the larger tombs at Helwan were often robbed soon after the burials were made, sometimes even several times.

98 Petrie et al. 1913, 27; Petrie and Mackay 1915, 10, 14–16 and tomb register plates 16–17; Clark 2016, chart P2.

99 Petrie et al. 1923, 21–24, tomb register plate 46; Clark 2016, chart P2.

100 Petrie and Brunton's (1924, plate 36) tomb register lists eight 'stairway' tombs dating to the Second Dynasty, but only five are drawn in detail. Some, such as tombs 568 and 569 (Petrie and Brunton 1924, plate 63), are included in those plans but do not appear in the tomb register.

101 Petrie and Brunton 1924, 2, plates 1.1–17, 2, and 8.

102 Petrie and Brunton 1924, plates 36 and 81.

103 Brunton (1927, 3) described the local geology: "The soil is unsuitable for graves, being a rather loose alluvial gravel for some depth. The substratum of marl is too deep to be reached by the grave diggers, and is waterlogged except on the hillside below the rock

tombs at the northern horn of the bay. As there was no high ground available, the main Qau cemeteries were placed on the rise to the north of the main wadi, to the south and east of the present village." Referring to Badari, he wrote: "This strip is composed of a series of spurs or foothills of limestone detritus."

104 Brunton 1927, 11–12 and 15, tomb register plate 10; Porter and Moss 1937, 15. The height of the burial chamber of tomb 438 is unpublished, but its floor was 3.04 m from the surface, implying an even thinner depth of cover (Brunton 1927, 15, plate 10).

105 Brunton 1927, 3 and 13–16 and tomb register plate 10; Porter and Moss 1937, 6.

106 Reisner 1908, 14 and 42; 1936, 129–31. In other tombs, it was sometimes simply built up to form a flat roof or given further layers of brick for added strength, as in N 1515 (Reisner 1908, 40).

107 As material proof of the improved strength and security achieved by using corbeling, Reisner (1936, 355) continued to cite the evidence of the excellent preservation of the corbeled tombs at Naga al-Deir itself.

108 Reisner 1908, 12–13. However, Reisner contradicted this statement when discussing tomb N 1513 and the likelihood of possible damage to its roof from water and cracking (Reisner 1908, 48). Indeed, more recent research into wood decay by Blanchette et al. (1994, 55–70) has demonstrated that wood in Egyptian tombs is frequently subject to brown rot, which is also related to termite attack and was a major cause of timber failure.

109 These are N 1513 and N 1586 (Reisner 1908, 41, 48).

110 Tawadros 2001, 159.

111 Myers and Fairman 1931, 224, plate 41.

112 Tawadros 2001, 163.

113 Quibell 1898, 7. This piece of information suggests that no trace of a superstructure was found.

114 Hendrickx and van Rossum 1994, 152, 184.

115 This calculation is based on the median figure of sandstone quarried from nearby Jebel al-Silsila, which weighs approximately 1.76 to 1.91 metric tonnes per cubic metet (Fitzner, Heinrichs, and La Bouchardiere 2003, 1093).

116 A collection of copper items hidden in the outer wall of the grave was dated by Needler to be no earlier than the Second and possibly as late as the Third Dynasty (Needler 1984, 146).

117 De Morgan 1984, 64–65.

118 Needler 1984, 122.

119 For example, the small tombs N 4370, N 4379, and N 4774 in Cemetery 3500 at Naga al-Deir (Mace 1909, 20–21) and Burial 28 at al-Masa'id, discussed below.

120 To be more precise, 0.99 to 1.07 metric tonnes if one assumes a scaled thickness of approximately 0.22 m and that the bulk density of Jebel al-Silsila sandstone is approximately 1.76 to 1.91 metric tonnes per cubic meter (Fitzner, Heinrichs, and La Bouchardiere 2003, 1093).

121 De Morgan 1984, 62–63; Needler 1984, 138.

Notes to Chapter 6

1 Porter and Moss 1974–81, 399–415; Martin 1979, 1.

2 Lauer 1936, 12–16 and 27–28; 1962, 70–72; Swelim 1983, 63–65. See Kaiser (1969, 16–17, fig. 4) for a possible reconstruction of the earliest layout of the complex.

3 Lauer 1936, 30–31, 32, n. 1, 102–104; 1962, 75–76.

4 Lauer 1936, 34–40; 1962, 75–81; Lehner 1997, 88.

5 Lauer 1936, 12–16, 30–31; 1962, 70–72.

6 Dodson and Ikram 2008, 142. Suggestions have included: its use by the king as a "stairway to the sky" (Badawy 1956, 182–83; Lauer 1962, 72; Radwan 2003, 90); that it was built to increase the "grandeur" and "monumentality of the tomb" (Stadelmann 1996, 798); and as "an increased claim to monumentality" (Arnold 2003, 229). Finally, Dreyer (2007c, 204) regards it as a monumentalized form of grave mound.

7 Stadelmann 1985a, 52; Dreyer in Haase 2006, 17–18.

8 Lauer 1962, 72. For a detailed discussion of these masonry arrangements, see Arnold (1991, 148–76) and Sampsell (2000, 2–6).

9 Lauer 1936, 2; 1962, 73; Lehner 1997, 17.

10 Although of course accessing the shaft by tunneling under the pyramid laterally is entirely possible, given enough time and resources, as the large passage created under the pyramid during the Saite Period demonstrates (Lauer 1936, 28–32 and 46; Smoláriková 2006, 43).

11 Firth and Quibell 1935, 29–31; Lauer 1936, 28–30. A very detailed description of the descent and passages can be found in Firth and Quibell (1935, 27–28).

12 Lauer 1936, 31–34, n. 1, and 41; 1962, 75–76.

13 Lauer 1936, 47; 1962, 80–90. They were equipped with limestone sarcophagi (Porter and Moss 1974–81, 401–402). Fragments of two were found in galleries I and III, as well as two limestone sarcophagus bases in gallery II and fragments of alabaster and limestone

sarcophagi in galleries III and IV. Gallery V contained a handsome alabaster sarcophagus with a lid (Lauer 1936, 47–62).

14 Lauer 1962, 91–92; 1976, 100; Porter and Moss 1974–81, 402–405.

15 Lauer 1936, 47, 50–57, 63; 1962, 84–86.

16 Lauer 1962, 91–92 and 95–98; 1976, 100.

17 Lauer 1936, 56–62; 1962, 86–90.

18 Lauer (1962, 131–42) discussed earlier theories regarding the South Tomb in depth. Ideas abound, among which are that it is: a tomb for the king's *ka* (Radwan 2003, 100); a cenotaph representing the king's tomb at Abydos (Lauer 1962, 141); and a tomb to house the canopics and internal organs of the king (Lauer 1976, 98). Dodson (1994, 6, n. 12; 2017, 13) believes that this last idea is extremely unlikely and that the South Tomb is a direct ancestor of the subsidiary pyramid, a view supported by Fakhry (1961, 31) and Lehner (1997, 92), who also see it as a forerunner of the later satellite pyramids. Finally, Dodson and Ikram (2008, 147) describe its function as a "dummy of unknown meaning."

19 Lauer 1936, 96–97; 1955, plate 1.2.

20 Lauer 1936, 99–100; 1962, 120–21.

21 Its internal dimensions were 1.6 m long, 1.6 m wide, and 1.3 m high (Lauer 1936, 98; 1962, 122–26; 1976, 96).

22 Lauer 1939, 46–48; 1962, 127. Interestingly, within the manoeuvring chamber itself, a furrowed wooden beam was discovered in situ whose wear marks had been caused by the friction of the ropes used to lower the plug (Lauer 1976, 95–96).

23 Lauer 1936, 106; 1962, 124.

24 Lauer 1936, 101–102. This may have been the same in the main pyramid, but there is no firm evidence to support it.

25 Firth and Quibell 1935, 18. It can be seen in Firth and Quibell's (1935, plate 46, 1–4) photographs that these large stones are least as big as a man (fig. 59, vol. 2), and thus would have presented a significant obstruction that was extremely difficult to move.

26 Lauer 1936, 100.

27 Firth and Quibell 1935, 19, n. 1; Lauer 1936, 102; 1976, 95.

28 Lauer 1936, 106; 1962, 127.

29 See Lauer (1936, 41–46) for a complete discussion of the explorations of the tomb by robbers—and the curious.

30 Porter and Moss 1974–81, 415–17.

31 Goneim 1957, 1; Lauer 1976, 138, fig. 9.

32 Goneim 1956a, 79; 1957, 11; Maragioglio and Rinaldi 1963, 21–22.

33 Maragioglio and Rinaldi 1963, plate 4; 1965, 4–5. The east–west

corridor measures 152 m and both the north–south 'arms' are 107 m (Goneim 1957, 15–16), while the rooms branching off it are on average 4.5 to 4.9 m long, 1.8 m wide, and 1.9 to 2 m high (Maragioglio and Rinaldi 1965, 9).

34 Goneim (1957, 12) suggested that the shaft was probably intended to serve as a route for removing waste material during the excavation of the substructure, whereas Lauer (1962, 189) proposed that it may have been built to provide ventilation. Baud (2002, 151) considered that the shaft served both functions, though he did not entirely exclude a religious purpose. Maragioglio and Rinaldi (1963, 37) speculated that the shaft's original purpose may have been to enable the lowering of a portcullis, as seen in similar shafts from the period at sites like Beit Khallaf and Reqaqnah. Edwards (1988, 60) and Dodson (2003, 45) supported this theory, but there is no concrete evidence for it.

35 Goneim 1957, 12; Maragioglio and Rinaldi 1963, plate 4.

36 Goneim 1956a, 79; 1957, 11; Maragioglio and Rinaldi 1963, 22. Underneath this lies another ramp leading to an unfinished nine-meter-long corridor, which was probably abandoned, filled in, and built over because of the poor quality of the rock (Goneim 1956a, 142, fig. 45).

37 Goneim 1956a, 84–85; 1956b, 98–99; 1957, 12–13; Maragioglio and Rinaldi 1964a, 4–5.

38 Goneim 1956a, 97; 1956b, 113–14; 1957, 18; Maragioglio and Rinaldi 1964a, 6–7; 1965, 8–9.

39 Goneim 1956a, 98; 1957, 18–19.

40 For a discussion of the sarcophagus in detail, see Goneim (1957, 18–19, plates 51–60) and Wissa (1997, 445–48). Lauer (1962, 194–200) believed that it was empty because the tomb had been robbed in the First Intermediate Period—a suggestion refuted by Maragioglio and Rinaldi (1965, 3–5).

41 Goneim 1957, 8–10, 12; Lauer 1962, 194; Maragioglio and Rinaldi 1963, 12, 25, 37–39.

42 Clark 2016, 266.

43 Lauer 1968, 100–101; 1969b, 464; 1972, fig. 1; 1973, 326–27; 1977, 202–203.

44 Lauer (1969b, 464–65, fig. 1; 1972, 579–80; 1976, 140) speculated during his excavations that, due to the huge quantities of marl found at the site, there may have been a set of subterranean 'comb' magazines attached to the South Tomb akin to those of the pyramid.

45 Lauer 1967, 502–505, plate 4b; 1968, 100–101, 4a and b, fig. 3; 1969b, 463.

46 Lauer 1969a, 124; 1976, 138; 1977, 202–203.
47 See Goneim 1957.
48 Lauer 1967, 502–505; 1969b, 463; 1976, 139; 1977, 202–203.
49 Goneim 1956b, 143.
50 Maragioglio and Rinaldi 1963, 47; Porter and Moss 1974–81, 313; Edwards 1988, 66; Lehner 1996, 511; 1997, 95; Dodson 2003, 46; Seidlmayer 2006, 122.
51 Baud 2002, 214; Dodson 2003, 46.
52 In the two excavation reports on the pyramid by Barsanti (1901) and Reisner and Fisher (1911), the drawings conflict extensively as to the layout of the substructure, as do the dimensions given by Reisner and Barsanti. However, Dodson (2000) has successfully demonstrated that Barsanti's layout is probably the correct one, so for the purposes of this discussion the Barsanti dimensions are used where possible, although they may be contradictory or inaccurate.
53 Barsanti 1901a, 92–94; Reisner 1936, 135.
54 This was a hundred and twenty meters east–west by thirty-eight meters north–south, and unlike in the pyramid of Sekhemkhet its magazines were only oriented toward the pyramid (Barsanti 1901, fig. 3).
55 Barsanti 1901a, 93–94, fig. 3.
56 Maragioglio and Rinaldi 1963, 42–43; Lehner 1997, 95; Dodson 2003, 46.
57 Alternatively, Dodson (2000, 86–87) suggests that a reason for the eastern approach of the pyramid's entrance may have been to ensure that access to these magazines was made easier for their provisioning, unlike in the pyramid of Sekhemkhet, where its tortuous route that doubled back on itself to reach the magazines would have undoubtedly demanded a far greater expenditure of labor.
58 Swelim 1987, 89; Swelim 2002, 444; Dodson 1998, 35; 2003 47–48. Although this is not universally accepted. For example, Lehner (1997, 96) writes, referring to the Brick Pyramid, "A further pyramid is tentatively assigned to Huni," and briefly discusses Swelim's work, but does not include the pyramid in the main corpus of his *Complete Pyramids*. Moreover, this attribution is also opposed by Verner (2003, 152), who feels that its location on the floodplain was wrong for an Old Kingdom pyramid, and Edwards (2005, 88), who thinks it may have been a large mastaba. Typologically, however, Dodson (1998, 35) has suggested that "the only place it would seem to fit into the overall sequence of pyramid evolution is the late Third Dynasty, when experimentation was

continuing in the design of these structures, and when truly massive pyramids were still being projected." Dodson (2000, 90, n. 44) further writes: "The sheer size of the Abu Rowash Brick Pyramid, and its 'mature' substructure, makes it impossible to attribute it to other than Huni."

59 Vyse 1840a, 193–94; Vyse and Perring 1842, 9.

60 Lepsius 1897, 11–12.

61 See Grinsell 1947, 99; Klasens 1957, 58.

62 Swelim 1987.

63 Vyse and Perring 1842, 193–94; Lepsius 1897, 12.

64 Dodson 1998, 36.

65 Swelim 1987, 22, 29.

66 Swelim 1987, 37–41. This helps with the pyramid's dating, as Dodson (2000, 89) writes: "The entirely-tunnelled form of the substructure makes it impossible to assign this structure to any period other than the end of the Third Dynasty, since such an approach was effectively abandoned after the time of Kheops."

67 Personal communication by Nabil Swelim (June 19, 2012).

68 Swelim 1987, 60; Lehner 1997, 109, 120–22, and 175.

69 Personal communication by Nabil Swelim (June 19, 2012).

70 Swelim 1987, 31, 39, 65.

71 Lepsius 1897, 11–12; Swelim 1987, 42.

72 Swelim 1987, 2, n. 1, 65–66, 88–9; Dodson 2003, 47.

73 Trimble 1964, 184; Badawy 1964, 203–206.

74 Stadelmann 1985a, 9 and 85; Lehner 1997, 28–29.

75 Edwards 1988, 278–79. This has been a subject of much debate since the nineteenth century. The great astronomer Sir John Herschel (1851, 191–93) originally suggested that the angle of the corridors in eight of the pyramids excavated by Vyse at Giza and Abusir was "doubtless connected" with the astronomical observation of the pole star. He later recanted his views in a letter to Sir Henry James of the Royal Ordnance Survey in September 1892, writing: "The inclination of the passages I used to think quite satisfactorily accounted for by being able to see *Alpha Draconis* through them; now you have shown a practical and assuredly very natural reason in pointing out 26° as the 'angle of rest,' facilitating the sliding down of great weights without incurring a '*down-rush*,' and directly subserving the intention of blocking up the access to the burial chamber" (published in *Daily Review Edinburgh*, October 9, 1869, and reprinted in Smyth 1870, appendices 16–17).

76 Walker 1984, 887; Brück 1995, 161–64; Krauss 2009, 151–60.

77 Sloping corridors are used in the majority of royal pyramids up until that of Amenemhat II, as can be seen in Lehner's (1997, 16–17) cross-section drawings of the pyramids. However, from the reign of Khufu onward their entrances are brought down to ground level, probably to permit the introduction of sarcophagi during their construction (Dodson and Ikram 2008, 160).
78 A subterranean substructure requires the surrounding geology to be largely self-supporting, and this would not be possible on a fifteen-meter-high sand gezira like that on which the Quesna mastaba is built.
79 Rowland 2011a, 10–13; 2011b, 12–23; Rowland and Tassie 2017.
80 Rowland 2011b, 16; Rowland and Tassie 2017, 374–76.
81 Porter and Moss 1974–81, 294; Jeffreys and Tavares 1994, 145. This is also known as tomb no. 1 or Mastaba T (Martin 1997, 281).
82 Bárta et al. 2010, 52 and 181. See also Bárta (2006) for a discussion on 'transitional tombs' at Saqqara North and Abusir South.
83 Jánosi 2006, 16–17.
84 Covington 1905, 195–96 and 208–10; Reisner 1936, 155–57.
85 Covington 1905, 210. This is presumably part of the "outcrop of the Upper Eocene Maadi Formation" to the southwest of the Giza plateau discussed by Lehner (1985, 114, figs. 2 and 3a), which is characterized by soft marly limestone strata with inclusive layers of shell beds and sandstones.
86 Covington 1905, 209–10.
87 Covington 1905, 214–15.
88 Covington 1905, 196.
89 Covington 1905, 203–204.
90 Covington 1905, 198–99; Jánosi 2006, 20.
91 Covington 1905, 208–10 and 213.
92 See for example tomb AS54, which dates to the reign of Huni (Bárta 2011a).
93 Porter and Moss 1974–81, 437–39.
94 Quibell 1913, 3, 11–12, and 37.
95 Jánosi (2006, 26) suggests that the lower two chambers are the result of Late Period alterations.
96 Reisner 1936, 158–59.
97 See Mariette and Maspero 1885, 80–82; Quibell 1913, 2–11, plates 4–23 and 29–32; Wood 1978; Davis 2003.
98 Barta 1963, 29; Bolshakov 1997, 34.
99 Jánosi 2006, 26.
100 Quibell 1913, 3–4 and 10–11; Reisner 1936, 270–73; Jánosi 2006, 26–27.

101 Reisner 1936, 285.
102 Martin 1974, 22–25, fig. 8A.
103 Emery 1968, 11–13, plate II.
104 Clark 2016, chart J1.
105 Spencer 1982, 74–75.
106 For a discussion of the increased incorporation of decorated rooms and spaces in the superstructures of elite private tombs of the Fifth and Sixth Dynasties and the concurrent changes in their significance, see Jánosi (1999, 34–7) and Bárta (2005).
107 Porter and Moss 1974–81, 448. Dodson and Ikram (2008, 146) suggest that this is a possible candidate for the tomb of Imhotep, on the basis of its date, great size, and the fact that it is oriented in the same direction as the Step Pyramid. Emery (1965a, 3 and 8; 1965b) had been searching for Imhotep's tomb from the mid-1960s and stressed in his later preliminary report on S 3518 (1970, 10–11), without actually claiming it to be the tomb of Imhotep, the significance of the tomb's orientation, its absolute dating from a jar seal with the *serekh* (a rectangular motif, usually surmounted by a falcon, in which the king's name could be written) of Netjerykhet Djoser, and the anatomical *donaria* (model body parts offered in the Greco-Roman Period to the cult of Asclepius, who was associated with Imhotep) found outside its entrance. Martin (1979, 17), however, writes: "But of his tomb or cult-area no trace has yet been found in the area of the Sacred Animal Necropolis so far excavated." Bárta (2003, 8) thinks it improbable in the light of the more modern understanding that S 3518 is the tomb of Imhotep. On the other hand, Nicholson (2005, 48) acknowledges that because of Imhotep's association with Thoth, the sacred ibis and baboon galleries may have been intentionally chosen to lie beneath the Third Dynasty cemetery where Imhotep's tomb may have been located. Therefore, the tomb's ownership remains unresolved and the subject of ongoing debate.
108 Emery 1970, 10.
109 Clark 2016, charts J1 and P3.
110 Emery 1970, plates 19–20.
111 Clark 2016, chart J1.
112 Saad 1951, 3–5, Plan 2; 1969, 32–37.
113 Petrie et al. 1923, 23.
114 Petrie et al. 1923, 22–24 and Tomb Register plate 46.
115 Brunton 1927, 3 and 14; Swelim 1983, 120.
116 Brunton 1927, 14 and Tomb register plate 11.

117 Brunton (1927, 15) wrote regarding 3227: "Probably the purpose of these brick walls was merely to surround the tomb, as seen in modern cemeteries at Badari today, and not to retain a *mastaba* of rubble. The area enclosed is far too great for that to be likely, being in one case (3227) 73 ft. *(22.25 m)* long in the side."
118 Reisner 1932, 220–21 and 229; 1936, 182; Clark 2016, chart P3.
119 Reisner 1932, 217–18; 1936, 181; Clark 2016, chart P3.
120 Reisner 1932, 17 and 226; Clark 2016, chart P3.
121 Porter and Moss 1937, 36.
122 Garstang 1904, 21–23; Reisner 1936, 179–80.
123 Garstang 1904, plate 4a and 4b; Clark 2016, chart P3.
124 Garstang 1904, 21–22, plate 4a; Reisner 1936, 179–80.
125 Garstang 1904, 30.
126 Porter and Moss 1937, 37.
127 Garstang 1903, 9–10; Reisner 1936, 172.
128 This consisted of eight hundred assorted offering tables and vases, pottery, and wine jars (Garstang 1903, 3).
129 Garstang 1903, 3–4 and 8–11.
130 Garstang 1903, 10.
131 Garstang 1903, 9; Clark 2016, chart P3.
132 The famous London Routemaster double-decker buses weighed between 7.46 tonnes (unladen) and 11.68 tonnes (laden).
133 Garstang (1903, 12) wrote concerning his excavation of nearby tomb K2: "The whole process by which these tombs were designed to be protected was made clear. The funeral ceremony performed, and the pathway laden with offerings, the slender walls of brick were removed, and the great stones fell into position before the successive doors, sliding in their grooves. The wells were then filled with mud of a hard and tenacious quality. The surface over all was probably bricked up, to finally conceal the approaches to the tomb."
134 Garstang 1903, 9–10, plate 7; Reisner 1936, 174.
135 Garstang 1903, 17.
136 Garstang 1903, 3.
137 Clark 2016, chart P3.
138 Garstang 1903, 11–2; Reisner 1936, 174–76.
139 Quibell 1898, 3.
140 Painted by Annie Pirie and redrawn by Margaret Murray (Quibell 1898, 7, plate 9).
141 Quibell 1898, 8.
142 Limme 2000, 27–29; 2008, 23; Huyge 2003, 29–30.

143 It is probably of this size and irregular because the sandstone at this depth is of low quality and highly fissured and contains many inclusions (personal communication by Dirk Huyge, September 4, 2012).
144 Although Hesyra's tomb is deeper overall, the fact that its lower chambers were probably Late Period additions makes this the main contender.
145 Personal communication by Dirk Huyge (April 20, 2013).
146 Limme 2000, 30; 2008, 23–24; Huyge 2003, 29–30.
147 Jánosi 2006, 16–17.
148 Hassan 1932, 5.
149 Grajetzki 2003, 14; Jánosi 2006, 25–26.
150 The author has been unable to find a single example of a granite portcullis in his research in either private or royal tomb contexts that predates Khufu's reign, with the exception of the stone plugs in the sarcophagi in the Step Pyramid, which do not take the usual form of a sliding slab.
151 Birrell 2000, 26.
152 Arnold 1991, 79–93; Blyth 2006, 219.
153 Arnold 1991, 269.
154 Emery 1949, plate 64; 1958, plate 119b.
155 Saad 1947, 173, plate 86.
156 See Arnold (1991, 74, fig. 3.2) for a suggested method.
157 Hassan 1960, 49, plate 17 a–b. See also Arnold 1991, 283, figs. 6.45–6.46; Isler 2001, 262, fig. 11.17a.
158 It has occurred to the author that there is a possibility that the packings in some of these tombs that are found under the portcullises were placed there by tomb robbers in order to gain access to the burial, rather than to assist in the lowering of the stones—for example those used to prop up the portcullis in the Middle Kingdom tomb of Senwosret-Ankh at Lisht (Arnold 2006, 22). Indeed, Belzoni (1835, 417) described that very method when he open the portcullis in the pyramid of Khafre: "The only method to be taken was, to raise it a little at a time; and by putting some stones in the grooves on each side, to support the portcullis while changing the fulcrum of the levers, it was raised high enough for a man to pass."
159 Arnold 1991, 74.
160 Lacher-Raschdorff 2014, 58–59.

Notes to Chapter 7

1 Stadelmann 1980, 442–43; 1985, 81–2; Lehner 1997, 97; Dodson 2003, 49; Verner 2003, 167.

2 Porter and Moss 1934, 89–90; Maragioglio and Rinaldi 1964b, 10 and 20–22.

3 Stadelmann (2011, 736–37) suggests that the pyramid may have been remodeled to provide a 'stand-by' tomb that conformed more with the new thinking on pyramid design while the work on the Bent Pyramid was ongoing at Dahshur, as the king would have been over fifty years old when the latter's construction commenced in year thirty of his reign.

4 Petrie 1892, 6, plate 2; 1910, 1; 1912, 25, plate 14; Borchardt 1928, 11–14, plates 3–4; Maragioglio and Rinaldi 1964b, 10–16.

5 Dodson 2003, 49–50. The reason for this collapse has been the subject of considerable debate among scholars. Petrie (1892, 4–5) noted that "the pyramid of Medum is the quarry of the neighbourhood" and thought that the casing was partially stripped in the Rameside Period, with the rest taken in the Middle Ages and in modern times. More recently, Mendelssohn (1973, 60–71) blamed heavy rainfall for washing away the pyramid's foundations, whereas others like Edwards (1974, 251–52) suggested it may be the result of an earthquake. See also Davey (1976, 178–79) regarding the structural collapse discussion. Finally, Stadelmann (2003, 114) concurs with Petrie and suggests that the pyramid was quarried for stone from the Greco-Roman Period onward.

6 There are numerous theories regarding the significance of the true pyramid. Reisner (1936, 340) was reluctant to accept any religious interpretations and suggested its design was intended to conceal the entrance to the descending corridor and that its steep slopes made an attack on the pyramid more difficult. Badawy (1957, 183) thought it "a monument of solar religion, the most perfect of all ascension devices." Fakhry (1961, 8) suggested that it was a rendition in stone of the *benben* (a pillar-like stone venerated at Heliopolis thought to represent the primeval mound) and a replacement for the sun's rays that would permit the king to ascend to heaven, while Stadelmann (1985, 86) believed it to be a symbolic representation of divine kingship. Edwards (1988, 277) proposed that it was a physical representation of the rays of the sun, which the king used as a ramp to heaven, but Brück (1995, 164) suggested it was an interpretation of the celestial sphere in stone. Lehner (1997, 35) writes: "The pyramid is a simulacrum of both the mound of primeval earth and the weightless rays of sunlight, a union of heaven and earth that glorifies and transforms the divine king and ensures the divine rule of the Egyptian household."

Finally, Dodson (2016, 18) considers it to be a solar symbol of the rays of the sun descending from the sky, via which the king could ascend to heaven.

7 Petrie 1892, 10.

8 Stadelmann 1985a, 83.

9 Petrie 1892, 10; Borchardt 1928, 13–14; Rowe 1931, 24; Maragioglio and Rinaldi 1964b, 8.

10 Maragioglio and Rinaldi 1964b, 18.

11 Rowe 1931, 24–25; Wainwright 1937, 128; Maragioglio and Rinaldi 1964b, plate 4. Stadelmann 1985a, 85; Lehner 1997, 98.

12 Known as the *angulus quietis*, the angle of this slope would naturally prevent a 'down-rush' of a plug-stone (Krauss 2009, 156). Its angle was undoubtedly determined by the exploitation of the coefficient of static friction that prevents objects from sliding down an incline of their own accord. The average angle of tilt for limestone to start sliding on an incline is thirty-six degrees, which gives it a coefficient of static friction of 0.73 (Stocks 2003, 195). This equation when applied to our twenty-eight-degree sloping corridor works out to 4.46 kilonewtons or about 446 kilograms of force required for a 2.6 tonne plug-stone, which would be difficult to apply in the cramped space of the corridor. However, if the slope is lubricated with liquid mortar or mud, the coefficient is reduced to 0.14 (Stocks 2003, 195), which would mean that the stone could be moved with a fifth of the force, about 90 kilograms, which two men could probably manage.

13 Rowe 1931, 24–25; Maragioglio and Rinaldi 1964b, 10 and 18; Dormion and Verd'hurt 2000, plate 10.

14 Swelim 1984, 12; Arnold 1991, 186. Recently, further corbel-roofed relieving chambers have been discovered at the northern end of the burial chamber and above the horizontal and descending corridors, which were used to bear the load of the pyramid and permit a flat roof in the corridor (Dormion and Verd'hurt 2000; 2003).

15 Reisner 1936, 201. Rowe (1931, 6) noted "the poor quality of the rock at Meydum, the existence of which is unhappily responsible for roof-falls."

16 Maragioglio and Rinaldi 1964b, 16.

17 Lehner 1997, 17.

18 Although this path of attack sounds unlikely, it was not beyond the bounds of possibility, as Wainwright demonstrated during his excavations by tunneling forty-five meters under the pyramid to expose its accretion layers (Petrie et al. 1910, 1; 1912, 25).

19 When the burial chamber was excavated by Petrie, there was no sign of a stone sarcophagus, but he did find fragments of a destroyed wooden coffin in the shaft (Petrie 1892, 11). These fragments are in the Petrie Museum, accession nos. UC 30876A–C.
20 Maragioglio and Rinaldi 1964b, 18.
21 The reasons for the move are unknown, but Stadelmann (1995, 726) suggests administrative and logistical reasons or simply a desire to keep the workforce employed.
22 Identified as Sneferu's by a cartouche in the upper burial chamber (Fakhry 1959, 52; Porter and Moss 1974–81, 877–82).
23 Dorner 1986, 54.
24 There are various theories as to why the second upper burial chamber was built. Stadelmann (1991, 380–87; 1995, 726–27) sees it as the final part of a three-chamber system common to all royal tombs, with the lower chambers having chthonic associations and the upper part connected to the king's ascent to the sky. Lehner (1997, 103) suggests that it may be reminiscent of the south–west-oriented South Tomb of Djoser, whereas Dodson (2003, 51) proposes that it was introduced after structural collapses occurred in the original structure.
25 Fakhry 1959, 46.
26 Maragioglio and Rinaldi 1964b, 94–96.
27 Maragioglio and Rinaldi 1964b, 64, plate 11, fig 4. The choice of this location was probably because of the ease with which these excavations could be undertaken in comparison to the more difficult sand gravel layers to the north. However, the unstable nature of this underlying geology and poor foundations led to serious problems with subsidence during the construction, which were visible as internal cracks in the substructure (Maragioglio and Rinaldi 1964b, 100; Stadelmann 1985a, 89; Dorner 1986, 44).
28 Maragioglio and Rinaldi 1964b, 62–64.
29 Fakhry 1959, 48; Maragioglio and Rinaldi 1964b, 104 B; Stadelmann 1985a, 92; 1995, 728.
30 Monnier and Puchkov 2016, 35.
31 Stadelmann 2004, 16.
32 Fakhry 1959, 52; Maragioglio and Rinaldi 1964b, 66; Monnier and Puchkov 2016, 34.
33 Fakhry 1951, 512; 1959, 67; Maragioglio and Rinaldi 1964b, 108, plate 11, fig 4.
34 Fakhry 1959, 52–59; figs. 19–24; Maragioglio and Rinaldi 1964b, 72. Stadelmann (1985, 94), Edwards (1988, 82), and Lehner (1997, 103)

suggest that these may have been intended to reinforce the chamber and prevent further cracking of the structure that had occurred as a result of structural instability, which was due to the poor ground on which the pyramid was built.

35 Vyse and Perring 1842, 69; Fakhry 1959, 52–59, figs. 20–23.
36 Fakhry 1951, 511; 1959, 49.
37 Fakhry 1959, 7, 46, and 49; Maragioglio and Rinaldi 1964b, 66.
38 Vyse and Perring 1842, 69; Fakhry 1959, 52.
39 Clark 2016, chart P3.
40 Dorner 1986, 51 and 54; Lehner 1997, 17.
41 Vyse and Perring 1842, 67; Maragioglio and Rinaldi 1964b, 94–96 and 110.
42 Fakhry 1959, 49.
43 Fakhry 1959, 94–96; Maragioglio and Rinaldi 1964b, 114. This jamming was probably caused by a combination of the shaft's angle of incline at thirty-two degrees thirty minutes being too shallow or it being insufficiently lubricated, as the average angle of tilt for limestone to start sliding on an unlubricated limestone incline is thirty-six degrees (Stocks 2003, 195).
44 Maragioglio and Rinaldi 1964b, 146; Porter and Moss 1974–81, 876; Stadelmann 2003, 183.
45 Stadelmann 1983, 234; 1985, 100; Edwards 1994, 160; Dorner 1998, 25; Jánosi 2004, 67.
46 Vyse and Perring 1842, 64; Maragioglio and Rinaldi 1964b, 128.
47 See Clark (2016, 256, n. 1974–76) for an in-depth discussion of these plug-stones.
48 Vyse and Perring 1842, 64–65; Maragioglio and Rinaldi 1964b, 130–36; Lehner 1997, 105; Dorner 1998, 27–29; Stadelmann 1985a, 104; Dodson 2003, 53.
49 Lehner 1997, 17.
50 Dorner 1998, 25.
51 Maragioglio and Rinaldi 1964b, 146; Stadelmann 2003, 183. For a discussion of the mummy see Batrawi (1951, 435–42).
52 Bárta et al. 2010, 52 and 57–67.
53 Bárta et al. 2010, 6–10 and 12–17.
54 Bárta et al. 2010, 12.
55 The tomb is so named because it sits on the western shore of the dried-up lake of Abusir (Bárta 2000, 335).
56 Bárta 2000, 335–37; 2001, 21–25.
57 Martin 1981, 7.
58 Jánosi 2006, 37.

59 Baud 1999, 67.
60 De Morgan 1895, 8–9; figs. 3–5; Clark 2016, chart P3. De Morgan (1895, 9, fig. 6) reported that nearby Mastaba 5 (Porter and Moss 1974–81, 890) also had a corbeled burial chamber, in which was found the earliest known reserve head (Cairo CG 519).
61 Stadelmann and Alexanian 1998, 316.
62 This is 17.95 by 9.2 m (Alexanian and Seidlmayer 2002, 3).
63 Stadelmann and Alexanian 1998, 302–303; Alexanian and Seidlmayer 2000, 292; 2002, 1–8.
64 In a similar way to those used in the later Great Pyramid and the pyramids of the Fifth and Sixth Dynasties (Arnold 1991, 191).
65 Barsanti 1902b, 200–201, figs. 5–6; Porter and Moss 1974–81, 894.
66 Alexanian 1999, 17; 2007, 162–64.
67 Stadelmann et al. 1993, 275; Alexanian 1999, 23–24.
68 Namely Mastabas I/1 and I/2. See Stadelmann et al. 1993, 272–78 and 284–88, respectively.
69 Stadelmann et al. 1993, 280; Alexanian 1999, 30, fig. 11a.
70 Clark 2106, chart P3.
71 Alexanian 1999, 23–24, n. 55.
72 Alexanian 1999, 22 and 26.
73 Alexanian 1999, 24. Fire was often used to shatter stone in ancient Egyptian quarrying. The technique of setting a fire to first heat stone and then pouring cold water on it to render it friable and removable by hand is known from the granite quarry at Aswan (Clarke and Engelbach 1990, 27). In addition, according to Diodorus Siculus in the first century BC, a similar technique was used by the Egyptians to break gold-bearing rock when mining (Diodorus Siculus in Oldfather 2007, Book III, 12, 2–6).
74 Petrie 1892, 16–17; Porter and Moss 1934, 90–92.
75 Spencer 1979, 29.
76 Petrie 1892, 15–17; Daninos-Bey 1886, 69–73; Reisner 1936, 223; Harpur 2001, 48–51.
77 Petrie 1892, 16.
78 Petrie 1892, plate 7; Reisner 1936, fig. 110; Clark 2016, chart J1.
79 Clark 2016, chart P3.
80 Petrie 1892, 16, plate 7.
81 Harpur 2001, 53–54, figs. 199–200.
82 Reisner 1936, fig. 110.
83 Harpur 2001, 53–54.
84 Reisner 1936, 223, fig. 111.
85 Clark 2016, chart J1.

86 Petrie 1892, 17–18, plates 5 and 7; Reisner 1936, 212–13.
87 Reisner 1936, 213, fig. 111.
88 Presumably, as the burial chamber was set approximately three meters up from the base of the shaft (Reisner 1936, fig. 111), the grooves stopped level with its floor, and their termination point may be indicated by the notches marked on the elevation. However, it is possible that the presence of portcullis grooves may just be wishful thinking on behalf of Reisner (1936, 213) and that the notches are precisely that, perhaps intended to support a beam of some sort, which in turn could have supported the portcullis before its final lowering.
89 Petrie 1892, 17.
90 Ikram and Dodson 1998, 86; Riggs 2014, 106.
91 Alexanian (1999, 18) suggests that the similarity of the grid-like layout of these tombs to those of the Lepsius' mastaba field at Dahshur indicates that the Meidum tombs were also intended to have superstructures, which for some reason were never built.
92 See Petrie et al. 1910, plates 17–18.
93 Petrie et al. 1910, 28. See Clark (2016, chart P4) for the portcullises' dimensions and weights.
94 Petrie et al. 1910, 24–25, 28, and plate 17.
95 Out of all of twenty-nine tombs that possessed a portcullis, only four—nos. 50, 60, 69, and 80—actually had their portcullises dropped into position. Among them, tombs 60, 69, and 80 had been robbed, the stone of 69 having been broken at the top to gain access. Tomb 50 was still intact and contained a contemporary burial (Petrie et al. 1910, 24–25).
96 Garstang 1903, 12.
97 Isler 2001, 71.
98 Petrie et al. 1910, 24.
99 Petrie et al. 1910, 24, 26, and 28.
100 Alexanian 1999, 18.
101 This situation may answer the question posed by Birrell (2000, 26) in his paper on tomb security, which was whether or not portcullis stones were put in place before the superstructure was built, as clearly in this case they were. Although this then brings up the issue of whether the Far Western Cemetery tombs were intended to have superstructures, or not, in the first place.
102 Warden 2013, 230–32. Although Reisner (1942, 150) suggested they may have been protected by a superstructure and accessed through its roof.
103 Petrie et al. 1910, 23–24, plate 15; Reisner 1936, 206–207.

104 Petrie et al. 1910, 22–24; Reisner 1936, 206–208.
105 See the tomb catalogue in Clark (2016, 478–81) for more details.
106 Strangely, Petrie wrote concerning these defences, "There seems no reason for excavating a trench in the rock twice as wide as necessary for the chamber, and then filling it up with huge blocks of stone," whereas it seems perfectly obvious to the author that the substructure's manner of construction and the use of stone would have improved the security of the tomb (Petrie et al. 1910, 5).
107 Petrie et al. 1910, 22–24.
108 Rowe 1930, 564.
109 Petrie et al. 1910, 13.
110 Porter and Moss 1934, 94.
111 Reisner 1936, fig. 105.
112 Petrie et al. 1910, 17.
113 Ikram and Dodson 1998, 246.
114 Petrie et al. 1910, plates 12–13.
115 Petrie et al. 1910, 14–18.
116 Petrie 1892, 11–12; Reisner 1936, 221. See Isler (2001, 208–209) for a detailed discussion of the method used by the builders to survey and then construct this feat of civil engineering.
117 These were probably the spoil from the excavation and building of the nearby pyramid (Petrie et al. 1910, 13).
118 Petrie et al. 1910, 3.
119 Petrie 1892, 13.
120 Petrie et al. 1910, 3, 13–14.
121 Petrie et al. 1910, 13.
122 Petrie et al. 1910, 14.
123 Porter and Moss 1934, 92–94; Reisner 1936, 222; Harpur 2001, 37.
124 Bárta 2011b, 132.
125 Petrie et al. 1910, 21.
126 Harpur 2001, 44.
127 Petrie et al. 1910, 18. In metric dimensions these limestone blocks were 1.52 by 0.91 by 0.61 m and would have weighed a considerable 1.43 to 2.2 tonnes each.
128 Harpur 2001, 283, n. 39.
129 Petrie et al. 1912, 25.
130 Harpur 2001, 44.
131 Petrie et al. 1912, 25, plate 16.I.
132 Petrie et al. 1912, 26; Clark 2016, chart J2.
133 Petrie et al. 1912, 26; Clark 2016, chart P4. Harpur (2001, 47) suggests that the height of the stone was intended to relieve pressure on

the roof of the chamber in the friable surrounding marl, a theory the author finds difficult to accept, especially as a shorter stone would have placed less pressure on the shaft in terms of weight. More likely it was to deter tunneling above by robbers.

134 Petrie 1892, 14. Layers of Aeolian sand between the successive coats of mud demonstrate that the structure took some time to build and that the coats were allowed to dry between them (El-Khouli 1991, 23).

135 Petrie et al. 1910, 4.

136 The rear wall of the chapel of Nefermaat weighed approximately eight tonnes, the two side walls weighed twenty tonnes each, and the roof weighed a remarkable thirty-three tonnes (Petrie 1892, 14).

137 Harpur 2001, 26–29.

138 One tunnel led from the southern chapel of Nefermaat 22.8 m northwest toward the axis of the mastaba and another from the southern chamber of the northern chapel of Atet (Petrie 1892, 2 and 14; Harpur 2001, 42).

139 Petrie (1892, 14–15) proposed three phases of development, whereas more recent research by Brock (in El-Khouli 1991, 23–24) suggests only two phases. See Harpur (2001, 35–44) for an in-depth discussion of this topic.

140 Petrie 1892, 14.

141 Petrie et al. 1910, 18; Petrie et al. 1912, 25–26; Harpur 2001, 18.

142 Petrie et al. 1910, 4 and 18; Harpur 2001, 47. See Harpur (2001, 46) for a detailed discussion on the possible perpetrators of the robbery.

143 Clark 2016, chart J2.

144 Reisner 1932, 238–39.

145 Reisner 1932, 248–49.

146 Reisner 1932, 208 and 231.

147 Porter and Moss 1937, 26.

148 Reisner 1932, 248.

149 Clark 2016, chart J2.

150 Reisner 1932, 231 and 238, fig. 161.

151 Clark 2016, chart J2.

152 Porter and Moss 1937, 175.

153 Quibell 1898, 3–4, plate 23.

154 Quibell 1898, 3.

155 Quibell 1898, 3–4. These grave goods included a stone dish with Sneferu's Horus name *Neb-Maat* inscribed on it, which provides an accurate date for the tomb (Quibell 1898, 4; Aston 1994, 133).

156 It is within the bounds of possibility that the descending corridor in the Brick Pyramid of Abu Rawash may have been intended to be blocked with plug-stones, bearing in mind its regular section and angle of descent.

157 Plug-stones are found in the pyramids of Amenemhat I and Senwosret I (Arnold, Arnold, and Dorman 1988, I, plates 89 and 69, fig. 26) and the tomb of Senwosret III at Abydos (Wegner 2009, 125, fig. 16c). They are also found in the private tombs of Intef and Senimeru at Lisht (Arnold 2006, 30, plates 35 and 72, plate 134).

Bibliography

Abłamowicz, R., J. Dębowska, and M. Jucha. 2004. "The Graves of Tell el-Farkha (Seasons 2001–2002)." In *Egypt at Its Origins: Studies in Memory of Barbara Adams: Proceedings of the International Conference "Origin of the State, Predynastic and Early Dynastic Egypt," Krakow, 28th August–1st September 2002*, edited by S. Hendrickx, R.F. Friedman, K.M. Ciałowcz, and M. Chłodnicki, 399–419. Leuven: Peeters Publishers and Department of Oriental Studies.

Adams, B. 1988. *Predynastic Egypt*. Princes Risborough: Shire.

———. 1996. "Elite Graves at Hierakonpolis." In *Aspects of Early Egypt*, edited by A.J. Spencer, 1–15. London: British Museum Press.

———. 2000. *Excavations in the Locality 6 Cemetery at Hierakonpolis, 1979–1985*. Oxford: Archaeopress.

———. 2004. "Excavations in the Elite Predynastic Cemetery at Hierakonpolis Locality HK6: 1999–2000." *ASAE* 78: 35–51.

Alexanian, N. 1999. *Das Grab des Prinzen Netjer-aperef: Die Mastaba II/1 in Dahschur*. Mainz am Rhein: Philipp von Zabern.

———. 2007. "Die Mastabagräber des Alten Reiches in Dahschur." In *Begegnung mit der Vergangenheit. 100 Jahre in Ägypten*, edited by G. Dreyer and D. Polz, 162–69. Mainz am Rhein: Philipp von Zabern.

Alexanian, N., and S.J. Seidlmayer. 2000. "Die Nekropole von Dahschur Forschungsgeschichte und Perspektiven." In *Abusir and Saqqara in the Year 2000*, edited by M. Bárta and J. Krejcí, 283–304. Prague: Academy of Sciences of the Czech Republic Oriental Institute.

———. 2002. "Die Residenznekropole von Dahschur Erster Grabungsbericht." *MDAIK* 58: 1–28.

Allen, J.P. 2005. *The Ancient Egyptian Pyramid Texts*. Atlanta, GA: Society of Biblical Literature.

———. 2006. "Some Aspects of the Non-Royal Afterlife in the Old Kingdom." In *The Old Kingdom Art and Archaeology: Proceedings of the Conference*

Held in Prague, May 31–June 4, 2004, edited by M. Bárta, 9–18. Prague: Publishing House of the Academy of Sciences of the Czech Republic.

Amélineau, E. 1899a. *Le tombeau d'Osiris: Monographie de la découverte faite en 1897–1898*. Paris: Ernest Leroux.

———. 1899b. *Les nouvelles fouilles d'Abydos [1895–1898]: Compte rendu in extenso des fouilles, description des monuments et objets découverts*. Paris: Ernest Leroux.

———. 1904. *Mission Amélineau: Les nouvelles fouilles d'Abydos 1897–1898. Compte rendu in extenso des monuments et objets découverts*. Paris: Ernest Leroux.

Anderson, J.B. 2000. "The Tomb Owner at the Offering Table." In *Egyptian Art: Principles and Themes in Wall Scenes*, edited by L. Donovan and K. McCorquodale, 129–40. Giza: Prism Publications.

Anderson, W. 1992. "Badarian Burials: Evidence of Social Inequality in Middle Egypt During the Early Predynastic Era." *JARCE* 29: 51–65.

Arkell, A.J. 1975. *The Prehistory of the Nile Valley*. Leiden: Brill.

Arnold, D. 1991. *Building in Egypt: Pharaonic Stone Masonry*. New York, NY: Oxford University Press.

———. 2003. *The Encyclopaedia of Ancient Egyptian Architecture*. London: I.B. Tauris.

———. 2006. *Middle Kingdom Tomb Architecture at Lisht*. New York, NY: Metropolitan Museum of Art and Yale University Press.

Arnold, D., D. Arnold, and P. Dorman. 1988. *The Pyramid of Senwosret I*. New York, NY: Metropolitan Museum of Art.

Assmann, J. 2005. *Death and Salvation in Ancient Egypt*. Translated by D. Lorton. Ithaca, NY: Cornell University Press.

Aston, B.G. 1994. *Ancient Egyptian Stone Vessels: Materials and Forms*. Heidelberg: Heidelberger Orientverlag.

Ayrton, E.R., and W.L.S. Loat. 1911. *The Pre-Dynastic Cemetery at El Mahasna*. London: Egypt Exploration Fund.

Badawy, A. 1954. *A History of Egyptian Architecture, vol. 1, From the Earliest Times to the End of the Old Kingdom*. Cairo: The Author.

———. 1956. "The Ideology of the Superstructure of the Mastaba-tomb in Egypt." *JNES* 15, no. 3: 180–83.

———. 1964. "The Stellar Destiny of Pharaoh and the So-Called Air-Shafts of Cheops' Pyramid." *MIO* 10: 189–206.

Baines, J. 1991. "Society, Morality and Religious Practice." In *Religion in Ancient Egypt*, edited by B.E. Schafer, J. Baines, L.H. Lesko, and D.P. Silverman, 123–200. New York, NY: Cornell University Press.

Bard, K.A. 1994. *From Farmers to Pharaohs: Mortuary Evidence for the Rise of Complex Society in Egypt*. Sheffield: Sheffield Academic Press.

———. 2005a. "Predynastic Period: Overview." In *Encylopedia of the Archaeology of Ancient Egypt*, edited by K.A. Bard, 31–35. London: Taylor and Francis E-library.
——— (ed.). 2005b. *Encylopedia of the Archaeology of Ancient Egypt*. London: Taylor and Francis E-library.
———. 2007. *Introduction to the Archaeology of Ancient Egypt*. Malden: Oxford and Carlton: Blackwell.
Bareš, L. 1999. *Abusir IV: The Shaft Tomb of Udjahorresnet at Abusir*. Prague: Karolinum.
Barsanti, A. 1901a. "Ouverture de la pyramide de Zaouiét el-Âryan." *ASAE* 2: 92–94.
———. 1901b. "Rapports sur les déblaiements opérés autour de la pyramide d'Ounas." *ASAE* 2: 249–53.
———. 1902a. "Fouilles autour de la pyramide d'Ounas." *ASAE* 3: 182–84.
———. 1902b. "Rapport sur la fouille de Dahchour." *ASAE* 3: 198–201.
Bárta, M. 2000. "The Non-Royal Cemeteries at Abusir South: The Early Fourth and the Early Fifth Dynasty at Abusir." In *Abusir and Saqqara in the Year 2000*, edited by M. Bárta and J. Krejcí, 331–46. Prague: Academy of Sciences of the Czech Republic Oriental Institute.
———. 2001. *Abusir V: The Cemeteries at Abusir South I*. Prague: Set Out.
———. 2003. "Imhotep, stavitel nejstarší pyramidy na svete." *Pražské egyptologické studie, suplementa* 1: 9–21.
———. 2005. "Architectural Innovations in the Development of the Non-Royal Tomb during the Reign of Nyuserra." In *Structure and Significance: Thoughts on Ancient Egyptian Architecture*, edited by P. Jánosi, 105–25. Vienna: Österreichische Akademie der Wissenschaften.
———. 2011a. "An Abusir Mastaba from the Reign of Huni." In *Times, Signs and Pyramids: Studies in Honour of Miroslav Verner on the Occasion of His Seventieth Birthday*, edited by V.G. Callender, L. Bareš, M. Bárta, J. Krejčí, and J. Janák, 41–50. Prague: Charles University, Faculty of Arts.
———. 2011b. *Journey to the West: The World of the Old Kingdom Tombs in Ancient Egypt*. Prague: Charles University, Faculty of Arts.
Bárta, M., F. Coppens, and H. Vymazalová. 2010. *Abusir XIX: Tomb of Hetepi (AS 20), Tombs AS 33–35 and AS 50–53*. Prague: Charles University, Faculty of Arts.
Barta, W. 1963. *Die altägyptische Opferliste von der Frühzeit bis zur griechisch-römischen Epoche*. Berlin: Bruno Hessling.
Batrawi, A. 1951. "The Skeletal Remains of the Northern Pyramid of Sneferu." *ASAE* 51: 435–42.
Baud, M. 1999. *Famille royale et pouvoir sous l'Ancien Empire égyptien*, tome 1, bde 126/1. Cairo: Institut Français d'Archéologie Orientale.

———. 2002. *Djéser et la IIIe dynastie*. Paris: Pygmalion.

Baumgartel, E.J. 1960. *The Cultures of Prehistoric Egypt*, vol. 2. London: Published on behalf of the Griffith Institute, Ashmolean Museum, by Oxford University Press.

Belzoni, G.B. 1835. *Narrative of the Operations and Recent Discoveries within the Pyramids, Temples, Tombs, and Excavations, in Egypt and Nubia; and of a Journey to the Coast of the Red Sea, in Search of the Ancient Berenice; and Another to the oasis of Jupiter Ammon*. Brussels: H. Remy.

Bestock, L. 2009. *The Development of Royal Funerary Cult at Abydos: Two Funerary Enclosures from the Reign of Aha*. Wiesbaden: Harrassowitz Verlag.

Birrell, M. 2000. "Portcullis Stones: Tomb Security during the Early Dynastic Period." *BACE* 11: 17–28.

Blanchette, R.A., J.E. Haight, R.J. Koestler, P.B. Hatchfield, and D. Arnold. 1994. "Assessment of Deterioration in Archaeological Wood from Ancient Egypt." *Journal of the American Institute for Conservation* 33: 55–70.

Blyth, E. 2006. *Karnak: Evolution of a Temple*. London, Routledge.

Bolshakov, A.O. 1997. *Man and His Double in Egyptian Ideology of the Old Kingdom*. Wiesbaden: Harrassowitz.

Bonnet, H. 1928. *Ein frühgeschichtliches Gräberfeld bei Abusir*. Leipzig: J.C. Hinrichs.

Borchardt, L. 1898. "Das Grab des Menes." *ZÄS* 36: 87–105.

———. 1928. *Die Entstehung der Pyramide an der Baugeschichte der Pyramide bei Mejdum nachgewiesen.* Berlin: Selbstverlag des Autor.

Brewer, D.J. 2005. *Ancient Egypt: Foundations of a Civilization.* Harlow: Pearson Education.

Brück, M.T. 1995. "Can the Great Pyramid Be Astronomically Dated?" *Journal of the British Astronomical Association* 105, no. 4: 161–64.

Brunton, G. 1927. *Qau and Badari*. London: British School of Archaeology in Egypt and Bernard Quaritch.

Brunton, G., and G. Caton-Thompson. 1928. *The Badarian Civilisation and Predynastic Remains near Badari.* London: British School of Archaeology in Egypt.

Butzer, K.W. 1976. *Early Hydraulic Civilization in Egypt: A Study in Cultural Ecology*. Chicago, IL: University of Chicago Press.

Castillos, J.J. 1982. *A Reappraisal of the Published Evidence on Egyptian Predynastic and Early Dynastic Cemeteries*. Toronto: Benben Publications.

Chłodnicki, M., and K.M. Ciałowicz. 2009. *Tell el-Farkha (Ghazala) 2009: Preliminary Report on the Activities of the Polish Archaeological Mission.* Poznan: Polish Archaeological Expedition to the Eastern Nile Delta.

Ciałowicz, K.M., and J. Dębowska-Ludwin. 2013. "The Origin of Egyptian Mastabas in the Light of Research at Tell el-Farkha." Études et Travaux 26: 153–62.

Clark, R.J. 2016. *Tomb Security in Ancient Egypt from the Predynastic to the Pyramid Age*. Oxford: Archaeopress.

Clarke, S., and R. Engelbach. 1990. *Ancient Egyptian Construction and Architecture*. New York, NY: Dover Publications.

Cobb, F. 2004. *Structural Engineer's Pocket Book*. London: Elsevier.

Connor, M.A. 2007. *Forensic Methods: Excavation for the Archaeologist and Investigator*. Lanham, MD: AltaMira Press.

Covington, L.D. 1905. "Mastaba Mount Excavations." *ASAE* 6: 193–218.

Daninos-Bey, A. 1886. "Lettre de M. Daninos-Bey à M.G. Maspero, directeur général des fouilles et musées d'Egypte, au sujet de la découverte des statues de Meidoum." *Rec. de Trav.* 8: 69–73.

Daressy, M.G. 1905. "Un édifice archaïque à Nezlet Batran." *ASAE* 6: 99–106.

Davey, C.J. 1976. "The Structural Failure of the Meidum Pyramid." *JEA* 62: 178–79.

Davis, W. 2003. "Archaism and Modernism in the Reliefs of Hesy-Ra." In J. Tait (ed.), *"Never Had the Like Occurred": Egypt's View of Its Past*. London: UCL Press.

De Morgan, H. 1908. "Notes sur les stations quaternaires et sur l'age du cuivre en Egypte." *Revue de l'Ecole d'Anthropologie de Paris* 18: 133–49.

———. 1909. "L'Égypte primitive: Le Néolithique et l'Énéolithique." *Revue de L'École d'Anthropologie de Paris* 19: 263–81.

———. 1984. "Archaeological Researches in the Nile Valley between Esna and Gebel es-Silsila (1908)." In *Predynastic and Archaic Egypt in the Brooklyn Museum*, edited by W. Needler, 50–66. Brooklyn, NY: Brooklyn Museum.

De Morgan, J. 1895. *Fouilles à Dahchour: Mars–Juin 1894*. Vienna: Holzhausen.

———. 1897. *Recherches sur les origines de l'Égypte, vol. 2, Ethnographie préhistorique et tombeau royal de Négadah*. Paris: E. Leroux.

Debono, F., and B. Mortensen. 1990. *El Omari: A Neolithic Settlement and Other Sites in the Vicinity of Wadi Hof, Helwan*. Mainz am Rhein: Philipp von Zabern.

Dębowska-Ludwin, J. 2009. "The Catalogue of Graves from Tell el-Farkha." *Recherches Archéologiques* SN 1: 457–86.

———. 2010. "The Necropolis at Tell el-Farkha Reconsidered." *Recherches Archéologiques* NS 2: 5–30.

———. 2011a. "Early Egyptian Tomb Security: Middle Class Burials from Tell el-Farkha." *SAAC* 15: 29–36.

———. 2011b. "Sepulchral Architecture in Detail: New Data from Tell el-Farkha." In *Egypt at Its Origins 3: Proceedings of the Third International Conference "Origin of the State. Predynastic and Early Dynastic Egypt," London, 27th July–1st August 2008*, edited by R.F. Friedman and P.N. Fiske, 257–68. Leuven: Peeters.

———. 2012. "The Cemetery." In *Tell el-Farkha I. Excavations 1998–2011*, edited by M. Chłodnicki, K.M. Ciałowicz, and A. Mączyńska, 53–75. Poznan: Poznan Archaeological Museum.

Dębowska-Ludwin, J., M.A. Jucha, G. Pryc, and P. Kołodziejczyk. 2010. "Tell el-Farkha (2009 Season): Grave No. 100." *SAAC* 14: 23–42.

Dębowska, J. 2008. "Burial Custom and Political Status of Local Societies: A View from Tell el-Farkha." In *Egypt at its Origins 2: Proceedings of the International Conference "Origin of the State: Predynastic and Early Dynastic Egypt," Toulouse (France), 5th–8th September 2005*, edited by B. Midant-Reynes, Y. Tristant, J. Rowland, and S. Hendrickx, 1107–17. Leuven: Peeters.

Diodorus Siculus in Oldfather, C. H. (ed.). 2007. *Diodorus of Sicily, The Loeb Classical Library*, vol. II. London: W. Heinemann and Harvard University Press.

Dodson, A. 1994. *The Canopic Equipment of the Kings of Egypt*. London: Kegan Paul International.

———. 1996. "The Mysterious Second Dynasty." *KMT* 7, no. 2: 26–60.

———. 1997. "The So-Called Tomb of Osiris at Abydos." *KMT* 8, no. 4: 37–47.

———. 1998. "On the Threshold of Glory: The Third Dynasty." *KMT* 9, no. 2: 26–40.

———. 2000. "The Layer Pyramid of Zawiyet el-Aryan: Its Layout and Context." *JARCE* 37: 81–90.

———. 2003. *The Pyramids of Ancient Egypt*. London: New Holland.

———. 2010. "Mortuary Architecture and Decorative Systems." In *A Companion to Ancient Egypt*, edited by A.B. Lloyd, 804–25. Chichester: Wiley-Blackwell.

———. 2016. *The Royal Tombs of Ancient Egypt*. Barnsley: Pen & Sword Archaeology.

Dodson, A., and D. Hilton. 2004. *The Complete Royal Families of Ancient Egypt*. London: Thames and Hudson.

Dodson, A., and S. Ikram. 2008. *The Tomb in Ancient Egypt: Royal and Private Sepulchres from the Early Dynastic Period to the Romans*. London: Thames and Hudson.

Dormion, G., and J.-Y. Verd'hurt. 2000. *The Pyramid of Meidum: Architectural Study of the Inner Arrangement*. Cairo: World Congress of Egyptology.

Dorner, J. 1986. "Form und Ausmaße der Knickpyramide." *MDAIK* 42: 43–56.

———. 1998. "Neue Messungen an der Roten Pyramide." In *Beiträge zur Kulturgeschichte Ägyptens: R. Stadelmann gewidmet*, edited by H. Guksch and D. Polz. Mainz am Rhein: Phillip von Zabern.

Dreyer, G. 1990. "Umm el-Qaab: Nachuntersuchungen im frühzeitlichen Königsfriedhof. 3./4. Vorbericht, mit Beiträgen von Joachim Boessneck und Angela von den Driesch und Stefan Klug." *MDAIK* 46: 53–90.

———. 1991. "Zur Rekonstruktion der Oberbauten der Königsgräber der 1. Dynastie in Abydos." *MDAIK* 47: 93–104.

———. 1992. "Recent Discoveries at Abydos Cemetery U." In *The Nile Delta in Transition: 4th–3rd Millennium B.C.: Proceedings of the Seminar Held in Cairo, 21–24 October 1990, at the Netherlands Institute of Archaeology and Arabic Studies*, edited by E.C.M. van den Brink, 293–99. Tel Aviv: Brink, distributed by the Israel Exploration Society.

———. 1993. "A Hundred Years at Abydos." *EA* 3: 10–12.

———. 1998. "*Umm el-Qaab I: Das prädynastische Königsgrab U-j und seine frühen Schriftzeugnisse*. Mainz: Verlag Philipp von Zabern.

———. 2003a. "Abydos/Umm el-Qaab." *DAIK Rundbrief* (December): 11–14.

———. 2003b. "The Tombs of the First and Second Dynasties." In *The Treasures of the Pyramids*, edited by Z.A. Hawass, 62–77. Vercelli: White Star.

———. 2004. "Saqqara." *DAIK Rundbrief* (September): 19–22.

———. 2005. "Abydos/Umm el-Qaab." *DAIK Rundbrief* (September): 13–15.

———. 2006. "Saqqara." *DAIK Rundbrief* (October): 19–20.

———. 2007a. "Ein unterirdisches Labyrinth: Das Grab des Königs Ninetjer in Sakkara." In Dreyer and Polz 2007, 130–38.

———. 2007b. "Friedhof B: Vom König zum Gott –Die Anfänge monumentaler Architektur." In *Begegnung mit der Vergangenheit: 100 Jahre in Ägypten: Deutsches Archäologisches Institut Kairo 1907–2007*, edited by G. Dreyer and D. Polz, 193–96. Mainz am Rhein: Philipp von Zabern.

———. 2007c. "Königsgräber ab Djer: Wege zur Auferstehung." In *Begegnung mit der Vergangenheit: 100 Jahre in Ägypten: Deutsches Archäologisches Institut Kairo 1907–2007*, edited by G. Dreyer and D. Polz, 197–204. Mainz am Rhein: Philipp von Zabern.

———. 2007d. "Saqqara." *DAIK Rundbrief* (September): 19–21.

———. 2008. "Report on the 20th Campaign of Reexamining the Royal Tombs of Umm el-Qaab at Abydos 2005/2006." *ASAE* 82: 49–59.

———. 2009a. "Saqqara." *DAIK Rundbrief* (January): 26–27.

———. 2009b. "Umm el-Qaab." *DAIK Rundbrief* (January): 17–19.

———. 2010. "Abydos/Umm el-Qaab: Frühdynastische Königsgräber." *DAIK Rundbrief* (January): 20–23.

Dreyer, G., and D. Polz, eds. 2007. *Begegnung mit der Vergangenheit: 100 Jahre in Ägypten: Deutsches Archäologisches Institut Kairo 1907–2007.* Mainz am Rhein: Philipp von Zabern.

Dreyer, G., A.I. Blöbaum, E.M. Engel, H. Köpp, and C. Müller. 2011. "Umm el-Qaab: Nachuntersuchungen im frühzeitlichen Königsfriedhof 19./20./21." *MDAIK* 67: 53–92.

Dreyer, G., A. Effland, U. Effland, U. Hartung, C. Lacher, V. Müller, and A. Porkony. 2006. "Umm el Qaab: Nachuntersuchungen im frühzeitlichen Königsfriedhof 16./17./18. Vorbericht." *MDAIK* 62: 67–129.

Dreyer, G., E.M. Engel, U. Hartung, T. Hikade, E.V. Köhler, and F. Pumpenmeier. 1996. "Umm el-Qaab: Nachuntersuchungen im frühzeitlichen Königsfriedhof 7./8. Vorbericht." *MDAIK* 52: 11–81.

Dreyer, G., U. Hartung, T. Hikade, E.V. Köhler, V. Müller, and F. Pumpenmeier. 1998. "Umm el-Qaab: Nachuntersuchungen im frühzeitlichen Königsfriedhof 9./10. Vorbericht." *MDAIK* 54: 77–167.

Dreyer, G., U. Hartung, T. Hikade, H. Köpp, C. Lacher, V. Müller, A. Nerlich, and A. Zink. 2003. "Umm el Qaab: Nachuntersuchungen im frühzeitlichen Königsfriedhof 13./14./15. Vorbericht." *MDAIK* 59: 67–129.

Dreyer, G., U. Hartung, and F. Pumpenmeier. 1993. "Umm el-Qaab: Nachuntersuchungen im frühzeitlichen Königsfriedhof. 5./6. Vorbericht." *MDAIK* 49: 23–62.

Dreyer, G., A. von den Driesch, E.M. Engel, R. Hartmann, U. Hartung, T. Hikade, V. Müller, and J. Peters. 2000. "Umm el Qaab: Nachuntersuchungen im frühzeitlichen Königsfriedhof 11./12. Vorbericht." *MDAIK* 56: 43–129.

Dupras, T.L., J.J. Schultz, S.M. Wheeler, and L.J. Williams. 2006. *Forensic Recovery of Human Remains: Archaeological Approaches.* Boca Raton, FL: Taylor and Francis.

Edwards, I.E.S. 1971. "The Early Dynastic Period." In *The Cambridge Ancient History*, vol. 1 pt. 2, edited by I.E.S. Edwards, C.J. Gadd, and N.G.L. Hammond, 1–70. Cambridge: Cambridge University Press.

———. 1974. "The Collapse of the Meidum Pyramid." *JEA* 60: 251–52.

———. 1988. *The Pyramids of Egypt.* London: Penguin.

———. 1994. "Do the Pyramid Texts Suggest an Explanation for the Abandonment of the Subterranean Chamber of the Great Pyramid?" In *Hommages à Jean Leclant*, vol.1, edited by C. Berger, G. Clerc, and N. Grimal, 159–60. Cairo: Institut Français d'Archéologie Orientale.

———. 2005. "Abu Roash." In *Encylopedia of the Archaeology of Ancient Egypt*, edited by K.A. Bard, 88–89. London: Taylor and Francis E-library.

Effland, A., and U. Effland. 2010. "'Ritual Landscape' und 'Sacred Space': Überle-gungen zu Kultausrichtung und Prozessionsach-sen in Abydos." *MOSAIK* 1: 127–58.

Emery, W.B. 1938. *Excavations at Saqqara: The Tomb of Hemaka*. Cairo: Government Press.

———. 1939. *Excavations at Saqqara, 1937–1938: Hor-Aha*. Cairo: Government Press.

———. 1949. *Great Tombs of the First Dynasty*, vol. 1. Cairo: Government Press.

———. 1954. *Great Tombs of the First Dynasty*, vol. 2. London: Egypt Exploration Society.

———. 1958. *Great Tombs of the First Dynasty*, vol. 3. London: Egypt Exploration Society.

———. 1961. *Archaic Egypt*. London: Penguin.

———. 1962. *A Funerary Repast in an Egyptian Tomb of the Archaic Period*. Leiden: Nederlands Instituut voor het Nabije Oosten.

———. 1965a. "Preliminary Report on the Excavations at North Saqqâra 1964–5." *JEA* 51: 3–8.

———. 1965b. "The Search for Imhotep in Sakkara." *Illustrated London News* 246 (March 6): 20–23.

———. 1968. "Tomb 3070 at Saqqâra." *JEA* 54: 11–3.

———. 1970. "Preliminary Report on the Excavations at North Saqqâra, 1968–9." *JEA* 56: 5–11.

Engel, E.M. 1997. "Das Grab des Qa'a in Umm el-Qa'ab: Architektur und Inventar." Doctoral dissertation, Göttingen University.

———. 2003. "Tombs of the 1st Dynasty at Abydos and Saqqara: Different Types or Variations on a Theme?" In *Proceedings of the Second Central European Conference of Young Egyptologists: Egypt 2001: Perspectives of Research, Warsaw 5–7 March 2001*, edited by J. Popielska-Grzybowska, 41–49. Warsaw: Institute of Archaeology, Warsaw University.

———. 2008. "The Royal Tombs at Umm el-Qa'ab." *Archéo-nil* 18: 30–40.

———. 2017. *Das Grab des Qa'a Architektur und Inventar*. Wiesbaden: Harrassowitz Verlag.

Eyre, C. 2013. *The Use of Documents in Pharaonic Egypt*. Oxford: Oxford University Press.

Fakhry, A. 1951. "The Southern Pyramid of Sneferu." *ASAE* 51: 509–22.

———. 1959. *The Monuments of Sneferu at Dahshur, vol. 1, The Bent Pyramid*. Cairo: General Organization for Government Printing Offices.

———. 1961. *The Pyramids*. Chicago, IL: University of Chicago Press.

Figueiredeo, Á. 2004. "Locality HK6 at Hierakonpolis." In *Egypt at Its Origins: Studies in Memory of Barbara Adams: Proceedings of the International Conference "Origin of the State, Predynastic and Early Dynastic Egypt," Krakow, 28th August–1st September 2002*, edited by S. Hendrickx, R.F. Friedman, K.M. Ciałowcz, and M. Chłodnicki, 1–23. Leuven: Peeters Publishers and Department of Oriental Studies.

Firth, C.M. 1927. *The Archaeological Survey of Nubia Report for 1910–1911.* Cairo: Government Press.

Firth, C.M., and J.E. Quibell. 1935. *The Step Pyramid.* Cairo: Imprimerie de l'Institut Français d'Archéologie Orientale.

Fitzner, B., K. Heinrichs, and D. La Bouchardiere. 2003. "Weathering Damage on Pharaonic Sandstone Monuments in Luxor—Egypt." *Building and Environment* 38: 1089–1103.

Friedman, R.F. 1997. "Excavations in the Predynastic Cemetery at HK43." *Nekhen News* 9: 2–3.

———. 1998. "More Mummies: The 1998 Season at HK43." *Nekhen News* 10: 4–6.

———. 2005. "Excavating Egypt's Early Kings." *Nekhen News* 17: 4–6.

———. 2006a. "Bigger Than an Elephant: More Surprises at HK6." *Nekhen News* 18: 7–8.

———. 2006b. "New Tombs and New Thoughts at HK6." *Nekhen News* 18: 11–2.

———. 2008a. "The Cemeteries of Hierakonpolis." *Archéo-nil* 18: 9–29.

———. 2008b. "Excavating Egypt's Early Kings: Recent Discoveries in the Elite Cemetery at Hierakonpolis." In *Egypt at Its Origins 2: Proceedings of the International Conference "Origin of the State: Predynastic and Early Dynastic Egypt," Toulouse (France), 5th–8th September 2005*, edited by B. Midant-Reynes, Y. Tristant, J. Rowland, and S. Hendrickx, 1157–94. Leuven: Peeters.

———. 2008c. "Remembering the Ancestors: HK6 in 2008." *Nekhen News* 20: 10–11.

———. 2011. "Perseverance Pays Off: Answers from Tomb 16 at HK6." *Nekhen News* 23: 4–6.

Friedman, R.F., and P.N. Fiske, eds. 2011. *Egypt at Its Origins 3: Proceedings of the Third International Conference "Origin of the State: Predynastic and Early Dynastic Egypt," London, 27th July–1st August 2008*. Leuven: Peeters.

Friedman, R.F., W. van Neer, and V. Linseele. 2011. "The Elite Predynastic Cemetery at Hierakonpolis: 2009–10 Update." In *Egypt at Its Origins 3: Proceedings of the Third International Conference "Origin of the State: Predynastic and Early Dynastic Egypt," London, 27th July–1st*

August 2008, edited by R.F. Friedman and P.N. Fiske, 157–92. Leuven: Peeters.

Gardiner, A.H., and K. Sethe. 1928. *Egyptian Letters to the Dead, Mainly from the Old and Middle Kingdoms*. London: Egypt Exploration Society.

Garstang, J. 1903. *Mahâsna and Bêt Khallâf*. London: B. Quaritch.

———. 1904. *Tombs of the Third Egyptian Dynasty at Reqâqnah and Bêt Khallâf*. London: A. Constable.

Gatto, M.C. 2003. "Hunting the Elusive Nubian A–Group." *Nekhen News* 15: 14–15.

———. 2006. "The Nubian A-Group: A Reassessment." *Archéo-nil* 16: 61–76.

Geus, F. 1991. "Burial Customs in the Upper Main Nile." In *Egypt and Africa: Nubia from Prehistory to Islam*, edited by W.V. Davies, 57–65. London: British Museum Press in Association with the Egypt Exploration Society.

Goneim, M.Z. 1956a. *The Buried Pyramid*. London: Longmans Green.

———. 1956b. *The Lost Pyramid*. New York: Rinehart & Company.

———. 1957. *Horus Sekhem-khet: The Unfinished Step Pyramid at Saqqara*: Cairo: Imprimerie de l'Institut Français d'Archéologie Orientale.

Görsdorf, J., G. Dreyer, and U. Hartung. 1998. "New (Super 14) C Dating of the Archaic Royal Necropolis Umm el-Qaab at Abydos (Egypt)." *Radiocarbon* 40: 641–47.

Grajetzki, W. 2003. *Burial Customs in Ancient Egypt: Life in Death for Rich and Poor*. London: Duckworth.

———. 2008. "The Architecture and the Signification of the Tarkhan Mastabas." *Archéo-nil* 18: 103–12.

Grinsell, L.V. 1947. *Egyptian Pyramids*. Gloucester: J. Bellows.

Haarlem, W.V. 1996. "A Tomb of the First Dynasty at Tell Ibrahim Awad." *OMRO* 76: 7–34.

Haase, M. 2006. "Vor der Pyramidenzeit: Bemerkungen zu den prä- und frühdynastischen Gräbern in Abydos und Sakkara: Interview mit Prof. Günter Dreyer." *Sokar* 12: 8–19.

Harpur, Y. 2001. *The Tombs of Nefermaat and Rahotep at Maidum: Discovery, Destruction and Reconstruction*. Presbury: Oxford Expedition to Egypt.

Hassan, F.A. 1988. "The Predynastic of Egypt." *Journal of World Prehistory* 2: 135–85.

———. 2000. "Kafr Hassan Dawood." *EA* 18: 37–39.

Hassan, S. 1932. *Excavations at Giza: The Offering List in the Old Kingdom*, vol. 6, part 2, 1934–35. Cairo: Government Press.

———. 1938. "Excavations at Saqqara 1937–38." *ASAE* 38: 503–21.

———. 1960. *The Great Pyramid of Khufu and Its Mortuary Chapel: Excavations at Giza, Season 1938–39*, vol. 10. Cairo: General Organisation for Government Printing Offices.

Hawass, Z.A., ed. 2003. *The Treasures of the Pyramids*. Vercelli: White Star.

Hays, H.M. 2009. "Unreading the Pyramids." *BIFAO* 109: 195–220.

———. 2012. *The Organization of the Pyramid Texts: Typology and Disposition*. Leiden: Brill.

Hendrickx, S. 1996. "The Relative Chronology of the Naqada Culture: Problems and Possibilities." In *Aspects of Early Egypt*, edited by A.J. Spencer, 36–69. London: British Museum Press.

———. 1999. "La chronologie de la préhistoire tardive et des débuts de l'histoire de l'Egypte." *Archéo-nil* 9: 14–81.

———. 2001. "Arguments for an Upper Egyptian Origin of the Palace-Façade and *Serekh* during Late Predynastic–Early Dynastic Times." *GM* 184: 85–109.

———. 2006. "Predynastic–Early Dynastic Chronology." In *Ancient Egyptian Chronology*, edited by E. Hornung, R. Krauss, and D. Warburton, 56–93. Leiden: Brill.

———. 2008. "Les grands mastabas de la Ire dynastie à Saqqara." *Archéo-nil* 18: 61–88.

———. 2011. "Sequence Dating and Predynastic Chronology." In *Before the Pyramids: The Origins of Egyptian Civilization*, edited by E. Teeter, 15–16. Chicago, IL: Oriental Institute Museum Publications.

Hendrickx, S., R.F. Friedman, K.M. Ciałowcz, and M. Chłodnicki, eds. 2004. *Egypt at Its Origins: Studies in Memory of Barbara Adams: Proceedings of the International Conference "Origin of the State, Predynastic and Early Dynastic Egypt," Krakow, 28th August–1st September 2002*. Leuven: Peeters.

Hendrickx, S., W. Van Neer, V. Linseele, and R.F. Friedman. 2004. "Animal Burials and Food Offerings at the Elite Cemetery HK6 of Hierakonpolis." In *Egypt at Its Origins: Studies in Memory of Barbara Adams: Proceedings of the International Conference "Origin of the State, Predynastic and Early Dynastic Egypt," Krakow, 28th August–1st September 2002*, edited by S. Hendrickx, R.F. Friedman, K.M. Ciałowcz, and M. Chłodnicki, 67–130. Leuven: Peeters Publishers and Department of Oriental Studies.

Hendrickx, S., and V. van Rossum. 1994. *Elkab. V, the Naqada III Cemetery*. Brussels: Musées Royaux d'Art et d'Histoire.

Herschel, J.F.W. 1851. *Outlines of Astronomy*. London: Longman, Brown, Green and Longmans.

Hoffman, M.A. 1982. *The Predynastic of Hierakonpolis: An Interim Report*. Giza: Cairo University Herbarium Faculty of Science and Department of Sociology and Anthropology, Western Illinois University.

———. 1990. *Egypt Before the Pharaohs*. New York, NY: Dorset Books.

Hussein, Y.M. 2011. "A New Archaic Period Cemetery at Abydos." In *Egypt at Its Origins 3: Proceedings of the Third International Conference "Origin of the State: Predynastic and Early Dynastic Egypt," London, 27th July–1st August 2008*, edited by R.F. Friedman and P.N. Fiske, 269–80. Leuven: Peeters.

Huyge, D. 2003. "An Enigmatic Third Dynasty Mastaba at Elkab." *EA* 22: 29–30.

Ikram, S., and A. Dodson. 1998. *The Mummy in Ancient Egypt: Equipping the Dead for Eternity*. London: Thames and Hudson.

Isler, M. 2001. *Sticks, Stones, and Shadows: Building the Egyptian Pyramids*. Norman, OK: University of Oklahoma Press.

Jánosi, P. 1999. "The Tombs of Officials: Houses of Eternity." In *Egyptian Art in the Age of the Pyramids*, edited by J.P. O'Neill, 27–40. New York, NY: Metropolitan Museum of Art.

———. 2004. *Die Pyramiden: Mythos und Archäologie*. München: C.H. Beck.

———. 2006. *Die Gräberwelt der Pyramidenzeit*. Mainz am Rhein: Philipp von Zabern.

Jeffreys, D. 2005. "Helwan." In *Encylopedia of the Archaeology of Ancient Egypt*, edited by K.A. Bard, 439–41. London: Taylor and Francis E-library.

Jeffreys, D., and A. Tavares. 1994. "The Historic Landscape of Early Dynastic Memphis." *MDAIK* 50: 143–73.

Junker, H. 1929. *Vorläufi ger Bericht über die Grabung der Akademie der Wissenschaften in Wien auf der neolithischen Siedelung von Merimde-Benisalâme (Westdelta)*. Wien: Adolf Holzhausens.

Kahl, J. 2006. "Inscriptional Evidence for the Relative Chronology of Dyns. 0–2." In *Ancient Egyptian Chronology*, edited by E. Hornung, R. Krauss, and D. Warburton, 94–115. Leiden: Brill.

Kaiser, W. 1964. "Einige Bemerkungen zur ägyptischen Frühzeit." *ZÄS* 91: 86–124.

———. 1969. "Zu den königlichen Talbezirken der 1. und 2. Dynastie in Abydos und zur Baugeschichte des Djoser-Grabmals." *MDAIK* 25: 1–21.

———. 1981. "Zu den Königsgräbern der 1. Dynastie in Umm el-Qaab." *MDAIK* 37: 247–54.

———. 1985. "Zu Entwicklung und Vorformen der frühzeitlichen Gräber mit reich gegliederter Oberbaufassade." In *Mélanges Gamal Eddin Mokhtar*, vol. 2, edited by P. Posener-Kriéger, 25–38. Cairo: Institut Français d'Archéologie Orientale.

———. 1994. "Zu den Königsgräbern der 2. Dynastie in Sakkara und Abydos." In *Essays in Egyptology in Honor of H. Goedicke*, edited by B.M. Bryan and D. Lorton, 113–23. San Antonio, TX: Van Siclen.

———. 1998. "Zur Entstehung der mastaba des Alten Reiches." In *Stationen: Beiträge zur Kulturgeschichte Ägyptens: Rainer Stadelmann gewidmet*, edited by H. Guksch and D. Polz, 73–86. Mainz: Philipp von Zabern.

———. 2008. "Zu überbauten Strukturen in den großen Nischengräbern der 1. Dynastie in Sakkara." In *Zeichen aus dem Sand: Streiflichter aus Ägyptens Geschichte zu Ehren von Günter Dreyer*, edited by E.M. Engel, V. Müller, and U. Hartung, 353–66. Wiesbaden: Harrassowitz Verlag.

Kaiser, W., and G. Dreyer. 1982. "Umm el-Qaab: Nachuntersuchungen im frühzeitlichen Königsfriedhof 2. Vorbericht." *MDAIK* 38: 211–69.

Kaiser, W., and P. Grossmann. 1979. "Umm el-Qaab: Nachuntersuchungen im frühzeitlichen Königsfriedhof 1. Vorbericht." *MDAIK* 35: 155–63.

Kanawati, N. 1987. *The Tomb and Its Significance in Ancient Egypt*. Giza: Ministry of Culture Foreign Cultural Information Department, Prism Publications Offices.

———. 2001. *The Tomb and Beyond: Burial Customs of the Egyptian Officials*. Warminster: Aris & Phillips.

Kemp, B.J. 1967. "The Egyptian 1st Dynasty Royal Cemetery." *Antiquity* 41: 22–32.

———. 1968. "Merimde and the Theory of House Burial in Predynastic Egypt." *CDE* 43: 22–33.

———. 1973. "Photographs of the Decorated Tomb at Hierakonpolis." *JEA* 59: 36–43.

———. 2006. *Ancient Egypt: Anatomy of a Civilization*. London: Routledge.

El-Khouli, A. 1968. "A Preliminary Note on the Excavations at Tura, 1963–64." ASAE 60: 73–76.

———. 1991. *Meidum*. Sydney: Australian Centre for Egyptology.

Klasens, A. 1957. "The Excavations of the Leiden Museum of Antiquities at Abu-Roash: Report of the First Season: 1957, Part I." *OMRO* 38: 58–68.

———. 1959. "The Excavations of the Leiden Museum of Antiquities at Abu-Roash: Report of the Second Season: 1958, Part I." *OMRO* 39: 32–55.

———. 1960. "The Excavations of the Leiden Museum of Antiquities at Abu-Roash: Report of the Third Season: 1959, Part I." *OMRO* 41: 69–94.

———. 1961. "The Excavations of the Leiden Museum of Antiquities at Abu-Roash: Report of the Third Season: 1959, Part II, Cemetery M." *OMRO* 42: 108–28.

Köhler, E.C. 1998. "Excavations at Helwan: New Insights into Early Dynastic Stone Masonry." *BACE* 9: 65–72.

———. 2000a. "Excavations at Helwan." *EA* 17: 38–40.

———. 2000b. "Excavations in the Early Dynastic Cemetery at Helwan." *BACE* 11: 83–92.

———. 2003. "Preliminary Report on the 4th Season of Excavations at Helwan/Ezbet el-Walda by the Australian Centre for Egyptology of Macquarie University in Sydney." *ASAE* 77: 85–90.

———. 2004. "On the Origins of Memphis: The New Excavations in the Early Dynastic Necropolis at Helwan." In *Egypt at Its Origins: Studies in Memory of Barbara Adams: Proceedings of the International Conference "Origin of the State, Predynastic and Early Dynastic Egypt," Krakow, 28th August–1st September 2002*, edited by S. Hendrickx, R.F. Friedman, K.M. Ciałowcz, and M. Chłodnicki, 295–315. Leuven: Peeters.

———. 2005. *Helwan I: Excavations in the Early Dynastic Cemetery Season 1997/98*. Heidelberg: Heidelberger Orientverlag.

———. 2007. "Final Report on the 9th Season of Excavations in the Early Dynastic Cemetery at Helwan/Ezbet el-Walda." *ASAE* 81: 191–215.

———. 2008a. "Final Report on the Tenth Season of Excavations in the Early Dynastic Cemetery at Helwan/Ezbet el-Walda." *ASAE* 82: 171–88.

———. 2008b. "The Helwan Cemetery." *Archéo-nil* 18: 113–30.

———. 2009. "Final Report on the 11th Season of Excavations in the Early Dynastic Cemetery at Helwan/Ezbet el-Walda." *ASAE* 83: 279–93.

Köhler, E.C., and J. Smythe. 2004. "Early Dynastic Pottery from Helwan: Establishing a Ceramic Corpus of the Pottery from Helwan." *CCE* 7: 123–44.

Krauss, R. 2009. "Weisen die Pyramidenkorridore den Weg zum Himmel?" *SAK* 38: 151–60.

Kroeper, K. 1992. "Tombs of the Elite in Minshat Abu Omar." In *The Nile Delta in Transition: 4th–3rd Millennium BC*, edited by E.C.M. van den Brink, 127–50. Tel Aviv: Van den Brink.

———. 2005. "Minshat Abu Omar." In *Encylopedia of the Archaeology of Ancient Egypt*, edited by K.A. Bard, 636–40. London: Taylor and Francis E-library.

La Loggia, A. 2008. "The Use of Stone in Early Dynastic Egyptian Construction." *BACE* 19: 73–89.

———. 2009. "Egyptian Engineering in the Early Dynastic Period: The Sites of Saqqara and Helwan." *BMSAES* 13: 175–96.

Lacher, C. 2008. "Das Grab des Hetepsechemui/Raneb in Saqqara: Ideen zur baugeschichtlichen Entwicklung." In *Zeichen aus dem Sand: Streiflichter aus Ägyptens Geschichte zu Ehren von Günter Dreyer*, edited by E.M. Engel, V. Müller, and U. Hartung, 427–52. Wiesbaden: Harrassowitz Verlag.

———. 2011. "The Tomb of King Ninetjer at Saqqara." In *Egypt at Its Origins 3: Proceedings of the Third International Conference "Origin of the State: Predynastic and Early Dynastic Egypt," London, 27th July–1st August 2008*, edited by R.F. Friedman and P.N. Fiske, 213–31. Leuven: Peeters.

Lacher-Raschdorff, C.M. 2011. "The Tomb of King Ninetjer and Its Reuse in Later Periods." In *Abusir and Saqqara in the Year 2010*, vol. 2, edited by M. Bárta, F. Coppens, and J. Krejčí, 537–50. Prague: Czech Institute of Egyptology.

———. 2014. *Das Grab des Königs Ninetjer in Saqqara: Architektonische Entwicklung frühzeitlicher Grabanlagen in Ägypten*. Wiesbaden: Harrassowitz Verlag.

Lacovera, P. 1988. "Funerary Architecture." In *Mummies and Magic: The Funerary Arts of Ancient Egypt*, edited by S. D'Auria, P. Lacovera, and C.H. Roehrig, 20–25. Boston, MA: Museum of Fine Arts.

Lauer, J.P. 1936. *La Pyramide à degrés: l'Architecture*, vol. 1. Cairo: Imprimerie de l'Institut Français d'Archéologie Orientale.

———. 1939. *La pyramide à degrés: Compléments*, vol. 3. Cairo: Imprimerie de l'Institut Français d'Archéologie Orientale.

———. 1955. "Sur le dualisme de la monarchie égyptienne et son expression architecturale sous les premières dynasties." *BIFAO* 55: 153–71.

———. 1962. *Histoire monumentale des pyramides d'Égypte*. Cairo: Imprimerie de l'Institut Français d'Archéologie Orientale.

———. 1967. "Recherches et travaux menés dans la nécropole de Saqqarah au cours de la campagne 1966–1967." *CRAIBL*: 493–510.

———. 1968. "Recherche et découverte du tombeau sud de l'Horus Sekhem-khet dans son complexe funéraire à Saqqara." *RdE* 20: 97–107.

———. 1969a. "Recherche et découverte du Tombeau Sud de l'Horus Sékhem-khet à Saqqarah." *Bulletin de l'Institut Egyptien* 48–49: 121–31.

———. 1969b. "Recherches et travaux à Saqqarah (Campagnes 1967–1968 et 1968–1969)." *CRAIBL*: 460–79.

———. 1972. "Recherches et travaux à Saqqarah (Campagnes 1970–1971 et 1971–1972)." *CRAIBL*: 577–600.

———. 1973. "Recherches et travaux à Saqqarah (Campagne 1972–1973)." *CRAIBL*: 323–40.

———. 1976. *Saqqara: The Royal Cemetery of Memphis*. London: Thames and Hudson.

———. 1977. "Rapport sur les travaux à Saqqarah (26 novembre 1969–25 mars 1970)." *ASAE* 62: 201–205.

———. 1979. "Le développement des complexes funéraires royaux en Egypte depuis les temps prédynastiques jusqu'à la fin de l'Ancien Empire." *BIFAO* 79: 355–94.

Leahy, A. 1977. "The Osiris 'Bed' Reconsidered." *Orientalia* 46: 424–34.

———. 1979. "Le développement des complexes funéraires royaux en Egypte depuis les temps prédynastiques jusqu'à la fin de l'Ancien Empire." *BIFAO* 79: 355–94.

Lehner, M. 1985. "The Development of the Giza Necropolis: The Khufu Project." *MDAIK* 41: 109–43.

———. 1996. "Z500 and the Layer Pyramid of Zawiyet el-Aryan." In *Studies in Honor of William Kelly Simpson*, vol. 1, edited by P. Der Manuelian, 507–22. Boston, MA: Museum of Fine Arts.

———. 1997. *The Complete Pyramids*. London: Thames and Hudson.

Lepsius, C.R. 1897. *Denkmaeler aus Aegypten und Aethiopien I*. Leipzig: J.C. Hinrichs'sche Buchhandlung.

Limme, L. 2000. "L'Elkab de l'Ancien Empire." *BSFE* 49: 14–31.

———. 2008. "Elkab, 1937–2007: Seventy Years of Belgian Archaeological Research." *BMSAES* 9: 15–50.

Lloyd, A.B. 1989. "Psychology and Society in the Ancient Egyptian Cult of the Dead." In *Religion and Philosophy in Ancient Egypt*, edited by J.P. Allen, 117–33. New Haven: Yale Egyptological Seminar, Department of Near Eastern Languages and Civilizations, the Graduate School, Yale University.

Mace, A.C. 1909. *The Early Dynastic Cemeteries of Naga-ed-Dêr*, Part II. Leipzig: J.C. Hinrichs.

Maragioglio, V., and C.A. Rinaldi. 1963. *L'Architettura delle Piramidi Menfite, Parte II: La Piramide di Sechemkhet, La Layer Pyramid di Zauiet-el-Aryan e le minori piramidi attribuite alla III dinastia*. Torino: Tip. Artale.

———. 1964a. *L'Architettura delle Piramidi Menfite, Parte II: Addenda*. Rapallo: Tipografia Canessa.

———. 1964b. *L'Architettura delle Piramidi Menfite, Parte III: Il Complesso di Meydum, la Piramide a Doppia Pendenza e la Piramide Settentrionale in Pietra di Dahsciur*. Rapallo: Tipografia Canessa.

———. 1965. *L'Architettura delle Piramidi Menfite, Parte II: 2 Addenda*. Rapallo: Tipografia Canessa.

Mariette, A., and G. Maspero. 1885. *Les mastabas de l'ancien empire: Fragment du dernier ouvrage de A. Mariette*. Paris: F. Vieweg.

Martin, G.T. 1974. "Excavations in the Sacred Animal Necropolis at North Saqqâra, 1972–3: Preliminary Report." *JEA* 60: 15–29.

———. 1979. *The tomb of Hetepka and Other Reliefs and Inscriptions from the Sacred Animal Necropolis, North Saqqâra, 1964–1973*. London: Egypt Exploration Society.

———. 1981. *The Sacred Animal Necropolis at North Saqqâra: The Southern Dependencies of the Main Temple Complex*. London: Egypt Exploration Society.

———. 1997. "Covington's Tomb and Related Early Monuments at Giza." In *Études sur l'Ancient Empire et la nécropole de Saqqâra: Dédieés à Jean-Phillipe Lauer*, edited by C. Berger and B. Mathieu, 279–88. Montpelier: Université Paul Valéry.

———. 2007. "The Early Dynastic Necropolis at North Saqqara: The Unpublished Excavations of W.B. Emery and C.M. Firth." In *The Archaeology and Art of Ancient Egypt: Essays in Honour of David B. O'Connor*, vol. 2, edited by Z.A. Hawass and J. Richards, 121–26. Cairo: Publications du Conseil Suprême des Antiquités de l'Egypte.

Mathieson, I., and A. Tavares. 1993. "Preliminary Report of the National Museums of Scotland Saqqara Survey Project, 1990–91." *JEA* 79: 17–31.

Mathieson, I., E. Bettles, J. Dittmer, and C. Reader. 1999. "The National Museums of Scotland Saqqara Survey Project, Earth Sciences 1990–1998." *JEA* 85: 21–43.

Mawdsley, L. 2012. "The Foundation and Development of Tarkhan during the Naqada IIIA2 Period." In *Ancient Memphis, 'Enduring Is the Perfection': Proceedings of the International Conference Held at Macquarie University, Sydney, on August 14–15, 2008*, edited by L. Evans, 331–48. Leuven: Peeters.

Mendelssohn, K. 1973. "A Building Disaster at the Meidum Pyramid." *JEA* 59: 60–71.

Midant-Reynes, B. 2000. *The Prehistory of Egypt from the First Egyptians to the First Pharaohs*. Malden, MA: Blackwell Publishers.

Midant-Reynes, B., Y. Tristant, J. Rowland, and S. Hendrickx, eds. 2008. *Egypt at Its Origins 2: Proceedings of the International Conference "Origin of the State. Predynastic and Early Dynastic Egypt," Toulouse (France), 5th–8th September 2005*. Leuven: Peeters.

Mond, R., and O.H. Myers. 1937. *Cemeteries of Armant*. London: Egypt Exploration Society, H. Milford, Oxford University Press.

Monnier, F., and A. Puchkov. 2016. "The Construction Phases of the Bent Pyramid at Dahshur: A Reassessment." *ENiM* 9: 15–36.

Montet, P. 1938. "Tombeaux de la Iere et de la IVe dynasties à Abou-Roach." *Kêmi* 7: 11–69.

Morris, E.F. 2007a. "Sacrifice for the State: First Dynasty Royal Funerals and the Rites at Macramallah's Rectangle." In *Performing Death, Social*

Analyses of Funerary Traditions in the Ancient Near East and the Mediterranean, edited by N. Laneri, 15–38. Chicago, IL: Oriental Institute.

———. 2007b. "On the Ownership of the Saqqara Mastabas and the Allotment of Political and Ideological Power at the Dawn of the State." In *Archaeology and Art of Ancient Egypt: Essays in honor of David B. O'Connor*, edited by Z.A. Hawass and J. Richards, 171–90. Cairo: American University in Cairo Press.

Mortenson, E. 2005. "El-Omari." In *Encylopedia of the Archaeology of Ancient Egypt*, edited by K.A. Bard, 715–17. London: Taylor and Francis E-library.

Murnane, W.J. 1983. *The Penguin Guide to Ancient Egypt*. London: Penguin.

Myers, O.H., and H.W. Fairman. 1931. "Excavations at Armant, 1929–31." *JEA* 17: 223–32.

Needler, W. 1984. *Predynastic and Archaic Egypt in the Brooklyn Museum*. Brooklyn, NY: Brooklyn Museum.

Nicholson, P. 2005. "The Sacred Animal Necropolis at North Saqqara." In *Divine Creatures: Animal Mummies in Ancient Egypt*, edited by S. Ikram, 44–71. Cairo: American University in Cairo Press.

O'Connor, D. 1991. "Boat Graves and Pyramid Origins." *Expedition* 33, no. 3: 5–17.

———. 2009. *Abydos: Egypt's First Pharaohs and the Cult of Osiris*. London: Thames and Hudson.

Peet, T.E. 1930. *The Great Tomb-Robberies of the Twentieth Egyptian Dynasty: Being a Critical Study, with Translations and Commentaries, of the Papyri in which These Are Recorded*. Oxford: Published in conjunction with the Provost & Fellows of Worcester College at the Clarendon Press.

Petrie, W.M.F. 1892. *Medum*. London: David Nutt.

———. 1900. *The Royal Tombs of the First Dynasty*. London: Egypt Exploration Fund.

———. 1901. *The Royal Tombs of the Earliest Dynasties*. London: Egypt Exploration Fund.

———. 1907. *Gizeh and Rifeh*. London: School of Archaeology in Egypt.

———. 1914. *Tarkhan II*. London: Bitish School of Archaeology in Egypt.

Petrie, W.M.F., and G. Brunton. 1924. *Sedment*. London: School of Archaeology in Egypt.

Petrie, W.M.F., G. Brunton, and M.A. Murray. 1923. *Lahun II*. London: School of Archaeology in Egypt.

Petrie, W.M.F., and A.C. Mace. 1901. *Diospolis Parva: The Cemeteries of Abadiyeh and Hu*. London: Egypt Exploration Fund.

Petrie, W.M.F., and E.J. Mackay. 1915. *Heliopolis, Kafr Ammar and Shurafa*. London: School of Archaeology in Egypt.

Petrie, W.M.F., E.J.H. Mackay, and G.A. Wainwright. 1910. *Meydum and Memphis (III)*. London: School of Archaeology in Egypt.

Petrie, W.M.F., and J.E. Quibell. 1896. *Naqada and Ballas*. London: B. Quaritch.

Petrie, W.M.F., G.A. Wainwright, and A.H. Gardiner. 1913. *Tarkhan I and Memphis V.* London: School of Archaeology in Egypt.

Petrie, W.M.F., G.A. Wainwright, and E.J.H. Mackay. 1912. *The Labyrinth, Gerzeh and Mazghuneh*. London: School of Archaeology in Egypt.

Phillips, J. 1992. "Tomb Robbers and Their Booty in Ancient Egypt." In *Death and Taxes in the Ancient Near East*, edited by S.E. Orel, 157–92. Lewiston, NY: Edwin Mellen Press.

Pinch, G. 2002. *Handbook of Egyptian Mythology*. Santa Barbara, CA: ABC-CLIO.

Podzorski, P.V. 2008. "The Early Dynastic Mastabas of Naga ed-Deir." *Archéo-nil* 18: 89–102.

Porter, B., and R.L.B. Moss. 1934. *Topographical Bibliography of Ancient Egyptian Hieroglyphic Texts, Reliefs, and Paintings, vol. 4, Lower and Middle Egypt*. Oxford: Clarendon Press.

———. 1937. *Topographical Bibliography of Ancient Egyptian Hieroglyphic Texts, Reliefs, and Paintings, vol. 5, Upper Egypt: Sites*. Oxford: Oxford University Press.

———. 1974–81. *Topographical Bibliography of Ancient Egyptian Hieroglyphic Texts, Reliefs, and Paintings, vol. 3, Memphis*. Oxford: Griffith Institute.

———. 1995. *Topographical Bibliography of Ancient Egyptian Hieroglyphic Texts, Reliefs, and Paintings, vol. 7, Nubia, the Deserts, and Outside Egypt*. Oxford: Griffith Institute and Ashmolean Museum.

Quibell, J.E. 1898. *El Kab*. London: B. Quaritch.

———. 1913. *Excavations at Saqqara, 1911–12: The Tomb of Hesy*. Cairo: Imprimerie de l'Institut Français d'Archéologie Orientale.

———. 1923. *Excavations at Saqqara, 1912–1914: Archaic Mastabas*. Cairo: Imprimerie de l'Institut Français d'Archéologie Orientale.

Quibell, J.E., and F.W. Green. 1902. *Hierakonpolis*, Part 2. London: B. Quaritch.

Radwan, A. 2000. "Mastaba XVII at Abusir (First Dynasty): Preliminary Results and General remarks." In *Abusir and Saqqara in the Year 2000*, edited by M. Bárta and J. Krejčí, 509–14. Prague: Academy of Sciences of the Czech Republic Oriental Institute.

———. 2003. "Step Pyramids." In *The Treasures of the Pyramids*, edited by Z.A. Hawass, 86–111. Vercelli: White Star.

Randall-MacIver, D., and A.C. Mace. 1902. *El Amrah and Abydos, 1899–1901*. London: Egypt Exploration Fund.

Ranke, H. 1926. *Koptische Friedhöfe bei Karâra und der Amontempel Scheschonks I. bei el Hibe*. Berlin: Walter de Gruyter.

Raven, M.J., H. Hays, C. Lacher, K. Duistermaat, I. Regulski, B.G. Aston, L. Horáčková, and N. Warner. 2009. "Preliminary Report on the Leiden Excavations at Saqqara, Season 2008: The Tomb of Ptahemwia." *JEOL* 41: 5–30.

Raven, M.J., R. van Walsem, B.G. Aston, and E. Strouhal. 2003. "Preliminary Report on the Leiden Excavations at Saqqara, Season 2002: The Tomb of Meryneith." *JEOL* 37: 91–109.

Reader, C. 2004. "On Pyramid Causeways." *JEA* 90: 63–71.

Regulski, I. 2009. "Investigating a New Dynasty 2 Necropolis at South Saqqara." *BMSAES* 13: 221–37.

———. 2011. "Reinvestigating the Second Dynasty at Saqqara." In *Abusir and Saqqara in the Year 2010*, vol. 2, edited by M. Bárta, F. Coppens, and J. Krejčí, 694–708. Prague: Czech Institute of Egyptology.

Reisner, G.A. 1908. *The Early Dynastic Cemeteries of Naga-ed-Dêr*, part 1. Leipzig: J.C. Hinrichs.

———. 1932. *A Provincial Cemetery of the Pyramid Age, Naga-ed-Dêr.* Berkeley, CA: University of California Press.

———. 1936. *The Development of the Egyptian Tomb Down to the Accession of Cheops*. Cambridge, MA: Harvard University Press.

———. 1942. *A History of the Giza Necropolis*, vol. 1. Cambridge, MA: Harvard University Press.

Riggs, C. 2014. *Unwrapping Ancient Egypt*. London: Bloomsbury.

Ritner, R.K. 1993. *The Mechanics of Ancient Egyptian Magical Practice*. Chicago, IL: Oriental Institute.

———. 2012. "Killing the Image, Killing the Essence: The Destruction of Text and Figures in Ancient Egyptian Thought, Ritual and 'Ritualized History.'" In *Iconoclasm and Text Destruction in the Ancient Near East and Beyond*, edited by N.N. May, 395–406. Chicago, IL: Oriental Instutute.

Rizkana, I., and J. Seeher. 1990. *Maadi IV: The Predynastic Cemeteries of Maadi and Wadi Digla*. Mainz: Zabern.

Rowe, A. 1930. "A Link between Ancient Egypt and Cyprus: A Cypriote's Tomb—and Other 18th Dynasty Intrusive Burials—in the Great Mastabah at Meydum." *Illustrated London News* 176 (April 5): 564–67.

———. 1931. *The Eckley B. Coxe, Jr., Expedition Excavations at Meydûm*. Philadelphia, PA: University Museum, University of Pennsylvania.

Rowland, J. 2011a. "A New Era at Quesna." *EA* 38: 10–13.

———. 2011b. "An Old Kingdom Mastaba and the Results of Continued Investigations at Quesna in 2010." *JEA* 97: 11–29.

Rowland, J., and G.J. Tassie. 2017. "A New Funerary Monument Dating to the Reign of Khaba: The Quesna Mastaba in the Context of the Early Dynastic Old Kingdom." In *Abusir and Saqqara in the Year 2015: Proceedings of the Conference held in Prague (June 22–26, 2015)*, edited by M. Bárta, F. Coppens, and J. Krejčí. Prague: Czech Institute of Egyptology.

Ryholt, K. 1997. *The Political Situation in Egypt during the Second Intermediate Period c. 1800–1550 BC*. Copenhagen: Museum Tusculanum Press.

Saad, Z.Y. 1947. *Royal Excavations at Saqqara and Helwan (1941–1945)*. Cairo: Imprimerie de l'Institut Français d'Archéologie Orientale.

———. 1951. *Royal Excavations at Helwan (1945–1947)*. Cairo: Imprimerie de l'Institut Français d'Archéologie Orientale.

———. 1957. *Ceiling Stelae in Second Dynasty Tombs from the Excavations at Helwan*. Cairo: Imprimerie de l'Institut Français d'Archéologie Orientale.

———. 1969. *The Excavations at Helwan: Art and Civilization in the First and Second Egyptian Dynasties*. Norman, OK: University of Oklahoma Press.

Sampsell, B.M. 2000. "Pyramid Design and Construction, Part I: The Accretion Theory." *Ostracon* 11, no. 3: 2–6.

Seeher, J. 1992. "Burial Customs in Predynastic Egypt: A View from the Delta." In *The Nile Delta in Transition: 4th–3rd Millennium BC*, edited by E.C.M. van den Brink, 225–33. Tel Aviv: Van den Brink.

———. (ed.). 1999. *Ma'adi and Wadi Digla*. London: Routledge.

Seele, K.C. 1974. "Excavations between Abu Simbel and the Sudan Border." *JNES* 33: 1–43.

Seidlmayer, S.J. 1998. "The Rise of the State to the Second Dynasty." In *Egypt: The World of the Pharaohs*, edited by R. Schulz and M. Seidel, 25–40. Cologne: Könemann.

———. 2006. "The Relative Chronology of Dynasty 3." In *Ancient Egyptian Chronology*, edited by E. Hornung, R. Krauss, and D. Warburton, 116–23. Leiden: Brill.

Smith, H.S. 1994. "The Princes of Seyala in Lower Nubia." In *Hommages à Jean Leclant* vol. 2, edited by C. Berger, G. Clerc, J. Leclant, and N. Grimal, 361–76. Cairo: Institut Français d'Archéologie Orientale.

Smoláriková, K. 2006. "The Step Pyramid: A Constant Inspiration to the Saite Egyptians." In *Abusir in the Year 2005: Proceedings of the Conference Held in Prague (June 27–July 25, 2005)*, edited by M. Bárta, F. Coppens, and J. Krejãí, 42–49. Prague: Czech Institute of Egyptology.

Smyth, C.P. 1870. *A Poor Man's Photography at the Great Pyramid in the Year 1865*. London: Henry Greenwood.

Smythe, J. 2004. "The Pottery from Operation 3/Tomb 1 at Helwan." In *Egypt at Its Origins: Studies in Memory of Barbara Adams: Proceedings of the International Conference "Origin of the State, Predynastic and Early Dynastic Egypt," Krakow, 28th August–1st September 2002*, edited by S. Hendrickx, R.F. Friedman, K.M. Ciałowcz, and M. Chłodnicki, 317–35. Leuven: Peeters.

Snape, S.R. 2011. *Ancient Egyptian Tombs: The Culture of Life and Death*. Chichester: Wiley-Blackwell.

Spencer, A.J. 1979. *Brick Architecture in Ancient Egypt*. Warminster: Aris and Phillips.

———. 1982. *Death in Ancient Egypt*. Harmondsworth: Penguin Books.

———. 1993. *Early Egypt: The Rise of Civilisation in the Nile Valley*. London: British Museum Press.

———. 1996. *Aspects of Early Egypt*. London: British Museum Press.

Stadelmann, R. 1980. "Snofru und die Pyramiden von Meidum und Dahschur." *MDAIK* 36: 437–49.

———. 1983. "Die Pyramiden des Snofru in Dahschur." *MDAIK* 39: 225–36.

———. 1985a. *Die ägyptischen Pyramiden: Vom Ziegelbau zum Weltwunder*. Mainz am Rhein: Philipp von Zabern.

———. 1985b. "Die Oberbauten der Königsgräber der 2. Dynastie in Sakkara." In *Mélanges Gamal Eddin Mokhtar*, edited by P. Posener-Krieger. *BdE* 97, no. 2: 295–308.

———. 1991. "Das Dreikammersystem der Königsgräber der Frühzeit und des Alten Reiches." *MDAIK* 47: 373–87.

———. 1995. "Builders of the Pyramids." In *Civilizations of the Ancient Near East*, vol. 2, edited by J.M. Sasson, 719–34. New York: Scribner.

———. 1996. "Origins and Development of the Funerary Complex of Djoser." In *Studies in Honor of William Kelly Simpson*, vol. 2, edited by P. Der Manuelian and R.E. Freed, 787–800. Boston, MA: Museum of Fine Arts.

———. 2003. "The Pyramids of the Fourth Dynasty." In *The Treasures of the Pyramids*, edited by Z.A. Hawass, 112–37. Vercelli: White Star.

———. 2004. "Dahschur: Knickpyramide und Taltempel des Snofru." *DAIK Rundbrief* (September): 15–18.

———. 2011. "The Heb-sed Temple of Seneferu at Dahshur." In *Abusir and Saqqara in the Year 2010*, vol. 2, edited by M. Bárta, F. Coppens, and J. Krejčí, 736–46. Prague: Czech Institute of Egyptology.

Stadelmann, R., and N. Alexanian. 1998. "Die Friedhöfe des Alten und Mittleren Reiches in Dahschur." *MDAIK* 54: 294–317.

Stadelmann, R., N. Alexanian, H. Ernst, G. Heindl, and D. Raue. 1993. "Pyramiden und Nekropole des Snofru in Dahschur. Dritter

Vorbericht über die Grabungen des Deutschen Archäologischen Instituts in Dahschur." *MDAIK* 49: 259–94.

Stevenson, A. 2011. "Material Culture of the Predynastic Period." In *Before the Pyramids: The Origins of Egyptian Civilization*, edited by E. Teeter, 65–74. Chicago, IL: Oriental Institute Museum Publications.

———. 2012. "The A-Group Cemetery at Tunqala West." *JEA* 98: 225–47.

Stocks, D.A. 2003. *Experiments in Egyptian Archaeology: Stoneworking Technology in Ancient Egypt*. London: Routledge.

Strudwick, N.C. 2005. *Texts From the Pyramid Age*. Atlanta, GA: Society of Biblical Literature.

Swelim, N. 1983. *Some Problems on the History of the Third Dynasty*. Alexandria: Archaeological Society of Alexandria.

———. 1984. "A Reason for the Corbelled Roof in Dynasty III and IV Pyramids." *JSSEA* 14: 6–12.

———. 1987. *The Brick Pyramid at Abu Rawash Number '1' by Lepsius: A Preliminary Study*. Alexandria: Archaeological Society of Alexandria.

———. 2002. "Pyramids on Lepsius, de Morgan and Later Maps." In *A Tribute to Excellence: Studies Offered in Honor of Ernö Gaál, Ulrich Luft, Láslo Török*, edited by T.A. Bács, 443–54. Budapest: Eötvös Loránd University.

Tassie, G.J., F.A. Hassan, J. van Wetering, and B. Calcoen. 2008. "Corpus of Potmarks from the Proto/Early Dynastic Cemetery at Kafr Hassan Dawood, Wadi Tumilat, East Delta, Egypt." In *Egypt at Its Origins 2: Proceedings of the International Conference "Origin of the State: Predynastic and Early Dynastic Egypt," Toulouse (France), 5th–8th September 2005*, edited by B. Midant-Reynes, Y. Tristant, J. Rowland, and S. Hendrickx, 1107–17. Leuven: Peeters.

Tassie, G.J., and J. van Wetering. 2003a. "Early Cemeteries of the East Delta: Kafr Hassan Dawood, Minshat Abu Omar, and Tell Ibrahim Awad." In *Egyptology at the Dawn of the Twenty-First Century*, edited by Z. Hawass and L. Pinch Brock, 499–507. Cairo: American University in Cairo Press.

———. 2003b. "Socio-Political Hierarchy of First Dynasty Sites: A Ranking of East Delta Cemeteries Based on Grave Architecture." In *A Delta Man in Yebu*, edited by A.K. Eyma and C.J. Bennett, 123–46. Boca Raton, FL: Universal Publishers.

Tavares, A. 2005. "Saqqara, North, Early Dynastic Tombs." In *Encylopedia of the Archaeology of Ancient Egypt*, edited by K.A. Bard, 854–59. London: Taylor and Francis E-library.

Tawadros, E. 2001. *Geology of Egypt and Libya*. Rotterdam: A.A. Balkema.

Taylor, J.H. 2001. *Death and the Afterlife in Ancient Egypt*. London: Published for the Trustees of the British Museum by the British Museum Press.

———. 2010. *Journey through the Afterlife: Ancient Egyptian Book of the Dead*. London: British Museum Press.

The Staff of the U.S. Bureau of Mines. 1996. *Dictionary of Mining, Mineral, and Related Terms*. Washington, DC: United States Department of the Interior.

Tooley, A. 1995. *Egyptian Models and Scenes*. Princes Risborough: Shire.

Trimble, V. 1964. "Astronomical Investigation Concerning the So-Called Air-Shafts of Cheops' Pyramid." *MIO* 10: 183–87.

Tristant, Y. 2008a. "Deux grands tombeaux du cimetière M d'Abou Rawach (Ire dynastie)." *Archéo-nil* 18: 131–47.

———. 2008b. "Les tombes des premières dynasties à Abou Roach." *BIFAO* 108: 325–70.

———. 2008c. "Un cimetière d'elite de la Ire dynastie a Abou Rawach." Égypte Afrique et Orient 50: 3–12.

Van Dijk, J. 2007. "Retainer Sacrifice in Egypt and in Nubia." In *The Strange World of Human Sacrifice*, edited by J.N. Bremmer, 135–55. Leuven: Peeters.

Van Walsem, R. 2003. "The Tomb of Meryneith at Saqqara: Results of the Dutch Mission 2001–2003." *BACE* 14: 117–34.

Van Wetering, J. 2004. "The Royal Cemetery of the Early Dynastic Period at Saqqara and the Second Dynasty Royal Tombs." In *Egypt at Its Origins: Studies in Memory of Barbara Adams: Proceedings of the International Conference "Origin of the State, Predynastic and Early Dynastic Egypt," Krakow, 28th August–1st September 2002*, edited by S. Hendrickx, R.F. Friedman, K.M. Ciałowcz, and M. Chłodnicki, 1055–80. Leuven: Peeters.

Verd'hurt, J.-Y., and G. Dormion. 2003. "New Discoveries in the Pyramid of Meidum." In *Egyptology at the Dawn of the Twenty-First Century: Proceedings of the Eighth International Congress of Egyptologists, Cairo, 2000*, edited by Z.A. Hawass and L.P. Brock, 541–46. Cairo: American University in Cairo Press.

Vermeersch, P.M., E. Paulissen, S. Stokes, C. Charlier, P. Van Peer, C. Stringer, and W. Lindsay. 1998. "A Middle Paleolithic Burial of a Modern Human at Taramsa Hill, Egypt." *Antiquity* 72: 475–84.

Verner, M. 2003. *The Pyramids: Their Archaeology and History*. London: Atlantic.

Vyse, H. 1840a. *Operations Carried On at the Pyramids of Gizeh in 1837, with an Account of a Voyage into Upper Egypt, and an Appendix*, vol. 1. London: Fraser.

———. 1840b. *Operations Carried On at the Pyramids of Gizeh in 1837, with an Account of a Voyage into Upper Egypt, and an Appendix*, vol. 2. London: Fraser.

Vyse, H., and J.S. Perring. 1842. *Operations Carried On at the Pyramids of Gizeh in 1837, with an Account of a Voyage into Upper Egypt, and an Appendix*, vol. 3. London: J. Weale.

Wainwright, G.A. 1937. "Einiges zur dritten Bauperiode der grossen Pyramide bei Gise by L. Borchardt." *JEA* 23, no. 1: 127–29.

Walker, R.L. 1984. "The Non-Astronomical Alignment of the Descending Passage in the Pyramid of Khufu." *Bulletin of the American Astronomical Society* 16: 887.

Warden, L.A. 2013. "Ceramics and Status at Meidum's Northern Cemetery." *MDAIK* 69: 227–46.

Wegner, J.W. 1996. "Interaction between the Nubian A-Group and Predynastic Egypt: The Significance of the Qustul Incense Burner." In *Egypt and Africa*, edited by T. Celenko, 98–100. Indianapolis, IN: Indianapolis Museum of Art.

———. 2009. "The Tomb of Senwosret III at Abydos: Considerations on the Origins and Development of the Royal Amduat-Tomb." In *Archaism and Innovation: Studies in the Culture of Middle Kingdom Egypt*, edited by D.P. Silverman, W.K. Simpson, and J.W. Wegner, 103–69. New Haven, CT: Department of Near Eastern Languages and Civilizations, Yale University, and University of Pennsylvania Museum of Archaeology and Anthropology.

Wendorf, F. 1968. "Site 117: A Nubian Final Paleolithic Graveyard Near Jebel Sahaba, Sudan." In *The Prehistory of Nubia*, edited by F. Wendorf, 954–95. Dallas, TX: Southern Methodist University.

Wendorf, F., and A.E. Close. 2005. "Paleolithic Cultures: Overview." In *Encylopedia of the Archaeology of Ancient Egypt*, edited by K.A. Bard, 6–15. London: Taylor and Francis E-library.

Wengrow, D. 2006. *The Archaeology of Early Egypt: Social Transformations in North-East Africa, 10,000 to 2,650 BC*. Cambridge: Cambridge University Press.

Wenke, R.J. 1989. "Egypt: Origins of Complex Societies." *Annual Review of Anthropology* 18: 129–55.

Wente, E.F. 1990. *Letters from Ancient Egypt*. Atlanta, GA: Scholars Press.

Wilkinson, T.A.H. 1996. "A Re-examination of the Early Dynastic Necropolis at Helwan." *MDAIK* 52: 337–53.

———. 1999. *Early Dynastic Egypt*. London: Routledge.

Williams, B. 1980. "The Lost Pharaohs of Nubia." *Archaeology* 33: 14–21.

———. 1986. *The A-Group Royal Cemetery at Qustul: Cemetery L*. Chicago, IL: Oriental Institute.

———. 1987. "Forebears of Menes in Nubia: Myth or Reality?" *JNES* 46: 15–26.

———. 1994. "Security and the Problem of the City in the Naqada Period." In *For His Ka: Essays Offered in the Memory of Klaus Baer*, edited by D.P. Silverman, 271–78. Chicago, IL: Oriental Institute.

Wissa, M. 1997. "A propos du sarcophage de Sékhemkhet." In *Etudes sur l'Ancien empire et la nécropole de Saqqâra dédiées à Jean-Philippe Lauer*, edited by C. Berger and B. Mathieu, 445–48. Montpellier: Université Paul Valéry.

Wood, W. 1978. "A Reconstruction of the Reliefs of Hesy-Re." *JARCE* 15: 19–24.

Yacoub, F. 1981. "The Archaic Tombs at Tura el-Asmant." *ASAE* 64: 159–61.

Žabkar, L.V. 1968. *A Study of the Ba Concept in Ancient Egyptian Texts*. Chicago, IL: University of Chicago Press.

Index

Numbers in italics refer to figures.

Abu Ghurab 51, 124; tombs: Mastaba XVII 51, *52*

Abu Rawash 19, 50, 81–86, 184; royal tombs: Brick Pyramid 186–89, *187*; private tombs: tomb 389 50, 82; tomb MO1 83–84, *83*; tomb MO2 *83*, 84–85; tomb MO3 84; tomb MO4 84–85; tomb MO6 84–85; tomb MO7 84–85; tomb MO10 84–85, *85*; tomb MO11 84; tomb MO12 84; tomb MO19 84–86; tomb MO25 82, *82*

Abusir 135, 140–41, 236–40; tombs: tomb 10B–4 140, *141*; tomb 11D–2 140; tomb 12B–6 140, *141*; tomb 13B–5 141; Lake of Abusir Tomb 1 239–40, *240*; AS 20 (Hetepi) 237–39, *238*; AS 33 236–37, *237*

Abydos 20, 25–26, 36–45, 64–65, 70–78, 122, 135–39; royal tombs: Cemetery U 25–26; U-j (Scorpion?) 25–26, *26*; Cemetery B, tomb B0/1/2 (Iry-Hor) 36–37, *36*; tomb B 7/9 (Ka) 37, *37*; tomb B17/18 (Narmer) 37–38, *38*; tomb B10/15/19 (Hor-Aha) 39–41, *40*; Umm al-Qa‘b, tomb O (Djer) 41, *42*; tomb Z (Djet) 41–44, *43*; tomb Y (Merneith) *44*, 45; tomb T (Den) 70–72, *70*; tomb X (Adjib) 72–73, 75, *73*; tomb U (Semerkhet) 74–75, *74*; tomb Q (Qa’a) 76–78, *77*; tomb P (Peribsen) 135–37, *136*; tomb V (Khasekhemwy) 137–39, *137*; private tombs: tomb I 122, *122*; tomb IV 64–65, *64*

Adjib (King) 72–73, 75, 78–79

akh 10, 275

al-Amra 123; tombs: tomb b 91 123, *123*

Armant 66, 162–63; tombs: tomb 1207 66, *67*; tomb 1208 66, *67*; tomb 205 162, *163*; tombs 206, 207, and 208 162–63

Awlad al-Sheikh 61–62, 118–19; tombs: tomb II 61–62, *62*; tomb III 118–19, *119*

ba 10–11, 275

backfills and blockings (excursus) 126–28

al-Badari 15, 159–60; tombs: tomb 3112 159, *161*; tomb 3227 203–204, *203*; tomb 3228 203, *203*; tomb 3229 203

Badarian 9, 15–18; tombs 15–16, *16*

Beit Khallaf 209–13, 220; tombs: tomb K1 209–111, *210*; tomb K2 211–13, *212*
Buto Maadi culture 19–20

Dahshur 226–35; 240–46; royal tombs: Bent Pyramid (Sneferu) 226–31, *227–28*, *230*, *232*; Red Pyramid (Sneferu) 231–35, *233–34*; Bent Pyramid satellite pyramid (Sneferu) 231, *232*; private tombs: tomb no. 1 241, *241*; Mastaba II/1 (Netjer-Aperef) 244–45, *244*; DAS 9 (Ipy) 242, *242*; DAS 32–34 (Iinefer) 242–43, *243*
Den (King) 70
Djer (King) 41
Djet (King) 41–42
Djoser (King) 169

Fayum culture 14

Giza 50, 135, 191–93, 220; tombs: Covington's Tomb (tomb no. 1, Mastaba T) 191–93, *192*; Mastaba V (Nazlet Batran) 50–51, *51*

Helwan 58–60, 107–17, 149–56, 200–202; tombs: 60.H.1 116; 553.H.2 112, *113*; 1371.H.2 112, *112*; 1390.H.2 (actually 1389.H.2) 107–108, *109*; 1502.H.2 112, *112*; 1.H.3 115–16, *116*; 40.H.3 (Op. 2/1) 114–15, *115*; 1.H.4 109–10, *110*; 68.H.4 59, *59*; 185.H.4 59–60; 355.H.4 111–12, *112*; 385.H.4 113, *114*; 407.H.4 110–11, *110*; 505.H.4 150, *150*; 1.H.5 155; 150.H.5 110, *110*; 785.H.5 111, *111*; 287.H.6 200–202, *201*; 256.H.8 155, *155*; 423.H.9 107, *108*; Op. 4/4 151, *152*; Op. 4/94 150–51, *151*; Op. 4/123 152–53, *153*; Op. 4/148 154, *154*
Hemamieh 15
Hierakonpolis 20, 21, 23–25; cemetery HK43 tombs 21; tombs: tomb 2 Locality HK6 30–32, *31*; tomb 11 Locality HK6 25; tomb 16 Locality HK6 25; tomb 23 Locality HK6 23, *23*; tomb 26 Locality HK6 23–24, *24*; tomb 100 the 'Painted Tomb' 24, 26; tomb 500 24
Hor-Aha (King) 26, 39–41, 65
Hotepsekhemwy (King) 129–31
Huni (King) 186, 310 n58

Iry-Hor (King) 36, 287 n1

Jebel Sahaba 13–14

ka 10–11, 275
Ka (King) 37
al-Kab 26–28, 163, 213–14; tombs: grave 64 163, *164*; grave 69 27; grave 85 27–28, *27*; tomb St. 2 163; tomb St. 9 213; tomb St. 12 213; tomb 274 Rock Necropolis 214, *215*; Mastaba A (Kamena) 263, *264*
Kafr Hassan Dawud 48; tombs: graves 913 and 970 48
Khaba (King) 184–85, 190
Khasekhemwy (King) 137–39
Kom al-Ahmar 30; tombs: burial 8 30, *30*

Lahun Bashkatib Cemetery 157–58, 202–203; tombs: tomb 735 202, *202*; tomb 769 202, *202*; tomb 771 157, *157*; tomb 785 158; tomb 821 *157*, 158

Mahasna 119, 121; tombs: M1 121, *121*
al-Masa'id 165–66, 285 n64; tombs: burial 28 165
Meidum xix, 223–26, 246–60; royal tombs: Pyramid of Meidum

(Sneferu) 223–26, *224–25*; private tombs: Mastaba no. 6 (Rahotep and Nefert) 247–49, *247*; Mastaba 9 (Ranefer) 249–50, *250*; Mastaba 16 (Nefermaat and Atet) 257–60, *258*; Mastaba 17 254–57, *255–56*; tombs 202, 277, and 393 254; tomb A, Great Western Cemetery 253–54, *253*; Great Western Cemetery tombs B and C 254; Far Western Cemetery tombs 251–52; tomb 51 252, *252*; tomb 63 251; tomb 68 251
Merimde Beni Salama 15
Merneith (Queen) 45
Minshat Abu Omar 79–80; tombs: grave 1590 80; grave 2897 80, *80*
mounding 17

Naga al-Deir 62–64, 119–21, 161–62, 204–207, 261–63; tombs: Cemetery 500–900, N 546 + N 604 261–62, *262*; N 573 + 587 205–206, *205*; N 574 204, *205*; N 593 206–207, *206*; N 599 204, *205*; N 629 261; N 739 261–63, *262*; Cemetery 1500: N 1506 63–64, *63*; N 1512 119, 121; N 1532 62–64, *63*; N 1581 119–21, *120*; N 1586 161–62, *162*; Cemetery 3500 307 n119
Naqada: Naqada I 20–21; Naqada II 21–25; Naqada IIIA–B 25–32; Naqada tombs: Cemetery 'T' tombs T10, T15, T20, and T23 22; 'Royal tomb' (Queen Neith-hotep) 65, *66*
Narmer (King) 35–38
Nazlet Batran *see* Giza
Nazlet Khater 13
Neith-hotep (Queen) 65
Ninetjer (King) 129, 131–34
Nubia (Lower) 13, 19, 28, 286 n79

al-Omari 18–19

Peribsen (King) 135–37
Plug-stones (excursus) 267
Portcullises (excursus) 218–21

Qa'a (King) 76–78
al-Qara 160; tombs: tomb 2 164–65, *165*
Qau 159–60; Cemetery 400 tombs: tomb 429 159, *160*; tomb 438 306 n104; tomb 507 159, *160*; tomb 562 159, *160*
Quesna 190–91
Qustul 28–29: tombs: L23 29, *29*; L24 29

Raneb (King) 129–31
Reqaqnah 207–209; tombs: R 1 and R 40 207–208, *208*
robbers' tunnels xix, 40, 45, 53–54, 57, 81, 107, *114*, 131, 149–50, *150–51*, *153*, 154, *154*, *155*, 166, *171*, 178, 231, *244*, 250, 254, 259, 292 n89

Saqqara 52–60, 89–107, 129–35, 141–49, 169–84, 193–200, 301 n4, 303 n46–47 and 52; royal tombs: Hotepsekhemwy/Raneb 129–31, *130*, *132*; Ninetjer 131–34, *133*; the Step Pyramid (Djoser) 169–76, *170–72*, *175*; the Step Pyramid, South Tomb 176–78, *177*; Pyramid of Sekhemkhet 179–83, *180*, *182*; Pyramid of Sekhemkhet, South Tomb 183; private tombs: S 2101 145, 148; S 2105 102, *103*; S 2171 143, 145–46, *146*, 148; S 2185 55–56, *55*; S 2307 143, 145, 148; S 2313 148; S 2322 143, 145, 148; S 2405 (Hesyra) 193–95, *194*, 315 n144; S 2429 143, 145; S 2452 145, 148; S 2498 143, 146; S 3024 141–42, *142*, 145, 148; S 3035 (Hemaka)

92–94, *93*; S 3036 (Ankhka) 95–96, *95*; S 3038 (Nebitka) 296 n102; S 3050 195, *196*; S 3070 196–98, *197*; S 3120 105–107, *106*; S 3121 104–107, *105*; S 3338 97–98, *98*; S 3357 (Hor-Aha) 53–54, *53*, 295 n96; S 3477 146–48, *147*; S 3500 99–101, *99–100*; S 3503 57, *58*, 295 n96; S 3504 56–57, *56*, 295 n96; S 3505 (Merka) 101–102, *101*; S 3506 92, *91*, 296 n111; S 3507 89–91, *90*, 296 n102; S 3518 198–200, *199*, 313 n107; tomb X 96–7, *97*
sebbakhin 60, 63, 109, 186
Sedment 158, 304 n84; tombs: tomb 94 158; tomb 560 158, *159*
Sekhemkhet (King) 179–84
Semerkhet (King) 74–75
Seyala 28; tombs: Cemetery 137 tomb no. 1 28; tomb no. 6 28, *28*
al-Siba'iya 160, 285 n64; tombs: al-Siba'iya brick tomb 164
Sneferu (King) 223–35

Taramsa Hill 13
Tarkhan 32, 60–61, 117–18, 156–57; tombs: Mastaba 852 32, 281 n3; Mastaba 1845 32, *32*, 281 n3; Mastaba 1060 60, *61*; Mastaba 2038 117, *118*; Mastaba 2050 117, *118*; grave 240 (Kafr Amar) 156, *156*; grave 545 (Kafr Amar) 156–57
Tell al-Farkha 46–48, 81; graves: grave no. 6 46; grave no. 9 46; grave no. 50 81, *81*; grave no. 55 81, *81*; grave no. 63 47, *47*; grave no. 99 48; grave no. 100 47–48
Tell Ibrahim 'Awad 48; tombs: tomb no. 1 Site B 48, *49*
tomb robbers 10–12, 17, 21–22, 41, 43–44, 48, 56–57, 60–61, 64–66, 78, 93–94, 97, 102–103, 107, 115–116, 119, 131, 139, 144, *152*, 155, 158, 176, 178, 184, 190, 194, 198, 208, 211, 213–14, 230, 237, 239–40, 245, 250, 254, 260–62, 281 n2, 282 n18, 288 n18, 289 n26, 294 n43, 308 n29, 315 n158, 322 n133; *see also* robbers' tunnels
tumulus 32, 39–41, 43, *43*, 45, 71–73, 75–76, 78, 90, 135, 138, 288 n20, 289 n26 and n32, 292 n17
Tunqala West, grave 3, Cemetery 268 28
Tura al-Asmant 86–89; tombs: tomb 130 87, *88*; tomb 249 87–88, *89*; tomb 986 86–87; tomb 1035 86; tomb 1056 86, *87*

Umm al-Qa'b 22, 25–26, 29, 36–45, 64, 70–78, 129, 135–39

Wadi Kubbaniya 13

Zawiyat al-Aryan 184: Layer Pyramid (Khaba) 184–85, 185